HARVARD HISTORICAL STUDIES · 147

Published under the auspices
of the Department of History
from the income of the
Paul Revere Frothingham Bequest
Robert Louis Stroock Fund
Henry Warren Torrey Fund

MARK LANDSMAN

Dictatorship and Demand

The Politics of Consumerism in East Germany

HARVARD UNIVERSITY PRESS

Cambridge, Massachusetts

London, England

MLC

Library of Congress Cataloging-in-Publication Data

Landsman, Mark, 1966–
Dictatorship and demand : the politics of consumerism in East Germany / Mark Landsman.
p.   cm.—(Harvard historical studies ; 147)
Includes bibliographical references and index.
ISBN 0-674-01698-X (alk. paper)
1. Consumption (Economics)—Germany (East).   2. Socialism—Germany (East).
3. Germany (East)—Economic conditions.   4. Germany (East)—Politics and government.
I. Title.   II. Series.

HC290.795.C6L36 2005   2004054334

To Jenny

Contents

Acknowledgments

In the course of writing this book, I have incurred many debts of gratitude. It is a great pleasure to acknowledge them here. To begin with—the money. I would like to thank Columbia University for a President's Fellowship in 1996–97, which enabled me to get started on the research. Most of the research, however, was funded by the Social Science Research Council's Berlin Program for Advanced German and European Studies in 1997–98. The Berlin Program was a unique experience, offering a stimulating intellectual environment and opportunities for making contacts at Berlin's Freie Universität, the Zentrum für Zeithistorische Forschung in Potsdam, and the Berlin branch of the Munich Institut für Zeitgeschichte. For their scholarly rigor and comradery, I would like to thank my fellow Berlin fellows; for their indispensable administrative assistance, I am indebted to Ingeborg Mehser and Dagmar Klenke. I would also like to thank Professor Peter Steinbach for allowing me to present some of my early findings to his seminar on East Germany at the Freie Universität.

Anyone who has done archival research knows how difficult the experience can be. Without the help of patient archivists the task would be impossible. I am deeply grateful to the staffs of the Bundesarchiv in Lichterfelde, the Landesarchiv Berlin (Breite Straße), and the Bundesarchiv Außenstelle in Dahlwitz-Hoppegarten. While in Berlin, I also benefited from countless discussions with several scholars—German and American, professors and doctoral candidates. For their advice, suggestions, and criticisms, I would like to thank Richard Bessel, Dierk Hoffmann, Patrice Poutrus, Judd Stitziel, Corey Ross, Paul Steege, and Peter

Steinbach. I would especially like to thank Philipp Heldmann, who has generously shared his research and insights with me. Throughout the research and writing, his help has been extensive, his comments invaluable.

Of course, the idea for the project took shape well before I ever got to Berlin, in the course of graduate work at Columbia University. When I returned from Berlin and began writing, I received indispensable criticism and encouragement from Fritz Stern, Volker Berghahn, Victoria De-Grazia, Richard Ericson, and Daniel Purdy. My time at Columbia, however, was most profoundly marked by my doctoral advisor, Fritz Stern. Repeated stints in his research seminar imparted a far deeper appreciation of the pleasures and burdens of history than I might ever have imagined when I entered graduate school. I owe him an intellectual debt that can scarcely be repaid.

After submitting my dissertation and while writing conference papers, drafting articles, and revising chapters, I continued to benefit from the helpful comments of several friends and colleagues: Volker Berghahn, Manfred Enssle, Martin Geyer, Maureen Healy, Philipp Heldmann, Dierk Hoffmann, Alexander Nützenadel, Jake Short, and Paul Steege. I would also like to thank Ken Barkin for permission to use here parts of an article I wrote that was published in *Central European History*.

At Harvard University Press, I am indebted to Kathleen McDermott for taking the project on, to Kirsten Giebutowski for seeing it through to publication, and to Professor Patrice Higonnet for including it in the Harvard Historical Studies series. In equal measure, I am grateful to the two outside readers of the manuscript, who provided highly perceptive comments and suggestions for improving it.

Finally, and most important, I have personal debts of gratitude. My parents, Faith and Mervyn Landsman, have shown exemplary patience and support during my years of graduate study and beyond. Anne and Warren Weisberg have offered additional and much-appreciated sympathy and encouragement. Last, I owe inexpressible thanks to my wife, Jennifer Weisberg, who, reading every page with an unerring eye for the infelicitious, has helped me to identify and remove several cognitive, technical, and stylistic blemishes. Without her patience, wit, and irony, the work would be immeasurably poorer. At every stage of the process, her emotional and intellectual support has been way above and beyond the call of spousal duty. I dedicate the book to her.

As convention dictates, I acknowledge sole responsibility for all errors of fact, form, and style.

Abbreviations

CARE	Cooperative for American Remittances to Europe
CDU(D)	Christian-Democratic Union of Germany
COMECON	Council for Mutual Economic Assistance (CMEA)
CPSU	Communist Party of the Soviet Union
DFD	Democratic Women's Federation of Germany
DHZ	German Trade Center
DVHV	German Administration for Trade and Provisioning
DWK	German Economic Commission
EDC	European Defense Community
ERP	European Recovery Program (Marshall Plan)
FDGB	Free German Federation of Unions
FDJ	Free German Youth
FRG	Federal Republic of Germany (West Germany)
GARIOA	Government Aid and Relief in Occupied Areas
GDR	German Democratic Republic (East Germany)
GHK	Wholesale Branch
HO	*Handelsorganisation* (Trade Organization)
HVHV	Central Administration for Trade and Provisioning
KKB	Coordination and Control Agency for Domestic Trade
KPD	Communist Party of Germany
KVP	People's Police in Barracks
LDP(D)	Liberal-Democratic Party of Germany
LPG	Agricultural Production Cooperative
SAG	Soviet Stock Company

SBZ	Soviet Occupation Zone
SCC	Soviet Control Commission
SED	Socialist Unity Party of Germany
SKHV	State Commission for Trade and Provisioning
SMAD	Soviet Military Administration in Germany
SPD	Social Democratic Party of Germany
SPK	State Planning Commission
VdgB	Association for Farmers' Mutual Help
VdK	Association of Consumer Cooperatives
VEB	People's-owned Enterprise

DICTATORSHIP AND DEMAND

Introduction

Erst kommt das Fressen, dann kommt die Moral.

Bertolt Brecht, *Die Dreigroschenoper*

In October 1999, as a way of marking the fiftieth anniversary of the founding of the German Democratic Republic, Berliners watched as more than forty Italian confectioners from Perugia built a chocolate facsimile of the Berlin Wall. The final product of their artful labors was a free-standing structure, thirty-nine feet long, consisting of four hundred blocks of chocolate, each weighing forty-five pounds—in total, thirteen tons of Italian chocolate. As an item in the *New York Times* blithely remarked, "Some eastern Germans have reacted to the anniversary with warm recollections of life before unification; others find nostalgia for a police state distasteful."[1]

Could Berliners have been treated to a more ambiguous symbol than a wall of chocolate? No doubt intended as a happy monument to reunification, to all the material pleasures so long denied East Germans by the actual Berlin Wall, the chocolate version offered the rather perverse spectacle of the Cold War's most despised symbol and instrument of tyranny cast in flavors of enticing sweetness. The incongruity of the monument was only heightened by the fact that it was also misleading: on the day being commemorated—October 7, 1949—there was no Berlin Wall. Not until August 1961 did the East German state physically seal itself off from West Berlin by erecting its self-described "antifascist protection wall." Perhaps worse still, the chocolate replica could so easily be interpreted as a symbol of remaining divisions: divisions between "eastern" and "western" Germans, the much-discussed "wall in the head" *(Mauer im Kopf);* and divisions between former East Germans themselves, between those whose memories of the German Democratic Republic flicker in the warm afterglow

1

of nostalgia and those who prefer the taste of chocolate to that of a "police state."

One can hardly blame the Italians. How could they have known that the new Germany would be no more immune to anxieties about the soundness of national unity than past Germanys have been? Yet to pause for reflection on the history of Germany since World War II is to recognize that issues of material well-being and consumerism form the theme of yet another chapter in the centuries-long story of Germany and its inner divisions. This book is an investigation into that theme. It explores the political consequences of frustrated desire in the German Democratic Republic (GDR) during the years between the Berlin Blockade and the building of the Berlin Wall.

The immediate setting is thus East Germany; the broader context is defined by the Cold War, the division of Europe, and the rise of distinct, new social orders on either side of the "Iron Curtain." The central tension driving the story arose from the confluence of an emerging, mass consumer society in the West and the crucial, destabilizing role of consumer dissatisfaction in the East. A product of research in recently opened East German state and party archives, this study depicts a regime caught between competing pressures: while East Germany's leaders received a Soviet model that fetishized productivity in heavy industry and rigidly prioritized the production of capital goods over consumer goods, they nevertheless had to contend with the increasingly tantalizing allure of consumer abundance in West Germany. As a result, the usual difficulties associated with satisfying consumer demand in a socialist economy acquired a uniquely intense political immediacy. From the very beginning, the regime found itself trapped in a contest of prosperity its leaders never expected, were loathe to engage in, but dared not ignore. Indeed, within their own painstakingly built bureaucracy—itself a perpetual work in progress—there soon emerged voices pressing the unsettling, almost taboo cause of consumer demand.

As in all the states of the Soviet bloc, the running discrepancy in East Germany between the regime's public promises to meet the material needs of its citizens and the chronic dearth of consumer goods called into question the political legitimacy of socialism on a daily basis. In this sense, the overall scope and implications of this work go well beyond the history of East Germany itself, raising larger questions about the nature of socialism and the East-West conflict that transcend the usual perspectives of political propaganda, military security, economic organization, and espionage. And yet the position of East Germany was especially difficult with regard to consumerism because of the magnetic prosperity generated by the West German "economic miracle" *(Wirtschaftswunder)*. Nowhere in divided Europe did the problem of consumption feature so prominently as a field of Cold War competition than in divided Germany, where nearly 3.5 million people fled across the open border to the West between 1945 and 1961. This book explores the ways in which the East German political leadership recognized, understood, and attempted to address one of the great weaknesses of the entire Soviet bloc.

My focus is therefore on the center, on those offices and departments within East Germany's ruling Socialist Unity Party (SED) concerned with consumer provisioning and on the central state ministries and planning authorities charged with carrying out, interpreting, and developing the policy directives of the central party leadership. I concentrate on particular moments in which the problem of consumer supply assumed great political significance and on specific efforts or campaigns associated with the regime's evolving consumption policies. The mode of the work is narrative, the argument cumulative. The problem of consumption is integrated into the larger, inseparable narratives of the Cold War and the history of divided Germany. Although we are beginning to see studies that highlight the significant role of consumerism in the fiscal crises and final collapse of the GDR, we still know little about the initial stages of the Cold War contest of prosperity as it played out on either side of Checkpoint Charlie.[2]

One point should be made clear at the outset: although this study offers, among other things, a critique of certain aspects of socialism, it is not intended as yet another (belated) warble in the glib chorus of Cold War triumphalism that greeted the fall of the Soviet Union over a decade ago. I have no interest in being a cheerleader for Western-style consumerism, which, as critics of various hues have long recognized, is so often cheap, loud, tasteless, offensive, manipulative, divisive, and endlessly insipid. Rather, my intention is to investigate the very real difficulties that postwar consumerism, for all its obvious shortcomings, created for the socialist world. Those difficulties constituted one of the crucial, if hitherto neglected, fault lines in the central geopolitical struggle of the second half of the twentieth century.[3] For our purposes, it is necessary above all to appreciate the profound difficulty of the position in which the leaders of East Germany found themselves from the very beginning, caught as they were between conflicting imperatives: on the one hand, "Sovietization"; on the other, the unprecedented, fitfully emerging, and only grudgingly understood challenge posed by postwar mass consumption in the West.

The step-by-step process of Sovietization began during the period of occupation immediately after the war under the authority of the Soviet Military Administration in Germany (SMAD). With the official founding of the German Democratic Republic in 1949, that process continued under the auspices of the Soviet Control Commission (SCC). Although in 1955 East Germany was nominally granted full sovereignty in domestic and foreign affairs, its sovereignty in practice was never more than partial, since Soviet influence remained pervasive and controlling, exercised through the Soviet embassy in East Berlin and through the activities of countless Soviet advisors in East Germany's leading political and economic administrations. Taken as a whole, the political, social, and economic changes introduced by the Soviets were nothing short of revolutionary. The Soviets presided over vast population movements, far-reaching land reform, the expropriation of large industries, the extraction of punishing reparations, the reorientation of foreign trade relationships, the abolition of "bourgeois" forms of justice, radical changes in the education system, the imposition of one-party rule, and the creation of a Soviet-style planned economy. With the exception of reparations, it must be added, none of this was anathema to SED leaders.

On the contrary, the SED leadership embraced these changes wholeheartedly and, with them, the economic and social priorities of productivism, by which I mean the classic Soviet-style emphasis on forced growth in heavy industry and the production of investment goods (in Marxist-Leninist terms, "the means of production"). For Marxist-Leninists the role of industry as the engine of growth, as the privileged core of the planned economy, was an article of faith derived from Soviet experience and inculcated under Soviet instruction. Productivism found expression not only in the division of scarce material resources and investments but also in the propaganda campaigns and socialist realist artifacts, which incessantly championed the virtues of productivity in labor and extreme modesty in material life. Productivism was at once an economic policy and a school of socialist virtue. Its heroes, typified by the Soviet coal miner Aleksei Stakhanov, were celebrated as models to emulate, their achievements immortalized in the glittering statistics of "overfulfilled" production quotas. This "proletarian mystique," so characteristic of Russian socialism, projected an idealized image of the working class as pure, ready for sacrifice, and unspoiled by materialism, "bourgeois" comforts, and selfishness.[4] Of course, the image was more goal than reality. Nevertheless, it remained an abiding mission, part and parcel of the Bolshevik dream of transforming people.

And yet it must also be remembered that for many on the Left austerity and sacrifice made up a great part of the appeal of socialism. As John Maynard Keynes recognized in the 1930s, after several trips to the Soviet Union, communism was "an appeal to the ascetic in us." Were Cambridge undergraduates disillusioned when they took their "inevitable trip to Bolshiedom" and found it "dreadfully uncomfortable?" "Of course not," Keynes suggested. "That is what they are looking for."[5] Socialism was to be not only more efficient and productive than capitalism but also more just, promising a moral renewal of which material sacrifice was an inseparable component, at least until the attainment of what Marx had called "a higher phase of communist society," a moment in which "society [would] inscribe on its banner: From each according to his ability, to each according to his needs!"[6] But this was a moment that could only be achieved through hard work and sacrifice, through saving and investing. On the path to that higher phase, a socialist society in the making would have to substitute the principle of work for that of need in the distribution of its "means of consumption." In Marx's words, "the individual producer receives back from society . . . exactly what he gives to it. What he has given to it is his individual quantum of labor."[7] In Leninist hands this principle found ready and exaggerated application.

To emphasize only the harshness and appeal of austerity, however, would be misleading. The Soviet Union and its protégé regimes in Eastern Europe did offer other, compensatory satisfactions, both material and nonmaterial, which helped to soothe the everyday frustrations aroused by chronic shortages in consumer goods. Professing a commitment to the brotherhood of mankind and to the breaking down of social barriers, socialist states extended to the lower orders of society unprecedented access to education, health care, and social welfare. Subsidized prices afforded an easy satisfaction of basic needs such as food, housing, and utilities. Never before had the working classes of Eastern Europe and east-central Europe enjoyed such material security. And although the constitutional "right to work" celebrated by socialist regimes came to be seen by their citizens as more of a duty than a right, socialism did provide full employment, an achievement that seemed particularly impressive after the chronic unemployment of the 1920s and 1930s. The relative neglect of private consumption wants reflected a contempt for consumerism as well as a desire to provide something loftier, to build a better, more egalitarian society in which the materialistic individualism that still plagued the West would finally be transcended.

East Germany's leaders, many of them only recently returned to Germany from extended periods of exile in the Soviet Union, were much beholden to this utopian impulse; they showed themselves to be avid pupils and enthusiastic practitioners of Soviet-style productivism. But complicating, even modifying, the process of Sovietization were developments in West Germany perhaps most easily grouped under the category of "Americanization."[8] There has been much debate about the extent and pace of Americanization in West Germany, particularly about the emergence of mass consumption. The most recent literature has argued that material prosperity and consumer abundance emerged more slowly in West Germany than previously assumed and that for most West Germans everyday life continued to be defined by material sacrifice, austerity, and hard work for most of the 1950s.[9]

Nevertheless, from the point of view of SED leaders, the pace of prosperity and mass consumption in West Germany was all too swift. As living standards in West Germany improved, especially by the mid-1950s, they became the primary point of reference not only for the East German people but for the SED regime itself. As often as they denounced the exploitative character of West German capitalism, as often as they heralded its imminent collapse, SED leaders found themselves confronted with a rival German society in the midst of an economic miracle that provided a measure of prosperity, material well-being, and social security its citizens had never known before. By 1956 Ludwig Erhard, West Germany's economics minister, could quite rightly encapsulate the strategy of West Germany's unfolding success story with the apt slogan "Prosperity for All" *(Wohlstand für alle)*. Erhard looms as a towering figure in the history of the Federal Republic. He is widely regarded as the father of the *Wirtschaftswunder.* Scholars differ on the extent to which his postwar nostrums were based on ideas already formed before 1945.[10] Few, if any, would dispute that by the time he assumed his duties as economics minister, he ascribed to the virtues of free trade and market competition and favored a consumption-oriented capitalism.[11] For Erhard the "will to consume" was a prerequisite for economic expansion and higher productivity; it was impossible to produce without consuming, he insisted, "except in a totalitarian system."[12] In addition, the "social market economy" over which he presided incorporated a system of "codetermination" *(Mitbestimmung)* between employers and organized labor, which helped to overcome the crippling industrial conflicts of the past. As Erhard suggested, it was more sensible to replace acrimonious squabbles over the distribution of wealth with a consensus on producing more of it: "It is considerably easier to allow everyone a larger slice out of a bigger cake than to gain anything by discussing the division of a smaller cake."[13]

Relative peace in industrial relations, a thriving capitalist economy, and hitherto unknown social security were, in turn, accompanied by the multiplying enticements of American-style mass culture and mass consumption. The 1950s brought not only rock 'n' roll, teen movies, and youth fashions to Europe[14] but also new products and modes of everyday consumption. For the first time in the history of Germany, indeed of Western Europe, households from all classes of society became able with the help of various consumer credit options to acquire refrigerators, washing machines, vacuum cleaners, and television sets. People found their ways of eating and dressing remade, as their wardrobes incorporated new artificial fibers and fabrics and as their cupboards filled with canned fruit and vegetables, tomatoes from Italy, and oranges and bananas from southern lands *(Südfrüchte)*. A rapidly expanding network of self-service stores lent new meaning to the idea of freedom of choice, providing unimpeded access to new, brand-name products. These were developments East Germany's leaders could ill afford to ignore. In fact, as this study shows, they made considerable efforts to respond in kind, by providing their own citizens with many of the same products and accoutrements of a modern consumer culture.

And yet if the challenges posed by West German prosperity and consumerism were undeniable, the ability of SED leaders to appreciate their significance was less straightforward. For in addition to the influence of the Soviet model they eagerly embraced, East German leaders were burdened by specifically German traditions that interfered with their understanding of the emerging "consumer society" in West Germany. In fact, there had long been a traditional ambivalence about, or aversion to, American-style mass consumption and mass culture, elements of which began to appear in Germany during the Weimar years.[15] Pejoratively tagged by cultural critics of the Left and Right as emblems of "Americanism," the harbingers of mass consumption were associated with many of the perceived spiritual and material ills of the modern age. Debates in the 1920s and 1930s about rationalization, standardization, Henry Ford, chewing gum—in short, "Americanism"—were at their core about Germany's confrontation with modernity. It was during these years that the future leaders of East Germany imbibed their political-cultural education. Once in power, they showed themselves ready and able to play upon deeply ingrained prejudices against "Americanism."[16]

Moreover, within the Left itself there was an ambivalence about what has come to be known as "Fordism." A different kind of productivism, Fordism linked mass production and mass consumption by combining standardized production with low prices and high wages. High output minimized costs per unit, as high wages sustained demand. It must be remembered that within the German workers' movement the enthusiasm for productivism had acquired deep roots well before the existence of the Soviet Union. Marx himself had been a champion of nineteenth-century advances in industrial production methods, identifying them as a necessary condition of increased production and greater efficiency. During the Weimar years the enthusiasm for production innovations was readily apparent in the pilgrimages of leading German socialists and labor organizers to the American Midwest, to the temples of Fordist mass production.[17] Those who visited were deeply impressed by Ford's plants at Highland Park and River Rouge and by the wondrous spectacle of perpetual motion facilitated by conveyors, railroads, and assembly lines. But it was primarily the production side of Fordism that appealed. Those who visited the United States displayed a pronounced myopia when it came to the central elements of Fordist-style mass consumption. Aside from admiring the comparatively high wages paid to American workers, they seemed to take little notice of the new forms of credit buying and advertising or the popularity of new consumer durables.[18]

Specifically German cultural traditions and habits of thought, therefore, combined with Marxist ideology and Soviet influence to leave SED leaders ill equipped to recognize the significance of mass consumption as it emerged in West Germany. Nothing in their past experience or within their ideological frame of reference prepared them for the impact of "the Fordist recipe."[19] The Marxist theoretical tradition they inherited had little to say about the sphere of consumption, except insofar as it reflected and disguised power relationships arising from the realm of production. Meanwhile, the experience of the Great Depression and fascism only confirmed their faith in the bankruptcy of capitalism and the promise of socialism. How could they have predicted that mass consumption would gradually replace the traditional, rigidly class-stratified patterns of consumption typical of Western Europe before the war? How could they have known that it would thus contribute to easing many of the classic problems of industrial capitalist society, above all those of rancorous class divisions and crises of overproduction?[20] The challenge they came to face was conceptual as well as material. Wedded to an understanding of capitalist society as one made up of distinct and opposing classes—that is, collective producing entities defined by their place in the hierarchical relations between forces of production—SED leaders were entirely unprepared to recognize the growing appeal of an emerging alternative view, one that substituted individual consumers for collective producers and proposed "prosperity for all" not as a vague, distant reward for prolonged, heroic sacrifice but as a real possibility in the immediate present.

It bears emphasizing: postwar mass consumption in Western Europe was a new phenomenon, at first dimly and then resentfully understood by the leaders of East Germany. And yet they could hardly escape the creeping challenge it posed. In fact, the demands for higher levels of consumption arising from the population very quickly found "representation" within the regime, as a consumer supply lobby began to emerge within the official planning and administrative apparatus responsible for domestic trade and provisioning (*Handel und Versorgung*). Scholars of Soviet-type systems have long acknowledged the existence of particular lobbies, or interest groups, within socialist regimes;[21] but in doing so, they have tended to recapitulate the dominant concerns of party leaders by focusing on the lobbying efforts of groups in heavy industry and the military. In contrast, they have had little or nothing to say on the subject of consumer advocacy. But as this study shows, a consumer supply lobby, however uncoordinated, emerged almost immediately within the GDR's Ministry for Trade and Provisioning. Motivated by the need to fulfill their sales plans and therefore to keep inventory moving, trade functionaries had a direct interest in satisfying consumer demand by supplying the goods consumers desired. In advancing their own interests, trade officials quickly developed a language and set of goals aiming toward a more generous array of consumption offerings. They called for improving market research, advertising, retail store decoration, and customer service. Most important, they pushed for greater control over the production of consumer goods, an effort that brought them increasingly into conflict with industrial manufacturers and the ministries under which they operated. As the pressure caused by growing prosperity in West Germany mounted, the claims of trade for the cause of consumption received added weight in the ongoing struggle with industry for control over consumer supply.

To be sure, additional interest groups within the system, played important roles in the planning of consumption. One can point, in particular, to the ministries of finance and foreign trade—in fact, at several moments in these pages, questions of finance and foreign trade assume great significance. The emphasis on the difficult relationship between domestic trade and industry, however, offers several points of unique insight. First, it affords a revealing view of the challenge posed by the consumer supply lobby to the otherwise uncontested official obsession with productivity in heavy industry. Second, the prolonged, unresolved nature of the struggle between trade and industry neatly parallels the SED leadership's own ambivalent and zigzagging strategies for addressing the problem of a consumer demand it could neither completely control nor satisfy. Third, drawing attention to this struggle not only sheds light on the inner workings of the GDR but may provide clues for the study of other Soviet-type regimes as well. Finally, understanding this struggle offers a broader political context for analyzing everyday consumer culture and assessing its importance in the history of divided Germany and the Cold War.

The attention to competing interest groups within the apparatus, in turn, has a direct bearing on the continuing debate about the type of regime East Germany's leaders fashioned and the nature of the relationship between rulers and ruled in the GDR. At the heart of this debate is the opposition between those scholars who focus on the state itself, proposing variations on the theme of totalitarianism, and those who insist on the importance of those aspects of social life that remained beyond the control of the state, allowing East German citizens to pursue daily lives largely imbued with self-generated direction and meaning (*Eigen-Sinn*). At issue is whether the East German people feature in their history as passive victims of totalitarian rule or as active subjects who were able to pursue their own interests within and beyond the claims of official ideology and institutions.[22] In fact, the debate is distorted by the assumption, false yet shared on both sides, that any study focusing its attention primarily on the state necessarily bolsters an understanding of the East German regime as totalitarian.[23] In truth, this need hardly be so. This book is a case in point: it shows quite clearly that there was a multiplicity of voices within the regime, and it highlights many of the limits hindering the successful implementation of various policies. In this sense, the following pages lay out a path leading beyond the confines of a debate that has long since grown rather sterile but that continues to cast its shadow over the expanding literature on East Germany.

The argument of this book is built into the narrative and may be summarized as follows. In the task of provisioning consumer goods to their citizens, East German political leaders found themselves confronted with a problem that they had never anticipated but that quickly acquired great political significance. Caught between the Soviet model they wanted to implement and the challenge posed by a new kind of prosperity in West Germany, SED leaders faced demands for a more-generous and higher-quality provisioning not only from the population but from within their own apparatus. As a result, an unresolved tension persisted between those voices arguing for ever-greater productivity in heavy industry and strict modesty in individual consumption, and those calling for a richer, more-developed set of consumption possibilities.

Between the poles of austerity and relative generosity, consumption policy swung back and forth, depending upon the amount of pressure at any given moment to address consumer dissatisfaction. The years until the uprising of June 17, 1953, have rightly been characterized as a time of austerity and reconstruction. And yet even in these years there were, for those who could afford it, means of satisfying desires that exceeded the most basic. Moreover, a consumer supply lobby, located in the Ministry for Trade and Provisioning, had already begun to develop a consumerist idiom and a set of arguments that, after the uprising in June 1953, were to receive, temporarily, official recognition and encouragement with the implementation of the "New Course." By the mid-1950s, however, after prewar consumption levels for many basic goods had been more or less equaled, party leaders abandoned the New Course and shifted the concentration of investment resources back to heavy industry. And yet despite the apparent return to productivism, East Germany's leaders, chastened by the uprising of June 1953, demonstrated an abiding concern for living standards and showed themselves to be increasingly beholden to the standard of material well-being emerging in West Germany, one against which they failed to pose a compelling alternative. Although the New Course disappeared from view, these were the years in which the regime expanded its consumer credit offerings, introduced the mail-order catalogue, and developed plans for establishing self-service stores. By 1956 even Nikita Khrushchev had come to see the need to turn the GDR into a "showcase" of socialist splendor in the Cold War competition with the West.

Within East Germany these conflicting impulses found their clearest expression in the relationship between trade and industry, with trade acting as a consumer advocate in the face of indifference on the part of manufacturers of consumer goods and the industrial ministries under which they operated. Strengthening the hand of industry in this struggle was the chronic weakness of trade within the structure of East Germany's political economy. Strengthening the hand of the consumer supply lobby, however, were the enticements of West German consumerism and the ever-swelling number of East German refugees fleeing to the West. Compelled to take action, the SED leadership proclaimed at the Fifth Party Congress in July 1958 its so-called Main Economic Task of surpassing West Germany in productivity and individual consumption by 1961–62. Although this bold move initially resulted in a decline in the number of refugees, another mounting provisioning crisis, brought on by the simultaneous drive to collectivize East

German agriculture, doomed the Main Economic Task to failure and precipitated the building of the Berlin Wall. Although the challenge posed by prosperity in the West would endure, and the issue of consumption would retain its political significance in East Germany right up until 1989, the building of the wall signified an important break. Having removed the immediate pressure caused by the open border between East and West Berlin, the SED would never again adopt as official policy the ambitious goals it had proclaimed in the Main Economic Task—it would never again boast of East Germany's ability to surpass West Germany in individual consumption. Here was a caesura that amounted to a concession of failure and as such marked the end of a crucial chapter in the Cold War contest of prosperity.

The implicit point of departure for this study is the recognition that in the bipolar world that emerged after the Second World War the issue of consumption came to delineate a crucial arena of Cold War competition. Nowhere was this competition more keenly felt than in divided Germany, where consumption emerged as a central, if hitherto neglected, factor in the Cold War crises of the late 1940s and 1950s. These crises serve as points of orientation in the narrative this study offers, and they allow us to trace the evolution in understanding and response on the part of the regime.

Chapter 1 introduces the problem of consumer provisioning under conditions of extreme scarcity and strict rationing in the Soviet zone of occupation and discusses the initial efforts on the part of authorities, Soviet and German, to grapple with the competing requirements of production and consumption. Chapter 2 highlights the emergence of the new contest of prosperity between East and West as occasioned by the June 1948 currency reform in the Western zones of occupation, which resulted in the overnight transformation of previously empty and forlorn shopwindows into tantalizing tableaux suddenly filled with all the consumer goods people had been forced to do without for so long. The chapter then follows this new contest as it resulted in the ensuing Berlin Blockade and in the introduction of the HO *(Handelsorganisation)*, a state-owned organization of retail stores that afforded Germans living under Soviet occupation the first legal opportunity to shop ration-free since the early war years. Chapter 3 outlines the overall process of consumption planning in East Germany, traces the emergence of the consumer supply lobby, and looks closely at the mounting provisioning crisis leading to the uprising of June 17, 1953. Chapter 4 discusses the subsequently pursued New Course and makes the argument that it was both more embattled and more enduring than scholars have previously suggested. Chapter 5 examines the GDR's system of market research, officially dubbed "demand research" *(Bedarfsforschung)*, and places it squarely within the context of the fateful struggle between trade and industry over control of consumer supply. Last, Chapter 6 discusses the ill-fated Main Economic Task and probes its meaning within the larger collection of simultaneously consumerist and productivist policies leading to the final crescendo that ended with the building of the Berlin Wall.

Before proceeding, however, it is necessary to set the stage for Chapter 1, which beginning in 1947, places the reader in a highly fluid moment, one in which several momentous changes had already been introduced in the Soviet zone of occupation but in which the future still remained profoundly uncertain as the Cold War lingered in its murky beginnings. Although by 1947 Soviet authorities had already embarked on policies of fundamental social and political transformation, they were not yet committed to an imposition of Soviet-style communism in their zone. In September 1945, under the slogan *Junkerland in Bauernhand!* they broke up the large landholdings of Prussian aristocrats, thereby crushing the position and power base of a class universally recognized as a traditional bulwark of authoritarianism and militarism in Germany. In July 1946, on the basis of a referendum in Saxony, the factories of "war criminals and Nazi criminals" were expropriated, a formula soon extended to the other provinces of the zone. As a result, by the beginning of 1947 the lion's share of industry in Eastern Germany was under the control of administrative authorities, either Soviet or German.

In the political sphere, the Soviets orchestrated the building of an "antifascist bloc of democratic parties," a constellation consisting of two new "bourgeois" parties, the Christian Democrats (CDU) and the Liberal Democrats (LDP), as well as the two main parties of the Weimar Left, the Social Democrats (SPD) and the Communists (KPD). Outwardly democratic, the bloc in fact served as a means for the KPD to establish its own political preeminence under the banner of "antifascism." Only the Social Democrats presented a potential challenge to Communist dominance. But with the forced merger of the SPD and the KPD into the SED in April 1946, that threat disappeared. Serving as cochairmen of the newly formed SED were Wilhelm Pieck (formerly KPD) and Otto Grotewohl (formerly SPD). But the person who quickly assumed real leadership of the party was Walter Ulbricht, a figure decidedly lacking in charisma and personal warmth but gifted in the arts of conspiracy and behind-the-scenes party politicking. Originally trained as a furniture maker, Ulbricht possessed an extraordinary capacity for hard work and soon became a master at matters of party organization. He had been a member of the KPD Politburo since 1929, and with several other leading Communists he had spent the war years in Moscow exile. It was the "Ulbricht Group" that entered Berlin with Soviet troops while the fighting was still going on, and it was Ulbricht himself who, following Soviet instructions, directed the creation of a new German administration in the Soviet zone.

The picture of SED preeminence was finally rounded out by the newly created, Soviet-style "mass organizations," which integrated important social groups and served as a means of communicating and facilitating compliance with party initiatives ("transmission belts" between the party and the masses). These included a new official trade union (the Free German Federation of Unions or FDGB), an official youth group (the Free German Youth or FDJ), a new women's group (the Democratic Women's Federation of Germany or DFD), and a new cultural association (the League of Culture or *Kulturbund*). Thus, by 1947 the process of Sovietization had taken great strides but was still far from complete. Nor was it at all certain that the process would continue, as Soviet and German officials began to grapple with the formidable task of building a future for the Germans living under their authority.

CHAPTER 1

Production and Consumption: Establishing Priorities

> But the point of departure must be to make do with what we have.
>
> Bruno Leuschner, July 1947

> The best provisioning to the best worker.
>
> *Die Versorgung,* November 1947

In the years immediately following the Second World War, Germany was a site of destruction, chaos, and misery. Its major cities were in ruins; its transport network was severely damaged; its economy had collapsed. Its inhabitants, uprooted and traumatized, presented a vision of the despairing and the demoralized: "rubble women" and refugees, returning soldiers and "displaced persons," the abject defeated and their foreign occupiers. Having controlled nearly the entire European continent at the apogee of its wartime power, Germany now found itself at the mercy of its wartime enemies.[1]

For most Germans everyday life was now defined by the struggle to survive in the face of chronic hunger, inadequate housing, a lack of heating fuel and other basic commodities. To capture the desperate, febrile quality of life in these years, historians have employed labels like the "survival society," the "society in collapse," the "rations society," the "society of provisioned classes."[2] With daily rations falling far below the two thousand calories calculated by the League of Nations as the minimum requirement for a working adult, people had no choice but to steal, engage in furtive black market exchange, make repeated foraging trips to the countryside in overly packed trains, and scrounge for heating fuel amid the twigs and tree branches of city parks.

Further heightening the sense of insecurity and confusion were the many administratively launched upheavals. Throughout occupied Germany authorities made efforts to denazify and reeducate, to dismantle industrial plant and extract reparations, to reform patterns of land-holding and reorganize business structures, to reestablish old political parties and create new ones. And if we widen the lens further, we bring into view the breakdown of the wartime alliance and the emergence of the Cold War, the fault lines of which, running through German territory, introduced cause for even more profound uncertainty about the future.

In histories of the occupation period the year 1947 is commonly viewed as the year of transition. Through a rapid succession of events it signaled an alarming increase in tension between the Allies, a shift on the part of occupiers from policies of punishment to those of reconstruction, and concomitantly a decisive shove forward along the path toward the division of Germany. The first half of the year alone witnessed the economic fusion of the American and British zones into the Bizone (January), the proclamation of the Truman Doctrine (March), the failure of the Moscow Foreign Ministers Conference (March–April), and the famous Harvard speech of U.S. Secretary of State George Marshall, announcing the plan that became most widely associated with his name (June).

On the eve of Marshall's speech, the Soviet Military Administration in Germany (SMAD) made its own contribution to the widening rift by creating the German Economic Commission (*Deutsche Wirtschaftskommission* or DWK). The DWK was to be the first centralized Soviet-zone administration run by Germans and, as such, the first forum for developing the principles and policies of economic planning. No task faced by the apprentice planners of the DWK was more formidable than that of provisioning consumer goods under the difficult living conditions of the immediate postwar years. Nor was their task eased by the vision for reconstruction pursued by Soviet-zone authorities. Under close Soviet supervision, DWK planners drew a road map marked primarily by metallurgy, machine building, coal mining, and electrical engineering. The path to a better future, as they conceived it, lay exclusively in the primacy of heavy industry. This emphasis on capital goods, however, necessarily came at the expense of consumption goods. And yet the consumption needs of Germans could not be entirely ignored. At the most basic level, workers had to be fed, clothed, and housed if they were to be productive. As the political confrontation between East and West intensified, Soviet-zone authorities had to take steps to garner the support of the inhabitants in their zone. This chapter shows how those authorities began to try to accommodate the requirements of consumption within the larger imperative of production.

One thing DWK planners had working in their favor was the fact that the experience of hunger and food shortages was hardly novel. For nearly thirty years the lives of Germans had been punctuated by food crises; for many, these decades had consisted of recurrent bouts of austerity.[3] Most adults in 1945 had personally lived through, or grown up hearing about, the terrible "turnip winter" of 1916–17. They remembered how slowly the food supply improved after the First World War, only to be again thrown into chaos by the Great Inflation of 1923. While the stabilization of the second half of the 1920s brought relief, even prosperity, to some, low-income earners continued to struggle to feed themselves and their families. Even during the "golden years" of the Weimar Republic, millions remained unemployed—2 million in 1926, that is, 10 percent of the working-age population and 18 percent of trade unionists.[4]

The onset of the Great Depression necessarily broadened and deepened their plight. In 1930 the number of unemployed reached 4.5 million; by January 1933, when Hitler became chancellor, it had grown to over 8 million.[5] Although the Nazi regime managed to put people back to work in the mid-to-late 1930s, there continued to be persistent complaints about shortages and rising prices for all kinds of basic commodities, as not only the reports of the German Social Democratic Party in Exile (SOPADE) but also those of the Gestapo clearly show.[6] For consumers the Nazi years were characterized by a combination of seductive promise and material frustration or, as one historian has recently put it, "enticement and deprivation."[7] The regime's propaganda tantalized with images of mass access to new kinds of consumer experience, most notably its "strength through joy" vacations, radios, vacuum cleaners, refrigerators, cars, and early television sets. But with the exception of the cheap, standardized "people's radio," which appeared to serve the propaganda needs of the regime, these promises were never, or only slightly, fulfilled during the Third Reich. With its economy geared toward preparing for war, its foreign currency reserves in desperately short supply, and its hope, never realized, of achieving a state of economic self-sufficiency, the regime did what it could to suppress private consumption. To soak up excess purchasing power, it increased taxes and allowed prices to rise faster than wages. In the hopes of "guiding" consumption, it appealed to consumers to "buy German" and to accept ersatz products in place of foreign or scarce commodities. It launched propaganda campaigns to encourage saving and to fight against all forms of waste.[8] Consumers were less responsive to these propaganda efforts than Nazi authorities had hoped they would be. Still, they faced shortages in textiles and foodstuffs. As early as 1937, butter, margarine, and other fats had to be rationed.

With the introduction of extensive rationing in August 1939, on the eve of the German invasion of Poland, there was much grumbling from the population. But the rationing system had been so painstakingly well prepared by Nazi authorities that people more or less grew accustomed to it. The Nazi leadership had been determined to avoid what it regarded as one of the great mistakes of the previous war—that is, allowing the food supply to deteriorate to the point that it weakened morale on the home front. Although there were complaints about the uniformity of rationed supplies, the regime managed in the first years of the war to feed its population sufficiently well, assuring "normal consumers" about twenty-three hundred calories daily. But as the tide of the war turned in 1943, and it was no longer possible to supply Germans with the goods plundered from the territories conquered by the Wehrmacht, the orderly system of provisioning gave way increasingly to improvisation and shortages.[9] By spring 1945 authorities had to extend the validity of ration cards already distributed in February and March, since it was impossible to allocate any new rations for the first week of April.[10] The ration cards themselves, meanwhile, had long since become worthless, as black markets flourished. In the end, as the military effort inexorably disintegrated, collapse on the home front could not be avoided.

Still, the Nazi system of rationing had functioned well for much of the war and, with its reputation largely intact, was continued in the Western occupation zones.[11] In the Soviet zone, however, the allocation of rations followed a combination of Soviet and Nazi wartime practices. Here the population was divided into three main groups: normal consumers (*Normalverbraucher*), partial self-providers (*Teilselbstversorger*), and self-providers (*Selbstversorger*). The normal consumers, who comprised the overwhelming majority of the zone's population, were then broken down into six smaller groups, each receiving a different ration card based on occupation and age. In order of decreasing rations, cards were distributed to workers performing the heaviest manual labor (Card I), those performing heavy manual labor (Card II), workers (Card III), employees (Card IV), children (Card V), and the rest of the population (Card VI).[12]

In the Western zones, too, there was a connection between heavy manual labor and better rations.[13] Workers performing heavy manual labor in Munich, for example, were "honored" in 1947 with 1,090 extra calories per day, which represented 83 percent of normal consumer rations. Similarly, miners in the Ruhr were rewarded according to a points system.[14] But in the Soviet zone, Cards I and II were also given out to engineers and technicians, political leaders and administration officials, intellectuals and artists, and even some professionals. The inclusion of these groups in the highest ration categories, justified by "the great economic and social significance of their work," reflected distinctly Soviet practices in the allocation of scarce commodities, one aim of which was to win over and build up a reliable leadership cadre.[15] In direct contrast, the members of these groups in the Western zones were among those at the bottom of the rationing hierarchy. Moreover, in the Soviet zone heavy manual labor did not in itself guarantee receiving Card I or II. One had to work in either mining or heavy industry. This requirement, too, reflected a particularly Soviet emphasis that, as we shall see, was soon extended on a far greater scale than was ever done in the West.

In addition to the categories of occupation and age, the size (and thus political importance) of one's place of residence also played a role in the early stratification of provisioning. The population was divided into a four-tiered residential hierarchy in which the Soviet sector of Berlin came first, followed by the two largest cities in Saxony, Dresden and Leipzig. These, in turn, were followed by the other sixteen large cities of the zone, which were finally followed by the smaller towns, rural communities, and villages. The differences between these categories, it should be added, were significant. For example, in January 1947 official daily rations ranged from nearly twenty-five hundred calories for a worker performing heavy manual labor in East Berlin to just over one thousand calories for a holder of Card V in one of the smaller locations of the zone.[16] Very often, however, even these desperately inadequate rations could not be fulfilled, and the actual amounts given out fell well below the official levels.

It was with the help of trusted house and block representatives that zonal administrators distributed ration cards to the population. Upon presenting their work certificates to these representatives, individuals would receive their corresponding cards.[17] The cards for most consumer goods retained their validity for a period of ten days, partly because officials wanted to limit attempts at speculation and partly because most food items would not keep for longer periods.[18] Not only were consumers required to shop within the circumscribed time period, but they also had to shop at designated stores in their immediate neighborhoods, where they were registered. Individual stores received their deliveries only after preregistering their customers' cards. (In East Berlin this system of binding consumers to particular stores lasted until 1951.) The shopping experience in these first postwar years was limited primarily to small, private shops. Department stores and specialized stores had not yet reopened, and not until the end of 1948 did authorities begin to create a state-owned retail chain. The only alternatives to traditional, small-scale private shopkeepers were the consumer cooperatives. Though once widespread and popular among the urban working classes, they had been "liquidated" by the Nazis and were only beginning to reestablish themselves in the postwar retail landscape.

Ration card coupons could also be used in exchange for additional meals at the workplace for adults and at school for children. Unfortunately, the quality of these meals was a source of constant complaint. Parents often preferred to feed their children at home rather than give up coupons for the watery soups prepared at schools. (Not until the end of 1949 would schoolchildren in East Berlin be assured of receiving at least one white roll [*Schrippe*] with their school meals.) Similarly, many adults refused to exchange ration coupons for workplace meals of equally poor quality and low nutritional value.[19]

Of greater use were the special workplace allocations of foodstuffs and other consumer goods, which could be used not only for personal consumption but also for exchange on the black market. These allocations, however, were sporadic and offered only temporary help. The black market itself was of limited value for most people, because of its prohibitively high prices. Generally, goods on the black market were more than one hundred times more expensive than rationed goods, the prices of which were officially frozen at 1944 levels. On the black market, in early 1947, a Berlin family with a middle-level monthly income of 200–300 *Reichsmark* (RM) would have had to spend about RM 40–60 for one pound of wheat flour, RM 35–45 for one loaf of rye bread, RM 250–350 for one pound of butter, RM 15–20 for one egg.[20]

Of course, most people could and did avail themselves of still other opportunities to supplement their meager official rations. They went foraging in the countryside, equipped with backpacks and potato sacks; they cultivated vegetables in small private gardens (in East Berlin, 26.5 percent of all households had a garden); they kept small farm animals on the balconies and in the courtyards of apartment buildings.[21] But these were efforts born of hunger, desperation, and uncertainty. Although they afforded intermittent alleviation of some of the harshest effects of living conditions in the Soviet zone, they could never be more than stopgap strategies in a prolonged, improvised struggle to survive. Deprivation, demoralization, and despair continued to shape the life of the Soviet zone.

For DWK planners intent on boosting industrial productivity, these material obstacles had to be addressed. Yet the problem of productivity comprised more than the material deprivations of individual Germans living under Soviet occupation. Here it is necessary to say something about the effects of Soviet demands for reparations on industrial productivity in the zone.

As the Soviet Union and the Western Allies failed to reach an agreement on the contribution of the Western zones to Soviet reparations claims, the Soviets saw no alternative but to satisfy their demands primarily in their own zone. Recent estimates of the total value of reparations extracted from the zone by the early 1950s range from $10 billion to $14 billion (1938 prices). If the latter amount is taken as accurate, the ratio of reparations ultimately paid by the Western and Eastern zones respectively is about 1 in 10. In the end, the Soviet Union took from the Soviet zone everything, if not more than, it had originally demanded from the whole of Germany.[22] The process of extraction proceeded in phases. The summer of 1945 was characterized by looting and plunder, as combat troops and "trophy battalions" swept through eastern Germany, taking everything, from food, watches, and furniture to military machinery, communications equipment, coal, iron, and steel. Thereafter, whole factories were dismantled and transferred to the Soviet Union. Finally, by mid-1946 the Soviets shifted to extracting reparations in kind, primarily through Soviet Stock Companies (*Sowjetische Aktiengesellschaften* or SAGs). The SAGs were German enterprises that had been transferred to Soviet ownership but that remained in the zone, producing goods to be sent back to the Soviet Union. By the end of 1946, the Soviets owned nearly 30 percent of all industrial production in the zone, including virtually all synthetic fuel, mineral oil, and industrial chemical production.[23]

The consequences of these measures on industrial production were catastrophic. By 1947 the Soviets had dismantled and removed nearly 80 percent of machine-tool productive capacity and 60 percent of light and specialized industrial productive capacity. As a result, spare parts were almost impossible to find, and new machines could not be ordered. Complicating matters further, the zonal divisions of the occupation disrupted the usual patterns by which raw materials and manufactured parts were delivered from west to east. Although the Soviets (and the Poles) took up some of the slack, supply problems persisted. Most typically, coal shortages simply brought production to a halt, even in large, state-run factories. The shortages, in turn, forced individual provinces to pursue protectionist economic strategies of their own, resulting in "trade wars." The chronic shortage of skilled labor, combined with disastrously high rates of absenteeism, added yet a further factor limiting productivity; in such key heavy industries as coal, metallurgy, and machine building, rates of absenteeism were over 20 percent.[24] Meanwhile, the SAGs not only represented a significant loss of productive capacity but also caused crippling dislocations throughout the rest of the economy—particularly in the production of spare parts, fuel, chemicals, and consumer goods— as a result of enjoying priority in the allocation of raw materials and labor.

Reparations and removals, the problem of productivity, the widespread sense of frustration and hopelessness all furthered the desire of SED leaders to develop some kind of centralized economic planning body. A plan, it was hoped, would help limit irregular Soviet removals and thus bring a more orderly character to the regrettable but unavoidable burden of reparations. SED leaders also believed that planning was indispensable for speeding up the process of reconstruction and giving workers the hope necessary to lift morale. In this regard, they were not alone. In fact, the belief in the desirability of some form of economic planning was shared across the political spectrum in all of the occupation zones.[25] For Communist leaders, however, the significance of planning far transcended considerations of short- and medium-term expediency. As both a mechanism of power and an instrument of idealism, planning *was* socialism. It would simultaneously bring the SED greater control over the economic life of the zone, and it would point the way to a new beginning, to transcending the anarchy and exploitation of the market, offering a chance to realize the greater efficiency and social justice held out by the promise of socialism. In the words of Bruno Leuschner, the future leader of the DWK planning department, economic planning was to signify "an economic invigoration and a moral impulse."[26]

Although Leuschner and others had been calling for more extensive economic planning for several months, the initiative for the creation of the DWK came from the Soviets.[27] Two factors, in particular, pushed the Soviets in this direction: their own inability to ensure the implementation of SMAD orders in the provinces; and the economic crisis resulting from (or vastly exacerbated by) the terrible winter of 1946–47. In January Major General Konstantin Koval, chief economics officer for SMAD, invited the presidents of the German central administrations (all but one SED members)[28] to work out proposals for increasing the power of their own administrations over that of their counterparts in the provinces. Secret negotiations continued through the spring, while the Soviets waited for an opportune moment to make a public announcement. On May 29, 1947, officials from the U.S. and British zones provided an opportunity when they announced the creation of the Frankfurt Economic Council for the Bizone. A few days later, on June 4, the SMAD responded by issuing Order no. 138, which authorized the formation of the DWK. Meeting for the first time the following week, the commission was made up of the presidents of five administrations (Industry, Transportation, Fuel and Energy, Agriculture, and Trade and Provisioning), plus the chief of the FDGB and the chairman of the Association for Farmers' Mutual Help (VdgB).[29] Bruno Leuschner served temporarily as head of the commission but later became leader of the planning section, and Heinrich Rau became DWK chairman.

Both Rau and Leuschner had spent the war years in prison and concentration camps. They both came from working-class backgrounds and had been active in the KPD before the war. Their life trajectories were on the whole typical of those veteran Communists who would come to rule East Germany.[30] Rau joined the KPD in 1919 at the age of twenty, was a deputy to the Prussian parliament from 1928 to 1933, and over the years acquired a certain expertise in questions of agriculture. He spent the years 1933–35 in prison in Germany. Thereafter, he went into exile, first to Czechoslovakia, then to the Soviet Union. After fighting in the Spanish Civil War, where he was wounded, he was arrested in France in 1939 and sent to the internment camp at Le Vernet, in the foothills of the Pyrenees.[31] There he remained until being handed over in 1942 to the Gestapo. He spent the rest of the war in Mauthausen concentration camp, after which he served in the Brandenburg provincial administration, first as second vice president, then as economics minister.

Leuschner, born in 1910, belonged to a somewhat younger generation of Communist functionaries. He joined the KPD in 1931 and within two years rose, while still in his early twenties, to the level of a district party leader in Berlin. He was arrested in 1936 for illegal propaganda activities and sent to prison until the last years of the war, when he was transferred, first to Sachsenhausen concentration camp and then to Mauthausen. Leuschner's formal education in economics was greater than Rau's. Originally trained in business, he worked in a clothing firm as a salesman and as an exporter. Until his arrest, he also took night classes in economics, philosophy, and psychology at the Lessing und Humboldt Hochschule in Berlin. Simultaneously, he studied Marxist literature at the Marxist Workers' School. After the war, he was immediately made leader of the Economic Policy Department of the KPD Central Committee; after the merger of the KPD and the SPD, he held the same position in the Executive Committee of the SED.[32] Within the newly created DWK, it was Leuschner who gradually came to run the economy of the zone. All significant questions of administration and implementation of policy were subject to his supervision. Erich Gniffke, a leading SPD official who had joined the SED briefly and then fled to West Berlin in 1948, described Leuschner as politically unpolished, "somewhat clumsy. He was too rigid *(Er klebte am Konzept)*."[33] It was Rau, the official DWK chairman, who tended to exercise more of a political function, representing the DWK in its dealings with the Soviets and with the SED.

It would be some time, however, before the DWK was able to exert anything like the kind of centralizing influence desired by SMAD and SED leaders, primarily because of the perceived need to demonstrate that the DWK in no way constituted a rump eastern German state (at least, not yet). Accordingly, the DWK was totally subordinated to the SMAD. Its work was placed under the direction of M. I. Perelivchenko, chief of the SMAD Economic Planning Department, and its administrations were forbidden from publishing their own directives without first obtaining approval from their SMAD counterparts. It was not until spring 1948 that the Soviets began to increase the DWK's authority over internal zonal affairs, in part as a response to similar moves in the Bizone and in part as a way of solving their own increasing personnel problems.[34] But not until the second half of 1948 was the DWK able to introduce, for the first time, a central economic plan to replace the self-contained quarterly plans hitherto produced by provincial governments.

Not surprisingly, there was little the DWK could do at first to alleviate the provisioning problems in the zone. Although the issue was raised early on, DWK leaders accepted with resignation the limitations imposed by the conditions of the occupation. At the DWK's fourth meeting, for example, when the question of food imports was raised, Leuschner quickly made clear to those present that food imports depended on what industry could offer in exchange. This was, of course, not much. "The point of departure," he instructed, "must be to make do with what we have."[35] Josef Orlopp, the leader of the Administration of Interzonal and Foreign Trade, elaborated: "If we import food then we can't import coal, and if we don't import coal then industry will come to a halt and we will no longer be able to exist."[36] Orlopp's comment was telling. It reflected not only the fact of the SMAD's control over the zone's foreign trade, but also the SED's own commitment to the primacy of heavy industry, that is, to Soviet-style forced growth.[37]

As Communist parties throughout the emerging Soviet bloc consolidated their positions, they elaborated similar programs emphasizing heavy industry, viewing it as both the engine of growth as well as a crucial lever for asserting greater control over their developing postwar polities. In many of the countries of Eastern Europe and east-central Europe, productivism was also motivated by the drive to modernize, as it had been in the Soviet Union. For many of these countries, prioritizing the raw materials and investment goods industries was seen as an indispensable step in the march of progress.[38] But this was considerably less true of what would become East Germany. Although the Soviet zone contained a relatively high percentage of agricultural land, combined with little in the way of basic and raw materials industry, it nevertheless already possessed a highly developed industrial base, above all in machine building, chemicals, nonmetallic minerals, electrical engineering, motor vehicles, precision mechanics, printing and paper, and textiles and clothing.[39] In fact, during the war, production in many of these industries had increased more quickly than elsewhere in Germany. Meanwhile, the effects of Allied bombing campaigns on industry in eastern Germany had been markedly less severe than in western Germany. (Ultimately, dismantling by the Soviets detracted more from East German industrial capacity than Allied bombings.)[40] Orlopp's seemingly exaggerated fear, therefore, reflected a clear recognition that coal shortages threatened to undermine the SED's attempt to build up a privileged, state-controlled heavy industrial sector as a base from which to dominate the economic and social life of the zone. With an acute perception of instrumental relations, he saw that productivism and power were intimately bound up with each other.

The coal-food dilemma, meanwhile, was hardly unique to the Soviet zone. Authorities in the Western zones, in particular the British zone, were in the difficult position of trying to boost coal production in the Ruhr in order to trigger a more general economic revival, while being unable to feed miners well enough to increase their productivity.[41] Because their zone was not self-sufficient in food, they were dependent on imports, mostly from the United States. The cost of imports, however, amounted to a huge dollar-drain, far outstripping the income derived from the zone's coal exports. With the goal of breaking through the coal-food cycle, officials in the British zone and London began to consider schemes for introducing a moratorium, or a ceiling, on coal exports so that British-zone coal could be used within the zone for producing more steel, agricultural machinery, and artificial fertilizer. The British zone, they hoped, might then be able to increase its own food production and thus reduce its dependency on American imports.

But these schemes met with immediate and stiff opposition from the French, who had just adopted the Monnet Plan for the modernization of the French economy and now required increased supplies of fuel. The French refused to countenance any reduction of coal deliveries from the Ruhr. The Americans, caught in the middle and fearful of an economic collapse in France brought on by lack of fuel, came up with an alternative solution. In the summer of 1946 Secretary of State James Byrnes made the offer of an economic fusion of the British with the American zone. The merger was supposed to relieve Britain of some of the burden for feeding its zone *and* assure continued coal deliveries to France. In view of their political and economic dependency on the United States, the British had no alternative but to agree. At a time of world hunger and food shortage, American control over food supplies gave the Americans the upper hand.[42]

At first, the merging of the two zones in January 1947 neither improved the food situation nor helped to increase the production of coal. The outlook for most Germans remained bleak. Nevertheless, there were important differences between the ways in which the Western Allies and the Soviets handled their consumption problems in Germany. In addition to the food and clothing donated by an array of private organizations in the United States, Switzerland, and Sweden, the Western zones received from the Western Allies deliveries of food, fertilizer, and other desperately needed supplies within the framework of the GARIOA (Government Aid and Relief in Occupied Areas) program. The Allies themselves financed German food imports, since the Germans were not yet able to export enough manufactured goods to pay for the imports themselves. Even as administrative collections of food produced in Germany declined after mid-1947 because of increased hoarding, the Allies were willing to make up the difference by increasing the amounts imported.[43] And in the second half of 1947 CARE packages began to arrive, providing further assistance. In contrast, leading officials within the SMAD and in Moscow continued to rule out supplying Germans in their zone with more food. Stalin himself insisted that even after reducing Soviet troops in Germany, any extra food they would have consumed should be sent to the Soviet Union rather than be left for the Germans.[44]

In their private and public statements, too, leading Western officials showed greater understanding for the need to improve the food supply. The heyday of Morgenthau-Plan notions of retribution had long since passed. If in July 1947 Orlopp insisted on the uncontested priority of coal over food, U.S. Military Governor Lucius Clay had come to the opposite conclusion a full year earlier: "Without food we cannot produce coal: without coal we cannot produce the fertilizer necessary to improve future food supply. Only food can prime the pump."[45] In a famous speech in Stuttgart in September 1946, Secretary of State Byrnes offered public support for Clay by pledging material American aid to Germany. Meanwhile, the political significance of the food question was abundantly obvious to German politicians in the Western zones. As Kurt Schumacher put it, "the question of bread and grain and potatoes is a question of the greatest political significance in Germany."[46] For Schumacher, no less than the fate of democracy in Germany was at stake. Meeting with American labor leaders during a trip to the United States in September 1947, he explained, "Hunger and the contraction and crumbling of the economy are the most dangerous enemies of freedom in Europe." The Soviet model, he argued, "is not the greatest danger; the actual threat comes from the political and economic failures of the powers that, in the eyes of the German people, are the representatives of democracy."[47] The announcement of the Marshall Plan in June 1947 amounted to an official recognition of what authorities in the Western zones had been saying for several months. Although it would be nearly a year before Marshall Plan aid began to reach Europe, the United States had made a bold, public commitment to offer substantial material help for the recovery of Western Europe. For those able to see beyond the formidable daily struggle to survive, there was a faint but visible glimmer of hope for real improvement in the not-too-distant future.

In contrast, the Soviet zone's emphasis on productivism consigned its population to an indefinitely prolonged condition of sacrifice and want, combined with vague promises of a better future. The nature of that future, however, remained as exasperatingly intangible as the path by which it was to be achieved. In August 1947 Fred Oelßner, a leading SED ideologist, made an attempt to suggest the outlines of what the future might look like:

> The task of the planned socialist economy is, first, to satisfy not the individual need, but rather the social need . . . It is the capitalist mentality that assumes that the most important task of the planned economy is the satisfaction of individual needs. That would be a relatively easy task. In a fully developed socialist economy these individual needs (housing, food, clothes, cultural goods of all kinds) will cause less confusion. An ever-greater part of human needs will then directly be-

come social needs, and society will set the tasks which enable humanity to complete the great leap from the realm of necessity to the realm of freedom.[48]

Oelßner's vision of freedom and the sacrifice it required was imbued with idealism. But as his rhetoric took flight, it left little place for the self, at least insofar as the self gave rise to "confusing" needs. His imagined "planned socialist economy," distinctly designed to appeal to what Keynes called "the ascetic in us," encircled the idea of socialism in a radiant nimbus of austerity.

But asceticism was a poor recipe for productivity, particularly in the Soviet zone. All hopes for raising productivity necessarily ran up against the problem of consumption. Even those capable of the greatest discipline and enthusiasm for work required food and clothing. According to a report from the FDGB-Berlin, even workers in the Soviet-zone's best provisioned city lacked what they needed, with serious consequences for their health. "All letters sent to us are cries of distress!" the report emphasized. "They show that the workers [*Werktätigen*] of Berlin, even with good work morale, no longer know how it is possible for them to carry on with their work as a result of the unfavorable conditions." The report produced a long litany of disheartening and gruesome grievances: the lack of warm outer clothing and sturdy footwear, combined with insufficient heat in work rooms, caused widespread pneumonia and pleurisy; shortages of work clothing, in particular protective clothing, left many workers exposed to corrosive chemicals and acids, resulting in burns, ulcers, furunculosis, and scabies; the absence of good soap and cleaning materials only heightened these afflictions, "bringing those affected to despair." In one particularly egregious case, ten workers in Lichtenberg were given the job of exhuming five hundred bodies that had been lying in a bomb crater since 1945. The workers, however, were given no protective clothing or gloves and no special cleaning materials of any kind. When their application for an increase in rations for the eight-week duration of the job was rejected, they finally threatened to strike. "The unhealthy results for the whole population of a work stoppage in the burial business (spreading of epidemics) need hardly be mentioned," the report noted. Of greater concern to the FDGB, however, was the prospect of "a great mass exodus from the economically most important industries, which demand the most difficult and dangerous work, to simple and easy jobs."[49] Indeed, this fear was shared by Soviet as well as German authorities. The strategy ultimately adopted for addressing this problem was SMAD Order no. 234.

Order no. 234 has most often been discussed in terms of the problem of productivity. And, indeed, it was conceived, first and foremost, as a mechanism for boosting productivity in those branches of industry that Soviet-zone authorities considered most important for rebuilding a viable economy in the zone. In typical Soviet fashion, the branches singled out were those of coal and metals, mining, machine building, electrical engineering, and transportation. Order no. 234 sought to achieve its aim, however, by offering material incentives to workers in these branches in the form of differential wages, an extra hot meal in the workplace, and a privileged supply of textiles, shoes, and other basic consumer items. In keeping with the slogan *"Mehr produzieren, besser planen, gerechter verteilen"* (Produce More, Plan Better, Distribute More Justly), higher wages and better rations would be the reward for greater productivity. Thus Order no. 234 also embodied the first attempt to introduce a more systematic, longer-term policy of supplying consumer goods to Germans living under Soviet occupation. It meant moving beyond limited, though successful, efforts at averting mass starvation, toward a mode of consumer provisioning that would contribute to the task of postwar reconstruction.

In view of the severe economic dislocations plaguing the zone, it was inevitable that questions of consumption be tied to those of production. Order no. 234 articulated that relationship in very clear terms: consumption, beyond the barest minimum necessary for survival, was to serve production. Order no. 234 was a moral injunction, an appeal to specific virtues combined with the prospect of a reward for those heeding the call. Above all, it demanded discipline, hard work, patience, a willingness to put the general need ahead of individual need and to endure continued sacrifice and profound modesty in personal consumption. Simultaneously, it appealed to traditional German values of industriousness and quality work. The immediate, if modest, reward was to be a foretaste of greater prosperity to come.

Unfortunately for the inhabitants of the zone, Order no. 234 proved to be a spectacular failure. The chief problem with the logic of the order was that Soviet-zone workers saw the fruits of their labor going straight to the Soviet Union in the form of reparations.[50] SMAD and SED authorities were, after all, calling for continued discipline and sacrifice *and* insisting on meeting Soviet reparations demands. And they were doing so months after the announcement of the Marshall Plan. As a result, attempts to rally work morale and to increase productivity were doomed from the start. Equally important, but hitherto neglected in accounts of Order no. 234, is the fact that the provisioning elements of the order also proved disastrous. Looking at the way in which they were carried out not only sheds further light on the failure of the order but, more interestingly, affords a vantage point on one of the first confrontations between an emerging, zone-wide provisioning policy and the skepticism, even hostility, with which it was received, both at the level of execution and at that of principle.

Issued on October 9, 1947, by Marshal Sokolovski, SMAD commander in chief, Order no. 234 represented the official adoption of Soviet-style "closed distribution."[51] Developed in the Soviet Union during the first Five-Year Plan as a means of protecting workers from the worst effects of shortages and of keeping them in the workplace, the system of closed distribution provided workers in specific enterprises with a privileged access to rationed goods sold in enterprise stores and cafeterias. According to the Soviet-approved guidelines of Order no. 234, the work kitchens of enterprises in the "leading branches of industry and transport" were to provide an additional warm meal in two forms: Form A "for highly qualified workers in the most important occupations, for workers [performing] heavy manual labor or labor injurious to [their] health, as well as for engineers and technicians"; and Form B for "other workers and employees of those firms chosen."[52] In either form, however, the meal would be denied to workers who failed to perform their duties, failed to meet their production norms, or otherwise violated the tenets of work discipline. In total, the order called for increasing the number of those Germans receiving a workplace meal from about 350,000 to 1 million.[53]

The carrying out of the order was left to the recently established administrations within the DWK and to the FDGB, both of which proceeded to evince a brand of organizational overactivity and duplication of bureaucratic responsibilities that was already becoming typical of the emerging SED regime. As a result, the array of acronyms involved verged on the bewildering. Responsible for coordinating the effort was the Department of Economic Questions, the nearest thing within the DWK to a central planning body. The Administration for Trade and Provisioning (DVHV, later HVHV) was in charge of making sure that the appropriate amounts of food, textiles, and other consumer goods were factored into the quarterly supply plans at the provincial level. This was to be done on the basis of lists of recipient firms drawn up by the FDGB or by the provincial ministries of work and social welfare or economics ministries. These lists, in turn, were to receive final approval at SMAD headquarters in Karlshorst, a suburb of East Berlin.[54] In addition, a special Committee for Overseeing the Measures of Order no. 234 was called into being; it included members from several different administrations within the DWK (Trade and Provisioning, Work and Social Welfare, Industry), as well as from the FDGB, and it produced yet more reports for DWK, SED, and SMAD leaders. Finally, watching over all of this activity was the SED itself, active at every level, whether monitoring reactions to the order, distributing questionnaires, or passing along guidelines. No less a figure than Walter Ulbricht was directly involved in issuing instructions to other members of the SED Central Secretariat and in directing the coverage of the order in the SED press.[55]

Initially, the Committee for Overseeing the Measures of Order no. 234 displayed guarded optimism. At the committee's first meeting, Dr. Herta Ludwig, an official in the Administration of Trade and Provisioning, reported that the supply of the workplace meal was assured. Nevertheless, there was cause for concern. As a result of late deliveries of food supplies, several firms in the province of Mecklenburg and in the city of Magdeburg would have to wait several weeks for the introduction of the workplace meal. Equally serious, she suggested, was the fact that textiles and shoes had yet to be distributed to workers.[56] The causes for concern soon multiplied. Nearly one month later, Walter Ulbricht received a particularly sobering report from the DVHV, furnishing information from an array of enterprises throughout the zone, for the vast majority of which there had still been no delivery of textiles and shoes. Moreover, those firms which did receive these goods received them in hopelessly inadequate quantities. The steelworks in Henningsdorf, for example, which did comparatively well, received two hundred pairs of socks, two hundred work suits, and five hundred pairs of wooden shoes; but this could hardly suffice for the four-teen hundred workers employed by the firm. Most firms, meanwhile, were far less fortunate. For instance, the AEG Henningsdorf, which employed twenty-eight hundred workers, received only six women's blouses, seventy dresses, three blankets, five men's suits, and equally small amounts of other goods. It was not uncommon for firms with as many as one hundred workers to receive no more than two pairs of leather shoes. Although there was more success in supplying meals in the workplace, there were shortcomings here, too. Weeks would go by without deliveries of potatoes; despite repeated petitions, there would be no milk. Often there would be no vegetables, or most of a given delivery would turn out to be garbage. Many firms had eating rooms, but no tables or chairs. Many had no work kitchens at all, and the introduction of the workplace meal had to wait until the kitchens were built.[57]

The amounts of manufactured goods distributed did eventually increase, but with the increase there emerged a new problem, that of assortment. More often than not, the goods delivered to factories failed to satisfy the needs of workers. Instead of work clothes and work shoes, workers would receive clothing and shoes for women and children. In a report to the SMAD Administration for Trade and Provisioning, Georg Handke, the leader of the DVHV, complained that although the provisioning of workers according to Order no. 234 "could be described as *quantitatively* satisfactory, the delivered assortments and qualities did *not* meet the requirements of a *demand-appropriate* [*bedarfsgerecht*] supply of workers."[58] As a result, the percentage of useless goods delivered to workers in factories was often extremely high. According to a report from one province, for example, several firms complained that up to 90 percent of the shoes distributed could not be used.[59] Estimating for the zone as a whole, the SED Department of Economic Policy reported to Ulbricht that more than 70 percent of the consumer goods distributed thus far were unusable.[60]

Criticism of Order no. 234 was not limited to shortcomings in its execution. While poor-quality goods and deliveries of the wrong sizes and assortments offered "points of attack to enemies of the new democracy,"[61] the order's key principles also met with objections from the workers it was supposed to benefit and with confusion from those charged with carrying it out. An article published in the *Tribüne*, the main organ of the FDGB, posed perhaps the most basic question in the most basic of terms:

"What is correct? First live and then work, or work in order to live bet-ter?" The chief editor passed along some of the "negative" answers to Ul-bricht, suggesting that they were nevertheless not without merit insofar as they pointed out deficiencies in the distribution of food, coal, and other basic goods and raised the question of special bonuses, "which contributed significantly to the lowering of work morale."[62] These letters serve as early examples of what became a common form of appeal in East Germany: letters to the editor that were never published but instead passed on to political higher-ups. The letter to the editor, in other words, became a letter of petition.[63] One of the letter writers, a former police of-ficer now working as a helper in an assembly plant, insisted that an "in-crease in the will to work can only be encouraged if the worker is given enough food . . . What use is it to have written constantly: destruction of bank monopolies, appropriation of the factories of war criminals, trans-fer of mines and so on." As letter writers often did, he then pointed to the authority of personal experience:

> The writer of the article appears to know little about hunger, because hunger hurts and dry bread offers no strength. From October 2 to October 9, I have gone to work every day with dry bread and my work isn't easy, and you'll have to admit that transporting oxygen bottles and heavy pieces of iron, often up three or four flights of stairs, is no small thing. Earlier one man could carry such things; today two or three men are needed to carry such burdens. Take one look around at the emaci-ated figures of workers as they stagger around in their work clothes. As the workers' new saying goes: "Gebt uns etwas auf dem Magen, dann können wir schwere Arbeit leisten und auch vertragen."[64]

Other letter writers took exception less to the principle of delayed grat-ification than to the privileging of certain groups over others. "We de-mand a unified working class [Arbeiterschaft]," proclaimed one letter, "and that means that we don't create two classes on the basis of provi-sioning: one better and one worse supplied. What little there is [must] be distributed equally and justly if we are to contribute to the lifting of work morale."[65] Very often workers simply refused to divide the work-place meal into Forms A and B. As authorities in the zone repeatedly complained, they persisted in "eating from one pot."

Three months later, the members of the Committee for Overseeing the Measures of Order no. 234 continued to show a basic confusion about these very questions. "Vagueness governs even the principles according to which distribution is carried out," complained one committee member. "Should the individual performance [*Einzelleistung*] be decisive or is neediness [*Bedürftigkeit*] also to be taken into account?" If individual performance was to be decisive, those who had an honest desire to increase their productivity but who were burdened with unfavorable circumstances (such as difficult living arrangements or lack of possessions) were being penalized. Members of the committee made reference to several cases in which large numbers of workers remained unemployed simply because they lacked suitable work clothing. The committee chairman, Erwin Lampka, also a member of the DWK Secretariat, agreed that need would have to be taken into account in a new ruling on distribution to be drafted by the Administration for Trade and Provisioning. However, it is not clear that such a draft was ever produced. If so, it was never adopted in practice.[66]

If the question of performance versus neediness *(Leistung v. Bedürftigkeit)* caused confusion, so too did the category of *Leistung* itself. In a report to the SED Central Secretariat, the DWK Department of Economic Questions pointed out that two different principles were currently at work in the distribution of consumer goods: first, the collective performance of the whole firm or of individual departments; second, the performance of the individual. "Taking into account merely the performance of the individual worker can lead to one-sided privileging," the report warned. Here, the question of *Bedürftigkeit* served to redefine that of *Leistung*: "If favorable conditions are not present, but the honest desire to increase productivity is, then these workers are disadvantaged from the beginning. One must, therefore, take as a basis the collective performance as well as the individual achievement."[67]

Causing yet further uncertainty about who exactly should be receiving consumption privileges was the fact that, at different points, Order no. 234 made reference to "leading enterprises," "leading occupations," and even to "leading building sites" without, however, defining more clearly what was meant by these terms. And because the German administrations, in practice, were unable to produce the required lists of firms in time, the Soviets ended up compiling their own lists and imposing them on the Germans.[68] Six months after the introduction of the order, German functionaries were still complaining about the lists drawn up by the Soviets. As the chairman of the FDGB, Herbert

Warnke suggested in a report to the SED Department of Economic Policy: "These lists are very much in need of improvement, and it would be especially desirable if the FDGB in the individual provinces and communities were given greater influence on the selection of enterprises. The FDGB in Saxony informs us that in February, as a result of the inexactness of the lists, an almost unbearable situation developed. In total, a series of enterprises received 16,000 more meals than they had employees."[69]

SED and FDGB leaders seemed able to do little more than lament the "ideological backwardness" and "weakened morality" of party members, union functionaries, and workers in general. They could, and did, insist on the need for "systematic enlightenment work." However, they themselves could not escape the questions and uncertainties occasioned by a task for which they were not prepared but which they had to carry out under patently impossible circumstances. The deepening division of Germany was about to complicate their task further. On June 20, 1948, the Western Allies introduced the deutschmark (DM) in the Western zones, and the Soviets responded with the Berlin Blockade.

CHAPTER 2

The Contest Begins: The Currency Reform, the Berlin Blockade, and the Introduction of the HO

There is a great danger in the West.

Paul Merker, March 1948

The significance of the June 20, 1948, currency reform in the historical consciousness of postwar West Germany can hardly be exaggerated. Later remembered as perhaps *the* event of the immediate postwar years, it became synonymous with its most dramatic and enduring image: the shopwindow, hitherto empty, suddenly and magically filled with all the foodstuffs and consumer goods people had been forced to do without for so long.[1] Those who experienced the currency reform remembered it as the point of passage from the myriad sacrifices of hunger to the pleasures of a prosperity without precedent, as the starting gun for the great *Wirtschaftswunder*.

Of course, memory distorts, and this one glossed over many of the difficulties involved in introducing the new currency.[2] Although the shopwindows did fill up literally overnight with goods, it would be some time before most people were able to purchase the items on such tantalizing display. Because of a continued wage freeze and the removal from circulation of 93.5 percent of the old Reichsmark (RM) volume, purchasing power remained chronically weak. And although basic foodstuffs continued to be rationed and sold at fixed prices, 48 percent of the population in the U.S. zone complained in July of being unable to pay for the goods they needed to subsist. In August that figure increased to 59 percent.[3] Meanwhile, the selling of certain goods (fruit, vegetables, and eggs) at unregulated and extremely high prices inflamed consumer rage, occasionally setting off riots.[4] The most serious problem resulting from the currency reform, however, was the

significant rise in unemployment. Because savings had been so drastically reduced, many firms and public administrations were forced to let
go hundreds of thousands of employees and workers.[5] Outrage at the
increase in unemployment and at the widening gap between wages and
prices led ultimately to a general strike on November 12, 1948. And yet
for all its problems the currency reform did help to open the way
toward economic prosperity; at the same time, it constituted a crucial
move toward the creation of a separate West German state, effectively
bringing to an end the prospect of German economic unity.

For the Soviets and the East German Communists the challenge was
serious and twofold: first, it brought one step closer to reality the nightmare scenario of a West German state fully integrated into an American-
led Western European bloc; second, the now copiously appointed
shopwindows of the Western zones opened up a whole new field for political competition. However high prices may have been, however widespread the sense of *Haben-Wollen und Noch-nicht-kaufen Können* (wanting
to have and not yet being able to buy), the visual evidence of abundance had a profound symbolic and psychological importance, holding out the credible promise of an end to years of scarcity and a return
to "normalcy." Such tangible proof that the Soviet zone was moving in
a similar direction was woefully lacking.

The immediate Soviet response to the currency reform was the
Berlin Blockade, partly a last-ditch effort to slow down the formation of
a West German state (with the population of West Berlin serving as
hostages), partly a means of extending SED control over the political
and economic life of the Soviet zone. In response to the newly filled
shopwindows in the West, authorities in the zone tried to pursue provisioning policies fully in keeping with the thinking behind Order no.
234, only in new form. Productivity in heavy industry would continue
to enjoy priority in economic planning, but where Order no. 234 had
failed, a new activist movement would be called into being as a means
of breathing new life into the idea of the differential wage. And to
serve as incentive for workers to boost productivity, the work kitchens
and clothing handouts of Order no. 234 would be superseded by the
Handelsorganisation (HO), a new state-owned, state-run organization of
retail stores offering Germans in the Soviet zone the first legal means
of shopping ration-free since the war years. And yet for all the continuity linking the activist movement and the HO to Order no. 234,

there was a growing recognition among Soviet-zone economic planners that the currency reform had thrown up a new challenge, one which required a fundamentally different response to the question of consumption than had hitherto been pursued in the zone.

The Berlin Blockade is an event no less endowed with the accretions of myth than is the currency reform it immediately followed. Through a flood of popular accounts, films, memoirs, and scholarly studies, we have received an image of the blockade featuring a West Berlin totally isolated from the outside world, its citizens entirely dependent on the airlift for their very existence. It is a story in which besieged but resolute and sacrifice-ready West Berliners, backed up by U.S. ingenuity, technology, and unyielding commitment, triumph over Soviet barbarism. Not only is West Berlin maintained as an island of freedom behind the iron curtain, but the threat of full-scale war with the Soviet Union is happily averted, if only for the time being.[6]

But, as has already occurred with the currency reform, the myth of the blockade is now beginning to break down. Recent literature on the blockade has presented a more ambiguous picture, one which shows that West Berliners were neither completely isolated nor entirely dependent on the airlift for their consumption needs.[7] William Stivers, for example, has offered the image of an "incomplete blockade," in which trade relations flourished between East and West Berlin, with the DWK-organized *Handelsgesellschaft Groß-Berlin* acting as chief intermediary. It is a blockade in which Soviet authorities, covetous of the new westmarks, not only tolerated but actively directed gray- and black-market trade, setting up special shops in East Berlin that were run by Polish, Bulgarian, and Yugoslavian front men. Here, West Berliners willing to pay exorbitant prices could shop for food, cigarettes, textiles, and luxury goods, even as Soviet cigarettes and Soviet-sector beer were being sold in West Berlin.[8] Stivers characterizes the relationship between West Berlin business and the DWK as one of "real symbiosis," as many firms in West Berlin profited from the blockade due to the parallel currency exchange system, which allowed them to be paid in westmarks by Soviet-sector authorities and to pay their own expenses in eastmarks,[9] while the DWK made use of much-needed business contacts with West Berlin as a means of making up for the damage done to the Soviet-zone economy by the West's counterblockade. Indeed, the

Soviet Union itself had a direct interest in continued contact, since production for reparations was also hurt by the counterblockade; as Stivers suggests, the Soviet joint-stock companies (SAGs) were "notorious for seeking contacts with companies in West Berlin."[10]

As individual consumers, too, West Berliners had access to goods from an array of nonairlift sources. Although it began officially on June 24, 1948, the blockade, according to Stivers, "leaked from all sides." Initially West Berlin residents were not even cut off from the Western zones of Germany. Until July 3 trains and barges continued to make their way to West Berlin. Postal shipments (letters and packages) were able to reach West Berlin legally by rail. Entrepreneurs in the Western zones even set up mail-order businesses, which shipped packages to all holders of Western currency. Until the end of August, "countless *hundreds* of trucks" poured into the ostensibly blockaded city. In mid-October a report prepared by U.S. military government-intelligence analysts carried the title, "Is Berlin Blockaded?"[11]

Although the Soviets did finally cut these supply lines off on September 1, the citizens of West Berlin could still avail themselves of the various Soviet-area channels for consumer goods. West Berliners turned to the black market and to the option of foraging in the surrounding Brandenburg countryside. In exchange for barter or coveted westmarks, West Berliners received significant amounts of provisions. The people of West Berlin are famous for having overwhelmingly declined the Soviet offer allowing them to register for rations in East Berlin; at no point during the blockade did more than 5 percent of them do so. However, what is usually left out of accounts of the blockade is the fact that they hardly needed to. In the ten and a half months of the blockade, roughly half a million tons of goods passed from the Soviet zone and East Berlin into West Berlin. According to an estimate prepared by American intelligence in early November, the daily flow of Soviet-area foodstuffs into West Berlin amounted to between six hundred and seven hundred tons through mid-October. Thus, at least one third of West Berlin's food supply during the first three and a half months of the blockade came from Soviet-occupied areas.[12]

Finally, with the opening of the first HO stores in mid-November, West Berliners were able to go shopping ration-free in the Soviet sector of the city and in nearby Potsdam, no questions asked, taking considerable advantage of the favorable exchange rate.[13] It is impossible to know the exact extent to which West Berliners used HO shops, because of the no-questions-asked policy. But there are clear indications that business from West-sector customers was significant. For example, in February 1949 rumors about the introduction of a new currency in the Soviet zone sent the value of the eastmark in West Berlin into a tailspin, causing a run on HO stores. Conversely, after the lifting of the block-ade in early May, and as cheaper West German goods flooded into West Berlin, HO sales and profits suffered a precipitous decline, falling al-most 50 percent in May and nearly 60 percent in June.[14]

It is, however, worth dwelling for a moment on the official Soviet sup-ply scheme, which went into effect on July 26, 1948. For the question inevitably arises: why did West Berliners prefer the illegal black market or the arduous foraging expedition to the Soviet offer of buying rations in East Berlin shops? Stivers suggests that the offer was partly an exer-cise in propaganda (it would have been a logistical nightmare for East Berlin food authorities if all of West Berlin had tried to buy rations in the Soviet sector); but he also makes clear that it was an effort seriously undertaken. The DWK and Soviet sector officials went to great lengths in their attempt to make the scheme work, and they did hope to draw large numbers of "customers" from West Berlin.[15] Indeed, the efforts they made attested to their recognition of the political importance of consumer supply. Involved in direct confrontation with the Western Allies, the Soviets clearly saw that it was essential to demonstrate that Germans living under their authority could expect to have their con-sumption needs met. Beyond the political symbolism, there was also the obvious and compelling economic incentive of luring large num-bers of West Berliners and their westmarks to East Berlin. The goal was not to starve West Berlin into submission, but rather to bring all trade into official channels and coffers.

But if, as Stivers suggests, the supply scheme was "born under an un-lucky star,"[16] it was the same star that consigned the rest of the Soviet zone to ill fortune. Ultimately, Soviet-zone officials were never able to sur-mount the sorts of problems hampering consumer supply throughout the zone: planning mix-ups, bureaucratic inefficiency, and chronic short-falls in the supply and quality of consumer goods. Despite the efforts made, the Soviets could not deliver on their promise, and the idea of drawing rations in East Berlin simply did not appeal to West Berliners.

The task of carrying out the supply offer was assigned to a special subdepartment created for just this purpose within the Food Office of the Berlin Magistrat. The subdepartment, consisting of twelve sections, was directed by Paul Letsch and his Soviet contact officer, Major Gubisch, chief of trade and provisioning for East Berlin.[17] One of the initial factors limiting their ability to draw people from West Berlin was the way in which the supply system was organized. Residents of each district *(Bezirk)* in West Berlin were supposed to go to the registration office of a specified "sister" district in East Berlin, where they would first exchange their Western ration cards for Soviet-sector cards. They were then supposed to register with a particular shop in that sister district, where they could purchase the food to which their cards entitled them. However, the specification of sister districts meant not only that West Berliners were unable to shop wherever they pleased in East Berlin but also that they faced the prospect of having to travel long distances—up to twenty kilometers, in many cases—to reach the appropriate store. In view of the state of public transport after the war, traveling long distances was a considerable inconvenience. Not until August 19 did Soviet-zone authorities realize their error and issue instructions for making shopping in the East a far less daunting endeavor for West Berliners. According to new regulations, West Berliners would now be allowed to exchange their cards in any registration office in the Soviet sector and to shop in any district they desired, regardless of where the card exchange had taken place. In addition, they were now entitled to the same special one-time handouts of extra food and heating fuel offered to East Berlin residents.

Nevertheless, the numbers of West Berliners going east remained (for the Soviets) embarrassingly low.[18] In addition to long travel times, potential customers from West Berlin faced a whole host of inconveniences in the Soviet sector. To begin with, they had to go through the process of exchanging their ration cards, an administrative challenge that East Berlin authorities never seemed able to master. Complaints about long lines and long waiting times were ubiquitous. As late as December, the food departments of all the district offices had to be reminded of the importance of minimizing the waiting times of West Berliners by introducing all possible organizational and personnel measures to speed up the process. Fritz Ebert, the mayor of East Berlin (and son of Friedrich Ebert, the first president of the Weimar Republic), instructed them: "It will be clear to you how significant it is in the present situation that the process of handing out the cards comes off smoothly."[19] Yet two months later, in a report to the head of the Magistrat Food Office, the fact that twenty thousand West Berliners were forced to wait outside in the freezing February cold for four to five hours before receiving their cards was simply mentioned in passing, with no further comment on how this might be avoided in the future.[20]

Possession of the new ration card, however, was only the beginning. One could hardly rest assured that the goods one wished to purchase would even be available. Ebert noted in December, "Among residents of the West sectors who have decided to draw their rations in the East the complaint is often raised that they must go repeatedly in vain to their designated shops before they receive the issued goods. The probable result of this shortcoming is that many people, especially old people, hesitate to register in the East sector."[21] Nor did it help matters that shopping in East Berlin very often entailed unpleasant brushes with surly salespeople. According to one report from late January 1949, poor and unfriendly service in the consumer cooperatives was a source of "constant complaint." "Whether in the weighing of bread, or including packaging material in the weighing of bread, or the unfriendliness of the sales personnel," the overall impression was one of "great indifference on the part of co-op employees towards customers."[22] And if the co-op salespeople could be unpleasant, so too could the co-ops themselves. The requirements of hygiene were not always observed to the letter. As an investigation of one co-op in the center of the city (a co-op with 90–95 percent West-sector customers) reported, "The varied array of goods on sale works to the disadvantage of the food department... [I]t is under no circumstances to be tolerated further that foodstuffs of all kinds like bread, butter, fat, cereals, sugar are mixed in with vegetables, potatoes and other goods which develop dust." The investigation took particular exception to a separate glass-enclosed room where meat, sausages, and other goods were sold: "It defies description that in this wet room sacks with sugar and other important foodstuffs lay on the floor so that their contents become completely wet and the customers rightly complain."[23]

For those who endured the long hours spent in transit and in endless lines waiting for new ration cards, the frequently fruitless trips to stores without goods, the overweening or indifferent salespeople, and the less-than-sparkling retail landscape, what must have been most disappointing was the often poor quality of the goods on offer. Throughout the blockade complaints flooded into Letsch's office, which he, in turn, passed on to his Soviet contact officer, Gubisch. For example, in August Letsch reported in frustration, "The complaints about bad quality processed foodstuffs [*Nährmittel*] will not end." Samples taken from storage warehouses in East Berlin showed that the complaints were, in fact, justified. Significant amounts had to be sorted out by consumers and thrown away. Letsch pleaded with Gubisch to do something so that "such things" were no longer delivered to Berlin.[24] Only a few days later, Letsch was again forced to turn to Gubisch, explaining that Soviet-sector bread was excessively water-heavy, and during the summer months grew moldy far too quickly. More seriously, it disturbed the digestion and thus posed a health risk to those who ate it.[25]

The following month Letsch found himself confronted with an alarming gap in meat, fish, and egg supplies. Because deliveries from the provinces and abroad were either canceled or diminished on short notice by the DWK, his subdepartment was without hundreds of tons of expected supplies. The supply of beef, fish, and eggs for the month of September could not be assured, and there were no fish supplies available for October.[26] Meanwhile, the Food Office was simultaneously obliged to distribute liverwurst and blood sausage from an East Berlin producer whose products were a source of repeated complaint. Ultimately, the population's unwillingness to purchase the sausage prompted the Food Office to carry out its own investigation, which determined that the sausage smelled strongly of intestines and was made with substandard innards. Their findings, moreover, were confirmed by the Berlin Health Office and the Veterinary Office of the district of Treptow. The commandant of Treptow even forbade the sale of the products. One month later, Letsch's request to be freed of the obligation to accept and distribute the sausage still remained unanswered.[27]

Nor were such instances merely characteristic of the first few months of the supply effort. Similar problems continued well into the winter. In December, for instance, the Food Office was inundated with complaints from West-sector residents about petroleum sold in the Soviet sector as a substitute source of energy for home-lighting purposes. (West-sector residents were limited to four hours of strictly rationed electricity per day.) According to a Food Office report,

The petroleum is actually industrial petroleum and is totally unsuited for use as a means of lighting. It immediately turns the lamp cylinders red and expels a noxious steam and gas. Those who happen to be in the room become immediately covered in soot, as do the furniture and laundry . . . In view of the situation it would be better to distribute none at all—all the more so since the petroleum distributed in the West sectors is of excellent quality.[28]

Examples of further shortcomings continued throughout the winter: in January there was no distribution of vegetables, even as rumors abounded that vegetables were to be had in West Berlin in exchange for westmarks; that same month complaints continued about the poor quality of processed foodstuffs.[29] Under these circumstances, it is not difficult to understand the readiness of West Berliners to reject the Soviet offer: in practice, it failed to entice.

To be sure, the citizens of West Berlin faced similar problems in their own sectors. There were complaints about poor-quality foodstuffs and shortages of vegetables and meat.[30] Moreover, they faced hardships unique to the blockade. With electricity limited to four hours per day and severe cuts in gas service, the task of cooking and heating meals required some ingenuity; meals often had to be eaten at midnight, while pots had to be packed in boxes with feathers and blankets to keep food warm. The lack of home heating fuel was also a serious burden. People spent their spare time pushing carts into the city's gardens and parks, foraging for wood to burn. The ubiquitous cold not only meant physical deprivation but posed a real threat to morale. Nevertheless, despite the hardships and sacrifices of West Berliners, if the Soviet supply scheme was to be successful—success being judged by the numbers of West Berliners seeking to take advantage of the Soviet offer—it had to provide something better; it had to offer a more tantalizing alternative to West-sector offerings. Here, it failed. For all the shortcomings of the airlift, West Berliners were receiving higher-calorie rations during the blockade than at any time since the war. Nor were Soviet aims helped by the noticeable improvements in the consumer provisioning of the Western zones of Germany, where the shopwindows now presented visions of abundance, where the average daily rations increased to eighteen hundred calories in August, and where potatoes ceased to be rationed in October 1948. The desire of West Berliners to remain firmly tied to the emerging West German state could only be strengthened by the tangible successes of the currency reform and its consequences for improving the supply of consumer goods.[31]

The consumption challenge opened up by the currency reform took the Soviet-zone propaganda machine completely by surprise. The major newspapers of the zone were filled with stories on the reform, but the full shopwindows of the West merited hardly a mention. For months the emphasis of the press campaign remained unchanged: the currency reform posed a mortal threat to German unity; it represented a brutal maneuver to subject the Western zones to the exploitation of "dollar-imperialism." The deutschmark was, in truth, nothing more than "the dollar-mark."[32]

Only after several months did a clear line begin to emerge on the effects of the currency reform for West German consumers. Latching on to some of the real difficulties bound up with the introduction of the new currency, SED propagandists pounced on the fact that the goods on display remained beyond the grasp of so many West Germans. They explained the reform as a "devilish plan" carefully developed by West German and American "monopoly capitalists." For months, even years, Germans in the Western zones were starved as reserves were hoarded in preparation for the day of the reform. It was of course true, they conceded, that the shops suddenly filled with goods, while in the Soviet zone enormous difficulties prevented an adequate supply of even basic foods such as potatoes and bread. As the political economist Dr. Alfred Lemnitz admitted, "At that moment there opened up between the Eastern zone and the Western zone not only a broad political, but also a deep economic chasm filled with doubts and disappointments."[33] But the "barrage of the full shops," at first so deafening, soon began to ease up. The "offensive" faltered; the "bombardment" became less constant. "The lines of the enemy," he wrote, "which for a short time appeared closed, fall apart. Masses of people stand before the full shops and are unable to buy anything. The prices rise, the reserves disappear. Factories are closed. The credit crisis begins. Unemployment increases."[34] In the end, the currency reform had thrown the Western zone into a state of "economic chaos," calling forth strikes and mass demonstrations.[35] It may have filled the shops with goods, but it also amounted to a "mass expropriation." In an obvious appeal to the traumatic memory of the currency stabilization of the mid-1920s, the currency reform was denounced for having taken everything from "the little man," from the "nineteen million small savers" with no more than RM 1000 in their savings accounts.[36]

In fact, the role of the past in the pronouncements of SED leaders was not limited to exercises in propaganda. The past affected their thinking profoundly, contributing particularly to the slowness with which they were able to recognize the challenge they faced on the battlefield of consumption. The first inkling of such a challenge had already appeared more than a year earlier with the emergence in the summer of 1947 of the broad outlines of the Marshall Plan. Official reactions had been similar to those greeting the currency reform. Somewhat more muted in tone, the SED's basic objection was the same: the Marshall Plan would tear Germany and Europe apart; it would constitute a giant sellout of West Germany to U.S. monopoly capital. The Marshall Plan was merely an extension of the Truman Doctrine, "the doctrine of the dollar." But as Marshall Plan aid actually began to reach West Germany in spring 1948, SED leaders began to consider the effects it might have on West German living standards.

A particularly revealing discussion took place in May 1948, only weeks before the currency reform, within the Economic Policy Committee of the German People's Congress.[37] After an opening speech from Walter Ulbricht, who served as the committee chairman, in which he denounced the transformation of West Germany into "a half colony of American finance capital," the discussion began in earnest. Jürgen Kuczynski, a leading economist and economic historian in the Soviet zone, insisted on the need to make clear that, all appearances notwithstanding, the Marshall Plan was really a plan for "the lowering of living conditions *(Lebenshaltung)* in the West." If any improvements were to emerge, they would affect only a small "workers' aristocracy." But this privileged group would differ from that of the past in that it would be based on "a general half-colonial living standard of the rest of the working class." Although the new workers' aristocracy would enjoy a higher standard of living *(Lebensstandard)* than that of the broad masses of workers, it would never attain that of the German working class in the Weimar Republic. The struggle against the Marshall Plan was thus a struggle for raising the living standards of workers in West Germany.[38]

Not entirely convinced by Kuczynski's argument, the deputy chairman of the committee and LDP leader, Dr. Alphons Gärtner, suggested

that an improvement of the living situation *(Lebenslage)* of the population might not work out badly for the countries taking part in Marshall
Plan aid: "We must pay attention to these things, too. We don't want to
see only one side, but the other as well."[39] Gärtner was hinting that it
might be in the interest of the Soviet zone to take the United States up
on an offer that had, after all, been extended to the countries of Eastern
Europe as well. But rushing to Kuczynski's defense was Josef Orlopp,
leader of the Administration of Interzonal and Foreign Trade, who argued that importing foodstuffs and consumer goods instead of raw materials would produce only a momentary improvement that would have
to be paid for later: "We import raw materials and phosphates that assure us a better food supply for years to come, whereas in the West
foodstuffs are imported that have a momentarily convincing effect, but
in one, two or three years the situation must deteriorate." According to
Orlopp, the task was to convince "the masses of our people" that in the
long run the course followed in the Soviet zone was the right one. But
Gärtner was not persuaded: "Experience shows that people are more
likely to follow the moment than to reflect on the longer term."[40]

Hoping to show that Gärtner's fears were exaggerated, Dr. Greta
Kuckhoff intervened. Kuckhoff was a member of the Secretariat of the
DWK and Leuschner's deputy in the DWK planning section. She had
studied economics in Germany and in the United States. She had also
lived for a time in Britain, working as an assistant to the sociologist Karl
Mannheim. During the Nazi years Kuckhoff worked as a translator in
the Racial Policy Office of the Nazi Party, while simultaneously being
active in the *Rote Kapelle* resistance group. Arrested in 1942 and originally sentenced to death, she spent the rest of the war in prison, her
sentence having been reduced to ten years. Although she had never
been a member of the Communist Party, she joined the SED in 1946.[41]
Exactly what constituted an improvement in the standard of living, she
suggested, was debatable. According to her, the foreseeable improvements discussed thus far amounted to no more than imports of raisins,
dates, and grapefruit juice in the British zone. "I believe that the population will not view that as a rise in the standard of living," she asserted. "Even if the stores should become fuller, we have shown the
prospect of unemployment to be an almost certain inevitability." Still,
she recognized that one could hardly wish away the popularity of the
Marshall Plan. The Western press, she noted, depicted the plan as one
that placed human beings at the center of the economy, as one that es-

chewed questions of dogma and sought to provide people with goods they could obtain immediately, not three years down the line: "I can say from personal experience that they have struck a vein that is extraordinarily popular. I think we put too much emphasis on economic facts, without examining them ideologically and discussing them in our press and in our speeches." On this point, Kuckhoff was joined by Professor Dr. Wilhelm Ziegelmeyer, vice president of the Administration for Trade and Provisioning, who described the situation somewhat more dramatically: "There is a great danger if living conditions improve only a little bit. We have over there [in the Western zones] a dulled, excitable mass that, as a result of hunger, is incapable of welcoming democratic ideas."[42]

The flow of the discussion had demonstrated a grudging recognition of a serious problem. But it was a recognition thoroughly conditioned by the struggles and crises of the 1920s and 1930s. First, Marshall Plan aid would benefit only the few, thus reintroducing old divisions within the working class. Second, those who might benefit would still lag behind the standard of living enjoyed by German workers during the Weimar years. For the implicit, if vague, understanding of "standard of living" was itself beholden to the past, to the longstanding, ingrained assumptions and ambivalence about consumption within the German Left. Material abundance was desired, but also regarded with suspicion, in part because it deceived and corrupted those whose task it was to enlighten the people—in this case, West German union functionaries willing to take part in preparations for Marshall Plan aid. But far more important for determining the "standard of living" were factors more directly connected to production: guarantees of steady employment, social insurance, collective bargaining—in short, many of the structural gains enjoyed by organized labor during the Weimar years only to be eroded, first during the Great Depression and then under Nazi rule. For SED leaders the working-class experience of hunger and long-term unemployment in the 1920s and 1930s was crucial. Their insistence on "the right to work" as a central element in judging living conditions cannot be understood without reference to that experience. In truth, SED leaders were only beginning to reconsider these questions, and they were doing so in a wholly unfamiliar context. The imprecision of their language—the interchangeable use of the German terms *Lebenshaltung, Lebenslage, Lebensstandard,*

Lebensverhältnisse—was itself indicative of their uncertainty. (As we shall see, the question of living standards would be both a source of further confusion and a call to action in subsequent years.) As the meeting came to a somber close, the horizon of their expectations for a West Germany on the receiving end of Marshall Plan aid was most vividly drawn by Paul Merker, a former member of the KPD Politburo and now leading SED figure:

> There is a great danger in the West. It was already said that here and there one can count on an improvement of living conditions *(Lebensver-hältnisse)*. I am of the opinion that this cannot be so important. Nevertheless, it cannot be entirely dismissed. In any case, one thing will occur; certain classes in the West will be helped to a better life. On the one hand, we will see an increase in poverty, and on the other we will see an increase in splendor. I can imagine that Frankfurt will become a city of lights as we have perhaps never seen before in Germany. But beyond the borders of Frankfurt it will grow that much darker.[43]

In contrast to the press silence that greeted the new shopwindows of the Western zones, the administrative bodies of the Soviet zone went into an immediate and focused flurry of activity. Only one day after the currency reform, Konstantine Koval, the SMAD economics chief, was instructing Heinrich Rau to stock up reserves for the winter, to make greater amounts of milk and fish available to the population, and to increase the number of East Berlin workers receiving the benefits of Order no. 234.[44] In addition, preparations were immediately initiated to increase rations for the whole population of the zone. By the end of June the Administration of Trade and Provisioning had already carried out investigations estimating the amounts of particular goods required. For the next two months Rau worked closely with the SMAD Administration of Trade and Provisioning, until, on September 3, the increases were finalized and set to go into effect on October 1.[45] According to the new regulations, the number of Order no. 234 workers was to be increased from 1 million to 1.5 million. In addition, the workers' communities on the outskirts of Berlin with populations of two hundred thousand or more were now to be provisioned as well as the sixteen large cities of the zone. Rations of bread, potatoes, and processed foodstuffs, meanwhile, were to be increased in varying degrees for all cardholders. A second round of increases the following spring continued the trend; special monthly packages of foodstuffs were to be distributed not only to the workers of Order no. 234, but also to railway workers and miners—in total, 2 million workers.[46] These increases represented a clear extension of the original premises of Order no. 234. The number of workers within its purview was substantially increased, and holders of the best ration cards received the largest ration increases.

Although SED and DWK leaders never questioned the reasoning behind these measures, they did try at times to obtain SMAD approval for either expanding the circles of those benefiting from the improvements or extending the improvements already introduced to particular groups, even if only marginally. For example, before the October 1 increases had even gone into effect, Rau was pressing the Soviets for a larger increase in bread rations for workers performing heavy manual labor in large cities than that provided for in the October 1 directive, which was considered so small that it had led to "countless complaints among workers in large industrial communities."[47] Although he had to wait a few weeks for an answer, Rau was eventually able to obtain Soviet approval.[48] Similarly, Rau took exception to SMAD plans for the introduction of point cards for rationing clothing, shoes, and household consumer items. According to an article published in the SMAD press organ, *Tägliche Rundschau,* unemployed adults (housewives and pensioners) were to be excluded from the distribution of the cards. "I have been informed that this is no accident," wrote Rau to the SMAD chief of trade and provisioning, I. Drofa, "but rather springs from principle. I should point out that this standpoint is not shared by the DWK."[49] Again, Rau got what he wanted. The point cards were to correspond hierarchically to the categories of food rationing; unemployed adults were thus to be included, albeit at the bottom of the hierarchy.[50]

At other times, however, SED leaders were not so lucky. In fact, SMAD actions could be extremely frustrating. In the weeks before Christmas, for example, the SMAD Finance Administration decided to recoordinate the hitherto state-subsidized retail prices for bread throughout the zone, with the aim of reducing public expenditures and eradicating the differences between the various provinces, for some of which the bread prices from October 1936 had remained in effect. This meant, however, increasing prices for consumers, which SED leaders considered particularly ill advised. Rau pleaded with Koval:

"The products of mass consumption like bread and potatoes should for political reasons be left untouched by any price increase."[51] German trade-and-provisioning officials were more emphatic: "The price of bread has always been a political price, and now more than ever since bread and potatoes form the basis of a nourishing diet."[52] But the Soviets were unyielding. As Rau learned from the SMAD Finance Administration one week later, the new price, after further review, had been confirmed and would go into effect on the first day of the upcoming new year.[53] The misgivings of SED leaders, however, turned out to be entirely well founded. As leaders of the SED in Saxony wrote to Ulbricht in January, "The mood of the population, which has been completely surprised by this measure, is, at the beginning of the Two-Year Plan, extraordinarily bad. The manner and way in which the price increase for bread was introduced has meant a very serious political burden for our party."[54]

And yet there were times when SMAD officials took Germans to task for their own failings in the area of consumer provisioning. For example, at a meeting of the leadership of the Association of Consumer Cooperatives, co-op officials found themselves being criticized for the poor state of many of the co-op stores. The Soviet official at the meeting was troubled, in particular, by the shoddy appearance and decoration of the stores, their lack of advertising, the fact that goods were not properly set out on display as a means of enticing customers and thus boosting sales. Commenting on the stores, he observed ruefully, "In the place of vitrines they are filled with metal grids." However, what the Soviet official seemed to find most distressing was the bad service: "The German has shown himself to have grown unaccustomed to saying thank you. One has the feeling that the salesperson finds his work to be a heavy burden—indeed, this is not the case everywhere, but it has become characteristic."[55]

Nevertheless, it would be a mistake to overemphasize the extent to which either SMAD or SED officials were willing to go toward redressing the sufferings and sacrifices of German consumers. Their major public pronouncements and policies continued to trumpet above all else the cause of productivity, as the Soviet zone moved economically and politically further along the path of Sovietization. Here, the Soviet zone fell within the overall pattern of Communist consolidation throughout Eastern Europe, a process pushed along by the intensification of the Cold War and by the widening split between Stalin and Tito in 1947 and 1948.[56] On June 30, 1948, ten days after the Western currency reform, the SED announced its intention to develop the first long-term economic plan for the zone, the Two-Year Plan for 1949–50. One month later, the SED adopted a resolution calling for the official transformation of the SED into a "party of the new type," that is, into a full-fledged Marxist-Leninist party.[57] During the next several months a series of articles appeared in the major journals and magazines of the zone, gushing with enthusiasm and pedagogy on the themes of work discipline, work norms, work morale. As if repetition were not enough, the message was now distilled into four simple words: "Produce more, live better."[58]

The ethos of productivity found its purest expression in the Hennecke movement, an officially organized and propagated Soviet-zone recapitulation of the Soviet Union's Stakhanov activist movement of the 1930s. The idea for launching a Soviet-zone version of Stakhanovism came from Otto Buchwitz, chief of the SED organization in Saxony. Buchwitz had been to the Soviet Union after the war and was deeply impressed by what he imagined to be the great successes of the movement. After a long search, Buchwitz and his assistants discovered and carefully groomed Adolf Hennecke, a coal miner, to be the personification of their own movement. Under specially prepared conditions and on the anniversary of the issuing of Order no. 234 (October 13, 1948), Hennecke performed his "great exploit" of labor heroism, mining 387 percent of his normal shift quota. The nascent Hennecke movement, initiated by Buchwitz, was then taken over by the Soviets, who did all they could to ensure its success. They showed old Stakhanovite films, trained trade-union delegations, prompted local newspapers to popularize the movement; they published songs, poems, and stories celebrating the accomplishments of Hennecke activists, first in coal mining, then in the other branches of heavy industry. No effort was spared to enhance the contagion of Hennecke's "work enthusiasm." Elevated to the status of heroes, the Hennecke activists were championed with typically Stalinist bombast and pathos: "Honor to the Hennecke activists, the heroes of the reconstruction, who, with brain and hammer, blaze a free trail to a better future for their nation!"[59]

The Hennecke movement was supposed to succeed where Order no. 234 had failed. But to improve incentives for workers to be more productive, a better means of distributing consumer goods had to be brought into being. Here, the activist movement intersected with parallel plans to establish a new state-run organization of retail stores and restaurants, the *Handelsorganisation*. It would be incorrect to suggest that the HO was merely the handmaiden of the Hennecke movement. In truth, the HO came to be associated with several, sometimes competing, aims. The story of its introduction is instructive in that it brings into focus many of the problems faced by the apprentice economic planners of the DWK, while laying out several of the themes and contradictions encountered in the course of this study.

The weeks leading up to the opening of the first "free shops," as the HOs were originally known, were characterized by a curious combination of intense anticipation and a distinct lack of information. Only two days before the first grand opening in Berlin's Frankfurter Allee on November 15, *Neues Deutschland* reported, "Over half of the letters that reach us, every second telephone call we receive and the steadily growing number of visitors to our editorial offices are concerned with the same subject: the free shops. When will they be opened? What goods will be sold? How high will the prices be?" No better informed than their readers, the editors confessed that they had to disappoint "because 42 00 18 (German Economic Commission) does not answer."[60]

The anticipation is easy to understand. The new stores were to offer Germans in the Soviet zone the first legal means of shopping ration-free since the war years. Consumers would still be able to buy rationed goods from their local shopkeepers and consumer co-ops, but now they would also have the possibility of making additional, ration-free purchases.[61] That much was known. The lack of detailed information is perhaps also not difficult to grasp. As this chapter has shown, Soviet-zone authorities had a great deal on their minds, attempting to steer their way amid the effects of the currency reform, the Berlin Blockade, preparations for launching the Two-Year Plan, and the transformation of the SED into a "party of the new type."

However, as this chapter has also shown, the opening of the HOs could hardly be unrelated to these events, in particular to the currency reform and its promise of a return to normalcy. Indeed, the attempt to reintroduce an element of normalcy into the daily life of the Soviet zone constituted one of the most important tasks of the HO. In addition, the new stores were supposed to be first-class establishments, catering to the most refined and exacting of consumer pleasures. Here, the need to answer the challenge posed by the Western currency reform was perhaps most apparent.

At the same time, it is important to recognize that the HO was understood as a mechanism for solving certain zone-specific problems that administrators had been hitherto unable to master. As indicated earlier, the HO was supposed to pick up where the workplace meals and clothing handouts of Order no. 234 had failed, thus helping to solve the problem of productivity. In addition, it was to serve as a means of fighting the black market and of absorbing excess purchasing power.[62] Although most prices for consumer goods had been officially frozen at 1944 levels, the imbalance between available consumer goods and the currency in circulation had created conditions for the emergence of hidden inflation (excess purchasing power) and a flourishing black market.

There had been previous attempts to address these problems. The black market, for instance, had been subject to repeated police raids, searches and seizures by volunteer groups, economic competition from "free" food markets (*freie Spitzen*) and from "free" exchange markets for secondhand goods organized by local authorities.[63] But none of these measures had succeeded. Nor had the currency reform in the Soviet zone succeeded in absorbing excess purchasing power, which not only went to feed the black market but in doing so disappeared from public use for the effort of reconstruction.[64] And, as discussed in the previous chapter, Order no. 234 had proven a total failure. Instead of productivity, all that had increased were wages and thus the amount of currency in circulation, which in turn only compounded the financial difficulties of the zone. It is in the context of these zone-specific problems, in addition to that of the Western currency reform and the ensuing blockade, that the introduction of the *Handelsorganisation* must be understood.

Katherine Pence has highlighted several paradoxes bound up with the introduction of the HO.[65] Its high prices, she rightly points out, served to reinforce provisioning hierarchies even as Soviet-zone authorities professed a desire for eradicating social differences.[66] As a state-owned institution, the HO was of a piece with the set of measures moving the Soviet-zone economy toward socialism; but to be effective the HO had to employ many of the selling strategies socialists had al-

ways denounced as capitalistic and therefore exploitative—in particular, the HO set out to "mobilize" and "enflame" the desire of consumers for luxury commodities, thus deploying the deceptive arts of
capitalist seduction as a means of making workers more productive.[67]
Above all, she argues, the HO set out to construct an "ideal socialist
consumer," one she identifies as a decidedly male activist–production
worker, pockets bulging with productivity wages, out on a leisurely spree
of pleasure shopping. Housewives and women generally, on the other
hand, tended to be excluded. Denied productivity wages, languishing
at the bottom of the rationing hierarchy, women were left with the arduous, unrewarding labor of standing in long lines while shopping for
basic rationed commodities.[68]

Pence's account of the introduction of the HO is fascinating. Nevertheless, I believe her picture is overdrawn, even at the level of official
intention. As the rest of this chapter tries to show, Soviet-zone economic planners and HO leaders had very little idea of the "ideal socialist consumer" they ostensibly hoped to "build." Hennecke was a
model for workers, not consumers. And while it is true that the HO was
intended to provide incentive for increased productivity, the notion
that consumer desire had to be mobilized, or enflamed, disregards the
context of extreme and chronic scarcity—as if the desire for all kinds
of consumer goods were not already there. If anything, Soviet-zone authorities hoped to keep consumer desire at a minimum, knowing full
well the constraints on their ability to satisfy consumption wants. It is
also misleading to suggest that the HO sold only luxury items. In fact,
a wide array of basic commodities were also available in HO stores, including basic foodstuffs, mending yarn, textiles, work clothing, and
shoelaces. As for the exclusion of women, especially housewives, one
may assume that many HO shoppers were women married or related
to high-wage earners and that such women did as much of a given
household's HO shopping as they did its normal rationed shopping.
Were male activist-workers likely to go out pleasure shopping for
bread, cooking oil, mending yarn, and women's shoes and underwear?
In fact, what becomes abundantly clear from Soviet-zone sources is the
high degree of uncertainty, confusion, conflicting information, and
competing goals that accompanied the introduction of the HO.

The initial planning meetings between leading DWK functionaries and
their Soviet counterparts took place in October 1948. At an October 5

meeting, I. Drofa, the leader of the SMAD Administration for Trade and Provisioning, opened with a succinct explanation of his own understanding of the purpose of the stores: "The goal of this organization must be clear. It is not only a question of the budget, of absorbing money and the support of the [Soviet-zone] mark, but also of the improved provisioning of the population, with the goal of getting rid of [ration] cards and of fighting the black market."[69] In the following discussion a wide array of basic questions was discussed: What kinds of goods should be sold in the stores: "specialty" items exclusively or basic goods such as potatoes and heating fuel as well? At what prices should they be sold? More specifically, how closely should the new stores approximate black market prices? Indeed, to what extent were black market prices known? What sort of organization should be in charge of the stores, with what structure, and under whose authority? How many stores should be opened at first, and where?

Without arriving at definitive answers to any of these questions, the meeting ended with Drofa reiterating his initial remarks. "Until now there has been no commercial activity [*Handel*] in the Soviet-occupied zone, only allocation [*Verteilung*]. We want to begin to trade [*handeln*] and thereby get rid of illicit trade. The free stores should be good stores, well appointed and with good-quality merchandise." Having acknowledged the financial uses the stores could be made to serve, Drofa chose to emphasize to DWK planners their primary significance in improving provisioning, fighting the black market, and reintroducing *real* retail trade.

Similar meetings took place in the following weeks and months, with the Soviets exercising close supervision over almost every aspect of the project, ranging from quality standards to price policy to the number and location of stores.[70] It became increasingly apparent that the HO was being modeled after the "commercial" stores of the Soviet Union. Emerging toward the end of 1929, the Soviet commercial stores had operated outside the Soviet rationing system, offering their wares at prices considerably higher than those charged in stores selling rationed goods.[71] Initially they offered only clothes and fabric but soon expanded their inventory to include vodka, cigarettes, and basic foods, as well as luxury commodities like caviar and smoked fish. Internal DWK memoranda sometimes even referred to the new "free stores" as "commercial trade" *(kommerzieller Handel)*.[72] The Soviet-zone trade journal, *Die Versorgung*, would later publish feature stories holding up the Soviet commercial stores as a model for the HO.[73]

As preparations proceeded, occupation authorities began to pass on information to the public about the free stores through the press. As suggested earlier, however, it would be entirely misleading to speak of a well-coordinated and clearly articulated press campaign. Rather, the information which appeared in Soviet-zone newspapers reflected the hesitancy and uncertainty of occupation authorities. On October 12, for example, an interview with Dr. Karl Steiner, vice president of the Central Administration of Finances, appeared in the *Berliner Zeitung*.[74] Steiner stressed the role of the new stores in fighting the black market and in using profits that otherwise would have gone to black marketeers for "productive purposes." He also indicated that to fight the black market where it was most rampant, the stores would have to be set up in the most important big cities in the Soviet zone, including two stores for the Soviet sector of Berlin. In a passing reference, however, he suggested that "little would be gained" by engaging private retail in the endeavor. Only "state shops" *(staatliche Verkaufsgeschäfte)* would guarantee the required "strict control" over ration-free trade. It was probably this remark that then set off a subsequent little feud between Steiner and Heinrich Rau. Until at least as late as October 15 Soviet authorities were planning to include private shops in the effort.[75] On the same day the interview appeared, Rau, perhaps under pressure from the Soviets, sent Steiner a letter (a copy of which went to Walter Ulbricht) in which he took Steiner to task for "lack of discipline" and fined him three hundred marks as a penalty for giving the interview without, he claimed, first getting permission from the Press Office of the DWK. Indignant, Steiner objected (a copy of his objection also going to Ulbricht), pointing out that the reporter from the *Berliner Zeitung* had in fact been sent to him by the DWK Press Office. A few days later Steiner was informed by the party's Central Secretariat that the fine had been lifted.[76] It is impossible to elaborate on this little feud, since the precise circumstances are unknown, but its mere occurrence was indicative of the confusion and lack of coordination among Soviet-zone authorities.

Subsequent press reports, too, were inconsistent in their information. Reporting on an October 15 meeting of the Economic Committee of the German People's Council, *Neues Deutschland* informed its readers that the new stores would be run by the FDGB and that rationed *Massengüter* (bread, potatoes, sugar, meat, fat) would be excluded from their inventory. The stores would instead sell "specialties," such as "high-quality [*hochwertige*] fruit, vegetables and tinned fish, as well as semiluxuries, high-quality textiles, cameras, accordions etc."[77] And although only a few days earlier Steiner had said that the stores would be concentrated in big cities, voices were raised in the ensuing discussion in favor of placing the stores primarily in factories for the benefit of workers. Not until October 27 did readers of *Neues Deutschland* learn that, according to an October 20 decree from the DWK, the stores would be run by a new *Handelsorganisation* to be organized and directed by the Administration for Trade and Provisioning and that the stores would sell manufactured consumer goods *(gewerbliche Gebrauchsgüter)* as well as foodstuffs, including potatoes but excluding meat, eggs, butter, fresh milk, and cheese.[78]

A day later, in an attempt to communicate the thinking behind the October 20 decree, Heinrich Rau published an article in *Neues Deutschland*. While offering little more in specific information, he did make an open comparison between the new policy in the Soviet zone and developments in the Western zones. "The available purchasing power in our zone presently exceeds the amount of goods offered," he pointed out. "We too could solve this problem of eliminating excess purchasing power in a simple way, as has been done in the west of Germany, through a general increase in prices without a corresponding rise in wages and salaries—thus, by lowering the real income of the entire nation. One would then see people standing before full shopwindows in our zone as well, most of whom, however, would not be able to buy the goods for lack of money." He added, "full shopwindows are only the expression of the fact that people can buy less, not the expression of an increased productivity."[79] If prices were going to be high in the new stores of the Soviet zone as well, he argued, at least the profits were going to be used in the reconstruction effort and, thus, for the benefit of all, whereas in the Western zones high retail prices merely served to line the pockets of "monopoly capitalists."

The most expansive press article on the introduction of the new stores was written by Erich Freund, the top SED official in the Administration for Trade and Provisioning. Previously screened by the SED Economic Policy Department and published on the eve of the opening of the first stores, Freund's piece hailed the *Handelsorganisation* as the embodiment of "a new era in trade," signaling the reestablishment of what he called "true trade for the satisfaction of the needs of the population."[80] The long years during which *Handel* had been reduced to performing a pure distributing function were coming to an end. Once again *Handel* would play its proper role in the dynamics of supply and demand: "The population desires nothing more than to be able finally to choose and shop for goods freely and in a legal manner." The emphasis here was clearly on the reintroduction of normalcy, on a partial lifting of the prolonged state of emergency in people's daily lives. But at the same time, he placed the introduction of the *Handelsorganisation* squarely within the series of profound political-economic changes that had already been introduced in the Soviet zone: "That which is represented by the people's-owned factories in the sphere of industry, and that which has been achieved by the land reform in the sphere of agriculture is now being completed in the sphere of *Handel* with the creation of free trade carried out by the people's-owned *Handelsorganisation*." Freund was presenting the HO simultaneously as a means of reestablishing a sense of normalcy associated with the past and as a vehicle for change in the construction of an uncertain future. Exactly what would it mean to have "people's-owned" retail stores was hardly clear. What role would they play in balancing supply and demand? What incentive would the managers and employees of the "people's-owned" shops have to ensure that demand be satisfied? What recourse would consumers have if supply and distribution were taken out of private hands?

Freund did not raise such questions, let alone address them. There was, however, a basic contradiction in his vision of the HO as a carrier of both old and new. Equally contradictory was his claim, on the one hand, that the stores were being called into existence for the improvement of the living standard of "all parts of the population" and his efforts, on the other hand, to highlight the significance of the stores in offering an incentive for greater productivity among Hennecke activists: "It is to be expected that an overwhelming portion of the shoppers [*Käuferschichten*] will be made up of activist workers in the Eastern zone and the Eastern sector of Berlin." This privileged recognition of activists was even to be reflected in the stores' late business hours, he wrote, "since a significant amount of their shopping time will be in the evening hours." Freund had thus inadvertently posed an important question: for whom were the new stores being established?

The contradictions and uncertainties that characterized the information disseminated in the press was itself a reflection of the ad hoc, improvised manner in which the introduction of the stores was carried out. On November 15, the day on which the first stores opened, Freund complained of this to the Economic Policy Department of the SED: "The *Handelsorganisation* works, in fact, under provisional conditions, but in theory doesn't yet exist since the three directors and the four procurers called for in the statutes issued by the German Economic Commission have not yet been named." The *Handelsorganisation,* he emphasized, due to its great financial significance would "tolerate no further improvisations."[81] Meanwhile, the deadlines for working out detailed plans for the amounts and kinds of goods to be sold, the extension of the retail net, the importing of goods from other countries, and other basic tasks extended well into December.[82] According to a paper *(Denkschrift)* produced by the special "Work Group HO" within the Administration for Trade and Provisioning, there had been an "alarming standstill" in the development of the *Handelsorganisation.* The paper went on to list the various measures pursued after November 22 to overcome this standstill and even spoke of a subsequent "new phase in the development of the HO." But the general tone of the paper was one of annoyance and impatience: "In view of the present situation and the slow tempo of development to be expected we must express the strongest objections to the fact that an orderly management of the HO is [only] possible after January 1, 1949."[83]

It was not until January 11 that the first session of the Administrative Council of the HO took place, presided over by Greta Kuckhoff. The council also included as members Hans Paul Ganter-Gilmans (leader of the Administration for Trade and Provisioning), Erich Freund, Willy Rumpf (leader of the Finance Administration), and Dr. Karl Steiner.[84] The newly appointed chief manager of the HO's Central Management Office was Hermann Streit, a man with no experience in trade but considerable experience as a union and Communist Party functionary. Like so many SED officials, Streit had spent most of the Nazi years in prison and in a concentration camp, with intermittent periods of exile and fighting in the Spanish Civil War. After World War II he served as a deputy minister for economic planning in Brandenburg.[85] His tenure as chief manager of the HO was to last only until April 1949, when he moved on to lead the agricultural section of the GDR's Ministry for Trade and Provisioning and was replaced at the HO by Paul Baender.

At the council's meeting, Streit reiterated the economic significance of the stores and assured his fellow council members that all HO stores throughout the zone, many of which had previously been forced to rely on their own initiative, were now firmly under the control of his Central Management Office. His assurances, however, proved premature. Despite the consolidation of the structure of the organization, serious problems continued to hamper its ability to function effectively. Not the least of these problems was that of financing. Nearly one month after the meeting of the council Streit was forced to appeal to Kuckhoff for increased credit.[86] An earlier appeal to the Finance Administration had produced a short-term credit from the Deutsche Notenbank for DM 50 million to be paid back with interest after one month. Accounting in some detail for the HO's income and expenses, Streit pleaded his case with Kuckhoff for either a larger, long-term, and interest-free credit or for an increase of the HO's principal capital assets to DM 100 million. Eventually the DWK did decide to increase HO's principal capital to DM 100 million. But the money was slow in coming, and one month later the HO Central Management Office was forced to turn to the Administration for Trade and Provisioning for additional money to purchase cash registers, telephones, and other supplies.[87]

The lack of adequate financing, in turn, had adverse effects on the carrying out of a variety of other tasks, as a result of which the HO was subject to repeated criticism from the Administration for Trade and Provisioning. In late February, for example, Freund complained that a number of stores and restaurants that were supposed to be opened by February 1 had not yet been opened, including two restaurants in Brandenburg, plus ten stores and two restaurants in Saxony.[88] Without the fulfillment of the planned extension of the retail net, he pointed out, the fulfillment of the sales plans was endangered.

In a long and revealing letter of complaint about those stores and restaurants that had been opened, Ganter-Gilmans took the HO managers to task for the fact that the stores and restaurants were not living up to what they were supposed to be: "especially cultivated establishments of the highest level." Ganter-Gilmans emphasized the need for "tasteful decoration and appointments, effective advertising, meticulous cleanliness, schooled, tactful and polite personnel, goods which satisfy the highest demands for quality, and a general atmosphere in which the customer feels comfortable."[89] He pointed to "countless reports" testifying to the fact that the stores and restaurants were falling far short of this ideal and focused in particular on an investigation of a Berlin restaurant carried out by Freund. In his letter, Ganter-Gilmans quoted Freund at length. It is necessary to do so here as well to show that there were voices within the emerging regime, even at this early date, insisting on the need to pay serious attention to the satisfaction of consumers' desires, both material and experiential. Freund wrote:

> I believe I am justified in saying that even among those working in the HO there still does not yet exist the correct attitude towards the great significance of the new path we have embarked on. Visitors of such restaurants are not going to be excited merely by the fact that goods are available ration-free, but rather by the general impression, by the atmosphere they encounter. This general significance, which is of great psychological value, appears to be completely trampled upon . . . Thus, the service was not obliging and pleasant, as it must be, but rather according to the old method, *"Kollege kommt gleich"* ["Someone will be with you in a moment"]. The management was nowhere in evidence to assure an orderly business and to give the customer the impression that in the case of unhappiness with the service there was a higher authority ready to intervene on behalf of the customer. The napkins had long since required a change. The coffee was served almost cold. Even the torte was tasteless, recognizable [as a torte] simply because it had been made from flour and butter . . . To the attentive visitor the general impression was of an old automat [*Aschingerfiliale*] that did not have the task of providing its guests with a pleasant experience [*Aufenthalt*] but was instead set up to process as great a number of customers in the shortest possible time.

It would be false, he warned, to judge such restaurants merely in terms of "their financial significance, of 'good business,' and of the large number of customers." On the contrary, Freund insisted on the importance of all those elements, as listed by Ganter-Gilmans, required to impart pleasure to the experience of consuming.[90]

On the morning of November 15, 1948, thousands of Berliners gathered in the Frankfurter Allee for the opening of the first "free store" in

Berlin. "It should have been a moment of celebration," reported *Neues Deutschland,* "but it didn't come to that." Because the crowd was so large, the police had to be called in to control the pushing, impatient customers waiting for the doors to open. The combination of the pressing multitude and police presence evidently soured the mood. Disgruntled voices, recorded in Berlin dialect, complained that the new stores must be only for "speculators and party bosses [*Bonzen*]," while others pointed out that there was but one, unhappy alternative, the black market: "*Ja, jeh'n Se man uff'n schwarzen Marcht, lass'n sich schnapp'n—und über's Ohr hau'n!* [Yeah. Go try the black market, get snatched up by the police—and cheated!]"

As soon as the doors opened, the throngs shoved their way in. According to *Neues Deutschland,* "It looked as if thousands of women, girls and men pushed themselves through the great swinging doors all at once. For minutes everything was confusion." Then the doors shut, leaving thousands still outside. For those who managed to squeeze in,

> the little "purgatory" was soon forgotten. In the brilliantly illuminated interior room the customers stood for a moment, shocked and still. Where should one turn to first? To the huge bundles of coat fabrics? To that corner where shoes in all sizes were piled up? To the high shelves, filled with ladies underwear, sweaters and—oh bliss!—countless boxes of stockings? Very quickly the points of "most burning" demand crystallized: shoes, stockings, mending yarn.[91]

Never mind the exorbitant prices: women's shoes in three styles for DM 160, 190, and 230; men's shoes for DM 240, and men's work boots in two styles for DM 180 and 210. Berliners in the Soviet sector were apparently only too happy to hand over their money for the goods offered ration-free in the new store. This at a time when the average gross weekly wages of an industrial worker came to only DM 47.74. A metal worker, in November 1948, would have had to work 19.7 hours in order to buy one kilogram of wheat flour, 32.5 hours to buy one kilogram of sugar, 78.9 hours to buy one kilogram of sausage, 128.1 hours to buy one kilogram of butter, and 108.4 hours to buy one kilogram of margarine in an HO store.[92] Nevertheless, according to *Neues Deutschland,* hours after the doors had first opened, the crowds waiting outside had still not diminished. Those customers coming out reassured them, saying, "The supply is inexhaustible. There is enough inside for the next three years!" In the words of Herr Behlow, the store manager, "All the pessimists who spoke out against the free stores have now been brilliantly refuted. The 'HO' (Handels-Organisation) is already popular in Berlin."

Soviet-zone authorities were keen to gauge the true reaction of the population to the new stores. Information on the reception of the HOs was channeled upward within the party itself, as well as within the Administration for Trade and Provisioning. Two weeks after the opening of the first stores, the SED Department of Propaganda, Press, and Radio compiled a general report based on individual reports from the different provinces.[93] Their general report was, in turn, sent directly to Walter Ulbricht. The findings of the report suggested "a very differentiated" reaction among the population, a "very divided opinion." The report listed the "most important" arguments both supporting and critical of the HOs. In support, people argued that the stores were the only means of fighting the black market; that even though workers were able to buy very little at first, the situation would improve in the future; that the ability of workers to buy something to supplement their food rations would contribute to increasing work productivity; that profits would no longer go to profiteers and speculators but rather would flow into state coffers for use in reconstruction and "social" purposes; and that the opening of the stores signified the beginning of normal trade. On the other hand, those criticizing the HOs argued that the "broad masses of the population" could buy nothing in the stores because of the high prices; the ability of the stores to fight the black market was doubtful; indeed, the stores themselves constituted a state-approved black market.

The report also contained a poll of 175 people, broken down according to political affiliation and occupation. They appear to have been chosen randomly. Of the total, eighty-nine were "in favor of" the new stores, sixty-seven were "against," eleven were "against with reservations," seven were "undecided," and one was "indifferent." The political breakdown was not particularly revealing, since nearly three-fourths of those polled declared no political affiliation. The occupational breakdown, however, was of interest because of the high percentage of workers voting against the HOs and the high percentage of white-collar employees *(Angestellte)* and officials *(Beamte)* voting for the stores. For those authorities counting on the HO functioning as a means of boosting the productivity of industrial workers, this information must have been sobering indeed.

In the following months complaints about high prices and poor-quality goods continued to demand attention.[94] There were even rumors that the Soviets were taking almost all of the income from the HOs. Party officials were convinced that these rumors were causing a decline in turnover.[95] In an attempt to refute the criticism, German authorities enlisted the press. If prices were high, they explained, that was because the HO was not a provisioning depot *(Versorgungseinrichtung)* but rather a trade establishment *(Handelsgesellschaft)* entrusted with the task of fighting the black market and of absorbing purchasing power. In any case, over time the HO prices would gradually be lowered, making HO goods more accessible to ever-wider sections of the population. If in the first few months the quality of merchandise was at times poor, all efforts would be made in the future to ensure that only "first-class" goods were offered for sale. If there were rumors that the Soviets were appropriating the profits of the HO, authorities insisted that such rumors were due to false information disseminated by Western newspapers. In truth, they intoned, all income from the HOs was exclusively at the disposal of the Soviet-zone economy.[96]

HO planners were themselves well aware of the sensitivity of the price question. What at times seemed to elude them, however, was the tension between the financial goals that high prices were supposed to serve and some of the other goals bound up with the entire HO endeavor. Above all, there was a basic conflict between the goal of absorbing "excess" purchasing power through high prices in a context of general scarcity and that of improving consumer supply for large sections of the population in the hopes of reintroducing a politically significant degree of normalcy into the daily life of the zone. HO planners, however, often seemed reluctant to recognize this difficulty. At the first session of the Administrative Council, for instance, Steiner held forth at some length on the financial tasks of the HO. Anticipating potential objections to price policy, he suggested that the emphasis should lie elsewhere, that is, with "a correct selling policy [*Absatzpolitik*]". If in one part of the zone certain goods were not selling because prices were high, one would simply have to sell them in another area where there were "better selling possibilities." At the very same meeting, meanwhile, Greta Kuckhoff highlighted the role of the HO in reintroducing normalcy. "Our present *Handel* is in no way 'normal,'" she pointed out. "Our economic goal lies rather in building up on an ever-broader basis a normal, ration-free provisioning of all goods with the help of our people's-owned *Handelsorganisation*. As Herr Dr. Steiner indicated, the financial policy measures also serve this goal."[97] Kuckhoff either appeared not to have heard Steiner, or she was bending over backwards to reconcile uncomfortably competing viewpoints.

The strict maintenance of high prices, moreover, could at times threaten to undermine the very financial goals these prices were intended to serve. Four months later, at the second session of the Administrative Council, the question of potato prices came up for discussion as "one of the most burning problems." Representatives from the provincial governments complained that the price of DM 24 per hundredweight was far too high, that as a result the potatoes were not selling, and that there was a real danger that they would rot in storage. As the representative from Mecklenburg pointed out, "One must not put the interests of finances over those of trade and provisioning." Kuckhoff, in turn, suggested proposing a price of DM 15 as a basis for negotiation with higher authorities in the DWK and the SMAD. This time it was Freund who spoke up for "the interests of finances." It was not the task of the council to discuss individual price proposals, he argued, but rather difficulties with price policy in general. In any case, DM 15 was too low in his opinion. One should not insist that the potatoes could not be sold before one tried to sell them: "That goes especially for Mecklenburg since there are centers of industry there where sales should be possible."[98]

The potato problem was simultaneously being discussed in the higher reaches of the SED. A few days after the Administrative Council session, the party's Economic Policy Department informed Walter Ulbricht that the 217,500 tons of potatoes intended for sale in the HOs were not selling, that they were in danger of rotting, and that the Soviets had rejected proposals to sell them at the normal (rationed) price.[99] Two days later Ulbricht learned from the editors of the Magdeburg *Volksstimme* that fifty tons of potatoes in a nearby county had already spoiled and had to be given to the local distilleries. The situation was known to the population and had aroused "a great unrest."[100] In the following weeks the price was then lowered, first to DM 18 and then to DM 9 per hundredweight. Still, sales failed to pick up. By May 20 the Economic Policy Department was recommending to Ulbricht a complete cessation of the sale of potatoes in the HOs; it went into effect in

August.[101] Financial goals had simply come up against objective "selling possibilities."

Nevertheless, by the end of its full calendar year, the HO could boast some real success, having fulfilled its overall 1949 sales plan by 119.5 percent, for a total sales volume of over DM 2.6 billion.[102] Sales were particularly strong in Berlin and Saxony (respectively 21 percent and 31.5 percent of total HO sales); and they were highest in the first and last quarters, having fallen off in the second quarter, partly as a result of the lifting of the blockade and the slowness with which price reductions were introduced.[103] According to a report from the Central Administration for Economic Planning, HO sales had also been hurt in the second and third quarters by limited and poor-quality merchandise, unqualified personnel, and strong competition from Western-zone retail offerings.[104] Still, the HO had exceeded its original sales-plan goals, accounting for about 26 percent of total planned retail sales for the zone.[105] By the end of April 1949, it had extended its retail net of department stores, specialized shops, restaurants, cafes, snack bars, and hotels to 343. As of March 31, 1951, that figure had grown to 2,294, accounting for a total sales of over DM 4.5 billion.[106]

The HO's one-year anniversary gala was held on November 17, 1949, at the Babylon, East Berlin's premier movie palace. Walter Ulbricht himself delivered the keynote speech. Full of praise for the HO's contribution to improving the provisioning of the population, Ulbricht celebrated the HO above all as a "great people's-owned enterprise" (*volkseigenes Unternehmen*). Like the newly created state-owned industries (VEBs), the HO belonged to the people and to the newly born "democratic state."[107] (The GDR came into being officially on October 7, 1949.) And like the VEBs, the HO too showed that economic policy was no longer in the hands of capitalists and shareholders but was instead determined by "men who come from the working people." As such, it featured prominently in the competition with West Germany. Ulbricht claimed that the "shareholders of the great department stores in West Germany" were "outraged over the success of the *Handelsorganisation*," particularly because its profits would help ensure early fulfillment of the Two-Year Plan. "The enemy," he pointed out, especially in West Berlin, was engaged in a "smear campaign" against the HO; the newspaper *Sozialdemokrat* had produced what Ulbricht called "the most fantastic report," claiming in bold headline, "Death by HO Cheese." For the authors of such "lying reports" he had only one piece of advice: "Watch out, my dear sirs in West Germany, that you don't die from the Marshall Plan!"[108]

If Ulbricht depicted the HO as part and parcel of the many changes introduced under Soviet occupation, he also hailed it as a vehicle of normalcy, highlighting its effectiveness as a tool in the struggle against the black market and as an indispensable mechanism in the step-by-step process of lifting rationing. Much of what he had to say had been said before: he defended the HO's high prices as a necessary source of income for reconstructing East German industry; he dismissed the calls of "reactionary forces" for egalitarianism (*Gleichmacherei*) in provisioning; and he defended the privileges enjoyed by certain groups (workers in heavy industry, engineers, technicians, the intelligentsia) as necessary for increasing productivity.[109] He reminded HO employees of their duties to provide good service and to ensure that they offered high-quality merchandise. He also made clear that the HO was not under any circumstances to exceed its investment plans: "Everyone must be conscious of his responsibility with regard to the use of the people's property. Everyone should be aware that expenditures for unnecessary investments [and] for unplanned investments come at the cost of investments above all for iron and steel and mining."[110] Priorities were still priorities.

The HO's success in meeting sales plans was in no small part due to a series of fourteen price reductions worked out by the Finance Administration and introduced gradually between May 1949 and December 1951.[111] On November 1, 1949, nearly one year after the opening of the first shops, HO prices stood at only 40 percent of their opening-day levels. By March 1950 prices for important foodstuffs had fallen by 80–90 percent, while prices for manufactured goods had fallen by up to 35 percent.[112] As a result, the HO was able to undercut the black market and thus contribute significantly to its demise. As Jörg Roesler has suggested, with HO prices falling and its retail net expanding, "the black market became proportionally less attractive as a place to procure extra consumer goods, particularly as it was associated with transactions which were not only more expensive, but were risky because they were illicit and because they involved the risk of being cheated over the quality of the merchandise." In the first half of the 1950s, the black market "ceased to function as a social phenomenon of politico-economic importance."[113]

But HO officials could hardly rest on their laurels. While customers and trade officials drew attention to many of the shortcomings of the stores themselves, central planning authorities took HO leaders to task for what they considered egregious waste, financial mismanagement, and lack of control over resources invested in the HO. According to reports from late 1949 and early 1950, the HO displayed a proclivity for rushing into building projects without obtaining cost estimates, an inexcusable ignorance of their own investments, and a regrettable habit of sloppy bookkeeping. From the point of view of the Ministry for Planning it was especially galling to have to observe that "this planlessness is characterized by frivolity [*Leichtfertigkeit*], if not irresponsibility."[114]

For their part, HO leaders argued that the speed with which the HO was forced to expand made it impossible to account for every penny and that, for the meantime, the HO could not be held to the same standards of accountability as other state-owned economic entities. Furthermore, in view of the importance of the organization and the tasks it still faced, investments would have to be increased. A law of February 22, 1950, called for the HO to expand its retail net to twenty-five hundred outlets.[115] Paul Baender, who had replaced Streit as head of the HO Central Management Office in April 1949, complained to Rau that if the HO was going to be able to comply with the new law, more resources would have to be put at its disposal. The HO's investment plan for 1950, drawn up before the new law was drafted, did not provide the necessary funds. Moreover, those funds contained in the plan had yet to be made available, as a result of which the HO had been forced to begin financing expansion from its own income. But the use of HO income for these purposes had undermined the ability of the HO to fulfill its sales and tax plans for the first quarter. Baender was fed up; he informed Rau that no more HO income would be used to expand the retail net, and he demanded an explanation for the fact that funds promised to the HO by the Ministry for Trade and Provisioning had not been made available.[116]

Rau, as the minister for planning, was not about to be intimidated by Baender's bluster. He pointed out to the trade functionary that the latter's own letter confirmed an "illegal" use of investments. The Ministry for Trade and Provisioning was, indeed, supposed to examine any plan proposed by the HO. But ultimate approval and coordination with the overall economic plan could only occur with the Ministry for Planning. "This long-standing practice," Rau instructed, "already normal in the DWK, would surely have to be known to a leader of such an important state trade organization." Like a prosecutor, he leveled accusations at Baender: "You have neglected your most basic duties and, unreliably, squandered money and materials in a manner worthy of punishment. Your actions demonstrate a total disregard for the laws of the democratic state, and disturb the course of the economic plan."[117]

For several weeks the matter remained unresolved. In June Baender informed Rau that he had appealed to Leuschner, who, in turn, suggested writing to Ulbricht.[118] In his letter to Ulbricht (a copy of which also went to Rau), Baender pleaded his case and explained that the earlier unavoidable "offenses to plan discipline" would be corrected with a promise of DM 48 million credit extended by the Finance Ministry. He requested that Ulbricht have the Ministry of Planning confirm the Finance Ministry's promise and plan an additional DM 45 million for the HO so that it could carry out the required expansion. It seems highly unlikely that Baender got everything he asked for, not least because by the end of the year the extension of the retail net had fallen short of the goal of twenty-five hundred.[119] Of greater interest perhaps than the outcome of this particular instance of wrangling over funds is the fact it was to continue in virtually identical fashion in subsequent years.[120] In short, the pattern had emerged: the HO played the role of supplicant, submitting its requests and appeals to unsympathetic central planning institutions; from their Olympian heights these institutions deployed the tactics of bureaucratic delay and taskmasterly condescension in their denials, critiques, and scaled-down revisions of HO proposals.

The difficulties of the HO were indicative of an administration being forced to deal with a problem it was both unprepared and reluctant to address: satisfying the material desires of its citizens above and beyond the bare minimum of nutritional sustenance. Conditions of scarcity, an ideology that privileged production over consumption, and the inescapable burden of reparations while under foreign occupation all worked to limit the amount of attention Soviet-zone authorities were willing to pay to the needs and desires of consumers in the Soviet zone.

It was the Western currency reform and the Berlin Blockade that forced the issue; the material well-being of Germans in all four zones suddenly became a crucial variable in a larger political contest.

The uncertainty, problems in coordination, conflicting information, and competing goals that marked the introduction of the HO were a result of the tension between the requirements of the political moment and the proclivities of an administration fashioned and directed by the Soviets. Had the task been merely to dry up the black market by absorbing excess purchasing power in the new stores, Soviet-zone authorities would have had an easier time of it. But in the context of the currency reform and the challenge posed by at least the visual evidence of abundance in the Western zones of occupation, the HO, as the site of *real* retail trade, was also invested with the hope of a return to some semblance of normalcy. Moreover, HO planners envisioned the new stores and restaurants as first-class establishments offering customers the finest service and the highest quality goods for the satisfaction of the most demanding desires. The HO was supposed to impart pleasure. Here was the rub. To succeed as a financial tool, its prices had to be prohibitively high, thus reducing access to an extremely limited range of customers. Simultaneously, Soviet-zone authorities, unable to escape their own ideological, material, and administrative constraints, were reluctant to provide the cash or credit needed to make the new stores the first-rate showcases of retail splendor required to compete politically in the emerging contest of prosperity. Although they recognized that some effort was absolutely necessary, a sustained, well-coordinated, and generously financed program was beyond their means and their inclination. This combination of reluctance and urgency, foot-dragging and intermittently intense response to crisis would go on to characterize the entire period under study here.

CHAPTER 3

The Planned and the Unplanned: Consumer Supply and Provisioning Crisis

Is fashion folly?

Die Waage, June 1952

How did the state attempt to plan individual consumption? How did its nascent, expanding, and unwieldy bureaucracy seek to plan how (and how much) individuals would consume, where and when they would go shopping, what they would eat, what kinds of clothes and shoes they would wear, how they would furnish and decorate their homes? The list of concerns was potentially endless. It was one thing to produce and find buyers for industrial machinery, spare parts, and raw materials, quite another to plan the individual consumption of goods which would be inescapably subject to the unpredictable fluctuations of fashion, of personal need, taste, and desire.

In truth, the effort to plan individual consumption showed the regime at its most ambitious and least effectual; the sphere of consumption was where its pretensions and its weaknesses found perhaps their most glaring expression. On the one hand, the endeavor marked a profound intrusion on the part of the state into the private sphere of individuals. On the other hand, even at the level of the plan, the regime could only exert a limited form of control. Through a combination of direct and indirect measures, economic planners sought to guide consumer demand. They continued to ration most consumer goods; they developed commodity supply and retail sales plans; they manipulated wages, prices, and taxes. But in doing so, they became ensnared in the contradictions of the system they worked so hard to build. As a result, the effort of planning looked far more like a prolonged exercise in damage control than the ideal of rational, efficient planning promised for decades by party ideologues.

In the wake of the Berlin Blockade, the young SED regime continued to face contradictory pressures. Inspired by a vision of prowess in heavy industry, its leaders preached the virtues of sacrifice, hard work, discipline, patience, and extreme modesty in personal consumption. But these virtues were fast losing their appeal. If the German people's long experience of material austerity had initially provided the regime a certain amount of breathing room in the area of consumer supply, that experience soon gave rise to increasing impatience with repeated homilies on the theme of sacrifice. SED leaders, positioned as they were at the center of the Cold War, and presiding over only a part of what had once been a united Germany, faced a sustained challenge to the legitimacy of their rule and their professed convictions. Nowhere in the Soviet orbit was the pressure as great to show that socialism, ushered in under Soviet auspices, would bring unsurpassed efficiency and prosperity to all.

The contradictory pressures of productivism and consumer supply not only heightened the strains on the fledgling planned economy, they introduced divisions within the regime itself. Between 1948 and 1953, the years in which the East German planned economy was built, there began to emerge within the official ranks of domestic trade a consumer supply lobby. However guarded in its argumentation, however uncoordinated in its approach, the consumer supply lobby nevertheless posed a challenge from within to those who insisted on the uncontested priority of productivism. In these years of intense Cold War competition, of remilitarization in both Germanys, of purges, show trials, and class confrontation throughout the Soviet bloc, the voices of the consumer supply lobby could not hope to shout down those of more Stalinist leanings. Still, they developed an idiom and a set of goals aimed at furthering their interests and, as a result, easing the plight of ordinary East Germans. When the emphasis on productivism was pushed to the extreme and workers across East Germany finally rebelled on June 17, 1953, SED leaders were forced to embrace the language and expressed goals of the consumer supply lobby. This chapter traces the early development of consumption planning, the emergence of the consumer supply lobby, and the mounting provisioning crisis that eventually forced the regime to shift somewhat the balance of its commitments from productivism to consumerism.

* * *

The process of consumption planning, like the rest of the East German planned economy, developed in keeping with the general goal projections of the early long-range plans, that is, the Two-Year Plan (1949–50) and the first Five-Year Plan (1951–55).[1] With the adoption of long-term planning, the Soviet zone took another significant step along the path of Sovietization, as did the other countries within the Soviet bloc. As in the "people's democracies" of Eastern Europe, the nature of the plans adopted in East Germany maintained and extended the regime's primary commitment to the priorities of productivism. The branches emphasized were those of heavy industry and heavy engineering: iron and steel metallurgy, energy and fuel, heavy machine building, and ship building. Investments during this period clearly reflected these priorities.[2] Although resources were limited, it was still possible during the Five-Year Plan to embark on ambitious new projects. With great fanfare the young East German state launched the impressive *Eisenhüttenkombinat* and built new metallurgical works in Calbe. And despite wartime destruction and dismantling by the Soviets, it resumed production at the giant Leuna chemical works, reconstructed heavy machine building plants, and built new extensions to already existing steelworks.

A number of specific material factors helped to reinforce the already ascendant emphasis on productivism. The need to repair war damage to the infrastructure and transport system required constant growth in the production of iron and steel. The Soviets, meanwhile, demanded reparations in the form of raw materials and capital goods. In addition, as a result of the Berlin Blockade the Soviet zone was increasingly detached from the capitalist world market, bringing about a fundamental shift in its foreign trade. In 1947 two-thirds of the zone's foreign trade had been with the West, above all with the Western zones of Germany. After 1950 nearly two-thirds of the GDR's foreign trade was with the socialist states of the Soviet bloc. But these countries, in less advanced stages of industrialization, had far less need for the textile and light industrial products traditionally produced in eastern Germany than they did for heavy industrial goods. To obtain from these countries basic materials such as coal, iron, and steel (previously supplied by the Ruhr), the Soviet zone (and later the GDR) now had to fulfill the particular needs of its new trading partners in the East.[3]

Consumer supply policy, therefore, continued to adhere to the imperatives of productivism, while making occasional gestures toward improving provisioning for the population as a whole. This meant maintaining the consumer hierarchy institutionalized by Order no. 234, offering better rations and higher wages to workers in heavy industry and mining, to political and administrative functionaries, and to the intelligentsia.[4] At the same time, it involved reintroducing through a series of step-by-step measures ever-greater increments of normalcy by removing various commodities from the constraints of rationing. In May 1949 vegetables ceased to be rationed; in the following month, tobacco, ersatz coffee, and vinegar. According to a November 1949 ordinance, based on a SED Politburo directive of the previous month, rationing was to be lifted entirely (except on meat and fat) after the 1950 harvest. In the meantime, a new rationing system was introduced in December 1949, according to which everyone over fifteen years of age was now issued a basic ration card *(Grundkarte)* as well as a supplemental card *(Zusatzkarte)* carrying additional rations based on occupation, thus maintaining all of the old distinctions.[5]

Unfortunately for East German consumers, the goal of lifting rationing by the end of 1950 could not be realized. By the beginning of 1951, not only meat and fat but also fish, eggs, milk, sugar, and everything made with these ingredients continued to be rationed, as did many manufactured consumer goods. Only gradually did various items come off the ration lists: in August 1950, laundry detergent; in February 1951, certain types of shoes and textile goods; in October of that year, marmalade, artificial honey, syrup, and soap; in March 1953, stockings and socks; one month later, leather shoes; in July, fish. Not until May 1958 did meat, milk, fat, sugar, and eggs cease to be rationed in East Germany, making it the last country in Europe to bring to a close what had begun twenty years earlier on the eve of World War II.[6]

Of course, many goods were now available ration-free in the HO stores. But because of its relatively high prices, the HO never served as more than a supplemental source of basic food purchases for most consumers during the 1950s. As late as 1957, the "average consumer" still used ration cards for two-thirds of the meat and sausage, three-fourths of the milk and butter, two-thirds of the margarine, and four-fifths of the eggs and sugar he or she bought.[7] In fact, rationing was the most effective means of limiting consumer demand, particularly in conditions of general scarcity.

Rather than give up rationing, therefore, the regime tried to improve the provisioning of the population by introducing a series of price reductions for nonrationed goods. To enable greater numbers of people to shop in the HO stores, finance planners carried out what one report referred to as thirteen "significant price reductions" between 1950 and 1954.[8] Gradually, the intense resentment of those initially excluded began to lessen. By middecade the prices for foodstuffs had fallen on average a little more than 50 percent, semiluxuries even further, and manufactured goods between 25 and 35 percent. In the immediate term, the price reductions were intended to garner support for the new regime.

In the longer term, the price reductions were necessary if prices were to play their proper role in the planned economy. In contrast to market economies, in which prices reflect the relative scarcity of goods and services (the relationship between supply and demand), prices in planned economies cannot convey this information. Instead, they are supposed to reflect "the socially necessary costs" of production and distribution.[9] In addition, they are to remain stable both to simplify the process of planning and to prevent inflation from eroding the purchasing power of consumers. However, since costs increase over time, these two principles contradict each other: if prices remain stable, they cease to reflect rising costs. In the GDR, as in all the countries within the Soviet imperium, political expediency dictated a commitment to price stability, at least for basic goods and services. As the gap between costs and prices widened, the regime tried to close it as much as possible through a complex system of subsidies and taxes. While subsidies supported artificially low prices for goods that satisfied basic needs—thus ensuring an affordable basic provisioning for lower-income groups—the prices for luxury goods were burdened with high consumption taxes.

This distinction between necessity and luxury was imbued with both financial-political and moral concerns. From the point of view of finances, high consumption taxes on luxury goods were needed for two reasons: first, to absorb excess purchasing power and to help stabilize the currency; second, to serve as a counterweight to expanding subsidies and thus to contribute to balancing the state budget. The moral impulse behind the distinction derived from the regime's paternalistic aspiration to define necessity and luxury for its citizens, an aspiration motivated in part by the need to exert some control over demand. As we shall see, however, there were several difficulties bound up with attempting to draw this distinction. To begin with, it meant that a system ostensibly devoted to egalitarian ideals created possibilities for the articulation of social differences through consumption. Subsidized prices for necessities also had socially regressive consequences in that they benefited all income groups, not just the needy, while higher-income groups had greater access to heavily taxed luxury items. In addition, subsidized low prices had the disadvantage of often causing demand to exceed supply: in East Germany goods that satisfied basic needs would be relatively cheap; for that very reason, they would also often be scarce. And yet, perhaps the greatest obstacle for SED leaders in attempting to draw the line between necessity and luxury was the fact that, in practice, they were in no position to do so, at least not by decree. Ultimately, the regime would have to take into account two interrelated factors: the expectations of its citizens and influences from the West, both of which were hardly static.

It would be nearly impossible to provide a detailed account of the entire administrative process of consumption planning, in part because the administration itself was an object of constant reorganization, a perpetual work in progress. What can be more easily, and perhaps more profitably, done is to sketch the broader and more consistent outlines of the process as it developed at the center.

Consumer supply planning was the province of functionaries within the DWK's Administration for Trade and Provisioning (with the founding of the GDR in October 1949, the Administration became the Ministry for Trade and Provisioning). Neither of the initial leaders of these bodies, Hans Paul Ganter-Gilmans and Dr. Karl Hamann, were members of the SED. Ganter-Gilmans, born in Vienna and the son of a merchant, had educational, professional, and familial experience in trade. Although "of bourgeois background," he was amenable to Soviet and SED officials due to a political record free of any taint of Nazi association. Indeed, in the 1920s and 1930s he had been a member of both the Red Falcons and the SPD. Two years after being drafted into the Wehrmacht in 1939, he was found guilty of "subversion" and imprisoned for a year. After being released, he returned to civilian life and work in trade, engaged in "illegal activities" toward the end of the war, and was a cofounder of the Brandenburg CDU in the summer of 1945.[10]

Hamann possessed a background in agriculture rather than in trade. He had studied agricultural science at university, and received his doctorate in 1933. He spent the Nazi years politically inactive and self-employed as a farmer in Thuringia. After the war, he was a cofounder of the Thuringian LDPD, and served as a member of that province's parliament. In 1947 he became a member of its Executive Committee, and in February 1949 the party's coleader, along with Hermann Kästner. With the founding of the East German state in October 1949, he became the minister for trade and provisioning. Unfortunately for Hamann, his tenure as minister coincided not only with a period of mounting Stalinist hysteria about "inner enemies" throughout the Soviet bloc, but also with the provisioning crisis caused by the SED's attempts to collectivize East German agriculture in the early 1950s. Amid the flurry of purges and paranoia, Hamann was arrested in 1952 for "sabotage of consumer provisioning." Originally sentenced to ten years' imprisonment, he was released in October 1956. Less than one year later, he fled to West Germany.[11]

The fact that the early leaders of trade and provisioning were not SED members was telling in several respects. First, it suggested that consumer supply would most likely not improve substantially anytime soon and that it would be best to minimize as much as possible the appearance of SED responsibility for the lack of improvement. Second, it lent credence to the fiction of the "antifascist, democratic bloc" of all Soviet-zone political parties. Third, it reflected the Soviet and SED assumption that the sphere of trade and provisioning was of lesser importance in the task of establishing SED dominance over the political-economic life of the zone.

Nevertheless, as in almost every other administration or ministry headed by a non-SED member, the occupants of the positions just below the leaders of trade and provisioning were not only SED members but those of KPD extraction. Erich Freund, encountered in the previous chapter as a propagandist for the HO, served as deputy to Ganter-Gilmans. Of working-class background, he joined the KPD in 1931, engaged intermittently in anti-Nazi activities during the 1930s, and as a result spent some time under arrest. After the war, during which he served in the Wehrmacht, he was assigned by the KPD to administrative work in Berlin, even though by his own admission he had no previous experience. Nor, it seems, did his total lack of experience or formal training in trade pose any obstacles to his being placed as Ganter-Gilman's deputy in 1948.[12]

Another appointee of political reliability and zero expertise was Emil Krüger, a trained glassworker, who had joined the KPD in 1919. Having spent the Nazi years engaged in the usual pattern of illegal activities, arrest, and emigration (first to Czechoslovakia, then to England), Krüger was shunted after the war, against his will, into trade and provisioning. "All I knew about trade," he later admitted, "was that it created no new social value, that it moreover fed on social surplus product [*Mehrprodukt*] and that therefore the social costs of trade had to be reduced to a minimum."[13] This from the man who, despite his repeated attempts to get out of trade and provisioning, claims to have in effect run the administration due to Ganter-Gilmans being either ill or otherwise occupied with his work in the CDU. The cause of trade and provisioning, it seems, had few committed believers within its leading ranks.[14]

However inexperienced and uncommitted, officials in trade and provisioning had the task of producing annual plans for commodity supply *(Warenbereitstellung)* and retail sales *(Warenumsatz)* for the entire Soviet zone, and later the GDR. It was these plans, for supply and sales, that constituted the main thrust of consumer supply planning at the center.[15] The commodity supply plans consisted of lists of goods to be made available to the population, measured in units of weight or volume, broken down quarterly and by province. Some of the early plans also took into account groups receiving special supplies, for example, Order no. 234 workers, "victims of fascism," war wounded, and pregnant women. Supply plans for manufactured commodities such as textiles and clothing were necessarily somewhat more detailed than those for food items, since these plans had to account for assortment, indicating, however roughly, the amounts of basic clothing items to be produced for men, women, and children. The retail sales plans listed commodities, which were measured in units of currency (usually per million DM) and broken down by quarter and by retail form, that is, HO, consumer co-op *(Konsum)*, and private retail. The goods themselves were grouped into two main categories: food and semiluxuries, and manufactured commodities *(Industriewaren)*. The second of these was then broken down into three subgroups: shoes, textiles and clothing, and "other" manufactured commodities. The categories, in other words, were *extremely* general. Planners at the center worked at an abstract level, thinking primarily in terms of broad headings and large numbers. The extent to which total quarterly and yearly fulfillment figures tallied with their basic supply and sales goals comprised the criteria for the success or failure of their supply and sales plans. More detailed planning was left to lower levels in the bureaucracy, as individual trade organs submitted specific, itemized orders to individual production units.

Initially, German trade-and-provisioning officials worked under the close control of their Soviet counterparts in the SMAD Administration for Trade and Provisioning. Together they drafted the plans, which were then sent to the DWK's Central Administration for Economic Planning. Here they were finalized and passed on to leading SMAD economic officials for final approval. Once approved, the DWK bore full responsibility for carrying them out.[16] After the founding of the East German state, the Soviets continued to exercise control, albeit in an attenuated form, through the Soviet Control Commission. On the German side, the coordinating functions carried out by the Administration of Economic Planning were taken over by the GDR's Ministry of Planning (renamed the State Planning Commission at the end of 1950), which continued to be run by Rau and Leuschner.

As might be expected of the regime's initial longer-term planning efforts, the process of organizing consumer supply during the Two-Year Plan was characterized by a host of administrative foul-ups and their attendant frustrations. As the Soviets insisted on the use of particular forms for planning, the information required to fill them out was invariably lacking.[17] Recriminations flew back and forth between the administrations of Economic Planning and Trade and Provisioning, each accusing the other of submitting plans too late and exercising poor coordination.[18] As Ganter-Gilmans objected to last-minute, drastic reductions of supply plans by Economic Planning, his assistants complained to him about the lack of coordination and qualified personnel within his own administration.[19]

The complaints of consumers, meanwhile, spelled out the effects of these organizational difficulties. As official "information trips" in the spring and summer of 1949 revealed, consumers faced continued shortages, poor-quality merchandise, and a pronounced lack of summer clothing, even in the HOs.[20] In September 1949 *Neues Deutschland* reported a number of serious trade-and-provisioning mix-ups in a leading article which ran under the headline, "Who's Sleeping Here?"[21] In Fürstenberg, July meat coupons had remained undelivered as late as August 18. In Rostock, inedible meat had been allocated to consumers, as had quark in exchange for meat coupons, despite specific DWK regulations forbidding the substitution. In Potsdam, city officials had been besieged with "countless complaints" from the population about poor-quality foodstuffs. The article assigned the blame to administrative lethargy and a proliferation of "bureaucratism." In particular, it singled out the Administration for Trade and Provisioning, "under the leadership of Herr Ganter-Gilmans of the Christian Democratic Union," describing the administration as a bloated apparatus, overly staffed with employees and drowning in its own paperwork.

Embarrassed and infuriated, trade-and-provisioning leaders shot off letters of protest to the editors of the newspaper. Ganter-Gilmans accused them of trying to undermine the authority of the DWK. On the contrary, they replied, their intention was to strengthen it: "You, yourself, will admit that the ordinances of the DWK are not carried out in the counties and communities and by the authorities in the provinces with the necessary punctuality and carefulness." Every day, the editors claimed, they received letters complaining about the failure of local administrative organs to manage an array of issues that directly affected the population, including the problem of consumer supply. With a perfect combination of cant, condescension, and self-righteousness, they explained, "It is necessary from time to time to bring into the light of publicity especially crass cases through the press and the radio, which no doubt best reach the ear of the population, in order, through a general discussion of these questions, to make the democratic administrative organs face the criticism of the public, and to encourage the population to develop its initiative in this direction."[22] The press, in other words, was to serve as both a safety valve and an instrument for applying pressure: it was an address to which the population could send its complaints, and it was a spotlight with which SED leaders could illuminate the failings of those deemed in need of critique, an art of which Walter Ulbricht, himself, was an occasional practitioner.[23]

More troubling for economic planners were the deeper problems and contradictions that could not be dismissed as mere start-up hitches. Perhaps foremost among these was the intractable monetary overhang, that is, the continued discrepancy between the amount of money in circulation and the availability of consumer goods. The Soviet-zone currency reform, the introduction of the HO, and the gradual diminution of the significance of the black market had not succeeded in bringing into balance commodity supply and consumer purchasing power. The gradual price reductions in the HO added to the imbalance. However, the problem also resulted from the fact that the wages of workers continued to rise faster than productivity. As Jeffrey Kopstein has argued, East German Taylorism was corrupted from the start due to the inability of shop floor managers to turn piecework and productivity wages into increased output per worker. In the context of the shortage economy, managers were compelled above all to secure the necessary labor inputs required to meet their production quotas. Their only rational strategy was to hoard labor. But hoarded labor became scarce labor. Under pressure to produce as much as possible at whatever cost, managers did everything they could to retain their workers. In part, this meant allowing work norms to remain weak. As Kopstein suggests, "here we find the origins of the East German soft budget constraint."[24]

Finance planners, meanwhile, tried to soak up as much purchasing power as possible through consumption taxes and the still relatively high prices for nonrationed consumer goods.[25] Thus, despite price reductions in the HO, consumers continued to face prices they considered exceedingly high, even for basic items. In spring 1949 Käthe Kern, a member of the SED Central Secretariat and head of the party's Women's Secretariat, pointed this situation out to the SED Economics Department. Women seeking to buy yarn for knitting and darning, she explained, "stood helpless" before the high prices. "This is one of the most indispensable and most in-demand materials," she stressed, "as much a necessity for living as a piece of bread."[26]

The regime believed its citizens had too much money even as they bemoaned their inability to buy the things they needed. Retail outlets soon began to report that high prices were undermining their sales plans. If only to move inventory, they pleaded, a more flexible price policy had to be introduced.[27] Central planners balked. Lowering prices, they argued, amounted to forfeiting the value of the labor and resources expended in producing the goods. More important, they knew that lowering prices increased demand, which in turn increased the pressure to supply yet more consumer goods. In the reports and memoranda circulating between the various offices and departments of the bureaucracy, purchasing power came to assume the contours of an unappeasable force; it inspired fear. Economic functionaries found themselves trapped in the untenable position of having to absorb as much of it as possible while simultaneously struggling to keep demand as low as possible. The outcome was most acutely registered in the sphere of retail in the form of expanding inventories, overly filled storage facilities, beleaguered salespeople, and frustrated customers.

Another major problem made its first appearance in the formulation of the early supply plans. Trade-and-provisioning planners had to work not only with their Soviet counterparts but also with the industrial administrations and ministries responsible for the production of the goods listed in the plans. In determining consumer demand, they faced the unenviable task of trying to reconcile what they believed the population needed with the limited production capabilities reported by industry officials.[28] As a result, the demands of trade and provisioning were frequently contested by manufacturers and more often than not scaled down, sometimes repeatedly, after top central planners intervened as final arbiters.[29] In fact, the relationship between trade and industry, which has been neglected in the literature on Soviet-type systems, was crucial. The chronic structural weakness of trade in relation to industry was perhaps the most significant factor in preventing the emergence of a more coordinated and effective effort to bring about a more consumerist orientation within East Germany's political economy. But this is to anticipate an argument developed more fully in Chapter 5. It must suffice for the moment merely to introduce it as a problem with which trade-and-provisioning planners were confronted from the very beginning.

In planning consumer supply, economic functionaries acted on the basis of several points of reference, the most significant being the living standards of the prewar period, with the year 1936 serving as the usual benchmark.[30] The prospect of attaining 1936 consumption levels by the end of the Two-Year Plan was ruled out immediately, since agricultural production could not pick up quickly enough and Soviet reparations demands would continue to limit the amount of supplies available to German consumers.[31] In June 1948, as Leuschner presented a draft of the plan for discussion in the SED Central Secretariat, he raised the question of the Two-Year Plan's goals for average daily calorie consumption. The plan, as it stood, projected a rise from sixteen hundred to two thousand calories by 1950, which Leuschner characterized as "insufficient." The problem was a serious one, he recognized: "One cannot simply say: we're stopping at 2000, and we'll discuss it no further." As he reminded his colleagues, the issue of work productivity was inextricably bound up with that of provisioning: "I would like to express doubts that work productivity can be increased without exceeding 2000 calories, even with an improved organization of work and an improved differential wage."[32] This discussion took place during the early stages of the Berlin Blockade. In addition to the question of productivity, that of the Western currency reform and its effects on consumer supply in the West no doubt also played an important, if unspoken, role in Leuschner's thinking.

What is noteworthy in the regime's focus on the prewar period as a point of reference is the concomitant lack of any larger vision for the role of consumption in East German society. Here, the official tendency to dismiss trade from the ranks of important sectors of the economy had its parallel in the regime's general ideological neglect of the sphere of consumption. And yet these were the years in which the SED embarked on the task of remaking East German society. The party's program for social revolution was ambitious and far-reaching, promising unheard-of social mobility for the members of those classes traditionally denied advancement in the past. The regime actively recruited its new leadership cadre from the working and peasant classes. In its education, employment, health, and social welfare policies, it tried to offer a measure of opportunity and security hitherto unknown to the lower orders of German society. Although these efforts were accompanied by systematic discrimination against members of the "bourgeoisie" and active participants in Christian institutions, many people found the regime's vision of a "classless" society, however vaguely defined, profoundly compelling. For those seeking a form of redemption after the disaster wrought by the Nazis, the "experiment" of the young GDR, its romantic rhetoric of the *Aufbau*, was a source of genuine inspiration. Christa Wolf, in her novel *The Quest for Christa T.*, captured perfectly the fervent idealism of the immediate postwar years: "She [Christa T.] joined in our discussions, those glorious rambling nocturnal discussions about the paradise on whose doorstep we were sure we stood, hungry and wearing our wooden shoes. The idea of perfection had taken hold of our minds, had passed into us from books and pamphlets; and from the rostrums at meetings came in addition a great impatience: verily, I say unto you, you shall be with me today in paradise!"[33]

Within the array of social innovations introduced by the regime, however, there was a complete absence of any new concept for the place of private consumption. In large measure, this absence is explained by the fact that Marxist-Leninist doctrine focused its economic program on production, relegating consumption to the margins. However, another factor that may also have contributed to this inclination derived less from conscious ideological intent than from the history and political culture of German Communism. As Catherine Epstein has recently suggested in her collective biography of veteran Communists, the party's self-image, dating back to its days as an embattled revolutionary movement in the 1920s, was decidedly masculine: "The party presented itself as a body of young, male, muscle-rippled proletarian workers."[34] While this self-image, according to Epstein, helps to explain why so few women came to hold leading positions within the party, despite its professed commitment to women's emancipation, it may also help to account for the relative lack of interest among party leaders in the sphere of consumption, a sphere traditionally belonging within the purview of women's work (shopping, cooking, mending clothes, keeping house, and so on). As is now well known, women in East Germany, despite being exhorted to work in the factories and fields of the young "workers' and peasants' state," were also expected to continue performing their traditional household duties.[35] It is fair to say that in failing to develop some new idea for the organization and role of private consumption in East German society—some concept and practice that might have relieved East German women of the "double burden" (Doppelbelastung) they carried in their everyday lives—the regime in effect squandered an opportunity to mobilize perhaps the greater portion of its population in support of an endeavor that might have served as at least part of a credible answer, or alternative, to the consumption challenge beginning to emerge from West Germany. As things stood, in the absence of such an endeavor, the privileges of particular groups undermined the promise of egalitarianism and aroused resentment. In the longer term, the regime would be left vulnerable to unfavorable comparisons with the West.

While preparing its first Five-Year Plan, the regime was ready to embrace the goal of surpassing the living standards of the prewar years. In doing so, SED planners were encouraged by the Soviets. After discussions in June 1950 with officials in the Soviet Control Commission, it was agreed that 1936 food-consumption levels were to be reached by 1952 and thereafter surpassed.[36] The Law on the Five-Year Plan promised wage increases and price reductions; it planned for a complete end to rationing by 1953, at the latest; it provided for substantial increases in the per capita consumption of foodstuffs such as meat and fat, as well as that of "the most important manufactured goods," above all, shoes, textiles, and clothing; and it projected an overall expansion in commodity supply and retail sales, as well as a widening of the HO and *Konsum* retail nets, especially in "important centers of industry."[37]

Unfortunately for the regime, few East Germans seemed to believe that the Five-Year Plan would achieve its proclaimed consumption goals. According to reports on the mood of the population from late August and early September 1950, there was widespread resentment about the state of consumer supply and a general skepticism about the ability of the regime to deliver on its promises, in particular those for lifting rationing. No doubt memories of consumerist promises broken during the Nazi years played a role in the skeptical attitude of East German citizens. But SED propaganda, as officials recognized, was proving "ineffective." This they attributed to the fact that "the overwhelming majority of the population of the republic" was listening to the West Berlin radio station, RIAS.[38] Discerning consumers of SED propaganda may also have been moved to skepticism by the party's continued adherence to a concept of "standard of living" in which an increase in the supply of goods was downplayed in favor of work and productivity. As Hanna Wolf, a leading SED ideologist and educator, instructed the readers of *Einheit,* "the most important aspect of an increase in the prosperity [*Wohlstand*] of a nation is the absence of unemployment, the absence of the possibility of unemployment, and the constantly increasing number of workers and employees required by the harmoniously expanding production process."[39] The emphasis on work allowed her not only to trumpet the cause of productivity but also to highlight the very real problem of unemployment in West Germany, which in the first quarter of 1950 had reached 12.2 percent. Unemployment, she argued, was chronic to capitalism and to "the American way of life," and therefore all countries "Marshallized" by the United States would be plagued by it.[40] In fact, as they held their ears (and eyes) to the West, populace and party alike revealed the force of an increasingly important point of reference underlying the entire discussion of living standards, namely, developments in West Germany.

After the currency reform, the Western zones seemed to offer an example of economic development directly opposed to the "Produce More—Live Better" blueprint espoused in the East. The lifting of rationing for most consumer goods, the filling of the shopwindows, the boom enjoyed by the consumer goods industries, and the surge in consumption all served to raise work productivity by providing a tangible incentive to work for money wages. Workers not only began turning up for work in increasing numbers, they worked longer and harder.[41] The long-awaited arrival of aid through the European Recovery Program (ERP), as the Marshall Plan was officially called, offered further cause to hope for a rise in the standard of living.

This is not to suggest that when the Bundestag met for the first time in September 1949, the West German *Wirtschaftswunder* was well underway. Quite the opposite was true. As the chief of economic affairs for the Marshall Plan in Germany, Robert Hanes candidly commented in early 1950, "Germany is flat on its ass."[42] Hanes was referring in particular to a number of serious economic problems confronting Konrad Adenauer's fragile coalition government. The newly established West German state faced intolerably high rates of unemployment, excessive inflation, a general lack of investment capital, regressive taxation, a severe housing shortage (45 percent of the housing in West Germany had been damaged in the war), and a steady influx of refugees from the East. There was widespread doubt about the likelihood of the Federal Republic achieving economic "viability" by the end of 1952, the cutoff date for ERP aid.[43]

In fact, the extent to which the Marshall Plan contributed to the West German economic miracle has been a subject of much debate. Werner Abelshauser has argued that growth began before the currency reform, that is, before any Marshall Plan aid reached European shores; and he has characterized West Germany as the "stepchild" of the Marshall Plan, since it received considerably less aid than the other countries of Western Europe.[44] Other scholars have argued that the aid given to the Federal Republic, though it was substantially less than that extended to other recipient countries, nevertheless targeted key bottlenecks and facilitated essential imports, provided better-quality foodstuffs and raw materials required for sustained industrial growth, offered political-psychological support (and thus helped stabilize confidence in the deutschmark), and ensured that the West German recovery meshed with (and helped fuel) that of Western Europe.[45]

Less disputed is the emphasis of the Marshall Plan on productivity in heavy industry and on high rates of capital formation, not only in Germany, but throughout Western Europe. Practicing what Charles Maier has called "the politics of productivity," Marshall planners "sought to transform political issues into problems of output, to adjourn class conflict for a consensus on growth."[46] By 1948–49 Europe was investing 20 percent of its GNP.[47] In France the industrial modernization drive embodied in the 1949 Monnet Plan drew 90 percent of its resources from Marshall Plan sources.[48] By 1951 Marshall Plan funds were facilitating similar modernization plans throughout Western Europe.[49] Productivity, meanwhile, meant not just higher production but increased output per worker. Here, the Marshall Plan played a pedagogical role. In all of the recipient countries, Marshall Plan officials created productivity councils and introduced productivity incentives. Both business and labor delegates took trips to the United States, touring American factories. In short, there was a "gospel of productivity" being preached on both sides of the Cold War divide.[50]

In West Germany, Marshall Plan aid followed a similar course, as did the changing drift of economic policy in general. Although the currency reform had diverted investments from the basic goods sector to consumer goods, authorities soon shifted the balance back. As a consequence, West Germany achieved exceedingly high rates of investment.[51] An equally crucial element in the "consensus" on productivity was the slow rate of wage growth accepted by weak labor unions throughout western Europe. In this regard, West Germany was no exception. Historians of the period have characterized the position of organized labor as one of "wage restraint," even "wage renunciation."[52] Like their East German counterparts, West German officials recognized the need for continued material sacrifice as an inescapable condition of recovery.[53] Ironically, the SED formula "Produce More—Live Better" seemed like a strategy more faithfully followed in West Germany than in the

East. Far from evincing the traits of a modern "consumer society," the Federal Republic of the early 1950s was, as one historian has suggested, more of "a 'work society,' the more so since working long hours was the only way for most workers to secure the bare means of existence for their families."[54]

Nevertheless, as grim as everyday life was for most people in East and West Germany—indeed, throughout Europe—in the early 1950s, the similarities should not obscure at least one crucial difference: in West Germany people *were* producing more and, as a consequence, they *were* beginning to live better—better, that is, than they had been living and better than their compatriots in the East. For with an effectively functioning incentive structure, there was now an obvious and direct connection between "producing more" and "living better." Between 1949 and 1952 West Germany's production index rose from 83 to 146 (1936=100). In 1952 the Federal Republic achieved the first in a long string of trade surpluses with its Western European neighbors. As the process of trade liberalization unfolded, total trade quadrupled to $1 billion annually, and unemployment was reduced by a third.[55] Working-class households in the West were able to spend lower percentages of their disposable income on food and clothing than those in the East.[56] Nor did West German consumers face the chronic shortages, poor-quality products, wrong assortments, and prolonged rationing with which East Germans continued to live.

Within the East German economic bureaucracy itself voices were now raised in opposition to the prevailing priorities pursued by the SED leadership, voices that pressed the unsettling, almost taboo, cause of consumer demand. Although the years before the uprising of June 1953 mark the period of most intransigent and unapologetic productivism, there was already emerging a nascent, uncoordinated consumer supply lobby within the planning apparatus. Located in the Administration (and later, Ministry) for Trade and Provisioning and finding its clearest outlet in specialized journals for domestic trade, that lobby was already developing a language and a set of goals aiming toward building a more articulated consumption regime, toward a wider and richer array of consumption offerings.

The question of consumer advocacy in the GDR is only beginning to attract scholarly attention, particularly from the perspective of gender studies and *Alltagsgeschichte.* As important as this approach has been for understanding consumer culture and gender relations in everyday life, however, it has been less fruitful for analyzing relationships within the state and its economic institutions. The emphasis has been on the role played by women's organizations and women officials as advocates for female consumers.[57] But the institutions and figures under study, in fact, had no sustained role in the planning of consumption, and in practice they acted far more as apologists for austerity than as consumer advocates. As these pages attempt to show, there was a more important and revealing source of consumer advocacy, one defined not by questions of gender but by those of institutional responsibility and function within the planned economy, in short, by the tasks and requirements of domestic trade.[58]

Admittedly, officials in domestic trade were concerned primarily with avoiding provisioning crises and fulfilling—or, in contemporary officialese, "overfulfilling"—their sales plans, an achievement that held out the prospect of bonuses. Moreover, it would be misleading to suggest that consumers themselves recognized in trade functionaries their champions vis-à-vis the state. For most consumers any over-the-counter interaction with retail employees tended to be characterized by either strictly personal relations and exchanges of favors *(Beziehungen)* or by a spectrum of hostility ranging from cool indifference to outright aggression. But in seeking to protect their own interests, trade functionaries also represented, by extension, those of consumers. If the interests of the two parties were not identical, they undeniably overlapped. It is in this sense that one can speak of a consumer supply lobby, though, again, one should understand it less in terms of particular individuals than in terms of a necessary function arising from within the structure of East Germany's political economy, a function left to domestic trade. For it is rare that one can identify and trace over several years the efforts of individual consumer supply lobbyists. Trade functionaries tended to be relatively poorly paid compared to their counterparts in industry, and as a result there was a relatively high turnover in trade personnel. Consequently, it is necessary to hold in view the task itself, the location within the bureaucracy where it was taken up, and, where possible, the series of individuals whose careers, for a time, intersected with the challenge of consumer supply.

In the midst of the preparations for the Two-Year Plan, for example, Ganter-Gilmans contributed an article to the official trade journal, *Die*

Versorgung, that explicitly challenged the SED's "Produce More—Live Better" mantra. The purpose and meaning of any state's economy, he stressed, "can only be to improve the living standard of the individual in order [then] to increase joy in work and work productivity."[59] His emphasis on the individual flew straight in the face of the ubiquitous calls for subordinating the individual need to the general need. Although he acknowledged the priority of developing industry in Russia (he avoided speaking of the Soviet Union), he insisted that for Germany the formula must be reversed, with industry taking consumer supply as its point of departure.

Constituting the front line of contact with consumers, domestic trade *(Handel)* was quickly assuming the role of advocate, or "representative," for their interests. No longer content with playing the part of mere allocator *(Verteiler),* trade now aspired to fulfill all the functions commensurate with its position as the point of contact between producers and consumers. Trade officials insisted with increasing frequency on the need for greater influence over the production of consumer goods. If manufacturers continued to deliver merchandise that was faulty, unsuitable, or late in coming, it was the duty of wholesalers and retailers to send it back where it came from.[60] If trade was denigrated as an "unproductive" part of the economic process, if it was castigated as a black hole where negligence and greed caused scarce commodities to be siphoned off into "dark channels," then trade functionaries highlighted the challenges they faced and the "creative" *(schöpferisch)* contribution they made to the economy as a whole.[61] Beyond the mere fact that consumer advocacy could serve the imperative of fulfilling sales plans, it also served as the only possible argument for highlighting the importance of trade and thus for bolstering its claim on resources, investments, and prestige. Here, trade functionaries could claim to be making their indispensable contribution to the appeal of socialism and thus to the legitimacy of the new regime. In the context of divided Germany, with the first signs of a return to normalcy in the West, it was an argument that possessed a force unique in the Soviet orbit.

Officials in trade also began to consider a number of ways to improve their own work. As early modernizers, they recognized the need for a more sophisticated "market observation" *(Marktbeobachtung),* and they suggested canvassing the opinions of consumers. They considered ways of improving advertising, sales organization, store decoration, customer service—in short, *Verkaufskultur,* a specifically East German term literally translated as "the culture of selling."[62] In spring 1951 *Die Versorgung* was replaced by a new trade journal, *Der Handel,* the title of which captured the rhetorical transition from the period of "provisioning" to a new era of real "trade." *Der Handel* served as a forum for discussing all of the problems bound up with trade and consumer supply. Through regular columns like "The Shopwindow of our Time" *(Das Schaufenster unserer Zeit)* and "Advertise and Design" *(Werben und gestalten),* it offered advice to retailers and salespeople on an array of questions affecting the quality of trade and the satisfaction of the needs of consumers.[63]

But the proponents of *Verkaufskultur* faced more than material and bureaucratic obstacles; theirs was a cause of considerable ideological ill repute. Official ideology explicitly excluded trade from the ranks of "important sectors" of the economy and repeatedly insisted on the need to keep down its costs. In popular consciousness, trade was associated with capitalist (if not Jewish) middlemen who drove up prices at the expense of consumers.[64] The constraints within which trade functionaries labored were readily apparent in their own argumentation. In an attempt to elaborate the concept of *Verkaufskultur,* for example, one contributor to *Der Handel* was compelled to distinguish explicitly between past and present, conceding at the outset that "the earlier *Verkaufskultur*" had been just another weapon in the arsenal of "lying advertising [*Reklame*], gushing compliments, and pushy subservience" with which "profit-seeking" retailers foisted "the lousiest junk" on their customers.[65] The new *Verkaufskultur,* though it embraced the same extra touches designed to make the retail experience as pleasant as possible for the customer—cleanliness, politeness, good service, useful advice, appropriate store decorations, and advertisement *(Werbung)*—constituted a genuinely disinterested service seeking only to accommodate the real interests of the customer by providing the best products for the best value.[66] Proper *Verkaufskultur* meant "advising correctly, serving individually, and so arranging the sale that the purchase is made as easy as possible for the working people."[67] The intended implication was clear: workers well served by *Verkaufskultur* would be happy shoppers and, consequently, more productive workers.

In addition to being well served, East Germans were also to be well educated as consumers. The suggestion that good *Verkaufskultur* meant providing what shoppers "really" needed hinted at a pedagogical impulse made more explicit on several occasions. With not a little condescension, consumer supply lobbyists spoke of the need to educate, or guide, taste (*Geschmacksbildung* or *Geschmackslenkung*). Contributors to the discussion suggested that consumer taste had not kept up "with the swift political and economic development" of the immediate postwar years and that the education of taste might take place in the press, in discussions with customers on the selling floor, and in advertisements for new products in which examples of "good" and "bad" production would "impart the necessary clarification."[68] Others claimed that not only had consumer taste not kept pace with postwar developments, it had in fact "been corrupted for generations by [the] commercially diligent advertising of entrepreneurs [*geschäftstüchtige Unternehmerreklame*] and through bad examples." Hence the persistence of "cultivated petit-bourgeois taste" and its hankering after "knickknacks and ornamentation [*Nippes und Verzierung*]."[69] The intended connection between petit-bourgeois taste and petit-bourgeois consciousness was self-evident.

To serve the aims of *Verkaufskultur* was also, apparently, to serve a yet higher ideal, that is, *Kultur* itself. No less a figure than the literary luminary Anna Seghers lent her voice to the cause: "In our society no artistic talent can be wasted that devotes itself to manufactured goods, stores, and shopwindows." At a moment in history pregnant with "complicated, still unanswered cultural questions," she opined, one should not "balk at directing one's attention to a frame [the shopwindow] that hangs in no exhibition but is able at every moment to educate countless people, politically and artistically." The overlapping of political, cultural, and *Verkaufs*-cultural messages was most clearly embodied in the more overtly political tableaux presented in the shopwindows of socialist countries. Slogans celebrating the achievements of the Five-Year Plan, the enduring friendship and brotherhood of the Soviet Union, and the virtues of hard work regularly accompanied displays of consumer goods. Seghers pointed to the shopwindows in Prague as particularly instructive in their felicitous, formal combinations of political message and consumer enticement. Hence this description of a display window for a store selling women's fashions:

In the foreground are some dress models, just a few, beautiful, beautifully presented. The emblem for the Five-Year Plan does not pop up inorganically, like some useless arabesque, [with] the decree from [Clement] Gottwald [placed] somewhere else. By drawing the [female] observer correctly into the construction of the shopwindow, it is clear from where she is able to buy all these good and lovely things to which she is entitled as a working woman of her people. What is important here is that the connection is so self-evident, the instruction so completely in the rhythm of the display, that it neither obtrudes, nor is it to be overlooked.

For Seghers the shopwindow at its best was like a miniature theater, static but enlightening, "an unobtrusive little stage on which a social scene rolls out" for the edification of passersby.[70]

Thus, although the consumer supply lobby challenged the productivist priorities of the SED leadership, it nevertheless reproduced in the sphere of consumption the paradoxical understanding of democracy inherent in the "antifascist" renewal prescribed by the regime. The sociologist Sigrid Meuschel has formulated that understanding in the following terms: "the people," having been "liberated" from fascism, was now supposed to decide its political fate for itself. But as long as the people failed to overcome its National Socialist tendencies, it required reeducation.[71] And as Meuschel suggests, in the context of the Soviet zone the distance separating the SED's notion of "antifascist reeducation" from a Marxist-Leninist proclivity to censure "false consciousness," never great to begin with, quickly narrowed. The proponents of *Verkaufskultur* posed a similar paradox: in one sense, consumers had a legitimate claim to have their needs satisfied, including those for good-quality merchandise, the correct assortments, good service, and a shopping experience that was as pleasant as possible; but in another sense, the deleterious effects of generations of lying advertising, corrupted taste, and debased consumer consciousness called into question their own knowledge of their needs and therefore made absolutely necessary the controlling tutelage of socialist tastemakers. In the end, it was as difficult to ascertain where "needs" ended and "taste" began as it was to know whose needs were in fact being discussed—the needs of citizens for consumer goods, their need for an education in taste (and politics), or the regime's need to control both needs and taste, however vaguely defined.

There was a recent German precedent for the notion that consumers could be educated and consumption guided in ways desired by the state. During the 1930s and 1940s the Nazi regime had attempted to subordinate consumption to the priority of rearmament. Hence its avowed goal of "consumption guidance" *(Verbrauchslenkung)*, however unrealized it was in practice.[72] But the decisive precedent for East German trade-and-provisioning advocates was the already extant but deeply conflicted Soviet idiom for discussing consumerism. As Sheila Fitzpatrick has shown, there emerged in the Soviet Union in the mid-1930s a drift away from the austerity and ascetic puritanism that had characterized the years of the first Five-Year Plan and the Cultural Revolution.[73] A new tolerance, even encouragement, of material pleasures was signaled by Stalin's famously self-serving observation: "Life has become better, comrades; life has become more cheerful." Presided over by Anastas Mikoyan, the Communist Party leader in charge of provisioning, the new trend embraced exotic new products, such as frankfurters and ice cream. Communist leaders abandoned the military style of dress favored in the 1920s and sought to popularize European-style clothing. Luxury goods such as silk stockings were again fashionable in elite circles. On the eve of the Great Terror, the Soviet Union seemed to be embarking on a belated jazz age, as a new leisure culture emerged, consisting of jazz music, fox-trots, tennis, and entertaining new sound movies like *Happy-Go-Lucky Guys* (1934) and *Volga-Volga* (1938).

But even this relatively happy interlude was complicated by a nagging unease and a compulsive need for control, as Soviet leaders insisted that Soviet consumers had to be educated. Hence the didacticism of Soviet advertising and the perceived need to subject consumption to the larger civilizing mission carried forward by the so-called vanguard elements in Soviet society. The proliferation of new products like ketchup and eau de cologne, as long as it proceeded under the control of Communist officials, was acceptable because, far from being a sign of "bourgeois decadence," it was actually a prerequisite for turning Soviet citizens into cultured people. Proficiency in the act of consuming was akin to mastering good manners, appropriate dress, and, at a more advanced level, the works of Pushkin.

The conflation of consumption and culture was also one of the ways in which Soviet leaders justified privilege amid scarcity. Stalin's appropriation of the term "intelligentsia" to encompass all Soviet elites served to confer on Communist officials the claims of cultural superiority enjoyed by intellectuals and artists. The Soviet social hierarchy, in other words, was "conceptualized in *cultural* terms." Stalin's intelligentsia, as Fitzpatrick suggests, "was privileged because it was the most cultured, advanced group in a backward society."[74] (Meanwhile, members of this intelligentsia were not above squabbling among themselves for privileges within privilege. As Nadezhda Mandelstam observed at the small, Crimean resort of Gaspra, near Yalta, "there were also disgusting scenes over the allotment of rooms in the rest homes, with everybody shrieking about the learned qualities which entitled him to a bigger and better one.")[75]

East German trade-and-provisioning advocates had to hold up the Soviet Union and Soviet trade methods as models to emulate. As the lead article in the February 1950 issue of *Die Versorgung* reminded its readers, those East Germans "lucky enough" to have visited the homeland of "triumphant socialism," whether as prisoners of war or as members of postwar delegations, invariably returned with accounts about "the abundance of commodities in the shops and department stores in all parts of the great Soviet land."[76] According to *Die Versorgung*, the Soviet retail landscape was a public mirror reflecting the wealth and wellbeing of Soviet life, a prosperity reserved not just for the few but for "every member of Soviet society." Other champions of Soviet trade contrasted it directly with the American nemesis. In the words of Greta Kuckhoff, chair of the HO's administrative counsel, "Our goal is not a Woolworth culture of standardization [*Einheitskultur*], but rather a richly articulated *Verkaufskultur* that does justice to the desires of our population." In her travels through the Soviet Union, she claimed, she was "repeatedly struck by the variety of goods offered; the colorful brilliance of the displays, which [drew] the population into the main streets until late in the evening for happy strolling, and which transform[ed] the walk through the shops into a journey of discovery."[77]

East German trade functionaries were called upon to make their own journeys of discovery as they adopted the methods of Soviet-style industrial labor competitions.[78] In April 1951 the trade union organization for workers in trade launched the first of what would be countless contests *(Wettbewerbe)*, in which individual HO and *Konsum* stores were exhorted to compete for the honorific title of "Retail Outlet with Excellent *Verkaufskultur*." The principal measure of success was the extent to which the stores were able to fulfill their sales plans and stick to their overhead cost plans. To awaken interest among retailers, sales instructor "brigades" were dispatched to stores to offer advice on how they might elevate the level of their *Verkaufskultur* and thus boost sales. But as *Der Handel* reported, entry registrations showed "that a large percentage of stores have not yet decided to participate in the competition."[79] Sales instructors were more often than not "received with some 'hostility,'" an indication that salesladies and store managers were "not yet clear about the meaning of the instruction."[80] By the end of the year, Dr. Karl Hamann, minister for trade and provisioning, bemoaned the dismal results: "Only a relatively small number of the HO and *Konsum* stores participated in the competition for the distinction of being a retail outlet with the best *Verkaufskultur*. That is an alarming signal for how the trade organs until now have misunderstood the significance of an improved *Verkaufskultur*."[81] On the contrary, they were most likely perfectly clear about the significance of *Verkaufskultur;* but they no doubt also understood only too well the significance of chronic shortages, poor-quality goods, and the wrong assortments and sizes.[82] After all, it was the salesladies and store managers who had to brave the criticisms, insults, and anger of dissatisfied customers. How were they to practice "the culture of selling" without suitable merchandise to sell?

In the following spring and summer, events unfolding on the international stage began to have significant repercussions on the little drama playing out in the shopwindows across East Germany. On March 10, 1952, as the Western powers neared the completion of negotiations on the creation of a European Defense Community (EDC), which was to include a rearmed West Germany, Stalin sent off the first in a series of notes offering to explore the possibility of establishing a reunited, neutral Germany. In what the British foreign secretary, Anthony Eden, called "the battle of notes," the West, skeptical of Stalin's motives, pursued a strategy of delay, keeping an ear open to Soviet proposals while simultaneously moving ahead with agreements to end the military occupation of the Federal Republic and bring it into the proposed EDC. In the meantime, Western leaders insisted on free elections as a prerequisite for creating an all-German government. The elections, they argued, would have to be held under the supervision of the United Nations and not under that of the four occupying powers, as the Soviets had suggested in a second note of April 9. But the final Soviet note, sent in late May, evinced a noticeable cooling of enthusiasm for the whole idea, and the initiative of March 10 was abandoned. Whatever

Stalin's motives may have been (and this question has been the source of much debate and speculation),[83] the more intimate, and now military, integration of the Federal Republic into the Western alliance triggered a chain of events in East Germany leading to a crisis that nearly brought about the collapse of the SED regime. The events preceding the uprising of June 17, 1953, are now familiar and need not be recounted in full here.[84] Of special interest to this chapter, however, is the provisioning crisis at its heart and the response of the regime to its increasing gravity.

The fateful moment invariably singled out in accounts of the uprising is the SED's Second Party Conference held in July 1952. Here, Walter Ulbricht proclaimed the GDR's readiness to embark on "the construction of socialism" and the creation of a national defense force. The era of the "antifascist, democratic order" would now give way to the regime's ambitions to take its place alongside the other "people's democracies" of Eastern Europe. Above all, this effort meant forcibly diminishing the extent of privately owned enterprise in those sectors of the economy where it still made up a majority, namely, in agriculture and handicrafts. Thus, in the countryside there was an intensification of the campaign against "large peasants" *(Großbauerntum)*, that is, those who owned more than twenty hectares of land. Their failure to make tax payments on time or to fulfill delivery quotas was taken as a pretext for outright confiscation of property and, in many cases, arrest. Simultaneously, a combination of material incentives and overtly applied pressure was employed to force smaller independent farmers and handicraft producers into joining state-sponsored cooperatives.

The economic strains introduced by the measures announced at the Second Party Conference were considerable. The effort to create a defense force, the *Kasernierte Volkspolizei* (People's Police in Barracks or KVP) was a serious burden which had to be borne by the GDR. Between the summer of 1952 and mid-1953, the rearmament effort claimed DM 2 billion in resources, as East Germany purchased World War II–era weaponry from the Soviet Union and paid for it with the products of its own machine-building and chemical industries.[85] The industrial potential required constituted a substantial drain on domestic needs for both capital and consumer goods. Moreover, as a result of reformulating the economic plan for 1953 to accommodate rearmament, imports were significantly reduced, including raw materials for producing manufactured consumer goods.[86] SED leaders, acutely aware of these burdens, sought help from Moscow in the form of consumer goods deliveries, a lessening of reparation demands, and the revision of other unfavorable export arrangements with the Soviet Union. But their requests went unanswered.[87]

In the meantime, they pressed ahead with the construction of socialism. Particularly harsh were their efforts in the countryside, which vastly inflated the number of East Germans fleeing to the West. Between 1950 and 1952 the monthly average had been approximately 15,000. In the first half of 1953, that number more than doubled to 37,500. In March alone 59,000 people fled the GDR.[88] As a result, by April 1953 over five hundred thousand hectares of productive farmland lay fallow.[89] Not only farmers fled, but also citizens in those nonworking-class groups targeted by an array of willfully punitive measures ranging from discriminatory taxation to the denial of ration cards. But perhaps the greatest incentive for flight was the rapid emergence of a provisioning crisis reminiscent of the worst moments of the occupation period. Brought on by the great disruption of agricultural production caused by the SED's attempts at forced collectivization, the crisis had disastrous results for consumers, only further intensified by simultaneous reductions in social services and increases in prices for health care, public transportation, and increasingly scarce consumer goods. Finally, in announcing a new, across-the-board, 10 percent increase in work norms for industrial workers, the SED leadership alienated its own ostensible constituency. The new work norms, combined with the increased prices for consumer goods, would have effectively reduced the real wages of many workers by 25–30 percent.

Why did SED leaders push so hard, with such apparently unthinking obduracy? In part, they were driven by ideology, in particular by that thesis of Stalin's according to which the transition from capitalism to socialism was inevitably accompanied by an intensification of class conflict, since all nonsocialist forms of production were viewed as obstacles to developing a socialist economy. Lending an especially vitriolic tone to the whole endeavor was the poisonous resurgence of the campaign against the "inner enemy" then raging throughout the Soviet bloc as a result of the Slansky show trial in Czechoslovakia. Not since the Stalin-Tito split had the search for "agents of imperialism," "saboteurs," and "party enemies" assumed such pathological and grotesque proportions. Within East Germany the slogan "Purity and Unity" accompanied the arrests of thousands, including even government ministers and Politburo members. By the end of 1952 the transformation of the SED into a "party of the new type," a project formally launched in 1948–49, had resulted in the purging of hundreds of thousands of SED members, most of them former Social Democrats.[90]

In its attempts to manage the mounting consumption crisis between the fall of 1952 and June 1953, the regime mustered a stunning display of intransigence, as it bore down and redoubled its efforts along all-too-familiar lines. On the one hand, through a program of "priority provisioning" *(Schwerpunktversorgung),* it further extended the productivist impulses behind Order no. 234. Priority provisioning would seek, in the midst of yet another round of austerity and belt tightening, to maintain the consumption privileges of workers in heavy industry and in the newly collectivized Agricultural Production Cooperatives *(Landwirtschaftliche Produktionsgenossenschaften* or LPGs). On the other hand, East German leaders simultaneously continued to pursue visions of socialist splendor, as they developed plans for the introduction of new luxury stores *(Luxusläden)* and as they moved forward with a "National Construction Program," the centerpiece of which was the much celebrated Stalinallee.[91] Hailed as "the first socialist street" and conceived as a showcase of socialist prosperity, the broad, expansive boulevard running through the heart of East Berlin turned out to be, at the time of its building, an untimely gesture of filial allegiance to the great Soviet leader, a case of contrived magnificence gone awry. Completed in the wake of the suppressed uprising, the Stalinallee seemed the very embodiment of Stalin's power, crushing in its monumentality, brutal in its demand for recognition as one of the finest, most dazzling jewels in the crown of socialist achievement.

A Politburo directive of January 1953 succinctly captured the role of trade in the construction of socialism and, with it, the essence of priority provisioning. "The development of commodity sales," it read, "must proceed in such a manner that it encourages to the utmost the swift development of the most important branches of industry and high levels of production."[92] Once again, a reminder: trade was to serve industry. In practice, however, the task was hardly so clear. At a meeting of the Kollegium of the Ministry for Trade and Provisioning in November

1952, a number of questions emerged that revealed several of the complexities involved.[93] How was the effort to be organized? Should there be a fixed list of firms slated for priority provisioning, or should the list be more flexible, that is, updated on a quarterly basis? Which firms should receive priority for which types of consumer goods? Should the priority-provisioning plan be based on a not-yet-formulated overall commodity supply plan, or should one go ahead and plan consumer supply for the privileged and then allocate whatever was left over to the rest of the population, knowing full well that the remainder would fall far short of satisfying consumer demand?

The task for trade was further complicated by the fact that in carrying out its new responsibilities it would have even fewer resources at its disposal than it had hitherto been granted.[94] At the same time, officials in the State Planning Commission took the Ministry for Trade and Provisioning to task for what they characterized as badly balanced, poorly coordinated, and irresponsibly inflated commodity supply plans for 1953. The ministry was thus forced to lower its supply plans, as well as its requests for investment funds.[95] Reeling from these setbacks, trade functionaries then had to cope with the imposition of an official "austerity regime" (*Sparsamkeitsregime*), according to which the costs of trade and provisioning had to be kept to an absolute minimum. And yet complaints about excessively low wages for sales personnel abounded. At a meeting of local trade-and-supply officials one HO food-store employee gave expression to the general frustration with the austerity regime:

> On austerity: How much does the half hour cost that delayed today's meeting? Where is the connection between the leadership and the sales personnel? Most of the salesladies don't even know the director. Where are the good salespeople? Because of the bad pay, they all go into production or into the administration . . . What does the Ministry for Trade and Provisioning plan to do? It saves at the expense of salesladies, but not at that of the administration.[96]

In addition, SED leaders plotted a further decline in the significance of private retail, in particular for the provisioning of manufactured consumer goods. For foodstuffs, however, they recognized that private retail would have to continue to play an important role. As a report from October 1952 on the development of private retail pointed out,

"A decrease in the contingents of these goods would damage the smooth provisioning of the population since the retail net of socialist trade, above all that of the consumer co-ops, is not yet sufficient to guarantee a satisfactory supply of foodstuffs."[97] Exactly how the regime hoped to maintain private retail as a smoothly functioning arm in the task of food supply while at the same time attacking private retailers as class enemies was a question the report did not address.

Its failure to question the assumption that the supply of manufactured items posed less of a challenge than food supply amounted to yet another instance of wishful thinking. One month earlier, trade and industry officials had explicitly discussed the likely drain on the supply of textiles and clothing for the population, resulting from government contracts for the production of uniforms for the KVP. "Through the government program," a representative of light industry admitted, "not only men's ready-made clothing but also women's ready-made would be affected." But, he added, "we are all clear-thinking political people, and we must know what receives priority in our present political situation. It's useless to produce fabric for coats and winter clothing if we haven't already taken measures for the protection of our republic." Trade officials could hardly disagree. In the words of one co-op *(Konsum)* representative, "The government measures are not to be seen as regular contracts. For us it is clear that in the planned construction of socialism measures must first be taken for the security of our new state." Another *Konsum* official suggested that the co-ops, as a mass organization, could also play a useful pedagogical role by explaining to customers why the provisioning of winter clothing would not be "as we wish and as trade demands." The co-ops would make clear to people the futility of producing "the most beautiful ladies' and men's overcoats in order that they be worn in air-raid shelters."[98] It was a suggestion that well reflected the deliberately invoked atmosphere of crisis and impending war.

In keeping with the construction of socialism, the regime had created several Coordination and Control Agencies *(Koordinierungs- und Kontrollstellen)* in the summer of 1952. The agency embracing provisioning, the Coordination and Control Agency for Domestic Trade (*Koordinierungs- und Kontrollstelle für Binnenhandel* or KKB) included representatives from several ministries (Trade and Provisioning, Light Industry, Finances) and from the State Planning Commission (SPK).

Although it did not formulate policy, the KKB, as its name would suggest, did try to ensure a more efficient coordination of the work carried out by the various administrative bodies involved in consumer supply. Thus, its leader, Herbert Strampfer, a former minister of labor in Thuringia, acted as the point man between Leuschner in the SPK and the different ministers involved in consumer supply.

The KKB also served as another funnel for information about the state of provisioning and the mood of the population. Already, in October 1952, Strampfer was receiving reports highlighting serious problems. In Erfurt, for example, "a catastrophic situation" had developed with regard to the supply of fat. At one HO department store, "enormous amounts of people" stood in line for hours trying "to force" the store to sell butter, margarine, and oil. According to the report, "agents" were leading discussions intended "to undermine the population's trust in the government." Invoking the "guns-and-butter" debate of the Nazi years, the waiting multitudes openly denounced the GDR's commitment to producing "guns instead of butter." Frustrated with waiting and "moved to exasperation," they eventually resorted to "acts of violence against salespeople."[99]

One week later, the KKB was reporting severe shortages in cotton underwear for the entire GDR. Orders originally planned for state-owned manufacturers had to be canceled so that they would be able to produce military uniforms, but private manufacturers were unable to pick up the slack. Consequently, millions of articles of cotton clothing could not be made available to retailers.[100] There were attempts to make up the difference by mobilizing hitherto unsold inventory held in warehouses by wholesalers and retailers. But the unsold merchandise dated back to 1950, if not earlier, and was more often than not of poor quality and thus unsellable at the prices demanded.[101] As trade organs pleaded in vain for a more flexible price policy,[102] embarrassing stories began to appear in the press. The *Berliner Zeitung* published an article under the headline "Millions of items stuck at the HO." The subheadline was explicit: "Bad Commodity Has the Highest Price/Finance Ministry Must Finally Undertake a Price Differentiation."[103]

Rather than bend their policies, SED leaders seemed more inclined to indulge their obsessions with "agents" and "saboteurs." According to Ulbricht, KKB leaders were failing to address the real problem. As he explained to Grotewohl, vast amounts of foodstuffs were being willfully "abandoned to destruction," and workers in the Ministry for Trade and Provisioning were pursuing "direct sabotage."[104] Local party leaders appeared to concur and passed along reports that seemed to confirm Ulbricht's own fears.[105] The number of trials against "economic criminals" escalated. In December 1952, Hamann was arrested, and responsibility for the chaos in consumer supply was attributed to him and his ostensibly agent-infested ministry.

Incongruously, the announcement of the construction of socialism, the elaboration of priority provisioning, renewed calls for material sacrifice, and the hysteria about "inner enemies" were accompanied by efforts to enhance the level of luxury available in HO stores. As Leuschner informed the ministers of trade and provisioning, light industry, and machine building, "In our state-owned trade there is a lack of luxury goods. We are of the opinion that we must as quickly as possible make the transition to producing such luxury goods." He produced a long list of the items he had in mind: high-quality gold watches and jewelry, automobiles, motorcycles, high fashion, silk underwear, high-quality shoes, excellent perfumes and soaps, leather goods of the highest-quality workmanship, expensive furniture, pianos, cameras, refrigerators, vacuum cleaners, hair blow-dryers, sumptuous delicacies, pastries, and chocolates. He invited the ministers to extend the list and insisted, "We can produce all these goods in the GDR. We are prepared to make available the necessary materials." Indicating the importance of the effort, he added, "We draw attention to the fact that the working out of these proposals can tolerate no delays."[106]

The ministers did produce revamped lists, and the discussions within the bureaucracy about the luxury stores continued through the fall, even as plans for consumption cutbacks in 1953 crystallized and the supply situation deteriorated.[107] In the meantime, the consumer supply lobby tried to press its cause within the confines of priority provisioning, hoping to expand the program's purview. HO shopping hours were extended in centers of industry to make shopping easier for workers. There were attempts to enhance customer service by offering free delivery of certain kinds of goods. HO stores organized fashion shows for gatherings of customers. And the HO announced the opening of new stores aimed at satisfying the demands of youth.[108]

But nowhere was the cause of the consumer supply lobby more officially embraced than in the Stalinallee, where the regime hoped to hold up a reflection of socialist success both to its own citizens and to the West. Accordingly, the HO, the VdK (Association of Consumer Co-operatives), and the Berlin Magistrat all collaborated closely with the East German Building Academy.[109] The HO established a special work "collective" to work with the Building Academy on plans for the interiors of the HO stores lining the boulevard. According to a July draft of the "National Construction Program Stalinallee," the sales personnel for the stores were to be enrolled in a special course of instruction. All of the normal administrative tasks involved in filling the stores with goods were to be accelerated. No efforts were to be spared in making the retail space of the Stalinallee a model for the entire GDR. To attract future customers, exhibitions were to be held, displaying models of the stores well before their scheduled pre-Christmas opening on December 20, 1952. In total, there were to be nineteen HO food stores and twenty-seven HO stores selling manufactured commodities, including special stores for motorcycles, sporting goods, jewelry, stockings, porcelain, high fashion, fur coats, cosmetics, and fine leather goods. The stores selling manufactured goods, alone, were to employ two thousand workers.[110] In addition to the HO stores, the retail space of the Stalinallee was to include thirty-one *Konsum* outlets, seven restaurants and cafes, three wash salons, two hair salons, the two-story Karl Marx Buchhandlung, and a children's department store (the unusual *Haus des Kindes,* modeled after a newly opened children's department store in Prague).[111]

But as the consumer supply situation deteriorated, all visions of socialist grandeur were eclipsed by the accelerating crisis. For the Stalinallee, difficulties in securing the necessary financing and an inability to obtain adequate commodity supplies made it impossible to realize the approved plans for its retail space. Despite repeated promises, the opening dates for the stores continued to be postponed. By the end of March 1953, only twenty-one out of the planned ninety-seven retail spaces had been opened.[112] For the GDR as a whole, there were now reports of shortages in an array of basic foodstuffs, including grain, legumes, meat, cooking oil, margarine, and butter. Even the modest commodity-supply plans worked out during the previous fall could not be fulfilled. For the first quarter of 1953, the supply of meat fell short by nearly 13 thousand tons, butter by 10.4 thousand tons, butcher's fat by 500 tons. The shortages were felt not only by private retailers and *Konsum* outlets but also by HO shops, where an indefinite ban on the sale of butter and sugar was introduced.[113] To make up for the scarcity of meat, consumers were offered eggs in exchange for meat coupons. Meanwhile, the shortages in textiles now forced substantial cutbacks in the production of work clothing.[114]

The regime's response to the crisis was to substitute bureaucratic reshuffling for substantive rethinking, as if it had only to find the magic formula for synchronizing the machinery to solve its deepening problems. Thus, in February 1953 the KKB was replaced by a new co-ordinating mechanism, the State Commission for Trade and Provisioning (*Staatliche Kommission für Handel und Versorgung* or SKHV).[115] The SKHV was created as an arm of the Council of Ministers, technically the highest executive organ within the East German state bureaucracy. With Elli Schmidt as its leader, the SKHV was charged with overseeing the carrying out of the council's directives on trade and provisioning. A leading Communist functionary during the Nazi years, Schmidt had spent the war in exile in the Soviet Union. After returning to Berlin, she took up leading positions within the KPD and the East Berlin Magistrat. Between 1946 and 1954 she was a member of the Executive Committee and then the Central Committee of the SED. Between 1950 and 1953 she was a Politburo candidate.[116] And as leader of the SKHV, she now held the rank of a government minister.

But these efforts at administrative makeover could not overcome the difficulties deriving from a set of essentially unchanged tasks stubbornly pursued in a context of rapidly worsening conditions. Soon after the creation of the SKHV, it became increasingly apparent that the program of priority provisioning was running into serious difficulties. The special department for the program that had been set up within the Ministry for Trade and Provisioning was seen as having failed to establish a "truly systematic priority provisioning."[117] The SED leadership struggled to balance contradictory pressures. While it remained committed to priority provisioning and sought to improve the program, it was confronted with an insupportable gap between purchasing power and commodity supply. Even as it urged economic planners to find ways to improve the provisioning of workers in the most important branches of industry, it planned price increases for butter, margarine, textiles, leather shoes, stockings, and an array of semiluxuries.[118] Simultaneously, Planning Commission and SED leaders dithered on producing a directive for improving the supply of what were now called "mass-demand goods" *(Massenbedarfsgüter),* a category the contents of which were at once self-evident and naggingly unclear.[119] An East German economic lexicon from the 1960s defined mass-demand goods vaguely as those "consumer goods which are constantly required for the satisfaction of the needs of the population, as for example, basic foodstuffs, clothing of standard quality, coal and electricity."[120] The problem was that "mass demand" was not static. As we shall see, over the course of the decade economic planners would continue to wrestle with the confines of the category, uncertain in many cases of what to include and exclude.

In any case, more notable than the actual measures called for in the final Politburo directive was the fact that industry and finance now accompanied trade (the usual whipping boy in complaints about consumer supply) as objects of top-level criticism. Thus, the directive reprimanded industry, which, it claimed, "has not seized the necessary initiative for fulfilling the plan in all its positions and has not, in the production of mass-demand goods, expanded assortments in a manner corresponding to the desires [*Wünschen*] of the population. On the contrary, the supply of commodities in certain assortments has become more limited, and the quality has in part deteriorated."[121] In similar fashion, finance was upbraided for its "inflexible price policy," as a consequence of which the work of trade and industry was made more difficult. And, as usual, trade was taken to task for its failure to press its demands on industry more forcefully and for its inability to distribute its supplies more effectively to those areas where they were most needed.

The fact that industry and finance, in addition to trade, came under fire reflected not only the seriousness of the crisis but also the involvement of the Soviets. Just as the outcome of the "battle of notes" had set into motion the chain of events that precipitated the crisis, yet another occurrence of world importance beyond the borders of East Germany was to have a rippling effect of seismic proportions on the SED regime: on March 5, 1953, Joseph Vissarionovich Stalin expired.

In the aftermath of Stalin's death, the beginnings of a thaw in East-West relations appeared to emerge. The now collective Soviet leadership of Malenkov, Beria, and Molotov began to seek not only a greater dialogue with the West but also an easing of Stalinist austerity in favor of greater attention to the consumption needs of Soviet and East-bloc citizens. Already, in April Soviet leaders were advising SED leaders to slow up on the forced tempo in their construction of socialism. But the SED leadership was divided. While Walter Ulbricht insisted on maintaining the commitment to hard-line policies, a group that centered around Rudolf Herrnstadt, the chief editor of *Neues Deutschland,* and Wilhelm Zaisser, a Politburo member and minister for state security, had come to favor, with Beria's encouragement, the new initiatives from Moscow. Recognizing the need for a more generous provisioning of consumer goods and a relaxation of the regime's harshest measures, Herrnstadt and Zaisser found sympathy from several leading SED figures, including Anton Ackermann, Hans Jendretsky, Elli Schmidt, Fred Oelßner, and Heinrich Rau. Herrnstadt, Zaisser, and Oelßner were especially critical of Ulbricht's dictatorial manner and personalization of power. Though they never aimed to purge him entirely from the ranks of the leadership, they were in favor of reasserting the principle of collective leadership and introducing a certain amount of democratization within the party. They also feared that Ulbricht's uncompromising stance on the forced construction of socialism would undermine any chance of achieving the reunification of Germany—at the very moment, no less, when certain Soviet leaders, particularly Beria, were interested in pursuing the possibility of creating a reunited, "bourgeois-democratic," and neutral Germany. Ulbricht, for his part, had no interest in sacrificing the GDR to this goal. Nor did he consider it realistic.[122]

At the May 13–14 conference *(Tagung)* of the SED's Central Committee, the ambivalence within the party leadership found telling expression. On the subject of trade and provisioning, Schmidt held forth, issuing a series of criticisms of the work of the industrial ministries. "We must express very serious criticism of our industrial ministries," she emphasized, "since in the production of mass-demand goods they have exhibited a punishable neglect. One has the impression that they consider their tasks in the production of manufactured consumer goods to be a burden."[123] She expressed outrage that "the criticism the population brings to bear on the quality of the ready-made clothing, knitted goods, stockings, and shoes produced by light industry is completely ignored." Her remarks extended to all the industrial ministries involved in producing consumer goods. It was only too evident, she continued, "that our ministers don't go shopping in order to see for themselves what our population lacks in the most important manufactured consumer goods that make life easier for people." She provided a short list:

"good" razor blades, pocketknives "that cut," bathing caps, screws and nails, thumbtacks, "different sized" pots and pans, curtain rods and accessories. "I, therefore, propose," she announced with mock gravity, "that our comrade ministers be sentenced to shaving every morning with the razor blades produced by their own factories so that they know what a punishment it is!"[124]

But there were limits to how far Schmidt was willing to press her case. Like the trade-and-provisioning advocates who contributed articles to *Der Handel,* she explicitly embraced the premises behind the priority provisioning program. And when she needed examples of greater success in consumer supply, it was to the East that she pointed, not to the West.[125] Thus, even those within the regime who had the greatest interest in bringing about the swiftest possible improvement in consumer supply were not yet ready to demand a radical change in policy, despite the depth of the crisis, despite the catastrophic rise in the numbers of East Germans fleeing to the West, and despite Soviet instructions to change course. For the moment, Ulbricht still held the upper hand. The hard-line ethos behind his thinking was further reinforced by the fact that at the very same meeting of the Central Committee, SED leaders also discussed the lessons to be gleaned from the Slansky trial. Their discussion highlighted the importance of vigilance, discipline, purity, and total commitment to the construction of socialism. On May 14, the final day of the conference, the members of the Central Committee made the fateful decision to introduce the infamous 10 percent increase in work norms. Appropriately, the increase was to go into effect on June 30, Walter Ulbricht's sixtieth birthday.

What followed is still a source of some puzzlement. As Soviet pressure increased, the SED response, reflecting the ambivalence within its leading ranks, was at once desultory, divided, and ultimately self-destructive. After returning from Moscow, where he reported on conditions in East Germany, the political advisor to the Soviet Control Commission, Vladimir Semyonov, called a June 5 meeting with the SED Politburo. There, SED leaders learned two things: they would receive no material assistance from the Soviet Union, and they now had to soften their hard-line policies and diffuse the atmosphere of class confrontation invoked by the construction of socialism.[126] Consequently, the Politburo issued a communiqué on June 9 announcing the adoption of a number of reforms intended to roll back the punitive measures directed at non-working-class groups. The Politburo admitted having made "a series of mistakes" resulting in "countless people" having left "the republic."[127] Self-employed persons would again be allowed to receive ration cards. Independent retailers and farmers were invited to return and take up their property and positions prior to the July 1952 announcement of the construction of socialism. The one-sided emphasis on the development of heavy industry would be reversed, and more attention and resources would be devoted to producing consumer goods.

But the Politburo, mysteriously, did not rescind the controversial increase in work norms. As a result, a paradoxical situation emerged in which the SED, once hell-bent on building socialism and rooting out capitalists and "saboteurs," was now making a series of concessions to "capitalist elements," while leaving its professed constituency to fend for itself in the face of renewed hardship. On June 11 *Neues Deutschland* reported the change of course but provided no elucidating editorial comment. Rudolf Herrnstadt, evidently unsatisfied with the limitations of the announced reforms, approved the publication of an article in *Neues Deutschland* on June 14, calling into question the wisdom of maintaining the new work norms. The article ran under the headline "It's Time to Lay Aside the Bludgeon." But only two days later, a leading trade unionist, Otto Lehmann, published an article in the trade-union newspaper, *Die Tribüne,* refuting Herrnstadt's article and defending the new work norms.[128] Appearing, as it did, right on the heels of Herrnstadt's article, the Lehmann piece revealed a regime accustomed to the practice of dictatorship but divided and without clear purpose; the mixed signals it conveyed, combined with the deep resentment its policies engendered, now rendered the leadership vulnerable. In this volatile mix of confusion and blustering, of uncertainty and profound frustration, Lehmann's article acted as the spark that ignited the explosion.

Until June 17, 1953, the SED regime attempted, first and foremost, to fulfill its commitment to productivism. Its investments were devoted primarily to heavy industry and heavy engineering. SED propaganda held up for adulation Hennecke activists and other "Heroes of Socialist Labor"; above all, it celebrated the construction of giant iron and steelworks and the "overfulfillment" of production quotas. SED leaders preached an ethos of work, sacrifice, discipline, and ascetic modesty in the consumption of scarce material goods. Individual needs were to be subsumed under the general need; selfless and maximum effort, expended for the good of the whole, was to serve as the benchmark of virtuous conduct and the criterion for reward.

But the array of obstacles to fulfilling this commitment was formidable and unyielding. How to increase labor productivity in the midst of a chronic, often severe scarcity of consumer goods? How to convince workers of the virtue of maximum effort when they saw the fruits of their labor being taken by the Soviet Union in the form of reparations? How to make shop floor managers ensure strict compliance with work norms when, in doing so, they drove their workers to those firms that allowed work norms to remain weak?

From the very beginning, the call for sacrifice and maximum effort had to be counterbalanced by a realistic assessment of material interest. Hence the emergence of a provisioning hierarchy (enshrined in Order no. 234) that favored those capable of making the greatest contribution to the power of SED leaders and the realization of SED goals. The ranks of the privileged included, in Soviet fashion, workers in "the most important branches of industry," as well as that cohort of white-collar toilers from which SED leaders hoped to fashion a new leadership cadre: political and administrative officials, intellectuals and artists, professors and engineers—in short, the intelligentsia.

But the June 1948 currency reform in the Western zones of Germany threw up a new challenge: the economic task for SED leaders was no longer merely to boost industrial productivity within the Soviet zone, but to present visual evidence as compelling as that trumpeted in the West of an end to shortage, of a return to normalcy, even of ways for satisfying the most demanding and luxurious of material desires. The introduction of the HO, the emergence of the consumer supply lobby, the development of plans for special luxury stores, and the relative lavishness of attention and resources devoted to the Stalinallee all reflected the intense pressure on the regime to meet this new challenge. But the insufficient financing, poor coordination, finger-pointing, and foot-dragging that accompanied these endeavors revealed the regime's lack of preparedness and ultimate unwillingness to allow the new challenge to dilute its primary commitment to productivism. It was the crisis of 1952–53 that changed the equation. The collapse of agricultural production, the neglect of the consumer goods industries, the dramatic disparity between purchasing power and commodity supply, the tens of thousands of people fleeing to the West every month, the attempt to increase and enforce the new obligatory work norms—all of these developments combined to transform the commitment to productivism into a stance that now threatened the SED's grip on power. With the death of Stalin and the policy shift in Moscow, that transformation made necessary the adoption of the New Course.

CHAPTER 4

The Rise, Decline, and Afterlife of the New Course

The basic line of the party was and remains correct.

Otto Grotewohl, July 1953

The fashion center, Paris, is an internationally recognized
reality . . . Until now our fashion creators have drawn
secondhand inspiration from fashion shows in Prague,
Warsaw, Budapest, Milan, Munich. As a result GDR
designs are always several months behind.

Ministry for Trade and Provisioning, July 1956

The New Course was marked immediately by uncertainty and ambivalence. The regime's first wary steps to pull back from the accelerated construction of socialism could not but arouse controversy, raise expectations, intensify power struggles, and betray disarray. Ultimately, the parameters of the New Course were determined by the outcome of the struggle between Ulbricht and his opponents, a struggle that, as recent research has shown, lasted several weeks beyond the uprising of June 17, 1953.[1] With Ulbricht's victory, and with the demise of Herrnstadt and Zaisser, the New Course was shed of the more politically far-reaching goals of its initial proponents: the curbing of Ulbricht's personal power; the hoped-for democratization of the party; the liberalization of intellectual and cultural life; and the pursuit of a reunited, "bourgeois-democratic," and "peace-loving" Germany. Instead, the New Course came to focus on improving the long-neglected living conditions of East German citizens. Even as SED leaders officially dismissed the events of June 17 as a "fascist provocation" instigated by "Western agents," they recognized them as, among other things, a violent eruption of consumer protest, a clear expression of the desire for a better life. Accordingly, they approved a number of measures designed to

115

make life easier for East German consumers. They raised wages, reduced prices, and transferred considerable effort and resources (previously devoted to heavy industry) to the production of consumer goods. The change of course reflected developments throughout the Soviet bloc after Stalin's death. In the Soviet Union itself a collective leadership presided over by Georgi M. Malenkov pursued policies that served as a model for the satellite regimes of Eastern Europe.

And yet, as this version of the New Course crystallized, the SED leadership evinced a deep-seated ambivalence about it. Although party pronouncements now embraced the goals of the consumer supply lobby, they displayed a reluctance to dispense with the old productivist ethos. The party endorsed wholeheartedly the goal of improving living standards but continued to posit any improvement as being dependent upon increased work productivity. In short, the SED brought together in its propaganda the idioms of consumerism and productivism, setting them side by side, suspended in an uneasy simultaneity. At the level of policy implementation, the regime offered an equally ambivalent show of conflicting impulses, assumptions, and imperatives.

Scholars have traditionally understood the demise of the New Course as a direct result of Malenkov's fall at the end of 1954 and the subsequent reversion to an emphasis on heavy industrial production in the Soviet Union, though they have taken Walter Ulbricht's hard-line remarks at the SED's Fourth Party Congress in early April 1954 as the first sign of Ulbricht's desire to turn away from the concessions promised after the June 1953 uprising.[2] In fact, internal SED reports show even earlier indications of the tenuousness of the New Course. Ulbricht's position at the Party Congress can now be seen as stemming not simply from his own hard-line intransigence and impatience with the New Course but also from earlier reports forecasting unexpected shortfalls in foreign imports so significant as to make it impossible to keep the promises made in the wake of the uprising. The beginning of the eclipse of the New Course can now be dated as early as January 1954, nearly a full year before the fall of Malenkov.

Of course, other factors too contributed to the attenuation of the regime's commitment to the New Course. As the trauma brought on by the uprising subsided, as SED leaders regained confidence in their own power—particularly by embarking on a new series of purges within the party and by expanding the power and resources of the Ministry for State Security *(Stasi)*—the New Course lost much of its urgency for them. It no longer seemed indispensable to their hold on power. Gradually, between 1954 and 1955 it receded from view. And yet to assume that its disappearance meant a return to the status quo ante would be incorrect. The New Course was not only more embattled than scholars have hitherto suggested but also more enduring. Having spotlighted the issue of individual consumption, the New Course, though eclipsed, was never extinguished. Not only had it raised expectations, it had conferred official sanction on them. The regime's rhetorical commitment to improving living standards, couched in the language of the consumer supply lobby, could hardly be retracted. Besides, as a result of the actual achievements of the New Course, East German consumption of basic consumer goods began to reach prewar levels by the mid-1950s. Economic planners could now begin to think about modernization rather than merely reconstruction.

Indeed, economic planners had no choice; these were the years during which the relative material prosperity generated by the West German *Wirtschaftswunder* began to replace memories of the prewar years as the most important measure of consumer well-being. The hopes raised among the East German population by the New Course, combined with the fears aroused within the East German regime by the relative prosperity of the West, produced a shift in frame of reference even after the official abandonment of the New Course. The shift was evident in the regime's efforts to introduce innovations in retail, to compile more detailed statistics on living conditions, and to compare living standards in East and West Germany. This chapter analyzes the evolution of the New Course, its successes and failures, and the subtle but significant shift in frame of reference it helped bring about, even as its name vanished from the directives, reports, and memoranda of economic planners and their political leaders.

As the previous chapter has shown, the New Course, though it had its supporters within the SED, was ultimately imposed on the Ulbricht-led party by Soviet pressure to repair the damage caused by the forced construction of socialism. After a series of hastily arranged meetings between Soviet and SED leaders in the spring of 1953, the SED Politburo issued its communiqué of June 9, in which it called for reversing most of the sweeping, hard-line measures taken since the SED Second

Party Conference of July 1952. Although the term "New Course" did not appear in the communiqué, the proclaimed intentions amounted to a significant change of direction. The communiqué recognized unequivocally the need for "a decisive improvement of the standard of life [*Lebenshaltung*] of all sections of the population," not just workers in "the most important branches of industry."[3] Consequently, the forced collectivization of agriculture and handicrafts was to be halted, and the property of private farmers and handicraft producers returned. Ration cards were once again to be issued to self-employed persons. Those who had fled to the West were invited to return to the GDR and take up their positions and property prior to the adoption of whichever punitive ordinances and regulations had targeted them. The existing plan for heavy industry was to be revised; a number of measures were to be adopted for increasing the production of consumer goods; and the recent price increases for consumer goods and public transport were to be reversed. The communiqué was published in *Neues Deutschland* and officially enshrined in a series of ordinances adopted by the GDR's Council of Ministers.[4]

But in view of the depth of the crisis caused by SED policies, the communiqué was a case of too little too late. It aroused in the population a mood of anticipation and uncertainty, of anger about the maintenance of the 10 percent increase in work norms, as well as rumors about a change of leadership in the SED. Finally, with the publication of the provocative articles by Herrnstadt and Lehmann, events quickly spun out of control. On June 16, 1953, construction workers on the Stalinallee joined construction workers from nearby building sites, and together they marched to the trade union headquarters and to the House of Ministries to protest the work norms. The regime's attempts at conciliation were desultory and unconvincing. Demonstrators called for a general strike the following day. Again, cries of "butter instead of cannons" were heard.[5]

On the next day, the protests and demonstrations, involving more than five hundred thousand people, spread spontaneously to over 350 cities and towns throughout the GDR.[6] Demands to cancel the new work norms and to raise wages quickly turned into broader political demands for free elections and, in places, reunification with West Germany. The regime's immediate response was characterized by confusion and wavering resolve. Lacking confidence in the loyalty of its own repressive forces (including the KVP), it was timid in deploying them.[7] Even political functionaries in whom SED leaders had more confidence sided at times with the demonstrators.[8] On the morning of June 17, 1953, the entire SED Politburo, under instructions from the Soviet High Commissioner Vladimir Semyonov, drove to Soviet headquarters in Karlshorst to wait out the disturbances under Soviet protection. In the end, only Soviet tanks were able to reestablish order, by suppressing the proliferation of uncoordinated demonstrations. Although there continued to be isolated strikes and disturbances across the GDR for several weeks, the moment of true danger for the SED leadership had passed. The combination of Soviet tanks and Western inaction had shown the demonstrators that there were fundamental limits to what violent protest could achieve. The SED regime, in other words, would retain its hold on power. What remained to be seen was what it would do to encourage its citizens to be more reconciled to that fact.

To ease the most pressing frustrations of consumers, authorities began almost immediately to distribute reserve food supplies held in storage for the third quarter of the year. They monitored closely the "fear purchases" *(Angstkäufe)* of shoppers, and they made every effort to avoid shortages of the most in-demand commodities, such as bread, canned goods, sausage, and baked goods. Nevertheless, items like margarine, sugar, and marmalade remained scarce.[9] Over the next few days the SED Central Committee formulated a brief but broadly encompassing report on recent events and the immediate tasks of the party. The document presented the regime's official understanding of the uprising *(der Tag X)* as a "fascist provocation" orchestrated by "Western agents" in order to sabotage any attempts made by the regime to improve living conditions in the GDR. In a tone of guarded assurance, the report made clear that order had been restored but also insisted that it was "in no way absolutely secure. The enemy carries on with his insidious agitation."[10] In response, the Central Committee announced another round of measures intended to build upon those of the Politburo's June 9 communiqué, including an immediate return to the calculation of wages based on the old work norms, a discount in the price of public transport for workers and employees in lower-income groups, an increase in pensions as well as health and social welfare expenditures, and a plan to increase housing construction.

According to the Central Committee, "in connection with the reduction of the plan for heavy industry, the main goal of the New Course [was] to improve the standard of life [*Lebenshaltung*] of workers, farmers, the intelligentsia, handicraft producers, and the remaining strata of the middle class."[11] Yet at the same time, the report reiterated the connection between living better and producing more: "this far-reaching initiative seized by the party and the government to improve the standard of life of all classes of the population can only succeed if the working population is convinced of the necessity of the constant increase in the productivity of work."[12]

The Soviet reaction to the SED report was positive, and the Soviets made a general promise to extend material help to the GDR. But they also criticized East German leaders for not doing more to regain control of their own apparatus: "We have gained the impression that there is still confusion within the leadership of the Central Committee of the SED about the most recent events. The practical work of repairing the situation proceeds very slowly. The work of the state apparatus and the party organs has become unreliably weak." In particular, the Soviets pushed the SED to consolidate its hold over the unions. Mindful of the need to make sure that the working class, the SED's own professed constituency, would never again rise up against the regime, Soviet leaders expressed dissatisfaction that the unions were "in strange hands" and that the party appeared to have no plan for bringing them back into its own. The general task for the SED, according to the Soviet Union, was twofold: first, the SED needed "to strengthen the influence of the party on the masses"; second, it had "to gain the trust of the masses for state power."[13] Control of the unions would bolster influence; the New Course would win trust. The explicit coupling of influence and trust captured perfectly the paternalistic mode of rule to which both the Soviet and East German parties aspired.

To ease the SED's ability to fulfill its paternalistic role, the Soviet Union announced in August its willingness to forgo further reparation demands as of January 1, 1954; it promised to return the remaining thirty-three SAGs to East German ownership (they accounted for 12 percent of industrial goods production); it offered a credit of a half million rubles, part of which would be in freely convertible currency; and it agreed to limit the East German share of Soviet occupation costs to 5 percent of the GDR's state revenue (in 1954 that figure still amounted to DM 1.6 billion).[14] Meanwhile, the further development of the New Course, its detailed formulation and implementation, required more time. Economic planners had to reconfigure their overall plans for the second half of the year, and SED leaders needed to come to an agreement with the leaders of the Soviet Union and the other East bloc countries about the form and amount of help the GDR would receive. At a meeting of July 4, 1953, the Politburo assembled a commission to revise the economic plan for the rest of the year.[15] In terms of consumer supply, the Politburo instructed the commission to follow the original plan for the third quarter but to increase food provisioning by 10 to 15 percent for the fourth quarter. The commission was also supposed to consider arrangements enabling a complete lifting of rationing in 1954. Such considerations came to nothing, as rationing was maintained until 1958. But they demonstrated the regime's continued embarrassment about the fact that rationing was still necessary. Could there have been a more glaring symbol of the scarcity still plaguing the East German economy?

From within the regime itself there were voices calling for swifter action in the area of consumer supply. Among them was Curt Wach, Hamann's replacement as minister for trade and provisioning. Wach was probably chosen for reasons of political reliability rather than those of expertise. Born the son of an agricultural laborer and trained as a machine fitter, Wach joined the KPD in 1927, spent the Nazi years in and out of jail, and joined the SED in 1946. Between 1946 and his appointment as minister for trade and supply, he held a series of local administrative posts, none of which were directly related to either agriculture or trade.[16] One can only assume that he was appointed minister in the midst of the 1952–53 provisioning crisis because he was considered sufficiently trustworthy and controllable. Still, as minister, he needed to try to improve the state of trade and provisioning. So in early July 1953 he lobbied for immediate and sweeping price reductions for consumer goods, especially textiles. But officials in the State Planning Commission insisted on the need to wait for the fourth quarter.[17] They remained convinced that the available supply of goods would not yet meet the expected rise in demand resulting from such far-reaching price reductions. Even months later, when plans for introducing price reductions were underway, the State Planning Commission expressed considerable caution: "Such a significant price reduction can be carried out painlessly only if one is entirely certain that in the fourth quarter the GDR will have at its disposal a commodity fund [*Warenfonds*] sufficient both to balance the price reduction and to cover the increased purchasing power of the population resulting from other measures passed by the government."[18]

In the meantime, doing nothing was hardly an option. The regime had to provide some show of immediate action. On July 25, 1953, the Council of Ministers, acting on a Politburo recommendation,[19] issued several ordinances increasing the wages of workers in all branches of state-owned industry, public transport, construction, agriculture, the HO, and the consumer co-ops. On the same day, it also reduced the prices of a limited group of consumer items, including rice, tea, nylons, soap, and lightbulbs. The price reductions, announced in the front page of *Neues Deutschland,* were considerable: the price of tea was reduced 50 percent; that of soap, 40 percent; nylons, 37 percent; typewriters, 40 percent.[20]

Simultaneously, SED leaders revealed more detailed plans at the Fifteenth Central Committee Conference. There, Otto Grotewohl laid out for party delegates the future shape of the New Course. According to Grotewohl, it would consist of two main elements: a broad set of price reductions and a determined effort to boost the production of "mass-demand goods." For the second half of 1953 alone, the price reductions were expected to leave consumers with an additional DM 500 million, while the increase in consumer goods production was to equal DM 900 million. These efforts were to be made possible by a combination of Soviet bloc help and a shift in the GDR's investment priorities. Grotewohl duly reported the Soviet Union's promise to deliver 230 million rubles' worth of foodstuffs for the second half of 1953. (Simultaneously, negotiations were underway with the "people's democracies" of Eastern Europe and China for further deliveries.)[21] He also announced a plan for significantly reducing heavy industrial production in 1954 and 1955 and for devoting the resources that would have been used by heavy industry to agricultural and consumer goods production.[22]

The report produced by the conference, *Der neue Kurs und die Aufgaben der Partei,* summarized the SED interpretation of the uprising, as well as the main elements of the New Course. Intended for a wide audience, it was published in both *Neues Deutschland* and *Einheit.* Although it celebrated the expected material benefits of the New Course for East German citizens, the report was still burdened with many of the moral catchphrases of preuprising work pedagogy: "the more that is produced, the more the living situation [*Lebenslage*] of the masses can be elevated"; "in order to bring more and better commodities to the market, the productivity of work is to be constantly increased and work discipline improved."[23] Although the Central Committee admitted past mistakes, particularly with regard to the accelerated tempo of its construction of socialism, it asserted unequivocally, "The basic line of the party was and remains correct."[24] As if to underscore the point, the document made public the Central Committee's decision to exclude Herrnstadt and Zaisser from its ranks. (By January 1954 they would be expelled from the party.)

For the next several months the pages of *Einheit* were open as they had never been before to discussions of consumer supply and the tasks of trade.[25] A series of articles reproduced many of the arguments previously made by the consumer supply lobby in *Die Versorgung* and *Der Handel*. They emphasized the importance of the role played by trade as "the connecting link between production and consumption." They insisted on the indispensability of trade for the success of the New Course. And they highlighted how it contributed to "the national struggle" by helping "Germans in the west of our country to discern in which part of Germany the working population lives better and where a truly stable economy exists."[26] Good *Verkaufskultur*, in other words, was a patriotic duty.

It was also a Soviet-bloc duty, as the Soviet minister of trade, Anastas Mikoyan, made clear on his now periodic visits to the GDR. Through published articles and publicized tours of retail outlets, Mikoyan imparted his message and weighty presence to East German trade-and-provisioning officials.[27] During a visit to the HO's flagship department store on Alexanderplatz in East Berlin, for example, Mikoyan found much to criticize in the store's *Verkaufskultur*. Although he had measured praise for the store's selection of high-quality watches (including Swiss watches), typewriters, nylon stockings, Meissen porcelain, and Jena glass, he was of the opinion that the store lacked "world-city character." He found it too dark; more light and advertising were required to give it a "friendlier" face. Nor did it help that the selling floors were too narrow and small and that the window displays offered nothing that was actually for sale in the store. Mikoyan was particularly irked by the fact that in certain departments cleaning ladies had already started their work before closing time and in the presence of customers. And he was disappointed by what he considered to be a meager selection of jewelry on offer: "In the Soviet Union considerably more attention is devoted to jewelry in department stores."[28]

The widespread attention to trade and consumerism would have been unthinkable before the uprising. Now the editors of *Einheit* embraced the cause, proclaiming the need for a wider assortment and better quality of consumer goods, a greater attention to fashion, design, and color. They stressed the importance of improving shopwindow displays, product packaging, and market research. Yet their discussions brushed the New Course with the same ambivalence evident in the Central Committee report. Like the Central Committee, the editors set these goals alongside the familiar imperatives of productivism: work discipline, socialist competition, the austerity regime, and increased productivity in heavy industry, all identified as prerequisites for "living better."

This ambivalence was, in turn, reflected in the unfolding of the New Course itself. First came the price reductions Grotewohl had announced in late July. In October 1953 the regime lowered the prices of twelve thousand different commodities (foodstuffs, semiluxuries, and manufactured items), adding an estimated DM 540 million to the purchasing power of consumers for the remainder of the year.[29] The HO prices for meat were to be reduced 10 percent, milk 20 percent, margarine 25 percent; the prices for ready-made clothing were to be lowered 15 to 25 percent, depending on the material used; the price of laundry detergent was lowered 15 percent, bicycles 15 percent, accordions 25 percent. The increase in purchasing power, according to Bruno Leuschner, was to be covered through the end of the year by deliveries of consumer goods from the Soviet Union.[30] In addition, the government announced plans to introduce a system for installment plan purchases to make it easier for East Germans to buy more expensive goods, such as furniture, radios, bicycles, and motorcycles.

The major newspapers celebrated the price reductions as the largest and most all-encompassing ever adopted in the GDR.[31] (In truth, the bulk of the price reductions of the first half of the 1950s occurred in the period before June 17, 1953.)[32] The press sent its reporters into the streets and stores to capture the excitement of the moment: salespeople happily engaged in redesigning their shopwindows; housewives rhapsodizing over being able to buy more margarine, smoked ham, and textiles; husbands thrilled to discover reduced prices for tools and materials needed for home repairs and craft hobbies. The press also took the opportunity to contrast the price reductions with the supposedly prohibitively high prices in West Berlin and West Germany.[33]

But as if to discipline the reported enthusiasm of consumers, as if to exert some control over the unending "flood of shoppers," the press simultaneously linked the price reductions to an ostensible upsurge in work enthusiasm: "price reduction awakens new initiative"; "workers express thanks through special work shifts."[34] The pleasures of shopping, in other words, had to be balanced by the commitment to work; the apparently rapturous exclamations of excited consumers had to be set alongside their supposed recognition that "something like this doesn't just fall from Heaven!"[35] In short, the press, even as it celebrated the new benefits for consumers, attempted to educate them as to how those benefits should be understood and acted upon.

Nevertheless, the significance of the New Course price reductions, combined with its provisions for increasing wages, should not be lost sight of. In fact, these measures confirmed the regime's commitment to breaking with past German traditions. Before World War II German industry had been characterized by highly cartelized organizational structures enabling employers to keep wages down and prices for consumer goods artificially high.[36] With the New Course, the SED continued to consolidate a consumption regime in which basic consumption goods were to be sold at subsidized low prices, theoretically assuring the satisfaction of basic needs. No less important, the price reductions constituted a recognition on the part of the regime that it would not repeat its preuprising attempt to balance excess purchasing power and insufficient commodity supply by means of price increases. In describing the relationship between industrial workers and the regime after the uprising of June 17, 1953, Jeffrey Kopstein has spoken of an "implicit 'labor agreement,'" according to which "production could rise so long as norms remained low and wages high, relative to productivity."[37] In similar fashion, one can say that the June uprising and the New Course brought about an implicit "price agreement." Henceforth the

SED leadership was perfectly clear that it could raise prices for consumer goods only at the risk of great social and political instability.

The regime's ambivalence about the New Course became yet more pronounced in its efforts to realize its second main element, that is, the attempt to increase significantly the production of "mass-demand goods." Announced in the press within days of the price reductions, the campaign to boost the production of mass-demand goods became identified with the future of the New Course. The Soviet High Commissioner Vladimir Semyonov, in particular, attached great importance to the effort, having his office direct the attention of the minister for trade and provisioning, Curt Wach, to an article recently published in *Tägliche Rundschau* that championed the effort to produce more mass-demand goods. "The production of mass-demand goods," the article insisted, "is an important and honorable task for every firm, regardless of its specialty."[38] There could be no patience for firms that tried to excuse their inability to produce enough high-quality consumer goods by pointing to a lack of materials:

> The population expects from industry that it produce greater quantities of beautiful and comfortable shoes, fabric in appealing colors and styles, lovely and practical furniture, flatware and other commodities. There can be no excuses for the fact that products of poor quality are still put on the market. The reason can only be that there is lack of a sense of responsibility in work and that the interests of the working people are ignored.

The public commitment to producing mass-demand goods notwithstanding, Wach's ministry soon ran into difficulties with the State Planning Commission, which drastically cut its commodity supply proposals for an array of foodstuffs, semiluxuries, and manufactured goods. In total, the Planning Commission sought to reduce the overall commodity supply plan from DM 41 billion to DM 38.2 billion. The difference was concentrated in fruits and vegetables, meat, eggs, butter, cocoa, coffee, and textiles.[39]

Trade-and-provisioning planners, moreover, were not alone in their disappointment. The Planning Commission also insisted on scaling back the investment proposals produced by the ministries of food and light industry. While the representatives of the food industry calculated an investment requirement of DM 275 million, the State Planning Commission approved only DM 193 million, even though a ministry investigation had concluded that the latter figure would make it impossible "to tackle a series of important measures for the year 1954." Similarly, the Planning Commission countered the Ministry of Light Industry's investment proposal of DM 394 million with an offer of only DM 145 million. Light-industry officials were despondent: "with DM 145 million the Ministry of Light Industry cannot even fulfill the most urgent tasks of the year 1954."[40] Although the negotiations within the bureaucracy were by no means over, the Planning Commission's drastic reductions might have made even the most fervently believing functionary question the regime's commitment to the New Course.

The official ordinance on the increased production of mass-demand goods was drafted in close cooperation with the office of the Soviet high commissioner and issued on December 17, 1953. It drew attention to the need not only to increase the quantity of consumer goods but also to improve their quality and assortment. The ordinance bemoaned the fact that East German textiles, clothing, shoes, leather goods, household items, kitchenware, shaving cream, and furniture still failed to measure up to prewar standards; it decried the ubiquity of shoddy workmanship, the lack of care for the outward appearance of commodities, evident in the woeful disregard of fashion and design, and in "the often loveless packaging" of products. For 1954 alone the ordinance promised a 25 percent increase in the production of mass-demand goods compared to 1953, with yet greater increases to follow in 1955. Yet in all of its fourteen pages, which reproduced much of the phrasing and touched on many of the arguments of the consumer supply lobby, there was no mention of additional investments in the consumer goods industries. Instead, the ordinance repeatedly insisted on the need to exhaust "all available production capacities," a formulation neither felicitous nor auspicious.[41]

To oversee the implementation of the ordinance, the Planning Commission set up a special department for mass-demand goods. Similarly, the ministries involved in producing mass-demand goods established special "work groups" to organize their respective contributions. Nevertheless, difficulties emerged immediately. In early January 1954 planners in the Ministry of Light Industry enumerated several factors hindering their efforts: the ministry oversaw the production of centrally led industry only, not of firms directed at the local level, and it was not yet clear how production would be divided between the different levels; the list of goods distributed by the Planning Commission differed from the items enumerated in the ordinance; the ministry was short of personnel; there were currently extraordinary difficulties in supplying materials to the textile and leather industries.[42] Within the Planning Commission itself there also seemed to be problems. Although the ordinance had gone into effect on January 1, 1954, as late as February 20 the commission's special department for mass-demand goods still consisted of only three people; as one of Leuschner's deputies pointed out, so few people were "not sufficient to fulfill the [department's] extensive tasks."[43] The department had hitherto failed even to produce a comprehensive report on the progress made by the ministries and local authorities involved in carrying out the ordinance. Arrangements were thus being made to enlarge the department to ten people.

But these administrative problems paled in significance compared to the unexpectedly bleak prospects faced by the regime in the area of foreign trade. As Leuschner informed Ulbricht on January 18, 1954, "The situation is very serious."[44] Without swift action, he warned, the GDR faced the prospect already in the first quarter of a significant decline in the production of consumer goods and the provisioning of the population. A shortfall in feed grain threatened to result in a loss of one hundred thousand tons of live-weight meat. Due to a shortfall in domestic supplies of rye, the bread supply was guaranteed only through the spring and early summer, after which there would be a six-week period when the supply could not be assured. To avert this disaster, Leuschner estimated, the GDR had to increase its imports by at least 120,000 tons. The amount of grain available for the production of processed foodstuffs and beer amounted to less than half of expected supplies. Leuschner predicted that by May beer production would cease in East Germany. Finally, economic planners found their expectations for imports of raw materials for the textile and leather industries rudely disappointed; Leuschner reported significant shortfalls in wool, cotton yarn, artificial silk, and leather hides. He estimated for the first quarter alone a DM 600 million reduction in the supply of light industrial consumer goods for the population. He therefore recommended immediate negotiations with the Soviet Union, especially to secure grain imports, before the Soviets made other export arrangements.

The future of the mass-demand-goods program, and thus New Course itself, was in obvious peril. Yet two months later it appeared that little or no progress had been made. According to a report compiled for Ulbricht in March 1954, the provisioning of the population in the second and third quarters of the year threatened to sink to levels reminiscent of the second quarter of 1953, that is, of the consumption nadir reached during the crisis preceding the June 1953 uprising.[45] The report warned of being able to supply consumers with only "very limited amounts of meat, butter, margarine, coffee, cocoa products, fruits from southern lands [*Südfrüchten*], cigarettes, and beer." It also added that the provisioning of manufactured goods would suffer significantly in quantity and quality. A calculated total purchasing power of DM 30.5 billion would be met by a commodity fund *(Warenfonds)* of only DM 29.5 billion, thus leaving unsatisfied DM 1 billion in purchasing power.[46]

Only in the context of these import shortfalls can we fully understand Walter Ulbricht's remarks at the SED's Fourth Party Congress (March 30–April 6, 1954), in which he reiterated the GDR's commitment to creating the foundations of socialism and reintroduced the language of austerity, cost-saving, and productivism.[47] Although he continued to give lip service to the mass-demand-goods effort, he was clearly preparing for a return to more hard-line policies. His remarks, in turn, came to serve as a point of reference in subsequent months for the regime's internal reports, bulletins, and memoranda. The shift in atmosphere had immediate repercussions on the mass-demand-goods program. In May 1954 the Politburo specifically lowered the 1954 production goals for several commodities listed in the December 17, 1953, ordinance.[48] The overall commodity supply plan for the second quarter was duly lowered, even though as Easter approached, trade-and-provisioning planners reported difficulties in covering consumer demand for meat and eggs.[49] And between March and May, the annual plan for total retail sales was reduced from DM 31.7 billion to DM 30.3 billion.[50] (In fact, according to the official *East German Statistical Yearbook*, the total figure for retail sales in 1954 ended up being even lower, that is, DM 29.7 billion.)[51]

The further eclipse of the New Course, meanwhile, was readily apparent in the succession of less-than-inspiring reports on the production of mass-demand goods in 1954.[52] By November one of the departments for manufactured goods within the Ministry for Trade and Provisioning had come to the conclusion that "among colleagues in the Ministry for Machine Building a disdain for the ordinance of December 17, 1953, prevails. From the conduct of colleagues in the production ministries one assumes that little or nothing has been done to mobilize workers in the production firms for the realization of this ordinance." Moreover, the initial 1955 goals for the production of mass-demand goods were already being drastically reduced. The ordinance, according to the report, was now viewed within the production ministries as a "historical document."[53]

And not without some justification. Not only had the Politburo modified the original goals of the ordinance months earlier, but now the Council of Ministers had just issued a new directive on "The Assurance of the Production of Mass-Demand Goods in 1954–1955."[54] But the new directive turned out to be of little significance. Again, a case of too little too late, it seemed to confuse rather than invigorate. In their subsequent reports, economic planners tended to conflate the new directive with the original ordinance. Their reports only confirmed what was already known: "Now as before, the production of mass-demand goods is viewed by the planning areas as a low priority [*Ressortarbeit*]."[55]

SED leaders, meanwhile, were neither of a mind nor in much of a position to bring about a change of attitude. By the beginning of 1955 they were again forced to turn to the Soviet Union for help. But this time they directed their plea to a Soviet leadership without its most committed proponent of the New Course, namely, Georgi Malenkov, who was officially ousted from power in February 1955. In a February letter to Nikita Khrushchev, Ulbricht and Grotewohl outlined their economic difficulties. Again, their concerns centered around foreign trade, on which the East German economy, they explained, was "extraordinarily dependent." Although imports in 1954 had fallen far short of expectations, the East German economy now faced yet lower imports in 1955. The seriousness of the situation was intensified by the fact that, according to East German calculations, consumer purchasing power had increased 20.8 percent since 1953. The overall commodity fund for 1955 was supposed to increase 10 percent, but that figure not only seemed impossible to fulfill in view of the looming decline in foreign trade but even if fulfilled would still leave a monetary overhang of DM 1.5 billion. As the SED leaders explained to Khrushchev, the economic plan for 1955 contained "great tensions."[56]

To relieve those tensions, Ulbricht and Grotewohl estimated that the GDR required an additional 740 million rubles in imports, mostly from the Soviet Union, to be paid back in the form of East German industrial products. The itemized list of imports included textiles, chemicals, steel and other metals, basic foodstuffs, and semiluxuries. In addition, the overall figure contained a request for a credit in hard currency (valued at 130 million rubles) for the purposes of buying an array of commodities from capitalist countries, in particular, wool, jute, leather hides, tobacco, cocoa beans, coffee beans, and brewing barley. (As we shall see, the problem of hard currency would come up again. Although East Germany had greater access than the other East-bloc countries to hard currency through its ongoing contacts with West Germany, those contacts simultaneously expanded East Germany's hard currency needs. As a result, SED leaders consistently bemoaned their chronically short supply.)[57]

Khrushchev's brief, unhurried reply came six weeks later. Although the Soviet leader believed it was "necessary to render assistance to the GDR," he offered far less than Ulbricht and Grotewohl had hoped for.[58] Of the dozens of goods requested, Khrushchev was willing to offer only a tiny portion; and of those items, he offered amounts considerably lower than East German needs as conveyed by Ulbricht and Grotewohl. In total, Khrushchev offered an additional 105.5 million rubles in imports, to be paid for with a sum total of 200 million rubles in East German machine goods. Finally, instead of the 130-million-ruble credit in hard currency requested by the SED leaders, Khrushchev offered, "as an exception," to buy a certain amount of East German exports to the Soviet Union with a hard currency sum valued at 75 million rubles. In short, Ulbricht and Grotewohl could expect to receive less than one-sixth of the additional imports and little more than half of the hard currency they needed to make their economic plan for 1955 work. It must have been a particularly trying moment for their faith in the leadership and brotherhood of the Soviet Union.

But just when their economic troubles seemed most insurmountable, the course of international events intervened. By the beginning of May 1954 the Western allies were finalizing arrangements for the signing of the Paris Agreements, under which they confirmed the end of their occupation of West Germany and recognized its sovereignty, thus preparing the Federal Republic to join NATO. With the signing of the agreements imminent, Ulbricht and Grotewohl received a second letter from Khrushchev, one that displayed a noticeable change of heart. As Khrushchev explained, "the Central Committee of the Communist Party of the Soviet Union [considered] it necessary, under the present conditions, to return again to the question of the provisioning of the population of the GDR." The Soviet leader was now prepared to come much closer to accommodating the original SED requests. He promised to make available an additional 62 million rubles in hard currency, a sacrifice that, as he reminded Ulbricht and Grotewohl, required the Soviet Union to sell off some of its gold reserves. The Soviet Union would also deliver an additional fifty thousand tons of wheat to the GDR. Finally, through its foreign diplomats in Eastern Europe, it would encourage the other "people's democracies" to increase their exports of foodstuffs to East Germany. The East Germans would be expected, "as compensation," to increase their shipments of machine goods to the Soviet Union. "In our opinion," Khrushchev wrote, "the assistance to be rendered to the GDR will assure a normal provisioning of the population with foodstuffs in 1955, and with such goods as fat and meat, it will even make possible a certain increase in consumption compared to 1954."[59]

It is impossible to know exactly what Khrushchev meant by "a normal provisioning of the population," but most likely something more modest than the big increases initially heralded by the New Course. Nevertheless, beggars could hardly be choosers. Ulbricht and Grotewohl accepted the offer with alacrity, great thanks, and an obligatory nod to the sacrifices made by the populations of the Soviet Union and the "people's democracies," without which such assistance would not have been possible.[60]

The New Course, now in full eclipse, gave way to preparations for the GDR's Second Five-Year Plan and its return to the priorities of productivism. As Leuschner confirmed to Ulbricht in June 1955, the plan emphasized investment and production increases in energy, mining, chemicals, metallurgy, machine building, and building materials.[61] In contrast, production in light industry and in the food and semiluxuries industries was to be "increased more slowly than [that of] the other branches of industry." Growth in individual consumption would, therefore, be significantly slowed down. As Leuschner made clear, in view of the new priorities, "a further robust increase of the presently achieved standard of living [was] not possible." Instead, economic planners would seek to increase the share of national income devoted to "accumulation" (that is, investment) from 12.7 percent in 1955 to somewhere between 15 and 17 percent annually during the Second Five-Year Plan.

It went almost without saying that the system of food rationing would be maintained. As Leuschner pointed out, "It is planned not to do away with the card system since the removal of the card system cannot be carried out without an increase in card prices."[62] In other words, without raising the prices of rationed goods, there would be an explosion in consumer demand that could never be met. As for increasing prices, he knew that was out of the question, particularly on the heels of the recent and loudly celebrated reductions of the New Course. The regime was stuck; price increases were taboo, and the rationing system would have to remain in place.

Nevertheless, even in Leuschner's report it was apparent that the concerns that had propelled the New Course could not be altogether ignored. For both ideological and power-political reasons, the SED could not escape the question of living standards. Even as they prioritized and understood economic growth primarily in terms of heavy industrial production, SED leaders held firmly to the belief that in the long term, living standards would have to improve, since socialism was by definition more efficient and productive than capitalism. However, what added urgency to the long-term, ideologically based expectations of SED leaders was the problem of West Germany and the challenge it posed in the area of consumer supply. As Leuschner duly explained to Ulbricht, he and his Soviet counterparts had devoted considerable time in Moscow to studying and comparing statistics on living standards in East and West Germany.

The trend recently has been to reassess the pace of prosperity in West Germany during the 1950s. Historians of everyday life have argued that the material fruits of the *Wirtschaftswunder* took longer than previously assumed to trickle down to the households of most West Germans. This reassessment has been part of an ongoing debate about the extent and nature of the "Americanization" of Germany and has served as a warning against projecting a 1960s-style image of modern mass consumption back onto what Arnold Sywottek has called "a society of deprivation, until the mid-1950s."[63] (In fact, there were some contemporary observers who emphasized "the limits of mass consumption" throughout western Europe.)[64]

But prosperity, always relative, is in the eye of the beholder. We must also consider how contemporary East Germans might have perceived the consumption achievements of the young Federal Republic. That they had ample opportunity to do so is beyond doubt. In these years before the building of the Berlin Wall, millions of East Germans were able to visit West Berlin and West Germany annually.[65] On a daily basis, fifty-three thousand "border crossers" (Grenzgänger) from East Berlin and the surrounding countryside went to work in West Berlin.[66] In the late 1950s approximately seventy-five thousand tickets for West Berlin's public transportation were sold against eastmarks every day. Even those East Germans denied official permission to travel to West Germany were able to do so by flying from Tempelhof airport in West Berlin; ten thousand East Germans did so every year to visit relatives. GDR citizens also came regularly to West Berlin for entertainment, enjoying a subsidized 1:1 currency exchange rate for theater, music, museum, and cinema tickets.[67] They came every year to be amazed by the newest, most modern West German industrial products assembled at the annual "German Industrial Exhibition" held in West Berlin. What kind of consumer landscape did East Germans encounter as they strolled through the shopping districts of West Berlin or other West German cities? What would they have seen, touched, and tasted in the homes of West German friends and relatives?

Here, the recent literature on West Germany is most instructive, providing a wealth of information on developing consumption patterns; leisure activities; household budget records; and innovations in packaging, distribution, and marketing. The resulting picture suggests that East Germans visiting the Federal Republic would have been struck by the rise of more sophisticated and aggressive forms of advertising, promoting new, technical kitchen appliances and installment plan purchases.[68] They would have noticed new artificial fibers and fabrics working their way into people's wardrobes, as well as the increasing ubiquity of brand-name items. Associated with higher quality and better hygiene, brand-name goods came prepackaged in enticingly modern and artificial materials like cellophane, polyethylene, aluminum foil, and colored glass. They conveyed a sense of modernity and attested to the pleasure of having been able to splurge.[69] They were also perfectly suited for distribution in the new self-service stores that, though still few in number, held out to the fingertips of consumers impressive, even overwhelming assortments of goods. The innovative stores offered a new freedom of choice; they saved time by freeing people of the need to stand in line.[70] For East Germans still chafing under the limitations imposed by ration cards and shortages, and all too accustomed to long hours spent waiting in line, the new stores must have seemed like the promise of some already partially achieved consumption utopia.

In the homes of friends and relatives they would have noticed several shifts in the balance in food consumption: from rye to wheat bread, margarine to butter, potatoes to meat. They would have seen more tomatoes from Italy, oranges and bananas from southern lands *(Südfrüchte)*, canned fruit and vegetables, and real, fresh coffee.[71] They would have noticed the appearance of more refrigerators, washing machines, and vacuum cleaners.[72] They would have seen television replace the radio as the dominant medium of evening home entertainment. At a more profound level, they might have noted a change in attitudes and assumptions, an attenuation of earlier moral and social constraints on consumption. A certain modesty no longer seemed to hold. As Georg Bergler, a leading West German market researcher, remarked with seeming dismay in 1956,

> Suddenly a great restraining threshold has fallen away. Who, now, would say, "That is not befitting our station"? An uprising would be called forth if we tried to say: "You are a girl of humble station, that does not suit you, you may not do that." Not only this measure of the permissible within a class [*Stand*], for which there is no law, but also morality, custom, tradition, religion, or cultural opinions are now almost entirely devalued.[73]

Bergler painted a picture of a new, modern market for consumer goods, featuring extreme competition, bewildering choice, and vastly differentiated selection. As markets were being "created," shopping patterns changed. As the influence of fashion increased, demand grew ever more mercurial. Consumers shopped more often but bought less per outing. The hardships of scarcity were being replaced by the vague, needling discontents of plenty: an accelerated turnover of desires, a never-ending quest for the new, a projection of inner dissatisfactions on an ever-proliferating array of material objects. In Bergler's words, "We burn today what we still worshipped yesterday." Perhaps most telling was the deceptively naive question he posed: "Why is no one happy today?"[74]

But these were the laments of the sated. From the other side of the iron curtain they could be sorely envied. Once confronted with these developments in West Germany, the SED could hardly return to the gross neglect that had characterized its pre–New Course handling of consumer supply. Its own recognition of this fact was reflected in its efforts to introduce innovations in the sphere of retail, to improve the bureaucratic process of consumer supply, and to compile more-detailed statistics for comparing the standard of living in East and West Germany. None of these tasks had been wholly inaugurated by the New Course, but they all acquired an urgency and coherence from it that continued even as the SED embarked on more austere policies.

Within East Germany's array of retail offerings, two new developments came to fruition in the mid-1950s: the mail-order catalogue and the installment plan. The mail-order catalogue, first introduced in Germany in the interwar years, reemerged in East Germany in the context of the New Course. SED economic planners initially envisioned it as a temporary means of supplying primarily the rural population with manufactured consumer goods. But once the retail net extended sufficiently into the countryside, they imagined, the mail-order catalogue would become superfluous. After a two-year test phase in the counties of Erfurt and Suhl, complemented by study delegations sent to West Germany,[75] the first republic-wide mail-order house opened on May 1, 1956, in Leipzig *(Versandhaus Leipzig)* under the auspices of the *Handelsorganisation.* The opening was accompanied by an extensive propaganda and advertising campaign, especially in the countryside.[76] In its first month, the *Versandhaus* received just under three thousand orders; nine months later, in December, it processed over sixty-seven thousand. In seventeen catalogues and prospects produced over the course of its first year, the *Versandhaus* offered clothing, shoes, kitchen appliances, wallpaper, cameras, children's toys, sporting goods, watches, cosmetics, and leather goods.[77]

The mail-order catalogue was an attempt to inject a greater degree of convenience into the lives of East German consumers, especially those living in thinly populated rural areas with limited shopping options. It also represented a modernizing impulse. Taking West German mail-order businesses such as Neckermann and Quelle as a model, the *Versandhaus* Leipzig tried to make available an equally attractive and modern selection of goods, combined with appropriate ease and time-saving benefits for its customers. For shoppers accustomed to chronic shortages and long lines, the prospect of "shopping" from a catalogue, in the comfort of home, was uniquely appealing. In its slogans, the *Versandhaus* placed special emphasis on these blessings: "shop in the coziness of home, without risk" *(Im behaglichen Heim ohne Risiko einkaufen);* "don't waste time, buy at the *Versandhaus*" *(keine Zeit verlaufen—beim Versandhaus kaufen).*

Nevertheless, the East German mail-order business faced serious obstacles. Since economic planners viewed it as a temporary effort, they neglected to outfit it properly with sufficient storage facilities and other technical equipment, a fact that detracted from its ability to operate efficiently.[78] Its own leaders repeatedly complained of unqualified personnel and poor organization, as a result of which catalogues invariably came out late.[79] Potential customers, meanwhile, had to be won over; they had to be convinced that they could trust the *Versandhaus* to deliver what it offered. But the *Versandhaus* was no more immune to problems in supply than other East German trade organs. Because manufacturers frequently failed to fulfill their orders, or because they delivered goods that differed in quality, style, or price from those items originally agreed upon, the *Versandhaus* was often unable to supply the products it advertised in its catalogues. Orders from customers flowed in but could not be fulfilled.[80] Under these conditions, trust remained elusive. Although by 1958 the *Versandhaus* counted 225,000 registered customers, or 3.3 percent of all East German households, its expected share of total retail sales came to only 0.06 percent. (In West Germany, the mail-order catalogue business accounted for 5 percent of total retail sales.)[81]

With the installment plan the regime had greater success, though its introduction was a source of some controversy. In official socialist thought and propaganda the installment plan traditionally suffered from a bad reputation, associated as it was with deceptive capitalist marketing strategies. The installment plan was believed to exert a corrupting influence: it kept workers in perpetual debt; it charged them unjustly marked-up prices and outrageous interest rates; if workers failed to keep up with their payment schedules, it cheated them out of the money they had paid, since sellers inevitably came to repossess the item purchased. The installment plan was understood primarily as that means by which capitalists tried to overcome the inescapable contradiction between chronic overproduction and the minimal purchasing power of workers who toiled for low wages.[82]

However, in the wake of the June 1953 uprising SED leaders found themselves confronted with increasing requests, in part from workers, to create some kind of consumption credit service to make it easier to buy more expensive consumer goods, such as furniture, radios, rugs, and motorcycles.[83] In the summer of 1953, in that moment of unusual vulnerability, SED leaders acquiesced, calling forth vehement objections from within the regime itself, particularly from finance officials. The Deutsche Investitionsbank protested: "In our economy hire purchases are in principle false. They are a typical result of capitalist overproduction [combined] with the wildest competition for sales hampered by insufficiently solvent demand."[84] But in the GDR, as the bank pointed out, the situation was reversed; there was no overproduction of "the most important consumption goods" but rather a significant shortage of commodities. Allowing installment plan purchases would dangerously inflate demand and consequently incite yet greater criticism of continued shortages in the supply of consumer goods. Besides, the bank continued, there was no installment plan in the Soviet Union, and with good reason: "It does not fit in the socialist economy. Even our Soviet comrades cannot recommend it to us."[85]

But the pressure of the moment proved decisive. In the end, government officials worked out a kind of compromise: the installment plan became a reality, but the banks retained control over the dispensing of credit. In keeping with the set of New Course measures adopted in the fall of 1953, the official ordinance allowing hire purchases in East Germany was adopted in October.[86] Consumers interested in buying on credit now had to arrange the details with their local bank, where they were required to save a down payment of at least 25 percent of the total price for a period of at least ninety days in a special savings account. After the waiting period, the bank loaned the balance to the buyer, who was then able acquire the item in question at whichever retail outlet (HO, *Konsum*, private) he or she desired. The credit limit was DM 2,000; the credit period could last no longer than two years. Payments were usually made on a monthly basis, and the bank charged 6 percent interest on the loan.[87]

Proponents of the new arrangement were careful to differentiate the East German installment plan from those versions available in West Germany, which, they duly reiterated, reflected "capitalist overproduction" and served as a means of "fleecing" the working class.[88] In the GDR, in contrast, credit buying would be a great boon to those in lower-income groups, in particular young married couples, allowing them to acquire furniture and other household items they would otherwise be unable to afford. Moreover, suitable controls were firmly in place to prevent East German citizens from falling into the vicious cycle of debt so ostensibly widespread in West Germany. The circle of goods one could buy on credit was limited to a few durable consumer goods. (In West Germany, clothing too could be bought on credit.) And most important, officials explained, the obligation to save the 25 percent down payment over a minimum ninety-day period helped to inculcate an ethos of saving. In other words, even as East Germans consumed on credit, they would be educated and forced to take part in the virtues of saving. For finance officials, meanwhile, the saving requirement was crucial in that it afforded them control over funds and helped chip away at the chronic monetary overhang.

In fact, in West Germany the installment plan also aroused controversy. Immediately after the June 1948 currency reform, a varied array of institutions emerged to facilitate credit buying; by 1955 33 percent of the West German population bought on credit. Nevertheless, in the early 1950s a "working group for marketing questions," led by the neoliberal economist Wilhelm Röpke, launched a high-profile publicity campaign against the installment plan. Fearful that widespread credit buying would interfere with the market-regulating function of prices, Röpke and the working group raised the specter of a nation of "installment payers" being transformed into one of debtors. "Prussia became great through saving," they insisted, "not through consumption credits."[89] East German officials, meanwhile, were perfectly aware of the West German debate, as well as the real contribution the installment plan made to raising the living standards of West Germans.[90] The objections of naysayers notwithstanding, the installment plan in West

Germany played a crucial role in broadening the circle of those able to benefit from the fruits of the *Wirtschaftswunder.*

In East Germany, on the other hand, the installment plan, as regulated by the October 1953 ordinance, seemed to play a far less significant role. I have been unable to find statistics on the extent to which consumers were able to take advantage of the new ordinance. But clear indications of the limited practice of credit buying in East Germany were the growing stockpiles of excess inventory in furniture. By the summer of 1956 officials in the State Planning Commission were urging trade functionaries to work out measures for the second half of the year to make it easier for consumers to buy furniture, suggesting that retailers themselves might offer consumption credits and that it might even be possible to forgo the initial saving period and allow people to make purchases immediately upon payment of the first installment.[91] Finance officials were quick to raise many of their old objections. Making credit buying easier, they argued, would result in throwing the entire population into debt. It would undermine the ethos of saving. It would inflate demand well beyond the extent to which it could be met by supply and thus exacerbate the monetary overhang. The very elements distinguishing the East German installment plan from its West German counterpart would be lost.[92] And behind these arguments lurked the unspoken objection: if retailers now presided over the installment plan, finance officials would lose control over the dispensing of credit.

Planning Commission and SED leaders, however, were more interested in moving inventory and increasing the share of manufactured commodities (relative to food and semiluxuries) in the overall consumption patterns of East German consumers than they were afraid that their installment plan might share too many similarities with practices in West Germany. In fact, the effort to expand the accessibility of the installment plan was driven by the recognized need to compete with the West German example. Consequently, as of October 1, 1956, East German citizens were allowed to buy on credit directly from state-owned retailers. The ninety-day saving period and the obligatory 25 percent down payment were abandoned, and the credit limit was expanded to DM 3000. To protect consumers from the danger of falling into excessive debt, the credit provided could not exceed 20 percent of the buyer's annual net income.[93]

The results of this loosening of the terms of credit were instantaneous. Installment-plan turnover in the fourth quarter of 1956 came to approximately DM 450 million, comprised of six hundred thousand installment plan contracts. The overwhelming portion of the buyers, nearly 60 percent of whom were workers, belonged to middle-income groups (monthly income between DM 300 and DM 400). Those items bought on credit included furniture (40 percent); radios (35 percent); nonclothing textiles, such as curtains and rugs (12 percent); and other manufactured goods, such as sewing machines and ovens (8 percent). The installment plan proved particularly effective in diminishing stockpiles of excess inventory.[94] In fact, the problem in subsequent months quickly became that of supply, as finance officials had predicted.[95] Nevertheless, installment plan buying continued at a brisk pace in the following year. Of all the furniture bought in state-owned retail, 60 percent was bought on the installment plan; 65 percent of all radio and hi-fi sets were bought on credit, as were 50 percent of all rugs and carpets, and 60 percent of all sewing machines. In total, installment plan turnover for 1957 came to nearly DM 720 million. But more important than the grand total, which amounted only to a little over 2 percent of total retail turnover, was the fact that millions of people were able to make use of credit buying and therefore to satisfy basic but relatively expensive and long-suspended household needs.[96]

The installment plan showed the regime trying to improve its provisioning of consumer goods. Efforts at improvement were also evident in simultaneously pursued organizational changes. At the end of 1955 the Council of Ministers created the new Government Commission for Consumer Goods Production and the Provisioning of the Population. The commission included all the ministers and state secretaries involved in the production and supply of consumer goods. As with previous commissions, this one, too, was supposed to facilitate coordination within the bureaucracy and to work out general problems and disagreements.[97] Indicative of the seriousness with which the SED took the new commission was its placement of no less a figure than Fred Oelßner at its head. A long-standing Communist leader, Oelßner joined SED Politburo in 1950. As the party's leading theoretician, he was the Central Committee's secretary for propaganda and the chief editor of *Einheit*. Like Walter Ulbricht, he was born in Leipzig and grew up in its working class milieu, joining the socialist youth movement towards the end of the First World War at the age of fourteen. His father, Alfred Oelßner, had been an active figure in the local SPD organization before the war. But as the fighting dragged on, Oelßner *père* and Oelßner *fils* joined the Independent Socialists (USPD) and then in 1920 the KPD. A conviction for conspiracy to commit treason landed him in jail between 1923 and 1925. Upon release, he traveled to Moscow, where he studied and taught political economy. After a period of further study and teaching in Paris and Berlin in the early 1930s, he returned to the Soviet Union, where he went under the Russian-sounding name of "Larev" and served as chief editor for German-language broadcasts on Moscow radio. In 1940 he even became a Soviet citizen and member of the Communist Party of the Soviet Union (CPSU), honors that served as sources of immense pride and prestige for German Communists. After returning to Germany with Wilhelm Pieck in July 1945, he immediately assumed leading functions as a KPD, and then SED, ideologist, propagandist, and educator.[98]

It was ironic and telling that Oelßner, first encountered in this study as a voice seeking to subordinate the issue of individual consumption to a diffuse and heady vision of individual needs transcended by the great leap into the realm of socialist freedom, should now preside over a commission charged with addressing those very needs. His own trajectory from a position of willful, ideological unconcern to one of official responsibility for consumer supply neatly described the SED's grudging but growing recognition of the problem it faced in supplying its citizens with consumer goods. And yet, as he took up his duties as head of the new commission at the end of 1955, Oelßner was losing ground within the SED leadership. As a frequent critic of Ulbricht, particularly before the June 1953 uprising, he had done much to alienate the party leader, who for his part had nothing but disdain for Oelßner's "intellectualism." Ulbricht saw to it that Oelßner lost his responsibility for propaganda in July 1954. In April 1955 Oelßner suffered another setback when he lost his position as Central Committee secretary for agitation. Oelßner nevertheless continued over the next few years to criticize Ulbricht for his arrogance and "egoism," for his dictatorial style of rule, and for policies that, he believed, contributed to the growing number of East Germans fleeing to the West. In the wake of Nikita Khrushchev's shocking "secret speech" at the Soviet Union's Twentieth Party Congress in February 1956, in which the Soviet leader denounced Stalin's "cult of personality," Oelßner and several other SED leaders were eager to apply its lessons to the GDR. In fact, Oelßner openly accused Ulbricht of indulging in his own personality cult. Though his position within the leadership was slipping, Oelßner remained a formidable figure until January 1958, when he was finally suspended from the Politburo for his alleged association with the "Schirdewan-Wollweber faction."[99]

As head of the Government Commission for Consumer Goods Production and Provisioning, Oelßner received repeated appeals for help not only from officials in trade but also from those in light industry. At times, they found his a sympathetic ear. At a meeting in July 1956, for example, in which the minister for light industry argued for a larger share of investments during the Second Five-Year Plan, Oelßner was in full agreement, acknowledging that "the investment sum for the Ministry of Light Industry, compared to the total investment sum of the GDR, reveals an underestimation of light industry. Several branches of industry [under] the Ministry for Light Industry have great political and economic significance, above all with regard to the swift rise in the standard of living of our population."[100] The dangers of neglecting light industry were especially evident in the continued problem of East Germans shopping for clothing in West Berlin, which resulted not only in a significant loss of revenue for the state's coffers but also in a loss of legitimacy for the state itself. As one particularly explicit report explained,

> The population hardly judges the worker-and-peasant state according to what it has created in the way of new factories, such as the ironworks in Stalinstadt, but rather according to how it perceives [the state] improving its living conditions, which, next to the provisioning of food, is reflected above all in the qualitatively better and less expensive provisioning of textiles. Here, especially in Berlin, a large part of the population of East Berlin and the surrounding area supplies itself with textiles from West Berlin, which, despite the exchange rate, are less expensive and often more tasteful than ours . . . The effects of shortcomings in the textile industry and the measures of the government in this area present a political situation that should be watched very closely by all members of the state and party apparatus.[101]

As this report and Oelßner's remarks suggest, there was now a perception shared by officials and consumers alike that decent, even fashionable textiles and clothing fell within the realm of basic needs that could no longer justifiably be denied. There could be no excuse for the fact that so many consumers in the GDR's best-provisioned city chose to clothe themselves across the open border.

Nor were the *West-Waren* purchases of East Germans limited to the more fashionable clothing and textiles available in West Berlin. Drawn by the higher quality, greater availability, and—despite the exchange rate—cheaper prices of many Western goods, East Germans regularly bought shoes, spare parts for bicycles, kitchen knives, lightbulbs, razor blades, zippers, toilet paper, children's toys, fashion magazines, bananas, oranges, spices, chocolate, cocoa, and coffee in West Berlin. Officials in East Berlin estimated that in 1954 East Germans were spending approximately DM 200 million (eastmarks) per month in West Berlin.[102] SED leaders were watching intently, assiduously compiling the statistics they needed for detailed comparisons. That the effort was driven by the competition with West Germany was openly admitted. A draft of an earlier ordinance on collecting statistics expressly stated, "The struggle for the peace and reunification of our fatherland is decisively influenced by the improvement in the living conditions [*Lebensverhältnisse*] of the population of the GDR. They must in every respect be elevated above those of West Germany."[103]

But perhaps the most high-profile concern about the standard of living in East Germany now came from the Soviet Union and its Communist Party leadership. In January 1956 Khrushchev openly recognized the economic "battle between socialism and capitalism" taking place on German soil: "There, the borders are simply open, and there is a constant contact with the capitalist world to which the German Federal Republic belongs . . . There, the comparison is made; which [social] order creates better material conditions: that in West Germany or that in East Germany. So stands the question today."[104] The following month Khrushchev delivered his "secret speech." Not only did he denounce Stalin's cult of personality, but he also adopted the doctrine of peaceful coexistence, thus rejecting Lenin's thesis that war, as "the midwife of the revolution," was inevitable. Instead, Khrushchev insisted, there could be a peaceful economic competition between the communist and capitalist worlds, as a result of which communism would be attained through peaceful, perhaps parliamentary, means. The only other alternative—"the most destructive war in history"—

was unacceptable.[105] Fully in keeping with the tenets of peaceful coexistence and economic competition, Khrushchev began to hold up a vision of the GDR as a "showcase" for the East Bloc.[106] The reverse image of this vision was the fear, heightened by West German economic success, that "the FRG could swallow the GDR."[107]

As part of this competition, the East German State Statistical Office was given the task of producing household budget studies based on representative samplings of different social groups within the GDR and of analyzing the income and expenditures of the entire population. In its analyses of the standard of living *(Lebensstandard)*, the Statistical Office took into account many of the categories one might have expected, including the development of real wages, prices, and the cost of living; total and per capita retail sales; imports of semiluxuries; the production of consumer durables; and state expenditures on health, social services, and housing construction. However, East German statisticians had as yet no distinct, explicit concept of the category "standard of living." Only in the late 1950s did East German economic planners begin to propose their own theoretical boundaries for the concept.[108] And only in later years, particularly in the 1970s, did party literature and propaganda present a consistent and distinct explanation of the category, one defined largely as an alternative to that which had emerged in the West, emphasizing, above all, social policies that assured employment, material security, health care, child care, educational opportunities, and easily affordable cultural offerings. But in the 1950s, East German statisticians were primarily interested in the levels of private consumption of material consumption goods. In their textual explanations of the figures and tables they provided, they tended to focus most of their attention on two aspects of the inquiry: the living conditions and consumption trends of East German workers as compared with the prewar period and statistical comparisons of present East and West German living standards.

Far less significant as an alternative point of reference in the minds of officials and population alike were living conditions in the other countries of the Soviet bloc. After all, during the 1950s, the political division of Germany was still an entirely new development; most East Germans continued to view the future of the "German question" as unresolved. Feelings of connection to West Germany, whether viewed in political, cultural, historical, or familial terms, remained preeminent.

The countries of east-central Europe, on the other hand, did not yet feature as prominently as they later would in the experience of most East Germans. Although little research has been done on the subject of East German tourism, there is sufficient evidence showing that only in the late 1950s and 1960s did East Germans begin traveling in large numbers to the "people's democracies."[109] In later years, the regime may have drawn some comfort from the fact that East Germans could view their own living standards as somewhat higher than those in Poland or Czechoslovakia. But in the 1950s such comparisons, to the extent that they were made at all, offered little in the way of stabilizing succor.

If anything, quite the opposite was true, as events in east-central Europe in the mid-1950s, particularly after Khrushchev's secret speech, offered a distinctly cautionary tale about the risks of imposing further hardships on already disgruntled and disaffected populations. In October 1956 popular protests against the government in Poland brought to power Władysław Gomułka, who promised greater independence from the Soviet Union and an end to Stalinist excesses. The following month, revolution erupted in Hungary, only to be violently suppressed by Soviet forces. As Peter Grieder has suggested, Ulbricht's "greatest fear" between 1956 and 1958 was that a "German Gomułka" might emerge to capitalize on popular protests and obtain Soviet approval for a change in leadership. Nor was Ulbricht's fear altogether ungrounded, as the upheavals in Poland and Hungary did inspire limited protests from workers and students in the GDR, raising the specter of another June 17.[110] There was, in short, pressure on the SED leadership from both the West and the East not to lose sight of the enduring imperative of the New Course.

Compared to the standards of the prewar period, the GDR had made undeniable progress during the first Five-Year Plan. The real wages of industrial workers *(Industriearbeiter)*—a category one report identified as "the decisive figure for judging the conditions of the working population [*Werktätigen*]"—had risen above prewar levels.[111] The cost of living for a four-person family (average monthly income of DM 390) had dropped considerably since 1950. And by 1955 retail prices for foodstuffs had fallen even further than the Five-Year Plan had foreseen.[112] Consequently, in 1955, ten years after the end of the war, East German consumption of butter, margarine, and sugar exceeded 1936 levels. The consumption of eggs and meat (a traditional indicator of living conditions in Germany) nearly equaled those levels. Conversely, the consumption of bread and potatoes, hitherto expanded due to shortages in meat and eggs, gradually sunk to prewar levels.[113] On the other hand, East German consumption of textiles, clothing, and many semi-luxuries remained well below 1936 levels.[114]

More important, comparisons with West Germany shed unfavorable light on East German achievements. Since retail prices in general and in every individual category of consumer goods (excepting rent, gas, and electricity) were higher in East Germany, the overall cost of living remained higher than that in West Germany. Taking 1936 prices as a basis, East German statisticians calculated that textiles and clothing were more than twice as expensive, semiluxuries were nearly twice as expensive, and foodstuffs, though still partly rationed, were in general about one-third more expensive in the GDR than in the FRG.[115] Meanwhile, West Germany in 1955 was importing six times more fruit *(Südfrüchte)*, three to four times more coffee, and four times more cocoa per head than East Germany. (For the first time, in 1955, the GDR imported more tea.) Finally, the Statistical Office noted the still early but swiftly widening gap between East and West German production of new consumer durables, in particular, television sets. In 1955, West Germany had produced over 300,000 TVs, while East Germany had produced only 38,610.[116]

East German achievements in the area of individual consumption were hardly negligible, particularly in view of the regime's overwhelming emphasis on heavy industrial production, combined with the vast resources extracted by the Soviets under the umbrella of reparations. But as the tempo of prosperity in West Germany began to accelerate, the West German example came to displace memories of the prewar years as a point of reference for regime and population alike. This shift was most dramatically evident in the dangerously upward trend in the number of refugees fleeing to West Germany.[117] If for that reason alone, the New Course, even in full eclipse, remained an enduring imperative. But, in fact, the cause of consumer supply had come to enjoy a legitimacy it had never known before the New Course, buoyed in part by Khrushchev's vision of the GDR as a showcase for socialism. In their subsequent appeals for aid from the Soviet Union, for example, SED leaders could now explicitly invoke the running competition with West Germany to leverage their pleas for material help. As the SED Central Committee explained to Khrushchev in May 1956, "a worsening of the provisioning" compared to 1955 would, "in view of the competition with West Germany, have very alarming results."[118] Moreover, the very task of consumer supply had become more elevated in nature, as traditional needs (bread, potatoes, work clothes) were increasingly joined by newer demands (fashionable clothing, refrigerators, TVs). At mid-decade the East German regime found itself in a precarious position, having embarked on a return to productivism after legitimizing concessions to consumerism. Nowhere within the SED state were these conflicting impulses more apparent than in the unhappy relationship between trade and industry.

CHAPTER 5

Demand Research and the Relations between Trade and Industry

The antagonistic contradiction between production and market is therefore alien to the planned development of the economy.

Der Handel, June 1952

In the course of the last century the attempt to understand consumer behavior gave rise to exceedingly fertile fields of scholarly and commercial inquiry. Whether motivated by disinterested, "scientific" curiosity or practical business interest, economists, social scientists, and professional market researchers developed an array of sophisticated quantitative and qualitative methods for analyzing and predicting how people shop, what they buy, why they buy what they buy, and how they might even be made to buy things they never intended buying. Market research evolved into a "science," a profession, an indispensable tool in the complex processes of producing, marketing, merchandising, and consuming commodities in modern societies. And yet it is also something about which we know astonishingly little. Its methods remain arcane and mysterious to most people, at times arousing suspicion and distrust. Its past is an amorphous expanse only beginning to acquire basic definition.[1] The subject of market research in the socialist countries of the Soviet bloc is terrain even more obscure.[2]

How, in the absence of a Western-style market mechanism, did socialist states understand and negotiate the complex relationship between supply and demand? How did economic planners attempt to observe and respond to the frequently, and often hollowly, invoked "ever-increasing material and cultural needs" of consumers? How did they define "needs" and "demand"? To what extent were they able to predict and, as they openly hoped, guide consumer demand? This chapter addresses these questions by exploring the development of "demand research" *(Bedarfsforschung)* in East Germany in the 1950s. Emerging with the step-by-step loosening of ration controls, East German demand research was the means by which trade-and-provisioning planners hoped both to know consumer demand and to pass that knowledge on to the production ministries. Backed by the irrefutable data of their research, officials in the Ministry for Trade and Provisioning hoped they would be better able to represent the demands of consumers vis-à-vis industry and as a result fulfill (if not "overfulfill") their sales plans. That, at any rate, was the idea. As we shall see, a host of obstacles intervened to frustrate their goals; foremost among these obstacles was the continued ability of industry to neglect the demands of domestic trade.

This is not the place for a detailed reconstruction of the history of market research in Germany.[3] Nevertheless, it is necessary to trace briefly the main lines of its development, which, like so many markers of modernity in German history, have their beginnings in the years immediately following the First World War. The best firsthand account of the early years is the chronicle provided by Georg Bergler, a leading practitioner in the field before and after the Second World War.[4] According to Bergler, the first tentative, uncoordinated efforts in market research were initiated by manufacturers of consumer goods and professional advertisers after the end of World War I, when entrepreneurs and advertisers began to analyze their markets more systematically by employing customer questionnaires, testing reactions to new brand-name products, and incorporating the findings of psychology and sociology. The impulse to do so grew out of the turbulence into which wartime and postwar economic difficulties had thrown traditional markets. By the mid-1920s, the influence of American advertising agencies and consultants in Germany also played an important role in these early developments. In addition, there emerged a body of specialized "scientific" literature on the subject, supported by several trade journals and by the Institute for the Observation of the Economy of German Finished Goods *(Institut für Wirtschaftsbeobachtung der deutschen Fertigware)*, founded in 1925.[5]

The institute's founder, Wilhelm Vershofen, deserves more than anyone to be designated the father of German "consumption research" *(Verbrauchsforschung or Konsumforschung)*. Vershofen's posthumous reputation is mixed. Former colleagues were filled with respect and admiration; Bergler described him as an important innovator, "the intellectual heart" of his institute, even as the "master and founder of European market research."[6] Historians interested in the pre–World War II career of Ludwig Erhard, whom Vershofen employed at the institute, have been more equivocal: some treat him seriously but acknowledge that he was "a prickly customer" and "not the easiest of masters to serve";[7] others write him off as an ungifted and unimportant economist, a dilettante who also wrote novels.[8] He was above all a man who straddled the worlds of business and the university, first making his reputation as the director of the Association of German Household-Porcelain Works *(Verband Deutscher Porzellangeschirrfabriken)*. In 1923 he was called to a professorship at the Nuremberg Hochschule für Wirtschafts- und Sozialwissenschaften, where, in 1925, he created the Institut für Wirtschaftsbeobachtung.[9]

The institute, like its creator, was as devoted to scholarship, research, and instruction as it was to their practical uses in the business world. It served, therefore, as a meeting point for market researchers, advertisers, and salesmen. From the very beginning Vershofen was clear that consumption research needed to be embedded in the larger task of marketing *(Absatzwirtschaft)*. He was particularly interested in the more obscure motives and irrational impulses behind consumer behavior. In Bergler's view, his was a kind of "motivational research" before the name, preceding by decades that brand of analysis associated most closely with Dr. Ernest Dichter and made so well known (and infamous) in the 1950s through Vance Packard's best-selling "exposé," *The Hidden Persuaders*. Most probably influenced by Georg Simmel, Vershofen believed that at the most basic level people were driven by the simultaneous and competing needs for conformity and distinction, for belonging and withdrawal.[10] In a book that appeared in 1930, *Wirtschaft als Schicksal und Aufgabe*—its title played on Walter Rathenau's famously melancholy observation that "the economy is our fate"—Vershofen wrote, "From the relations to the whole there arises the need for recognition [*Geltungsbedürfnis*] that, in turn, appears in the double quality as the need for adapting [*Angleichungsbedürfnis*] and as the need for standing out [*Abhebungsbedürfnis*] (based in the drive for acceptance and the drive for distinction)."[11] It was the job of market research to hold in view this "polar tension" between the individual and the community and, in doing so, to probe the deeper motives guiding consumer behavior.

In Vershofen's thinking and practical work the task of consumption research acquired even greater urgency with the onset of the Great Depression. He believed that the study of consumption and marketing would help avoid, or minimize, the problems of overproduction and mass unemployment and that the only way out of the slump was to increase the purchasing power and spending of consumers.[12] These were unpopular ideas under Nazi rule. Nevertheless, the institute maintained its commitment to consumption research, establishing in 1935 the only institution of its kind in Germany: the Society for Consumption Research *(Gesellschaft für Konsumforschung)*, led by Vershofen, Erich Schäfer, and Ludwig Erhard. The society counted among its members individual scholars, businessmen, advertisers, and business associations. It held conferences and seminars, and it carried out research projects at the behest of companies as well as its own scholarly impulses.[13]

Among the society's most important innovations was its organization of consumption "correspondents." The society divided the entire country into a collection of "correspondent districts" *(Korrespondenten-Bezirke)*, based on the most important economic and sociological characteristics of particular regions. Each district was assigned one correspondent or in some cases two if a district was very densely populated. The entire system, which initially required approximately five hundred correspondents, allowed the society to develop its famous purchasing-power map of Germany. The correspondents' training consisted of intermittent weekend seminars and printed materials distributed by the society, with the help of which they carried out extensive interviews *(Befragungsgespräche)* with consumers. Depending on the project in question, the society would usually have its correspondents carry out between five and ten thousand "representative" interviews nationwide.[14] According to Bergler, the society did meet certain obstacles, including a general skepticism about the uses of its work, official suspicion on the part of the Gestapo, and the Nazi regime's increasing subordination of consumption to other economic priorities, especially the rearmament effort, which began in earnest in the mid-1930s. Still, the society was able to continue and develop its work nearly right up to the end of the war. After the Anschluss it had even expanded its activity; by 1941 it counted within its purview eight hundred "consumption districts."[15]

After the war, the society resumed its work in the Western zones of occupation. The society's approach, with its emphasis on the deeper psychological motives driving consumer behavior, soon regained preeminence, buoyed by the vogue of Ernest Dichter's "motivational research." The Germans, after all, could (and did) claim to have practiced it for decades. Developments in East Germany, of course, took quite a different turn.

Already by the beginning of the 1950s, the SED leadership had realized that some form of market research was needed to help bring production and consumption into smoother alignment with each other. Most immediately, it was necessary to overcome the chronic, embarrassing problem of the so-called *Überplanbestände* (inventories in excess of the plan), a phenomenon that has since come to be recognized as one of the signature paradoxes of Soviet-type economies: alongside chronic shortages in consumer goods there existed large stockpiles of conspicuous waste, items which remained unsold because they were of poor quality, were considered too expensive or unfashionable, or came in the wrong styles, sizes, colors, and so on. In East Germany, from the very beginning, even as most consumer goods continued to be rationed and conditions of extreme austerity prevailed, the fledgling planned economy delivered piles of unwanted merchandise. As Grete Wittkowski openly admitted in the pages of *Einheit*, "commodities are produced for which there is actually no demand."[16]

Wittkowski was one of the few women in East Germany to have achieved a leading position within the state apparatus. She was Bruno Leuschner's deputy in the DWK and the Ministry of Planning (the precursor to the State Planning Commission). She had studied economics in Berlin and Basel, receiving her doctorate in 1934. A Zionist since the age of twelve, she began to study Marxism-Leninism in the early 1930s and joined the KPD in September 1932. During the Nazi years she moved back and forth between Switzerland and Berlin, carrying out "small jobs" for the party and editing party propaganda. She spent the war in England and returned to Berlin in 1946. At the time she was writing about *Überplanbestände* in late 1951, her position within the apparatus had slipped as a result of the Stalinist purge of "Zionist conspirators" then sweeping through the Soviet bloc.[17] Now serving as the president of the Association of Consumer Cooperatives (VdK),

Wittkowski fully recognized that the failures of the planning apparatus were a source of serious embarrassment for the SED. Socialism, as party leaders genuinely believed and endlessly repeated, would not only provide greater social justice than capitalism but would also enhance economic efficiency, all awkward evidence to the contrary notwithstanding. The problem of *Überplanbestände* was further complicated by a combination of recent wage increases and price reductions in the HOs. As Wittkowski suggested, "Our workers, though they possess sufficient purchasing power to satisfy their demand, do not find the goods they desire to purchase."[18] Conspicuously absent from the planning equation was a real "analysis of demand." The task was clear and simple: "to determine the demand and the desires of our population at the lowest levels of trade, and to see that what is produced corresponds to this demand. Today this is not the case."[19] In short, Wittkowski was calling for an enlistment of socialist retail (HOs and consumer co-ops) in the task of ascertaining consumer demand. It was those who worked in retail, after all, who had the closest view of the desires of consumers.

Wittkowski was hardly the sole driving force behind the development of East German demand research. In fact, she was giving expression to sentiments that had been aired several months previously at a meeting of the SED Central Committee, where party leaders assessed the results of the first months of the Five-Year Plan.[20] In their discussions it became abundantly clear that the combination of growing purchasing power resulting from wage increases and price reductions, the expanding *Überplanbestände,* and the ongoing step-by-step process of removing individual consumer items from the constraints of rationing made it necessary to establish some means of monitoring the selling and buying of consumer goods within the planned economy. Officials in trade, for their part, greeted the new task with enthusiasm. In fact, for years they had themselves been calling for the creation of a system of market research.[21] While they shared the hopes of SED leaders that such a system would help rationalize the relationship between production and consumption, they also hoped that it would provide them with the data they needed to press their demands more forcefully on manufacturers of consumer goods. Such a system, in other words, was seen as a prerequisite for strengthening the position of trade in relation to industry.

Building the system of demand research was a gradual process beginning in early 1952 under the guidance of Werner Kelch, head of the newly created Department of Demand Research within the Ministry for Trade and Provisioning.[22] As Kelch explained in January 1952, "For retail trade the most important side of demand research is the observation of the unsatisfied demand of the population . . . More than ever retail must turn its ear to the consumer, the salesman must follow closely the demands of customers and pay careful attention to their observations and desires."[23] At every stage the East Germans were careful to distinguish their own demand research from "bourgeois market research," which they derided as a "tool of the class struggle," employed by the ruling class to increase profits and intensify the exploitation of the proletariat.[24] According to Kelch, demand research was to be carried out daily, in a systematic manner, on a scientific basis. Most ambitiously, demand research would seek not merely to follow the mysterious and complex variations in consumer demand but also to exert an active influence on it, thus performing "a demand-guiding function."[25] As we have seen, this last professed goal could draw on both Nazi and Soviet precedents, but it was the Soviet example that featured in East German sources and discussions.[26] They did not specify exactly how the research would help to guide consumer demand. Nor is it clear how seriously trade functionaries took the goal of guiding demand. In these early years of East Germany's history, the belief in the efficacy of scientific planning in all aspects of social and economic life was still widely held within and outside the ranks of officialdom. At the very least, proclaiming the goal was viewed as a necessary part of legitimizing the task.

But what did the East Germans mean when they spoke of "demand"? As an economic category, East German demand bore little resemblance to what Western economists understand by the term. The difference had partly to do with the different roles played by prices in socialism and capitalism. In capitalism, prices fulfill allocating and communicating roles; they reflect scarcity (supply and demand) and indicate the extent to which particular products are profitable. In contrast, prices in East Germany performed neither of these roles. Rather than reflect supply and demand, prices were supposed to reflect costs, though in truth the prices for most basic consumer goods had to be subsidized for political reasons as the costs of labor and raw materials increased. As a result, the information conveyed by market prices was lost, and the plan took over the task of allocating goods and services.

The East German understanding of demand was further complicated by the alternating use of two different German words, *Nachfrage*
and *Bedarf*. The first is generally used in the standard phrase, supply
and demand *(Angebot und Nachfrage)*. The second term, *Bedarf*, is very
close to *Nachfrage* but also connotes need, *(Bedürfnis)* and is therefore
used to express demand for specific commodities. As such, *Bedarf* represented needs appearing in the marketplace already shaped by certain factors, such as purchasing power, sex, age, taste, and fashion. But
Bedarf differed from *Nachfrage* in two other ways as well: first, in being
closer to *Bedürfnis*, it occupied a higher moral ground; second, it was a
quantity to be determined by authorities or suppliers. Thus, East German demand researchers very often spoke of *Bedarfsermittlung* or "demand inquiry." Where *Bedarf* was calculable, *Nachfrage* was mercurial;
where *Bedarf* could be planned, *Nachfrage* had to be accommodated. It
is perhaps most useful to see *Bedarf* as occupying a space between *Nachfrage* and *Bedürfnis*, as a metaphor for the regime's ambivalent, ongoing
struggle with a consumer demand it needed to keep within limits but
also desired to satisfy. Of course, the connection between *Bedarf* and
consumers could hardly be ignored. For their part, East German officials, in practice, often used *Bedarf* and *Nachfrage* interchangeably, recognizing demand as a dynamic, complex, and varied phenomenon,
anything but stable.

How was "systematic demand research" supposed to work? According to guidelines produced by Kelch, published in *Der Handel*, and
passed down to local trade organs, the process began in the individual
retail outlet and extended all the way to the upper reaches of the planning bureaucracy.[27] Retail sales personnel had the daily task of writing
down the comments and criticisms of customers on specially prepared
note slips. To ensure prompt attention to problems, they were obliged
to include the date on which the note was taken and their own names
as note-takers. They were to classify complaints as either common and
ongoing or one-time only, as coming from regular customers or ran-
dom passersby, as justified or unjustified in the context of the store and
its assortment of goods. Signs were to be posted in the stores, prompt-
ing customers to make sure that employees were writing down their
comments. Every week's accumulated notes were then to be discussed
at store meetings or "demand consultations" *(Bedarfsberatungen)*, where
employees discussed the notes they had taken as well as the comments

written down by customers in the so-called desire and complaint books *(Wunsch- und Beschwerdebücher)* supplied and maintained on the selling floor by the stores.[28]

At every level of the bureaucracy, trade functionaries were to address a prescribed set of concerns: achieved satisfaction of demand *(Bedarfs-deckung)*, attitudes of customers to commodity supply, unexpected changes in demand and their causes, and measures taken to overcome shortcomings in commodity supply. The information would make its way finally to the Department for Demand Research in the Ministry for Trade and Provisioning, which would in theory be able to piece together a coherent view of consumer demand, the extent to which it was being satisfied, and the measures required for improving the provisioning of the population.[29] And, in fact, the reports produced at the local levels did enable the department to summarize their findings, incorporate them into the ministry's overall commodity supply plans, and submit the information to the State Planning Commission on a regular basis.

The summaries produced by the department conveyed essential, if often sobering, information, ranging from the general to the specific, from the basic to the more nuanced. For example, reporting on demand research to the State Planning Commission in February 1953, that is, in the midst of the provisioning crisis brought on by the regime's decision to accelerate the tempo of the construction of socialism, Kelch highlighted many of the shortfalls in the supply of foodstuffs.[30] Yet, even at this moment, with food items becoming increasingly scarce, Kelch also devoted attention to questions one might have considered less pressing.[31] In his discussion of leather shoes, for example, he began by noting that the supply had been helped substantially by the availability of imports (from where he did not say). The imported shoes sold quickly; they were "much desired." Customers repeatedly praised their high quality. However, moving easily from the issue of quality to that of fashion, he also made a point of adding, "In this connection it has been pointed out that *our products are often behind the imported products in their fashion development.*" Getting more specific, he continued, "Now, as before, in men's and women's shoes the sporty models are most in demand, especially brown colors, *California* models, and pumps. Already the demand for spring and summer models has set in, with a particular emphasis on fashionable colors and styles."[32] Of course, in February 1953 neither Kelch nor anyone else in East Germany had an inkling of the uprising to come. Nevertheless, one is struck—despite the characteristically neutral, bureaucratic tone—by the range of information supplied through the system of demand research, even at this moment of mounting crisis in the provisioning of the population.

In less acute moments, the reports generally monitored the influence of seasonal changes on consumer demand; they took note of the price ranges most desired for particular commodities; they observed that consumers were willing at times to pay higher prices for better-quality goods, particularly if they were imported from West Germany or other Western countries.[33] The reports showed how the available supply of goods might induce variations or substitutions in consumer demand (for instance, the greater the amount of fresh food items available, the lower the demand for canned goods). The reports also passed on complaints about faulty merchandise and shortcomings in commodity supply. Frequently they made reference to ugly scenes in which frustrated shoppers became outright nasty.[34]

But what the reports failed to provide was a clear picture of these customers, nasty or polite, real or imagined. Skulking in the background as faint shadows behind the abstract categories of demand and purchasing power, consumers did not appear as identifiable embodied beings. Beyond the most basic differentiation of demand according to age, sex, and region, there was no sustained, systematic attempt to break down consumers and their desires into discrete groups according to income, occupation, level of education, or any other typology that might have provided a fuller image of the carriers of demand. Here, demand researchers may have been victims of official ideology: how could a state ostensibly devoted to breaking down social divisions reinforce them by catering to a stratified set of habits, tastes, and mentalities of consumption?

Nor did the reports take the research project beyond the actual sale of commodities. That is, there was little attention to how people consumed. Were shoppers happy with their purchases? What might their purchases have meant to consumers? What deeper psychological processes may have been at work?[35] These questions were not asked. The limited criteria of fulfilling specific plans encouraged a narrow focus on the rate and extent of sales turnover. Demand researchers took no interest in the postpurchase relationship between a commodity and its consumer. Perhaps the emphasis on *Bedarf* instead of *Nachfrage* reinforced a neglect of these questions. It is hardly surprising, therefore, that the research failed to play its assigned role in the task of demand guidance (*Bedarfslenkung* or *Bedarfsbildung*). The sad irony for demand researchers was the fact that two of the most important factors influencing demand—wages and prices—were largely beyond the control of the ministry under whose auspices they labored. Any true description of the process by which consumer demand emerged must take into account the regime's overall amalgam of planning, improvisation, and attempts (successful and unsuccessful) to respond to the demands of consumers. We will return to this problem at the end of the chapter.

In the meantime, officials in the Ministry for Trade and Provisioning soon faced a problem of a more immediate and galling nature. As a report from the Association of Consumer Cooperatives explained, "We cannot help gaining the impression that the demand investigations carefully compiled by us from the sales level do not receive the necessary consideration from the responsible ministries ... In order that the entire demand research not become a [merely] formal affair, we are obliged, and our stores demand, to be informed of the measures introduced for the realization of the desires [of consumers]."[36] At the crux of the whole endeavor was the extent to which the results of demand research actually influenced the production of consumer goods. Were that influence to prove chimerical, the entire effort would have been little more than an exercise in futility. What recourse did trade possess in the event of indifference on the part of industry?

In practice such indifference was hardly hypothetical, nor was it infrequent. Trade officials had been complaining for years about manufacturers delivering to wholesalers and retailers merchandise that arrived late, was faulty, or consisted of goods that simply hadn't been ordered. Repeatedly, they had insisted on the need for trade to assume a more assertive role in its relations with industry, as well as greater initiative in its knowledge of and advocacy for the demands of consumers. The two tasks were seen as inextricably connected.[37] With the complexities arising from the removal of items from rationing controls, the expansion of the HO, and the lowering of its prices, the relationship between trade and industry cried out for a fixed and articulated mode of regulation. By the summer of 1951, complaints from trade about industry failing to fulfill its agreements, combined with articles in the press reflecting those complaints, forced leading officials in the State Planning Commission to address the situation.[38]

Over the course of the following months they drafted the outlines of a legal system of contracts for regulating relations between the various economic entities throughout the economy. The results of their efforts were two laws adopted in December 1951, the first providing for the terms of the contracts and the second for creating a set of courts to adjudicate any disputes which might arise.[39] According to the first law, all contracts were required to be in keeping with already approved economic plans. In the event of one party's failure to meet the terms of a contract, the law provided for the application of contract penalties. It also allowed for the possibility of changing contracts in response to changes in economic plans. The second law provided for the establishment of a system of contract courts at the central and regional levels to preside over contract disputes.[40] Because their jurisdiction covered the economy as a whole, cutting across the activities of nearly all state ministries, the courts functioned under the Council of Ministers. The council appointed the president of the Central State Contract Court; the president, in turn, appointed all of the judges on the court, as well as the directors (presiding judges) of the fifteen district courts.

The authority of the courts was broadly conceived, extending into that area where adjudicating disputes overlapped with overseeing the implementation of economic plans. The courts could not only order an enterprise to comply with an existing contract but also change that contract if they judged that it contradicted a plan. The central court could go a step further, recommending changes to the plan itself in light of difficulties revealed by a particular case.[41] In a limited sense, therefore, the courts had considerable leeway in resolving disputes. There was no need to confine their role to deciding whether one party had violated the terms of a legally binding contract. If necessary, for economic or political reasons, the courts could simply change the contracts. In the larger sense, however, that leeway was constrained by the Council of Ministers and its economic and political priorities. The courts, in other words, constituted yet another malleable instrument in the hands of the SED leadership, to be employed in enforcing the priorities of the moment.

For those working in trade, the contract system was initially seen as a great boon, as an opportunity for increasing the influence of trade on industry and thus for helping to ensure a supply of "demand and quality-appropriate" consumer goods.[42] But these initial hopes were soon disappointed as reports began almost immediately to flow in, highlighting the failures of manufacturers to meet the terms of contracts. As a May 1952 report from the Brandenburg Association of Consumer Cooperatives pointed out in frustration, "The introduction of the contract system with the imposition of contract penalties is supposed to ensure that the contract partners fulfill with the utmost care the tasks incumbent upon them and take all the steps necessary to make sure that the preconditions for the fulfillment of contracts have been created."[43] And yet, as the report made clear, the fulfillment of first-quarter contracts for textiles fell well below the commodity supply plans, in some categories by as much as almost 50 percent. As a result, the consumer co-ops were unable to fulfill their own sales plans. For their part, manufacturers complained of not receiving the necessary raw materials to produce the goods required by the plans. Hence the report's reference to the "preconditions" necessary for fulfillment.

The report was typical. Disillusionment with the contact system soon found expression in the pages of *Der Handel.* By the summer of 1952, the editors were complaining about "shortcomings in the application of the contract system" and "insufficient influence on production."[44] A little over a year later, one writer depicted a system awash in paperwork and bureaucracy, serving little purpose, since most cases were thrown out anyway as enterprises convinced the courts of their inability to meet their contracts due to a chronic lack of promised materials.[45] Subsequent reports in the following years testified to an unchanging deadlock. From the perspective of trade, the system failed to protect its interests; even retailers and wholesalers paid it increasingly less attention, since it afforded no remedy for what trade functionaries alone seemed to recognize as "the political significance" of shortcomings in the supply of consumer goods.[46] Although this apparent disaffection brought on charges that trade failed to apply the contract system with sufficient vigor, even officials in the SED and the Planning Commission had to acknowledge that its ability to do so was seriously complicated by the role played by industry in canceling contracts and delivering unacceptable merchandise.[47]

It was no doubt true that in many cases bottlenecks in the supply of materials interfered with the ability of manufacturers to meet the terms of their contracts with trade organs. Nevertheless, lack of materials was hardly the whole story, and with constant repetition the refrain came to strain the credulity of SED leaders themselves. In fact, as students of Soviet-type economies have long known, there were other important factors hindering a "demand-appropriate" flow of consumer goods from producers to retailers. Perhaps most important was the lack of incentive on the part of state-owned manufacturers to perform as required. The shortage economy created a seller's market, as a result of which individual enterprises felt no real compulsion to perform based on a fear of losing buyers to competitors. Neither the danger of incurring losses nor the potential appeal of making profits played a motivating role.[48] In fact, in some respects, enterprises had a distinct interest in underperforming as a means of avoiding more demanding plans in the future. In other words, the individual firm had a clear interest in receiving from superior authorities as easy a plan as possible and as great a supply of materials and labor as possible. Performing "too well" was a disadvantage because it encouraged central planners in the future to maintain, if not increase, the pressure on the firm to show optimum output with minimum inputs. The result was a perpetual process of vertical bargaining within the system, in the course of which information about production capacity and input requirements became increasingly distorted.[49] And beyond the level of the actual enterprise, that is, within the ascending hierarchy of the administrative planning bureaucracy, planners were most concerned with increasingly abstract aggregate indicators and broader categories of production value, to the obvious neglect of the vast quantity of itemized details pertinent to satisfying the particular desires of consumers for particular kinds of consumer goods, their styles, sizes, designs, colors, and so on. Here, meeting the plan meant meeting the target for aggregate output. Lost was the finer focus required for the particularities and vicissitudes of the consumer economy.

Contributing significantly to the weakness of trade in its relations with industry was its inability to present a united front. Had all trade organs been able to maintain a shared steadfastness in their demands, they might have been able to put more pressure on manufacturers of consumer goods to comply with the contracts as written, for example, by simply rejecting unacceptable deliveries. Within the ranks of trade there were certainly calls to do so.[50] In practice, there were instances where deliveries were rejected, but they were rare. The seller's market allowed manufacturers to find buyers elsewhere if their original contract partners refused to accept what they had to offer. The refusers, meanwhile, ran the risk of losing those refused manufacturers as suppliers in the future.

The ease with which manufacturers found other buyers was in no small part due to structural divisions within the edifice of East German domestic trade. Put more precisely, at the beginning of the 1950s the Ministry for Trade and Provisioning, though it presided over the HO and the Association of Consumer Cooperatives, did not possess monopoly control over the distribution of consumer goods. Instead, it shared this task with wholesalers over whom it had zero control and private retailers, who in 1952 still accounted for nearly 30 percent of total retail sales.[51] At the time of the introduction of demand research and the contract system, East German wholesale trade was divided between private wholesalers and state-owned wholesalers, with the state-owned under the authority of the industrial ministries responsible for the production of the goods they distributed.[52] Although by 1952 the significance of private wholesale was rapidly declining, it maintained a share in wholesale turnover that hovered between 4 and 5 percent for most of the decade.[53] Although seemingly small, that share was large enough to help manufacturers and the industrial ministries under which they operated to get around the contract system. Meanwhile, state-owned wholesalers, organized in a series of "German Trade Centers" (*Deutsche Handelszentralen* or DHZs) trading in both capital and consumer goods, functioned much more as representatives of the industrial ministries than they did as representatives of trade.[54]

Consequently, when state-owned retailers (HOs and consumer co-ops) tried to reject deliveries of goods that failed to meet the terms of already accepted contracts, the DHZs could turn around and sell those goods to private retailers. In a typical report from June 1952, for example, the Ministry for Trade and Provisioning complained of the DHZ-Textiles taking commodities rejected by the HO for not meeting contract requirements and selling them to private retailers. "As a result," the report bemoaned, "the purpose of the contract system in relation to industry is not applied; on the contrary, the DHZ, which is under the Ministry for Light Industry, has come into the possession of additional profit margins through which the profitability of the trade center [the DHZ] is improved."[55] Three months later, a report from the State Commission for Trade and Provisioning characterized private retail as a "safety valve" (*Ventil*) for industry in those instances in which the HO and the consumer co-ops rejected its deliveries. The DHZ, meanwhile, seemed "to support the unsatisfactory work of industry without any concern for the interests of the population."[56] As even one DHZ functionary admitted in early 1954, the industrial ministries "viewed the DHZs placed under them as their sales organ (*Absatzorgan*)."[57]

Within the ranks of trade there soon emerged calls for transferring control of wholesale trade in consumer goods from the industrial ministries to the Ministry for Trade and Provisioning, especially after the June 1953 uprising. At the crucial Fifteenth Conference of the SED Central Committee in July 1953, Elli Schmidt, in her capacity as head of the State Commission for Trade and Provisioning, emphatically endorsed the transfer: "Then the state wholesale organ will no longer try to sell what industry produces, but will instead force industry to produce in a manner corresponding to the actual demand and desires of the population."[58] By October 1953 the Council of Ministers was considering a draft of a directive on the transfer as part of the New Course. The draft explicitly recognized the need for a "better and demand-appropriate supply of retail" and a "strengthened influence of trade on the production of commodities of individual consumption."[59] The transfer, however, took time. Not until the end of 1954 and the beginning of 1955 did the responsibilities of the DHZs for consumer goods pass into the hands of the Ministry for Trade and Provisioning, receiving new form as a series of "Wholesale Branches" (*Großhandelskontore* or GHKs).[60] Yet even this new arrangement failed to achieve the desired end. The GHKs, it turned out, were sufficiently numerous and varied in their administrative ties to allow industry to elude any significant pressure from trade. Meanwhile, private wholesale maintained its 4 percent share in wholesale turnover. In addition, the consumer co-ops possessed their own wholesale organs. As a report from the State Planning Commission concluded in June 1958, the coexistence of these many different kinds of wholesale "[hindered] the necessary influence of trade on the production of consumer goods and as a result the safety of a stable and continuous provisioning of the population."[61]

Finally, there existed still another distribution outlet for consumer goods over which the Ministry for Trade and Provisioning had no control: the so-called industry stores (*Industrieläden*). Serving as retail outlets for specific state-owned enterprises, the industry stores were placed under the authority of the industrial ministries to which those enterprises belonged. The first stores began to open at the end of 1952 and the beginning of 1953, though planning for them had begun over a year earlier.[62] According to a set of early guidelines, the stores had a double task: first, to bring producers and consumers closer together by giving industry direct access to the needs and wants of consumers; and second, to provide a model assortment of consumer goods, showing by virtue of its own exemplary performance the possibilities for retail that were ostensibly neglected by the other trade organs. In other words, the industry stores were to serve as the embodiment of an implicit, standing reproach of those trade organizations under the authority of the Ministry for Trade and Provisioning.[63] How else could the fledgling East German state show that shortcomings in consumer supply were due not to any factors associated with its new and much loved state-owned industries but rather to failures on the part of trade, a sector of the economy far less dear to the hearts of SED leaders?

The actual share of total retail sales taken over by the industry stores was hardly significant, ascending to a plateau of 0.4 percent from 1955 to 1959. The stores sold mostly textiles, clothing, and "other manufactured goods," though they also sold foodstuffs and semiluxuries.[64] Located in large cities, they never grew vastly in number. By September 1953 there were only four in Berlin: a shoe store, a leather-goods store, a fabric store, and a clothing store. For the following year city officials planned to open ten more stores.[65] By March 1955 there were a total of only seventy-nine industry stores throughout East Germany.[66] Nor did they always live up to the high standards articulated in their official guidelines.[67] Nevertheless, even at this limited scale, they acted as a thorn in the side of the Ministry for Trade and Provisioning. The problem was partly symbolic, a matter of prestige. There was, for instance, considerable bureaucratic wrangling in the fall and winter of 1953 over the allotment of retail space in the Stalinallee, East Berlin's showcase avenue of socialist prosperity.[68]

But the issue was also one of real power. By their mere existence, the industry stores offered manufacturers an alternate retail outlet, thereby further undermining the ministry's hopes for consolidating its position in the distribution of consumer goods. Hence its attempts to incorporate the stores into its own HO retail net. The industry stores, the ministry charged, were privileged in their supply of goods, thus causing imbalances throughout the rest of the retail landscape. These privileges had, in turn, led to "serious discussions among the entire population." The stores had also failed to play the role they were assigned as a consumer advocate, neglecting the task of exerting pressure on industry and concerning themselves solely with fulfilling their sales plans.[69] The industrial ministries were perfectly aware of the stakes involved and emphatically resisted attempts on the part of the Ministry for Trade and Provisioning to take over their stores. With varying degrees of diplomatic tact, the Ministries for Light Industry, Chemicals, Food, and General Machine Building defended themselves against the charges from Trade and Provisioning. The industry stores, they maintained, were popular among the population, fulfilled their tasks for the most part with aplomb, mustered an enviable *Verkaufskultur,* and exerted a positive influence on commodity supply and demand research.[70]

The standoff continued for years until the State Planning Commission became involved. In a letter to Curt Wach, minister for trade and provisioning, the Planning Commission's own recently established Department for the Provisioning of the Population suggested that because of continued shortcomings in the HOs it did not yet make sense to incorporate the industry stores into the HO system. Only when the performance *(Handelstätigkeit)* of the HOs improved would it be possible to make the transfer. Wach was outraged by this condescending reproach. In a fit of anger, he accused the Planning Commission's special department of displaying gross ignorance: "The better performance of the industry stores," he complained, "is a result of the best people from the HO going over to the industry stores because they can get better salaries there." The industry stores enjoyed the significant advantage, he added, of dealing in shortage commodities, which helped immeasurably to boost their sales figures. Wach's arguments, though true, proved futile. The Planning Commission stood behind the collective defense of the industrial ministries.[71]

In the end, trade remained splintered in its organizational framework, with the HO, the Association of Consumer Cooperatives, and the

GHKs under the Ministry for Trade and Provisioning, the industry stores under their respective industrial ministries, and private wholesalers and retailers holding on to that share of the market afforded them by the state. The result was a structural power imbalance between trade and industry abundantly clear to all those employed in the consumer economy. And yet, by the mid-to-late 1950s, there emerged within the regime a growing intolerance for the effects on consumer supply of the relationship between trade and industry. As Chapter 4 indicated, the New Course, combined with the progress of prosperity in West Germany, had brought about a shift in frame of reference from memories of the prewar period to the hopes engendered by postwar developments. The cause of consumer supply enjoyed a new legitimacy; the task of consumer supply reflected new, more elevated needs and wants. Simultaneously, the swelling numbers of East Germans fleeing to the West posed an immediate challenge to the forces of complacency in consumer supply.

The regime's growing unease with the status quo was particularly evident in its concern for the supply of new consumer durables—what more obvious symbols of modernity and progress, of the GDR's ability to compete in the contest of prosperity? (Durables also had the practical value of freeing up workers, especially women workers, from many time-consuming household chores, allowing them to spend more hours at the workplace.) When it came to durables, the State Planning Commission, so often the defender of industry against the complaints of trade, now began to display increasing impatience with industry's shortcomings. In early 1955, for example, the Ministry for General Machine Building came under criticism from the Planning Commission for having fallen considerably short of its 1954 production plans for a number of consumer goods, especially refrigerators, radios, and motor vehicles. The Planning Commission, moreover, refused to accept the usual argument that shortages of materials had prevented fulfillment.[72]

Production shortfalls in durables and other manufactured goods, in turn, transformed annual retail sales plans into works of fiction. As the Ministry for Trade and Provisioning observed in August 1956, the inability to supply enough durables was directly responsible for the fact that sales plans remained unfulfilled.[73] The lack of durables also helped explain the stubbornly high percentage of consumer spending on foodstuffs. As the ministry explained, purchasing power was stratified, displaying "such peculiarities" that "the highest purchasing power reserves" were held by the technical intelligentsia, well-paid white-collar workers, independent farmers, craftsmen, and private manufacturers. Without durables to entice them, these groups had little incentive to part with their savings. Meanwhile, families of four with monthly incomes between DM 350 and DM 450, the vast majority of families in East Germany, devoted between 65 and 70 percent of their expenditures on foodstuffs.

Nor was criticism of industry limited to the problem of durables. In these mid-decade years the number of reports highlighting shortcomings in the supply of textiles and clothing proliferated, reflecting growing frustration in the population and mounting exasperation among top-level planners and SED leaders. Production was dropping off in terms not only of quantity but also quality; and manufacturers proved unable to keep their promises for developing the production of new, modern, synthetic fibers.[74] The problem of quality, in turn, exacerbated the problem of *Überplanbestände*. Once again, the paradoxical coexistence of shortages and surplus demanded attention. In a speech to the Council of Ministers in August 1956, Fred Oelßner, in unusually candid form, shared his thoughts on the running discrepancy between commodity supply and purchasing power, and the resulting shortcomings in the realization of retail sales plans. The lack of durables he identified as an important failing: expensive goods, he said, "which we need for certain classes of the population, are simply not delivered by production. Here there are large gaps in the commodity supply plan. We don't receive automobiles and motorcycles, and televisions are also missing."[75] But most of his speech was devoted to textiles and clothing. *"The fact is,"* he admitted, *"our commodity supply in this area is bad and far too expensive."* The quality of textiles had declined in comparison with previous years, and yet prices for these goods were *"two to five times higher than in the West."* Hence the surplus inventory. Even though "certain needs of our population[,] especially in the textile market" remained unsatisfied, East German consumers would not buy poor-quality merchandise at prices they considered too high, especially if cheaper and higher-quality goods were to be had in West Berlin.[76] Oelßner himself appeared to share their viewpoint and spent much of his talk badgering the minister of finance to lower the prices of those goods piling up in inventory.[77]

Indeed, the question of prices was vexing for several reasons, perhaps the foremost being the basic lack of clarity about the locus of ultimate responsibility for setting and controlling prices for consumer goods. Officially, that responsibility was divided among several state and party institutions: the Ministry of Finance, the State Planning Commission, the Ministry for Trade and Provisioning, the Council of Ministers, and the SED Central Committee Department for Planning and Finances.[78] The division of competencies, however, was hardly clear and rarely stable over the course of the 1950s, though in practice the Finance Ministry often held the upper hand. Its position of preeminence among state actors was perhaps most evident in complaints like Oelßner's about its "inflexible" price policy, even in the face of growing *Überplanbestände*. Officials in trade, unable to fulfill their sales plans, most commonly argued that the only way to move excess inventory was to reduce prices, by either lowering trade margins or reducing consumption taxes.[79] Finance officials, however, were loathe to reduce prices, which from their point of view would mean forfeiting the value already invested in the commodities, allowing demand to increase further, and thus contributing to the ever-present monetary overhang. Besides, they had no desire to cede any of their control over price policy.

And yet there were distinct limits to the control exercised by the Finance Ministry over consumer prices. In fact, trade officials regularly carried out end-of-season sales *(Saisonschlußverkäufe)* and inventory clearance sales *(Inventurausverkäufe)* to move excess inventory at reduced prices. Between 1957 and 1959 there was even a special chain of stores (the so-called *Biwa-Läden*) that sold *Überplanbestände* at reduced prices.[80] (These sales and special stores were, in themselves, an indication of the limits of the regime's ability to guide demand; instead, it had to improvise in its attempts to react to the shifting, unforeseeable demands of consumers.) Beyond these actions on the part of trade, the effective authority of the Finance Ministry was limited by the vastness and complexity of the market for consumer goods; the ministry simply lacked sufficient information about the array of producers and products involved. Many of the enterprises producing consumer goods were not centrally organized; many still belonged to the private sector.[81] Perhaps most worrisome were the so-called creeping price increases, particularly for textiles and clothing. Because individual producers calculated their prices on the basis of different guidelines and costs, the same goods, produced by different producers, could have different retail prices (*Einzelhandelsverkaufspreise* or EVP).[82] Thus, if retailers had to change their suppliers, consumer prices could go up. If subsidies suddenly fell away, either prices would rise or production of the item in question would cease. This situation was especially true for private producers, since they had to operate as efficiently as possible. In addition, many producers increased their prices by using higher-quality materials, a strategy which diminished the supply of cheaper goods.[83] In short, market forces were at work in the planned economy, causing uncontrolled price increases and calling into question the regime's commitment to price stability.

The problem of consumer supply, however, exceeded questions of price policy and finances. As internal reports from 1956 show, industry was coming under increasing criticism, even from sources outside the ranks of trade. A report from the Central Administration for Statistics concluded, "Commodity turnover to the population shows considerable shortcomings due in part to poor distribution, but overwhelmingly to mistakes in production." It was precisely in the supply of textiles that the report found "great failings," dismissing the usual cry of an insufficient supply of raw materials as "no argument for the insufficiently demand-appropriate provisioning of the population."[84]

In May, Oelßner received from the editors of the East German economics journal *Die Wirtschaft* a draft of an unpublished article offering a substantive critique of relations between trade and industry. Significantly, the article was written by an economist, one Dr. Hartwig, employed in industry. As Hartwig explained (and Oelßner duly underlined), the initial postwar years of "commodity hunger," in which "the consumer swallowed everything placed before him and was happy if he received anything at all," had passed. "The consumer" had grown more discriminating and now rejected products which failed to meet "certain minimum conditions of quality," consigning them to the category of *Überplanbestände*.[85] Enlisting Oelßner's own published words for support, Hartwig went a step further, arguing that "the present system of commodity flow from production to consumer must be fundamentally reviewed and adapted to the changed circumstances."[86] Hartwig objected in particular to the fact that trade had become "the whipping boy for all difficulties" because of its inability to fulfill "the role of mediator between consumer and production." Indeed, how could it fulfill that role? "In view of the existing arrangement of the relations between trade and industry, the task assigned to trade of pressing the desires of consumers on production is impossible [*unlösbar*]." The real task, according to Hartwig, was to make industry take on responsibility for the fact that goods did not sell: "If sales difficulties become felt immediately in the production enterprise, then measures can be introduced quickly for adjusting production."[87] Only through tangible pressure to perform, concluded Hartwig, would performance truly improve.

Oelßner was finding himself increasingly caught between the competing claims of trade and industry.[88] But what could he do? To apply pressure on manufacturers was to make things "very uncomfortable" for industry, as it would require attempts to impose greater discipline on industrial workers.[89] For SED leaders the memory of June 1953 was still far too fresh to consider such an option.[90] On the other hand, internal pressure on them to do something was clearly mounting as *Überplanbestände* piled up, as enterprises found alternate buyers when their contract partners rejected their deliveries and as trade organs increasingly refused even to conclude contracts with suppliers.

And yet even these pressures might have been ignored indefinitely. While the obvious shortcomings of demand research represented serious limitations in the efforts of the consumer supply lobby, the weakness of trade vis-à-vis industry delineated a boundary beyond which SED leaders were not prepared to address that lobby's demands. This boundary, in turn, constituted a crucial element in their control over demand. Although in practice the regime neither guided consumer demand nor educated consumers in a manner in keeping with its more intoxicated claims, it did exert control over demand by channeling it into a cul-de-sac, into the arms of advocates deprived of the means of advocacy. Admittedly, it is debatable whether a truly effective system of demand research carried out by trade officials with real power to press their demands on industry would have made much of a difference in view of the regime's limited ability to ensure a steady supply of raw materials, to counteract the lack of incentive for individual firms to perform as required, and to impose discipline on industrial workers. But by assigning responsibility for demand to a chronically weak trade apparatus, the regime tamed demand, preventing it from becoming too powerful a challenge from within, even as it allowed SED leaders to pay lip service to "the ever-increasing material and cultural needs" of East

German citizens. As a result, consumer demand remained subject to an unhappy process of "demand adjustment," emerging as a mixed product of the regime's consciously pursued goals, its improvisations, its shortcomings affording uncertain redress, and a relationship between rulers and ruled in which the demands of the ruled, voiced by atomized supplicants, passed within view of the rulers only at the threshold of critical mass.[91] And even at that stage their needs and wants, however defined, may or may not have found satisfaction. As we have seen, the regime could only provide so much. Did it matter? Soviet tanks had brutally demonstrated the limits of open, collective protest. What choice did individual consumers have?

There was but one real choice in the 1950s, namely, flight. In 1955 252,870 East Germans fled to West Germany; in 1956 that figure rose to 279,189, no doubt boosted by the Soviet suppression of the uprising in Hungary; in 1957 another 261,622 GDR citizens opted for life in the Federal Republic.[92] To appropriate the eloquent terms of an old book, in the absence of an effectively functioning "voice" mechanism, East German consumers increasingly embraced their only "exit" option, substituting flight for the suppressed market.[93] The numbers, moreover, were greater than the sum of their parts, comprising as they did a high percentage of the young, the talented, and the educated—in short, East Germany's future.[94] Ultimately, it was this reinvention of "exit" that jolted SED leaders out of their post–New Course complacency.

CHAPTER 6

Crisis Revisited: The Main Economic Task and the Building of the Berlin Wall

Whether you like it or not, history is on our side. We will bury you.

Nikita Khrushchev, November 1956

With Hitler, during the war, we at least had meat and bread regularly!

East German shopper, May 1961

We are entirely lacking in ideas.

Erich Apel, June 1961

Between 1958 and 1961 the problem of consumption again featured in the wider narrative of high international politics and superpower confrontation. The events of these years, crowded and still puzzling, reached a pitch of intensity and contradictoriness remarkable even by the standards of the time. If in past years SED leaders wavered back and forth between the competing claims of productivism and consumerism, their policy mix of the late 1950s seemed to give equal expression to both imperatives.

In the spring and summer of 1958 SED leaders made promises outstripping even the wildest dreams of the consumer supply lobby. In May they lifted the last remnants of rationing, and in July, at the SED's Fifth Party Congress, they unexpectedly and boastfully proclaimed the "Main Economic Task." According to Walter Ulbricht, East Germany would surpass West Germany in per capita consumption of "almost all foodstuffs" and "the most important industrial consumer goods by 1961–62."[1] As if to strengthen the impression of confidence and resolve, SED leaders quickly eliminated the relative uncertainty of their deadline—1961–62—and fixed unequivocally on the year 1961 as the projected arrival time of socialist consumer abundance. In either case, the policy was bold, significant, and exceptionally concrete. And yet SED leaders simultaneously embarked on a hard-line course of confrontation that threatened to sabotage the professed goals of their new Main Economic Task. Intent on settling the Berlin question once and for all, they applied pressure on their Soviet sponsors to confront the Western powers over the fate of the divided city. Determined to build socialism in the countryside, they renewed their efforts to collectivize forcibly East German agriculture. The result was a catastrophic combination of provisioning crisis and *Republikflucht*, each so great and mutually reinforcing as to threaten the collapse of the GDR. In the end, to stop the bleeding and to prop up the hopelessly overextended SED regime, the Soviet leadership finally acquiesced to the solution for which SED leaders, above all Walter Ulbricht, had been pleading for some time: the building of the Berlin Wall.

The Main Economic Task, in other words, is a puzzle; several questions remain unanswered. Were SED leaders serious? Did they really believe that East Germany could overtake West Germany in per capita consumption? If so, why did they then pursue policies that were sure to undermine this aim? If, on the other hand, they were not serious, why did they proclaim a goal they knew they could never fulfill and give themselves a deadline they were certain they could never meet? In short, what were they thinking? Further, what was the relationship between the Main Economic Task and the Berlin Crisis? And what role did the Soviet leadership play in the crowded succession of events in East Germany between 1958 and 1961?

These questions fall into a gap left open by two sets of recent scholarship on the period. The first, dealing with consumption and consumer culture in East Germany, has tended to neglect the Main Economic Task, touching on it only briefly and in a vacuum, without reference to the broader political context driven by the collectivization of agriculture and the Berlin Crisis.[2] The second set, which reexamines the Berlin Crisis itself, has tended to ignore the unraveling of the Main Economic Task and has thus failed to incorporate it into the story of the unfolding crisis and the responses of political leaders.[3] While this chapter cannot hope to close this gap entirely or to answer fully all the questions involved, it seeks to make a beginning by offering a narrative of the Main Economic Task, itself a missing piece of the puzzle. Recounting its story, from bold inception to spectacular demise, enables us to sharpen the focus of the questions asked here, to suggest answers to some of them, and to pose others for further analysis. And it allows us to bring together the various and ambivalent elements contributing to this final crescendo in our narrative of the Cold War contest of prosperity.

On May 28, 1958, thirteen years after the end of the Second World War, the GDR's People's Chamber passed the law that brought to a close almost twenty years of food rationing in East Germany.[4] Effective the following day, it finally removed sugar, meat, milk, eggs, butter, and other fats from the constraints of coupons and customer registration. The prices for these items would now be higher than their rationed prices but lower than their HO prices had been. To ease the transition for lower-income groups, the law promised wage and salary increases, expanded social benefits, and price reductions for manufactured consumer goods. In addition, it left untouched the array of subsidized low prices for basic foodstuffs such as bread, cereals, and potatoes, as well as for such services as electricity, gas, and public transportation. Rationing had always been a symbolic sore point for the regime; its promises to lift rationing dated back to 1950. Throughout the decade economic planners had made preparations and sat on commissions charged with the task of removing this eyesore from the public face of socialism. Food rationing in West Germany, it must be remembered, had ended in January 1950.

The timing of the May 1958 law can perhaps be best explained by a combination of pressure and confidence. Pressure came most urgently in the form of the refugee problem, pushing the SED to take some kind of action in the area of consumption. It also came in the form of Khrushchev's vision of the GDR functioning as a "showcase" for socialism and thus as a vanguard in the struggle against capitalism. Confidence, on the other hand, derived from real and recent economic successes: industrial production had risen by 8 percent in 1957 and 12 percent in the first half of 1958; a currency reform in October 1957 had substantially (if temporarily) reduced the monetary overhang.[5] Already in the summer of 1957 reports from trade officials greeted the prospect of an end to rationing with perfect equanimity, indeed, enthusiasm. In response to a query from the Secretariat Ulbricht in July 1957, the minister for trade and provisioning, Curt Wach, could foresee no serious problems with the removal of rationing. He recognized that in past years previous commissions had insisted that the end of rationing would have to be accompanied by price reductions for manufactured goods as a means of guiding demand away from newly unrationed food items. Otherwise, it had been feared, demand for the latter would quickly exceed available supplies. But Wach was now confident that "the situation ha[d] changed significantly." He even predicted a surplus in foodstuffs of DM 500 million in 1957. Only with regard to butter did he betray any concern, suggesting that "good-tasting" margarine be readily available to offset what might be too great an increase in the demand for butter.[6] As we shall see, butter was only the beginning of his problems.

The pace and vigor of preparations picked up through the fall and winter of 1957. In October Otto Grotewohl informed the Ministry for Trade and Provisioning that a new "central commission" with Fred Oelßner at its head was to be formed to preside over the initiative.[7] The commission concerned itself with working out many of the details relating to retail prices, wage increases, social benefits, and taxes. It studied recent household budget analyses that tracked the effects of previous HO price reductions on the consumption of meat, sausage, eggs, sugar, butter, margarine, and oil.[8] The problem of Berlin also featured in the commission's deliberations, as recent investigations predicted a likely increase in the speculation in foodstuffs by West Berliners. In other words, with the aid of the favorable currency exchange rate, speculators from West Berlin would have a greater opportunity to buy up items cheaply in East Berlin and then turn around and sell them at a profit in West Berlin. The spot checks carried out by East German border patrols were less than systematic, affording ample opportunity for smuggling.[9] According to a September 1957 report from the Ministry for Trade and Provisioning, speculators were already making handsome profits in sugar, meat, eggs, and fat, even at current HO prices. Lifting rationing and reducing prices below their HO levels would assuredly exacerbate the problem.[10] For SED leaders it must have been mildly excruciating to think of West Berlin speculators capitalizing on the very goods whose supply the regime could not sufficiently guarantee to hold on to millions of its own citizens.

The problem of West Berlin was soon joined in the apprehensions of SED leaders by the question of the relationship between the consumption of foodstuffs and that of manufactured consumer goods. Reporting to the Politburo in January 1958, Oelßner's commission now predicted a DM 500 million increase in the demand for manufactured items, resulting from the rise in prices for those foodstuffs soon to be freed from rationing. Here was cause for considerable concern, since the 1958 supply plan for these articles (shoes, textiles, clothing, household items) fell way below the expected rise in demand. The alternative to increasing their supply, the commission suggested, was to appeal to the Soviets for approximately 65 million rubles in convertible currency to pay for imports of *Südfrüchte,* cocoa, tobacco, and other semiluxuries. This option had the added advantage of bringing "*the consumption structure in the GDR* still closer to *West German consumption.*"[11] In the following months, however, SED pleas for additional help from the Soviets and the other Warsaw Pact countries fell for the most part on deaf ears.[12] Presumably even Khrushchev's vision of the GDR as a showcase for socialism ran up against the limits of the Soviet capacity for generosity. It was, therefore, with some trepidation that the SED gave up its most effective means of controlling consumer demand. The anxiety was readily apparent in the closing of a May 1958 letter from Ulbricht to Khrushchev:

> In carrying out this complicated task it is difficult to assess accurately how the consumption of individual commodities will develop. It is possible that our funds in particular commodities are too small. We will, however, do everything we can to solve these problems on our own. Nevertheless, there is the possibility that we will not be able to solve all problems. In this case we would turn to the Central Committee of the CPSU and the Council of Ministers of the USSR with a request for help in commodities and currency.[13]

In the short term, Ulbricht's worries seemed exaggerated. To be sure, technical difficulties remained. Not less than thirty-three laws and ordinances had to be changed in the months before the law was passed.[14] On the eve of May 29, 1958, there was a rush on the stores, with consumers buying as much sugar, meat, butter, and margarine as they could before prices went up. Although economic planners had expected the rush, they were surprised by the amount of ration coupons consumers were able to produce. During the first few days after the law went into effect there were the inevitable administrative difficulties that needed to be overcome: communicating the correct price information to the stores, redecorating shop windows, redressing scattered shortcomings in supply.[15] In addition, broad sections of the population greeted the end of rationing with skepticism and resentment, fearing too steep a rise in prices.[16] Nevertheless, the transition to completely unrationed provisioning appeared to be carried off with success. In an August 1958 report to the Politburo, the State Planning Commission exuded complete confidence. Contrary to expectations, the consumption of foodstuffs had not increased alarmingly. The report even recommended lowering planned imports of foodstuffs, increasing exports of meat and fat, and devoting the added resources to importing semi-luxuries and raw materials for the production of shoes, textiles, clothing, and consumer durables.[17]

The apparent confidence of the moment found its boldest expression in the announcement of the Main Economic Task at the SED's Fifth Party Congress in July 1958. In the words of Walter Ulbricht,

> The economy of the German Democratic Republic is to develop in such a manner in the next few years that the superiority of the socialist social order of the GDR over the rule of imperialist forces in the Bonn state is unequivocally proven, and, as a result, the per capita consumption of our working population of all important foodstuffs and consumer goods reaches and surpasses the per capita consumption of the entire population of West Germany.[18]

Again, the questions posed at the beginning of this chapter leap immediately to mind. Was the Main Economic Task realizable? Did Ulbricht believe his own words? Did anyone else in the SED believe him? Did East German citizens believe the SED? How could they, in view of its track record in the area of consumption, its accumulated backlog of promises deferred? Western historians of East Germany have long dismissed the Main Economic Task as entirely unrealistic. Recent research has confirmed this view. The questions of sincerity and belief, however, are more difficult to answer with real certainty. In his recent history of the Berlin Crisis, Michael Lemke has called the Main Economic Task a "lie—even if several leading politicians in the SED were not or may not have been entirely conscious of it as such."[19] The SED leadership knew the GDR lacked the necessary raw materials, modern technologies, and resources for investment required to overtake West Germany. Nor were SED leaders under any illusions about the gap in work productivity between East and West Germany. Why, then, did they trumpet a task they knew to be impossible? Why did they impose a deadline they knew they could never meet?

André Steiner has suggested the opposite, arguing that the majority among the SED leadership believed that as long as the Soviet Union provided the necessary assistance, the goals of the Main Economic Task could be realized. He attributes this belief partly to the performance of the East German economy in 1957 and 1958, pointing to high growth rates for industrial output. These successes, meanwhile, were matched by a period of relative stagnation in West Germany. But more important, he argues, SED leaders were emboldened by recent Soviet successes in rocket and space technology.[20] In the summer of 1957 the Soviets successfully tested the world's first intercontinental ballistic missiles (ICBMs). This impressive display was followed by the spectacular launching of Sputnik in October 1957. Soon thereafter Khrushchev offered a bracing image that perfectly conveyed the combined promise of the technological and consumerist future in the socialist world: the Soviet Union, he said, would turn out missiles "like sausages on an assembly line."[21] (In private Khrushchev showed far less confidence. Knowing full well that Soviet ICBMs were not yet operational weapons, he openly admitted that they "represented only a symbolic counterthreat to the United States.")[22] Steiner speaks of a "Sputnik-euphoria," which bolstered the confidence of SED leaders that the Main Economic Task would be fulfilled; he maintains that their confidence lasted well into 1960. To be sure, the launching of Sputnik was a great boon to the entire East bloc. That the excitement, even euphoria, greeting this success necessarily translated into a belief among SED leaders in the attainability of the consumption goals of the Main Economic Task, however, is highly questionable. Certainly their anxiety about the lifting of rationing indicated something less than complete confidence with regard to the sphere of consumption.[23] In the following pages it will become clear that whatever optimism existed at the outset faded quickly, indeed, well before 1960.

As for the population, it is impossible to know if in July 1958 most East Germans believed that by 1961 they would be better fed, clothed, housed, and equipped with consumer durables than their West German counterparts. It is hard to imagine that very many people believed this would happen.[24] On the other hand, it is plausible to think that many people did expect their material circumstances at least to improve. The Main Economic Task, after all, sounded very much like the New Course. Much of the same language was employed, many of the same promises made. The New Course, for all its shortcomings, had meant real, material improvements in people's lives. What is certain is that in the short run the announcement of the Main Economic Task was followed by a substantial decrease in the number of refugees fleeing to West Germany. Sixty thousand fewer people fled the GDR in 1958 than in the previous year. In 1959 the total figure declined by another sixty thousand.[25] If emigration is the result of a combination of push and pull, the SED clearly achieved a temporary attenuation in the factors of push.

And yet for all its continuities with past SED promises, the Main Economic Task did promise something new, that is, a significantly improved provisioning of modern, industrial consumer durables: refrigerators, vacuum cleaners, washing machines, motorcycles, automobiles, and televisions. It was clear from the very beginning that these items fell under the rubric of "most important" consumer goods. In fact, internal reports show that preparations for substantially increasing their production were well underway months before the announcement of the Main Economic Task.[26] Although recent research on West Germany has emphasized the material austerity of the 1950s, it still shows that West Germans were further along than East Germans in acquiring these goods, a fact of which SED officials were painfully aware. Moreover, West German purchases of durables increased dramatically in the last third of the decade.[27]

With the inauguration of the Main Economic Task, it was now the expressed goal of East German economic planners that these goods acquire the same "mass-demand" status as shoes, textiles, and basic clothing. That this shift had yet to occur was well illustrated by the lengths to which consumers still had to go to obtain them. An instructive anecdote is provided by correspondence surviving in the files of the former Magistrat of East Berlin; it traces the unusually persistent efforts of one woman to acquire a television set for her ill, apartment-bound mother. The story it uncovers is revealing on many levels and, therefore, merits reproducing here. The documentation begins with a March 1957 letter from Frau B., a secretary in the social services department of the municipal district of Prenzlauer Berg, to the "little bear" *(Bärchen),* a column of the *Berliner Zeitung.* As Frau B. explained, her efforts to buy a television first took her to one of the industry stores in the Stalinallee, where she learned that she would have to put her name on a list and wait two years for delivery of the TV she desired. Her only alternative, the store suggested, was to turn to local authorities for possible preferential treatment. This she did, explaining in a letter to district officials that her mother's illness had reached the point where she could no longer leave the apartment: "That means that she can no longer visit the cinema or the theater, which is very saddening for a 64-year-old person." Frau B. requested a privileged delivery of a TV and, in particular, asked for the Dürer model. To her dismay, however, district officials rejected her request, pointing out that due to the large number of applications, it would be impossible to meet her wishes. Nevertheless, they added, if she were willing to forgo the Dürer, they were prepared to offer her swift delivery of another model, namely, the Rubens. But this counteroffer only aroused Frau B.'s indignation. The Rubens came with a smaller picture tube; it could hardly serve as an adequate substitute for the Dürer. In Frau B.'s own words,

> On the one hand something is denied, on the other hand, something is offered that does not fulfill the purpose it is supposed to fulfill. I am now supposed to accept the smaller picture tube, even though it means that my mother would not have the desired pleasure she should actually have. I would not like to leave unmentioned the fact that *my mother was totally bombed out in 1944 and no longer possesses anything she can enjoy. She has only her illness and the fact that she is chained to the house.*[28]

A telephone call to the district offices only resulted in more frustration, particularly when one functionary made the impertinent suggestion that she wanted the Dürer not for her sick mother but really for herself, her husband, and her child. Her subsequent appeal to *"liebes Bärchen"* had been her next step.

Here, there is a gap in the documentation, which only picks up one year later. Presumably having received no word in the meantime from the newspaper, Frau B. herself finally turned to the city's Department for Trade and Provisioning, retold the sequence of events, and emphasized once again her mother's desire "to be able to take part in cultural life."[29] And once again, her request was refused with the same explanation: supply, though increased, still fell far short of demand.[30] However, as the department pointed out, the offer of the Rubens still stood.[31] But Frau B., determined to obtain the Dürer, persisted, appealing in the following months to yet more officials within the city administration. But her efforts yielded only further denials of the Dürer and reiterated defenses of the Rubens. Finally, fifteen months after her first letter to the little bear, she acquiesced and agreed to accept the Rubens. One can readily imagine her outrage, then, on learning that the TV actually being held for her at an industry store in the Stalinallee was in fact not a Rubens, but rather an Iris, a model city officials praised as the new-and-improved version *(Weiterentwicklung)* of the Rubens. "I cannot understand," Frau B. fumed, "how every authority I addressed offered me only a 'Rubens,' which they were never able to deliver anyway. Now that I have finally decided on a 'Rubens,' I am offered a model which isn't even a 'Rubens.'" If it was really impossible to supply a Rubens, she now insisted, only a Derby would do. The Derby, she claimed, was the actual new-and-improved Rubens.[32] Fittingly, the final letter in the correspondence was a brusque refusal from city officials:

> Unfortunately, it is not the case, as you seem to imagine, that televisions with small picture tubes are available in unlimited supply. When you were offered privileged access to a "Rubens," it was available on sale for you. As I wrote to you on June 4, 1958, we can now offer you an "Iris" until *June 12, 1958.* If this model should not be acceptable to you, then you must wait for a delivery in the order in which you have registered.[33]

Did Frau B. give in and accept the Iris? We cannot know for sure. Due to her persistence, however, we have an especially well-documented account of an all-too-common tale of frustration, certain aspects of which are worth noting. As we have seen, the letter of complaint *(Eingabe)* was a common form of appeal in East Germany, one that functioned as a form of petition within the framework of a paternalistic exercise of authority. In Frau B.'s case, one is struck by the prominence of *Kultur* in her quest for a TV, in the model names ("Dürer" and "Rubens"), and in her emphasis on her mother's ostensible longing to be reconnected with "cultural life." Here we have an example of a supplicant shrewdly, if rather transparently, couching her appeal in terms corresponding to the party's avowed ideological moral code: put crudely, cultural consumption was an inherent good, as long, of course, as the culture in question was party-approved—hence the widespread practice in East Germany of subsidized ticket prices for concerts, theater, and other cultural offerings; material consumption, on the other hand, if it exceeded the amount required for the reproduction of labor power, was, to say the least, suspect. The use of the names of old master painters as model names for TVs was particularly indicative of the deep ambivalence with which the East German regime took up the consumption challenge posed by its Western neighbor. The fact that in the course of this competition "Dürer" and "Rubens" were soon replaced by names like "Iris" and "Derby" reflected the SED's creeping loss of control over its own terms of moral virtue. Finally, thanks to Frau B.'s efforts, we have a kind of slow-motion view, in a Soviet-type setting, of what economists call "demand adjustment": an initial want thwarted, appeals to a higher authority that an exception be made in one's case, grudging acceptance of a proposed alternative, discovery that even the alternative is not available, the final unhappy choice between a lower-grade alternative or indefinite suspension of the want.[34] More often than not, this entire process lasted only a few minutes, between the time one entered and exited any particular store. Frau B.'s efforts were unique only in their duration, their obduracy.

The Main Economic Task was supposed to bring an end to this stingy mode of provisioning scarce durables. As Erich Apel explained to the Politburo's recently established Economic Commission, over which he presided, "The questions of industrial consumer goods are of decisive importance for the resolution *(Lösung)* of the Main Economic Task."[35] Apel and his commission were relative newcomers to the problem of consumption, having more or less taken over for the now fallen Oelßner and his Government Commission in the spring of 1958. Apel, born in 1917, represented a younger generation within the state apparatus, one which came of age under Nazism. Apel himself had been a member of the Nazi Party and had worked during the war as an engineer on a rocket project in Peenmünde, contributing to the design of Hitler's "miracle weapons." After the war the Soviets put him to work in the Soviet Union as a chief engineer. Only in 1952 did he return to the

GDR, and not until 1957 did he become a member of the SED. Nevertheless, his rise was swift. Already in 1953 he was a deputy minister for machine building. Between 1955 and 1958, he served as minister. A candidate for the SED's Central Committee by 1958, he became a full-fledged member in 1960, remaining so until his death by suicide in 1965.[36] Apel's relevance for us derives from his role as the increasingly despairing head of the Politburo's Economic Commission, which played a central role in overseeing and coordinating the Main Economic Task.

As the summer of 1958 passed, so, too, in degrees, did the bold optimism that had characterized it. For all their hopes to introduce modern consumer durables into more and more East German households, economic planners soon found themselves challenged on humbler grounds. By the fall of 1958 it had become clear that the end of rationing had, indeed, resulted in a significant increase in demand for foodstuffs.[37] For the fourth quarter of the year, the SED's Department for Trade and Provisioning expected an increase of ten thousand tons in the consumption of meat, requiring additional imports from West Germany, other western countries, and the Soviet Union.[38] There were shortages in the supply of fat, cheese, and milk. A poor potato harvest caused unexpected shortfalls. Trade functionaries reported difficulties in covering demand for fowl, butter, and eggs. In fact, these problems resulted not only from the end of rationing but also from shortages in the supply of manufactured goods. Wage increases associated with the Main Economic Task had substantially increased the purchasing power of many consumers. Without the requisite increase in the supply of manufactured goods, demand inevitably concentrated in foodstuffs. And yet the unsatisfied demand for shoes, textiles, clothing, and household items was keenly felt. Reports of "negative discussions" in the population multiplied, particularly due to shortages in lightbulbs, leather shoes, ready-made clothing, and bicycles.[39]

By the beginning of 1959, SED leaders were forced, as Ulbricht had predicted they might be, to turn to the Soviet Union for help. Ulbricht and Grotewohl explained to Krushchev that merely to cover the GDR's "most pressing" demand, they required an additional 250 million rubles in hard currency for additional imports of *Südfrüchte*, seed oil, cooking oil, brewing barley, animal feed, and an array of raw materials required for the production of consumer goods.[40] In addition, they requested that Soviet deliveries of wool to the GDR be made up of a higher percentage of finer material; Soviet deliveries consisted primarily of a prickly wool that resisted attempts to be finished into clothing items acceptable to the population. Continuing such deliveries, they complained, threatened to diminish the quality of East German woolen products. The Soviets, however, were not immediately forthcoming. As Leuschner explained to Ulbricht in March, the GDR was still in no position to guarantee payment for imports from capitalist countries, even as East German needs for those imports continued to expand.[41]

Meanwhile, reports flowed in steadily detailing difficulties in meeting the increased demand for foodstuffs. In March Ernst Lange, the Central Committee's secretary for trade and provisioning, informed Apel of shortcomings in the supply of meat, butter, and milk in the first quarter of the year.[42] In April the Ministry for Trade and Provisioning prepared for the Council of Ministers a report highlighting similar gaps in supply. As the food situation gradually deteriorated, internal reports kept SED leaders equally well appraised of shortages in shoes, textiles, and clothing. As Grete Wittkowski reported to Apel in July 1959, recent price reductions for manufactured goods had so inflated demand that, despite increased supply compared to previous years, it could not be satisfied.[43]

These difficulties, in turn, brought to the fore more fundamental questions. The Main Economic Task was supposed to bring East German consumption levels above those of West Germany. The goal was to demonstrate the higher standard of living afforded by socialism. But as the stream of disappointing early reports flowed in to the center, economic planners were led inexorably to the conclusion that they were being driven by a Western, "bourgeois" concept of standard of living, one against which they had hitherto failed to develop a compelling alternative. This state of affairs was perhaps most painfully clear to those responsible for compiling standard of living statistics, for quantifying East German successes and failures in the contest of prosperity. As the Central Administration for Statistics explained, "the concept, standard of living, is not originally a concept of scientific Marxist political economy, but rather originates from bourgeois economics, which exploits thoroughly the indeterminacy of the concept to whitewash capitalism and slander socialism." Associated primarily with quantifiable features such as real wages, per capita consumption, and the cost of living, the concept neglected less quantifiable but equally important factors such as "the social position" of the working class, its "political and economic role in society, state and enterprise," as well as "the cultural level" of the population, that is, "the extent to which the broad classes of the people take part in science and art."[44]

In subsequent months East German statisticians continued to debate the theoretical parameters of the concept.[45] But in their work, they maintained an overriding focus on the material and the quantifiable: per capita consumption, real income, and the cost of living.[46] Indeed, what else could they do? Their theoretical qualms notwithstanding, they could hardly ignore the "bourgeois" understanding of standard of living, nor could they elude the unrelenting challenge it posed. The SED-regime had allowed itself to become fully and publicly beholden to a standard of well-being not of its own devising.

In the midst of these mounting difficulties, the regime's concern for at least the appearance of prosperity encouraged it to focus on retail trade as an important, highly visible site for advertising material well-being. The adoption of the Main Economic Task now made it essential "to develop new forms and methods of trade, and in particular to modernize the material-technical basis in socialist trade, equipping it with the newest technology."[47] In part, this effort entailed the rationalization of wholesale and retail administrative structures. In part, it meant modernizing storage and selling spaces. It also meant building upon earlier innovations in retail. Soon plans were underway, for example, to set up a second mail-order catalogue business under the auspices of the Association of Consumer Cooperatives. Preparations included more special trips to West Germany, where trade representatives studied first-hand the operations of the largest West German mail-order businesses.[48]

But it was the self-service store that quickly emerged as the most important and dramatic retail innovation of these years. Associated with modernity, abundance, and freedom of choice, the self-service store in 1958 was still a relative newcomer throughout Germany. Although a handful of self-service stores had been introduced during the interwar years, they remained something of a novelty.[49] Even after World War II, it took some time before West Germany was ready to embrace the new retail form. As a distribution outlet, self-service made sense only once manufacturers had made the transition to producing and marketing standardized products for mass-consumption markets. In 1955 there were still only 203 self-service stores in West Germany. Only in the second half of the decade did the decisive transformation occur; by 1960 there were 17,132 self-service stores accounting for 62 percent of retail sales.[50] East German trade officials watched this development with a keen, if apprehensive, eye, eager to follow suit as soon as possible. One East German functionary's description of some of the early self-service stores in West Berlin provides a sense of the profound newness of the phenomenon:

> The stores with self-service, which have already been introduced on a test basis with insufficient means in the democratic sector [East Berlin] and in several cities in the GDR, must be mentioned as an innovation in West Berlin retail trade . . . Except for meat and sausage, which are sold by salesladies, all manner of commodities are made available for self-service in shelves made of wire . . . All kinds of foodstuffs are offered such as legumes, flour, sugar, condensed milk, fresh milk in bottles, sweets, coffee, canned vegetables, freshly cut vegetables in cellophane pouches, fruit and potatoes in bags. In order to ease the selection, the goods are packed in different quantities, so that the contents of the packages can either be seen from the outside or determined from labels. The selling proceeds as follows: the customer takes a wire basket supplied at the entrance, one corresponding to the extent of the intended purchase and the desired selection of goods. At the cash register a saleslady calculates the prices of the goods and hands them to the customer, taking back the wire basket. These stores enjoy increasing favor because the goods on offer are easily assessed and the purchase proceeds relatively quickly.[51]

The painstaking exactness of the description, its detailed emphasis on the presentation of goods and the new mechanics of shopping, suggests how unfamiliar the experience still was to those accustomed to addressing salespeople from the other side of the sales counter.

Preparations for setting up self-service stores in East Germany date back, at least, to 1955.[52] But progress was slow. By the end of 1956, there were only two in East Berlin, though both reported increased sales.[53] In the following year, the Magistrat of East Berlin, eager to expand self-service, developed further plans for study trips in West Berlin and West Germany.[54] Still, its goals were relatively modest. In January 1958 its program for further development envisioned only thirty-eight self-service stores in East Berlin by 1960.[55] It was the Main Economic Task that brought a new vigor and an accelerated tempo to the whole endeavor. Self-service quickly became the most obvious emblem of an improved "material-technical basis" in retail.[56] By May 1959 the Magistrat could report that the number of self-service stores in East Berlin had grown to seventy-six, and that plans were being developed to increase their number to over four hundred by the end of the year.[57] The parallel expansion of self-service in West Germany and West Berlin also added incentive to East German efforts. According to West Berlin radio broadcasts, to which leading SED officials paid careful attention, the number of self-service stores in West Berlin had reached 350 by April 1959, enjoying "great popularity," especially among working housewives.[58] Spurred on by the competition, the Magistrat could boast, by the end of September, 399 self-service stores comprising 22,917 square meters of selling-floor space, and producing a third-quarter turnover of DM 63.7 million (nearly 10 percent of total retail sales).[59] By the end of 1961 there were, in the whole of East Germany, nearly thirteen thousand self-service stores, making up 15 percent of the HO retail net, and 26 percent of *Konsum* retail outlets.[60] Self-service had clearly arrived in East Germany.

In view of the SED's previous record in consumer supply, combined with the chronic weakness of trade within the bureaucracy, one is struck by the success and speed with which East Germany was able to meet this new challenge in the sphere of retail. However, one should not be too surprised; success in establishing self-service demonstrated the extent to which the interests of the consumer supply lobby and those of the SED leadership overlapped. From the point of view of trade functionaries, the ideal of an increasingly modern and elevated *Verkaufskultur* and certainly the investment of material resources to that end always held great appeal, even more so at a moment in which the image and importance of retail trade held such a prominent position in the concerns of SED leaders. Conversely, those leaders had from the very beginning shown genuine regard for outward appearances. Hence the discussions surrounding the introduction of the first HO stores, the efforts expended on the Stalinallee, and the pedagogical tenor of East German shopwindow displays. The Main Economic Task and the pressures leading to its adoption only heightened an already existing commitment to the public countenance of socialism, as regarded by both its own population and the capitalist world directly across the open border. Self-service, in theory, was perfectly suited to serve this commitment. It provided a kind of staged exercise in legitimacy or transparency, with the state openly displaying its provisioning achievements directly to the gaze and grasp of consumers. Self-service offered direct access. It embodied the promise of modernity, abundance, and, above all, freedom of choice.

But could the SED deliver on that promise? Once again it is necessary to emphasize where the interests of trade officials and SED leaders diverged. Even in the context of the Main Economic Task, no new substantive efforts were made to lift trade out of its structurally subservient position. The system of demand research remained ineffectual.[61] Reports of industrial enterprises failing to meet their obligations in the production of consumer goods continued to flow in.[62] By the summer of 1959, even some SED leaders were running out of patience. After receiving a complaint from the director of the HO mail-order house in Leipzig about an insufficient supply of goods for the fall 1959 season, Erich Apel turned directly to Bruno Leuschner, imploring him for help: "Here, the entire drama of our light industry becomes very clear . . . Perhaps it is possible for you, on the basis of this example, to become personally involved and to lay down measures so resolute that they will quickly bring us out of this whole situation."[63]

Looking back on the year that had elapsed since end of rationing and the adoption of the Main Economic Task, the SED leadership was clear that things had not gone as promised. And yet the questions of consumption and living standards were more than ever in the public eye, as U.S. Vice President Nixon traveled to Moscow in July 1959 to open the American National Exhibition. There, he and Khrushchev famously engaged in a series of debates about the relative merits of their respective social systems, most notably during a visit to the exhibition's model American kitchen, with all its modern consumer durables and labor-saving devices.[64]

In East Germany, at the end of that same month, a large, much publicized trade conference was held in Leipzig, ostensibly to assess present difficulties and breathe new life into efforts to achieve the goals of the Main Economic Task.[65] The months preceding the conference entailed extensive preparations, the drafting of programmatic theses, and the mounting of a broad press campaign.[66] Held in one of the main auditorium spaces usually reserved for the biannual Leipzig Trade Fair, the conference was attended by 2,871 delegates, most of them trade officials.[67] Among those present were several leading SED figures, including Walter Ulbricht. In total, thirty people gave speeches over a two-day period, the evening hours of which were devoted to a full cultural program of musical and theatrical entertainment. (In addition to the overture from Carl Maria von Weber's *Oberon* and an aria from Otto Nicolai's *The Merry Wives of Windsor,* the delegates were treated to Slavic dancing, proletarian work songs, and an act featuring roller-skating on three tables.)[68]

Despite the avowed purpose of the conference, its main speakers spent more time trying to revive the flagging spirits of trade functionaries than they did discussing openly the causes of the difficulties they encountered. This fundamental omission characterized the speeches of Grete Wittkowski, Wilhelm Feldman (minister for light industry), and Curt-Heinz Merkel (Curt Wach's recent replacement as minister for trade and provisioning). Perhaps the omission was inevitable, given the guiding hand of the SED Central Committee in sponsoring the conference. However, what might have been an occasion for real debate quickly revealed itself to be an extended pep rally for those working in trade. Even those who addressed the problem of the relationship between trade and industry downplayed the confrontation, focusing primarily on the obligations of trade for improving the relationship.[69] As a remedy for overcoming what were regarded as essentially ideological shortcomings, conference speakers emphasized the virtues of the classic methods of "socialist competition"; like workers in industry, those in trade had also to compete for the coveted title "socialist work brigade."[70] In short, the conference quickly degenerated into a ritualistic attempt to will into existence an atmosphere of enthusiasm and renewed resolve.

Only momentarily did the sound of genuine frustration and impatience cut through the general hum of repeated platitudes, when a trade official named Dümde, representing wholesale trade in textiles, insisted that "one side of our work has not yet been firmly and clearly discussed."[71] Launching into an attack on light industry, he told of production enterprises delivering the wrong assortments of textiles to trade organs under his authority and of his attempts both to reject the wrongly delivered items and to arrange for production of the correct assortments. But just as his efforts appeared on the verge of yielding successful results, he explained, a letter from his supplier arrived like "a thunderbolt." With a flair for drama, Dümde produced the letter and, reading it out loud, showed how his efforts had been nullified. Citing a higher authority, the letter simply demanded that he accept the original deliveries. That higher authority was none other than Grete Wittkowski, who had only just spoken on the first day of the conference. (This revelation, according to the protocol, created "movement in the auditorium.") Dümde was willing to admit that the supplier may have been using Wittkowski's name without having consulted her at all. But he was adamant in the rightness of his position: "we declare unequivocally that we will not back off from our justified demands and will enter into no contract for such *Überplanbestände.*" (Here, the protocol records "applause" from the delegates.)[72]

But Dümde's was a lone voice, and the trade conference achieved nothing. The stream of reports highlighting gaps in the provisioning of foodstuffs continued its unceasing flow. In October 1959 the Ministry for Trade and Provisioning identified "considerable difficulties" in supplying butter, margarine, and pork during the third quarter of the year.[73] It had been necessary to increase the supply of beef and mutton to make up for shortages in pork. Butter could no longer be sold in butcher shops. Advertising for butter ceased, as attempts were made to intensify advertising for margarine. Bakeries and pastry shops now had to substitute margarine for butter. And sales personnel were offered bonuses for selling margarine instead of butter. But these attempts to increase the consumption of margarine at the expense of butter ran into their own problems: many shops very often had no margarine to sell, and there were a series of complaints from consumers about margarine speckled with strange, blue spots causing it to taste like soap. In a letter to Leuschner, Wittkowski predicted similar difficulties for the fourth quarter of the year.[74] Worse still, there appeared to be no remedy in sight. She recognized perfectly well that the GDR could not rely on help from the other "people's democracies." Nor was it clear whether the Soviet Union would provide the necessary assistance.

The inability to meet consumer demand for an array of foodstuffs was not solely the result of the end of rationing, the introduction of wage increases, and the concomitant increase in purchasing power. An important cause of the disruption in provisioning, one which would become decisive in the following months, was the much-delayed but now vigorously revived effort to collectivize forcibly East German agriculture. Of course, the "socialist transformation" of agriculture was a long-standing SED goal, an indispensable cornerstone of the "worker-and-peasant state" it was committed to building. Halted after the uprising of June 17, 1953, the effort resumed only gradually in the following years. But between January 1958 and January 1960, the pace of collectivization quickened dramatically, as the portion of agricultural land collectivized jumped from 25.2 to 45.1 percent.[75] This development necessarily took a large toll on the domestic supply of agricultural products, just as it had in the months preceding the uprising in June 1953. But from the very beginning there was a strict taboo within the regime on speaking openly about the effects of collectivization on consumer supply. One spoke of "measures introduced," and one tracked shortfalls in agricultural production. But the connection between the two developments could never be made openly, not even in internal reports and memoranda.[76] In fact, doing so was tantamount to spreading subversive propaganda. Eric Apel stated clearly at a meeting of the Politburo's Economic Commission, "Everything now has to do with the socialist transformation of agriculture. The enemy is active not only in trade, but also elsewhere. He says: everything [the shortages in consumer supply] has come about because you have socialized agriculture. That is why the people now receive less."[77] Apel was adamant; only "the enemy" said such things.

Even in denial, however, the regime's internal communications continued to paint a sobering picture, one that grew more dismal in the spring and summer of 1960. For these were the months of the most intensive collectivization, the officially propagated "socialist spring in the countryside." Within a mere five months, between the beginning of January and the end of May, the portion of agricultural land collectivized in East Germany leapt from 45.1 to 83.6 percent. Under an atmosphere of threats, intimidation, and persecution of those farmers who resisted, the number of collectives almost doubled from 10,465 to 19,345.[78]

As a direct consequence, domestic production of basic foodstuffs, including meat and potatoes, declined sharply. Rice imports had to be increased to make up some of the difference, despite the damage done to the balance of foreign trade. In some instances those agricultural goods that were produced simply disappeared in the countryside, leaving stores in urban areas without expected deliveries. At a meeting of the Politburo's Economic Commission, for example, one official reported a particularly embarrassing story. While driving through the Saxon countryside with officials from Czechoslovakia and Poland, the visitors complained of being unable to buy cherries in Leipzig, despite having seen trees in the area full of cherries. The East German official suggested that the cherries were probably not yet ripe and then quickly changed the subject. But soon thereafter, as they continued their drive, they saw "countless" groups of children with faces smeared blue from the juice of stolen cherries, as well as groups of adults on their way home, their pockets bulging with the stolen fruit.[79]

Meanwhile, attempts to steer purchasing power toward manufactured goods were unsuccessful due to insufficient supplies.[80] According to a June 1960 report from a special Politburo commission, the supply of many manufactured goods, especially textiles, failed to reach the levels of the previous year.[81] Not only was supply down; so too was quality. Similarly, the supply of many durables declined, including automobiles, electric stoves, radios, and television cabinets. The bleak news contained in the report moved the Politburo to draft a directive for addressing the situation. But the measures it proposed displayed a habitual vagueness and a distinct lack of new thinking.[82]

Was it any wonder that the élan of those working in trade seemed at a low ebb? Reports showed that whatever boost in enthusiasm that might have emerged from the trade conference of July 1959 had since played itself out. Where there had once been a flurry of activity in the form of "socialist competition" and the building of "socialist brigades," there was now an unmistakable atmosphere of indifference and flagging morale.[83] Meanwhile, consumers complained of shortages, long waiting lists, poor-quality merchandise, and a lack of spare parts. Their grievances ran the entire spectrum of commodities, from basic foodstuffs to modern durables.[84] Even in Berlin and in the areas surrounding the city, where it was most imperative to demonstrate the success of the Main Economic Task, officials had to contend with insufficient resources, cuts in commodity supply plans, and wholesalers failing to fulfill contracts for the delivery of consumer goods.[85]

*   *   *

In the wake of the July 1959 trade conference, the SED finalized arrangements for its new Seven-Year Plan, which linked the planning cycle of the East German economy more closely with that of the Soviet Union. (In January 1959 the Soviet Union had adopted its Seven-Year Plan, which boasted that the socialist countries would surpass the capitalist world in industrial productivity by 1966. By 1980, Krushchev claimed, the construction of Communism in the Soviet Union would be complete. Exactly what that meant, however, was hardly clear.) The new East German plan, announced in October 1959, maintained its professed commitment to the Main Economic Task, although Ulbricht appeared to modify its initial claims when he said that by 1961 the provisioning of the population with all important foodstuffs and consumer goods would equal, and in some categories surpass, that in West Germany. The emphasis, in other words, was now on equaling consumption in West Germany, not necessarily on surpassing it. Equally indicative of a weakening in the SED's public adherence to the Main Economic Task as originally articulated were the new plan's ambitious goals for increasing industrial production. Focusing investment on energy, chemicals, and electrical engineering, the plan called for an increase in total output of nearly 90 percent by 1965.[86]

The Seven-Year Plan had involved extensive negotiations in Moscow, during which the Soviets promised to deliver foodstuffs and raw materials to East Germany at a value of 250 million rubles in 1960, 200 million in 1961, and 120 million in 1962. The promised commodities included raw materials for fertilizer and textiles, aluminum, paper, fat, leather hides, coffee, and *Südfrüchte*. During the negotiations in June 1959, Bruno Leuschner still seemed to think that by 1961–62 it would be possible to reach, and in some cases surpass, West German consumption levels in milk, meat, cheese, fish, eggs, butter and other fats, sugar, fruits and vegetables, cotton and silk fabrics, furniture, carpets, underwear, wristwatches, household porcelain, bicycles, televisions, motorcycles, and scooters. On the other hand, he recognized that, despite increases in supply, it would be impossible to catch up to West Germany in consumption of automobiles, refrigerators, and washing machines. East Germany would also remain behind in semiluxuries and other goods that could be acquired only from the capitalist world, with hard currency: coffee, cocoa, *Südfrüchte*, woolen products, and shoes made of high-quality leather.[87]

A telling sign of the regime's gradual, tacit disavowal of the initial goals of the Main Economic Task was the increasing prominence of what had originally constituted one of its less-noticed extras, that is, the campaign for improving the supply of the "thousand little things of daily demand" *(die tausend kleinen Dinge des täglichen Bedarfs)*. Nuts, bolts, screws, sewing needles, shoelaces, buttons, spare parts, miscellaneous kitchen items—these were the sorts of unglamorous articles promised by the thousand-little-things campaign, along with an emphasis on improving the array of repair and other services bound up with their supply.

Already in September 1959, at a meeting of the SED Central Committee, Walter Ulbricht complained of a general neglect of this campaign, a tendency to underestimate its importance for the Main Economic Task. "The provisioning of the thousand little things, repairs and services, has become a basic problem within the framework of the Main Economic Task," he instructed. "We must prove the superiority of socialism in this area as well."[88] Adding some urgency to the task, as he openly admitted, was the recently accelerated process of collectivizing the handicraft trades. Although it moved ahead at a much slower pace than the collectivization of agriculture, this process nevertheless brought disruptions in its wake.[89] Nor was Ulbricht alone in his grasp of the importance of the campaign. Many SED leaders assumed rightly that shortages in the supply of modern durables were regrettable but certainly more understandable—even excusable—than shortages in the supply of the thousand little things. In the words of one trade union official, "Our workers definitely have understanding for the fact that there are still not enough televisions, that we still can't cover the demand for automobiles . . . But they have no understanding for the fact that hundreds of small items, which one could manufacture, are missing."[90]

Accordingly, in the fall of 1959 economic planners devoted increasing attention to the thousand little things, producing investigative reports and drafts of programs for bringing the campaign forward.[91] As one draft explained, "the achievements in the improvement of living conditions *(Lebenslage)* are measured not only by a high per capita consumption of high-grade consumer goods. They are now judged increasingly by the satisfaction of the needs of working people for the thousand little things of daily demand, as well as repairs and services that ease and enhance daily life."[92] Study groups were dispatched to

West Berlin and Sweden to investigate Laundromats, dry cleaners, and shoe repair services.[93] In Sweden East German officials were particularly impressed by the widespread do-it-yourself *(Hilf Dir selbst)* approach to home repairs and hobbies and by the abundant supply of tools and hardware parts. They were equally fascinated by new residential building projects featuring communal washing machines and apartments with central heating, eat-in kitchens, and built-in closets. In their reports they showed a readily apparent enthusiasm for what they regarded as the obvious blessings of practicality, efficiency, convenience, and comfort.

In February 1960 the Council of Ministers approved a program produced by the State Planning Commission for transplanting these blessings to East German soil.[94] Translating it into practice, however, proved enormously difficult. Due to the worsening provisioning crisis, economic planners had to cope with drastic cuts in material supplies, an increasingly overwhelmed bureaucracy, and a lack of incentive on the part of manufacturers to produce thousands of little things, which, being subject to price subsidies, held out little hope of profitability.[95] The program depended to a large extent on the efforts of local administrative organs, but reports indicated that they mostly failed to take up the initiative.[96] SED leaders were perfectly aware of the damage these setbacks inflicted on their prestige. In July 1960, at a meeting of the Politburo's Economic Commission, Apel's frustration approached the boiling point: "These thousand little political pinpricks are unbearable."[97] Above all, they were embarrassing: "The opponent says this: you can plan and build power stations and chemical factories etc. no worse than us—on the contrary, even in a shorter time and probably better. But the thousand little things which the population needs, that you can't manage!"[98]

Subsequent reports expanded the list of formidable obstacles: insufficient administrative cooperation, lack of materials and productive capacity, negligent quality control, the proclivity of manufacturers to ignore the demands of trade organs.[99] The State Planning Commission's program had called for the establishment of new, special stores for selling the thousand little things, but even these stores were often unable to secure their inventory.[100] The program was not without modest successes. In 1960, overall production of the thousand little things increased 6.5 percent compared to 1959. Certain consumer service industries were able to report increased activity, particularly the repair industries, beauty salons, and Laundromats.[101] But these gains were a small consolation, a far cry from the hopes and boastful challenges of July 1958. With foodstuffs increasingly scarce and the pace of collectivization in the countryside proceeding at full speed, the less-than-brilliant campaign for the thousand little things could hardly drown out the rising chorus of dissatisfaction.

In keeping with the scaling back of its consumption goals and the general drift towards retrenchment, the SED leadership began to revert to old form by resuscitating a policy of "priority provisioning" (*Schwerpunktversorgung*). As in the months preceding the uprising in June 1953, the regime again prepared plans for privileging heavy-industrial workers with a larger share of the insufficient supply of consumer goods. Yet the language of prosperity, so prevalent for the past few years, could scarcely be excluded. The result was an updated version of priority provisioning, the official logic of which suggested a kind of Main Economic Task limited to the factory floor: "Workers in the main enterprises of our republic create the most important preconditions for the further building of socialism. They have the first claim on a priority provisioning of foodstuffs, semiluxuries, and manufactured goods with the help of the most modern forms and methods of trade as well as exemplary repair and [other] services."[102] The emerging plans envisioned an array of stores and restaurants in the enterprises and in the residential areas surrounding them. They were to display the highest *Verkaufskultur;* many were to feature self-service. The stores were to have special business hours to accommodate all workers' shifts. There was also to be a special order and delivery service, allowing workers to order items while at work and have them delivered to their homes.

The reemergence of "priority provisioning" can be traced back to the trade conference of July 1959. Among the many tasks it had bequeathed to the Ministry for Trade and Provisioning was that of "complex provisioning in the enterprise." Again, the hand of Walter Ulbricht was evident, as he called on the ministry to enhance the consumption offerings available in factories.[103] If the ministry had any doubts about the importance of this task, they were quickly dispelled by a follow-up intervention from Ulbricht. Erich Apel explained the situation to Minister Merkel in October 1959: "In connection with the provisioning of the population comrade Ulbricht has criticized the fact that the provisioning of the large enterprises no longer stands at the level it once did."[104] According to Apel, Ulbricht had been particularly dismayed by the fact that there had been a decline in provisioning even at such flagship enterprises as the Kombinat Schwarze Pumpe and, worse yet, his namesake VEB Leuna-Werke "Walter Ulbricht."

Despite Ulbricht's involvement, preparations dragged on into the spring and summer of 1960. As late as September, government officials were still unable to narrow down the list of potential participants. The various districts (Bezirke) had proposed a total of seventy-eight enterprises. By August, officials from the State Planning Commission, the FDGB, and the Ministry for Trade and Provisioning were able to bring that number down to forty-six.[105] Their task, however, had been to reduce the list to a maximum of fifteen to twenty firms. Meanwhile, only very few enterprises, those certain of a place on the final list, could begin to implement some of the aspects of priority provisioning.[106] Consequently, the policy failed to get off the ground before SED leaders seemed to steer their ship of state into yet another economic tidal wave. In September 1960, in response to some public but uninfluential denunciations of the Oder-Neisse border by West German *Landsmannschaften*, the SED introduced a required visitor's visa for West Germans seeking to enter East Berlin. In retaliation for this official restriction of freedom of movement, West Germany announced that at the end of the year it would cut off all trade with East Germany.

This new confrontation is only understandable within the context of the Berlin Crisis. And although by September 1960 the crisis was already nearly two years old, it now began to play a significant role in the course of East Germany's deepening provisioning debacle. The crisis had begun with Khrushchev's ultimatum of November 1958, in which he threatened the Western powers that if they refused to begin negotiations with the Soviet Union on preparing a German peace treaty and on turning West Berlin into a demilitarized "free city" within six months, the Soviet Union would hand over to the GDR all rights and responsibilities over Berlin, including control over Western access routes connecting West Germany and West Berlin. With his usual gift for brutal metaphor, Khrushchev described West Berlin as "a sort of malignant tumor" on which the Soviet Union had "decided to do some surgery."[107] This is not the place to address in detail the overlapping and divergent motives and interests of all the actors involved in the crisis. Recent research, however, has highlighted a hitherto underestimated factor that is of concern to us, namely, the growing pressure exerted on Khrushchev during the crisis by the SED, in particular by Walter Ulbricht.[108] While Khrushchev had hoped to use West Berlin as a means of leveraging the Western powers into a broader German peace settlement, Ulbricht, for obvious reasons, pressed Khrushchev to resolve the problem of West Berlin immediately and independently of a larger treaty with the Western powers.[109]

How was the small, satellite East German state able to put pressure on its superpower patron? In fact, there were several factors that allowed it to do so. The open border and the annual flight of hundreds of thousands of East Germans directly undermined Khrushchev's concept of the GDR as a showcase for socialism in the peaceful struggle against capitalism. The forward strategic position of East Germany with regard to NATO heightened the importance of internal stability, which was obviously threatened by the open border. The widening rift between the Soviet Union and China over leadership of the socialist world, combined with Mao's increasingly hard-line stance toward the West, made it necessary that Khrushchev not appear too soft in his dealings with the capitalist world. Finally, declining economic conditions in East Germany put pressure on Khrushchev to do something about West Berlin.[110] As Khrushchev's six-month deadline elapsed without eliciting the desired Western response and as the East German Main Economic Task disintegrated, the SED leadership was emboldened to act with increasing independence, even as it grew more economically dependent on the Soviet Union. Hence the introduction in September 1960 of the visitor's visa. (Later, the GDR began cultivating closer relations with China, without Soviet approval.)[111]

The West German threat of a trade cancellation, however, came at a terrible time for the GDR's economy. Shortages in food items were increasingly exacerbated by the forced collectivization of agriculture. These shortages, in turn, contributed to the refugee crisis, which took yet a further toll on the economy by worsening labor shortages.[112] (The Berlin Crisis, too, now began to push even more East Germans into fleeing to the West, as a kind of panic took hold among the population that this might be the last chance to escape before the border was closed.)[113] Internal reports to Ulbricht showed that the meat supply was "very strained," so that a "demand-appropriate" supply was "not assured." The situation had given rise to "political discussions" in the population. Attempts to steer demand toward poultry by lowering prices had proved ineffectual.[114] Any hope that the other socialist countries would help with increased exports to East Germany was dim. East German leaders had grown accustomed to seeing their expectations of aid from COMECON disappointed. As recently as July 1960 Minister Merkel had complained bitterly to Ernst Lange about Bulgaria backing out of promised tomato deliveries to East Germany. The tomatoes were desperately needed as a means of steering demand away from meat. Merkel's anger only intensified when he learned that there were so many Bulgarian tomatoes in West Germany and West Berlin that price reductions had been announced in the West German press.[115] In any case, imports from West Germany consisted mostly of commodities unavailable from the COMECON countries. The prospect of a West German trade embargo would mean not only the loss of 10 percent of East Germany's imports but, more important, an especially disruptive loss of such economically "strategic" goods as high-grade steel, sheet metal, and spare parts.[116]

As the East German economy reeled and as reports of "negative discussions" in the population multiplied, the meetings and memoranda of SED leaders displayed a greater sense of frustration and panic.[117] At the center of the regime's provisioning problems was the upheaval in agriculture. As Wittkowski explained at a November meeting of Apel's Economic Commission, shortfalls in planned deliveries of meat and milk had reached 150,000 and 170,000 tons respectively.[118] Although silent on the role of collectivization in these shortfalls, she did mention that large numbers of farmers no longer appeared in the marketplace as suppliers. Other members of the commission emphasized those factors that contributed to shortages in manufactured commodities: a lack of raw materials interfered with meeting demand for textiles, clothing, shoes, and household chemical products; cooperation between trade and industry was virtually nonexistent; a lack of packaging materials prevented many goods from reaching retail outlets. Wittkowski complained of prices being too low for the thousand little things of daily demand. There was an irrational fear of raising prices, she suggested. But how else could one exert control over demand and provide incentive for manufacturers to increase production?[119] Apel, as head of the commission, was exasperated; the list of problems seemed endless. "What's the point?" he asked. "For the party leadership the point is that all of these little pinpricks that cut to the quick be overcome in our entire policy, through our own efforts; with correct order and discipline, with the right organization, we must begin the work."[120] As so often in the past, the atmosphere of deepening crisis drew SED leaders ever closer to the magic words "organization," "discipline," "through our own efforts." By invoking them—by relying on them—Apel showed the limitations of his, and the party's, thinking. At the end of the meeting, he asked Wittkowski to draw up proposals for the Central Committee. She again brought up the problem of agriculture. He told her to include it in her report. "With agriculture I know of no way out," she continued. "Good," he interrupted, "but in other areas we can do something." Several months later, intending to rebuke those working for him, he unwittingly described the leadership when he said "We are entirely lacking in ideas."[121]

In 1960 nearly sixty thousand more East Germans fled to West Germany than in 1959.[122] In November, two and a half years after the lifting of rationing, several *Bezirke* reintroduced it in new form by instituting customer lists for the retail sale of butter.[123] How else to assure a "just" distribution of a scarce commodity? But as an admission of the failure of the Main Economic Task, it could not have been clearer. SED leaders turned to their only option for help, the Soviet Union. Initially, the Soviet leadership seemed to underestimate the severity of the unfolding crisis in East Germany. In November 1960, at a meeting in Moscow, Khrushchev admitted to Ulbricht that he had not realized how dependent the East German economy had become on West Germany: "For the time being Adenauer didn't give it to us on the nose." Generally, Khrushchev showed sympathy for East Germany's economic problems: "The GDR's needs are also our needs," he recognized.[124] Still, he tended to underestimate the role of West Germany as a major cause of difficulties for the SED. Moreover, his relations with Ulbricht had been strained for some time, at least since 1956, when Khrushchev delivered his secret speech and Ulbricht resisted the drift of de-Stalinization.[125]

Although the West Germans agreed in December 1960 to renegotiate the inter-German trade agreement, Ulbricht felt compelled in January 1961 to reiterate to Khrushchev East Germany's urgent need for assistance. Ulbricht recounted at length its myriad economic woes. He spoke of chronic shortfalls in plan fulfillment and widespread unhappiness among workers and the intelligentsia. But his emphasis was on the unexpected advances in productivity and consumption in the Federal Republic. The goals of the Main Economic Task, he admitted, had presumed economic stagnation in the FRG. Instead, East Germany was confronted with the "constant political pressure" exerted by continued West German successes, which, as he pointed out, were "visible to every citizen in the GDR" and constituted "the main reason for the fact that in the course of ten years about two million people have left our republic."[126] In view of the disparity in living standards, the East Germans had been forced to take steps to increase individual consumption. But these efforts had come at the expense of modernizing and reinvesting in "our production apparatus." This state of affairs was not sustainable. The implication was clear: without Soviet help, the situation in East Germany threatened to spin out of control, with disastrous results for the entire socialist bloc. Ulbricht proposed a change of course: a return to emphasizing investment over consumption, extensive deliveries of goods from the East, and a more integrated East German–Soviet "economic community." Picking up on proposals discussed back in November at the meeting in Moscow, Ulbricht was preparing for economic life in a world in which the problem of West Berlin would be solved in one way or another.

Over the next several months the East German economy did become more tightly linked to that of the Soviet Union, but not quite as Ulbricht had imagined. Khrushchev's sensitivity to East German needs notwithstanding, the Soviet Union had its own economic interests to pursue as well. Moscow came to treat the GDR increasingly as "a Soviet union republic."[127] This meant that in return for deliveries of commodities from the Soviet Union, East Germany had to deliver finished machine goods to the Soviets. However, to produce these items, materials and parts had to be imported from Western countries, including West Germany, and paid for with hard currency. Thus, the East German "production program" geared itself increasingly toward Soviet demands requiring imports from the West. Mindful of price advantages for themselves, Soviet trade officials encouraged the East Germans to expand their Western trade as much as possible. They suggested buying commodities, particularly steel, from West Germany on credit, without worrying too much about paying off their debts. In the words of Anastas Mikoyan, now Soviet premier, "It does no harm to have debts with West Germany."[128] A feeble, offhand joke from a deputy chairman of the Soviet Council of Ministers indicated how far expectations had slipped from the heady optimism of July 1958: it was "necessary to assure three basic factors," he said. "The sufficient supply of foodstuffs, the satisfaction of housing needs, and love. For the last one, however, the economists are not responsible."[129] Here was the festive embrace of Gosplan.

This change of economic course, however, did little to alleviate East Germany's provisioning crisis. Reports of insufficient food supplies multiplied in the first months of the year. As economic planners complained of excessive purchasing power, consumers found their shops lacking in meat, butter, milk, and coffee; in many places, there were shortages of potatoes, bread, noodles, and vegetables.[130] By May, Merkel was growing desperate. In a letter to Wittkowski, he emphasized that the supplies of meat and butter had declined compared to 1960, giving rise to yet more "negative discussions" in the population. Attempts to substitute fish and margarine foundered on lack of supplies and poor quality. Shortages in foodstuffs were only exacerbated by a further downturn in the supply of manufactured commodities.[131] As Merkel pleaded for Wittkowski's personal intervention, local party officials conveyed the repeated cries of discontent from consumers: "Not only do things not go forward, they go constantly backwards"—"Conditions like 1945!"—"With Hitler, during the war, we at least had meat and bread regularly!"[132] To ease the demand for meat, officials in the State Planning Commission toyed with the idea of trying to popularize a "meatless day." There was concern within the party leadership, however, that such a measure would be ill advised; people might associate it with either Nazism or Catholicism.[133] A clear indication of the severity of the shortages was the fact that HO and consumer co-op sales personnel and store managers were quitting in record numbers. In East Berlin alone nearly eight hundred people left their retail jobs between April and June 1961.[134]

As the provisioning crisis intensified, so too did the Berlin crisis, both of which found common expression in the rising number of refugees. Between January and July over one hundred thousand East

Germans fled to West Germany. In his dealings with Khrushchev, Ulbricht continued to pressure him for some action on West Berlin. He
reminded Khrushchev that two years had elapsed since his original ultimatum; he argued that the time was favorable for action since the
Adenauer government was gearing up for elections in September and
U.S. President Kennedy would be loathe, in the first year of his presi-
dency, to antagonize the Soviet Union.[135] When Khrushchev and
Kennedy met in Vienna in June 1961, they failed to reach an agreement on Berlin and Germany, and Khrushchev issued another six-
month ultimatum. East German citizens feared this might be their last
chance to escape before the border was closed. In fact, the Soviet
ambassador to East Germany informed Ulbricht in early July that
Khrushchev had finally agreed to Ulbricht's request to seal the border.[136] That very month one thousand people left the GDR every single
day. In a television address of July 25, 1961, Kennedy outlined his three
"essentials," making it clear that the United States was committed to
maintaining Western rights in West Berlin, the freedom of West Berlin,
and freedom of movement between West Germany and West Berlin.
What he neglected to mention—the question of freedom of movement
between East and West Berlin—was painfully audible to everyone
watching. (Five days later, a public statement from Senator William
Fulbright echoed Kennedy's position.) This opening certainly contributed to Khrushchev's willingness to acquiesce to East German pressure to seal the border. The SED's Department for Security had already
determined the amount of building materials it required, including
485 tons of barbed wire and 51.9 tons of wire fencing.[137] As many as
forty-seven thousand East Germans fled to West Germany in the first
two weeks of August. The parallel flurry of correspondence and meetings among Soviet bloc leaders is well documented. It was at a three-
day meeting (August 3–5) of the Political Consultative Committee of
the Warsaw Treaty Organization that East German requests were formally approved; there, the leaders of the socialist world officially decided to close the border between East and West Berlin on the night of
August 12–13, 1961.

Having at long last reached the building of the Berlin Wall, we must
now address several long-deferred questions. How was it possible that
within the short space of three years—between the summers of 1958

and 1961—East Germany fell so precipitously from public optimism to patent desperation, from the lifting of rationing and the adoption of the Main Economic Task to the ignominy of retreat behind the Berlin Wall? And how do the constituent events and policies of these years— the Main Economic Task, the collectivization of agriculture, the self-service store, the Leipzig trade conference, Khrushchev's ultimatums, the Seven-Year Plan, the thousand little things of daily demand—take their places in this trajectory of rapid decline?

The available evidence suggests that the SED leadership never for a moment believed in the possibility of realizing the goals of the Main Economic Task. In fact, one wonders if the party's leaders even considered its goals desirable, at least in the short term. In the years covered in this study, Walter Ulbricht and those loyal to him came down repeatedly on the side of productivism. Their visions of economic prowess and socialist superiority were consistently wedded to the realm of investment goods and heavy industry. Meeting the needs of consumers was at best a distraction, at worst a profligate waste of scarce resources. Only the challenge of prosperity in West Germany wrenched their attention from the indices of productivity, forcing their grudging participation in a contest of material well-being they resented and despised. In the late 1950s the collectivization of agriculture most clearly demonstrated the SED's lack of commitment to the goals of the Main Economic Task. How, with the experience of the early 1950s in recent memory, could its leaders have pursued a policy certain to disrupt consumer supply if they were truly intent on surpassing West German consumption levels? And how can we explain the intensification of the collectivization campaign even as it brought chaos to the provisioning process and drove increasing numbers of East Germans across the open border?

Further research may provide definitive answers to these questions. However, the most recent research on the Berlin Crisis offers grounds for plausible speculation. The evidence it has uncovered pointing to the assertive role played by SED leaders, above all by Ulbricht, in pressuring Khrushchev to take action on the question of Berlin encourages one to see the Main Economic Task primarily as a temporary, stopgap measure. Ulbricht never intended to pursue its expressed aims. Its purpose was rather to limit the flow of refugees from East to West by serving as a kind of modernized New Course, the essence of which was neatly conveyed by attempts to increase the supply of modern durables and to develop retail innovations such as the self-service store. But the emphasis on consumption would last only until the problem of the open border was solved.

The precise nature of that solution, however, remained uncertain. Ulbricht hoped to incorporate West Berlin into the GDR and to sign a separate peace treaty with the Soviet Union. Khrushchev, seeking improved relations with the West, wanted to settle the Berlin question within the context of an overall treaty on Germany with the Western powers. Ulbricht chafed, knowing that the Main Economic Task was a gamble that grew riskier with each passing day. When Khrushchev's first ultimatum elapsed without result, the East Germans took the initiative by engaging in provocative, unilateral actions. Trying to maintain pressure on Khrushchev, for example, they introduced gratuitous bureaucratic obstacles for western officials and West Germans seeking to enter East Berlin; later they cultivated closer relations with China.[138] The collectivization of agriculture, which accelerated dramatically after the elapsing of Khrushchev's first ultimatum, can also be seen in this light, as it intensified the atmosphere of confrontation and increased the pressure on Khrushchev to do something about Berlin.[139] The effect was to sabotage the spirit of East-West cooperation and to exacerbate the refugee crisis. The SED, out of increasing desperation, had raised the stakes, embarking on a high-risk effort to force Khrushchev into making a move. (The thousand little things of daily demand and priority provisioning were part of this general drift into hard-line retrenchment.) It was perhaps reckless for the SED leadership to have taken so risky a course of action.[140] On the other hand, did it have an alternative? In any case, it was not the first time, nor would it be the last, that party leaders, enamored as they were of "discipline," "will," and "struggle," chose the path of unyielding confrontation to achieve their objectives, even at the risk of spiraling chaos and violence.

Admittedly, this scenario too raises questions. One wonders if Khrushchev himself ever believed in the plausibility of the Main Economic Task, if he simply assimilated it into his vision of East Germany as a showcase of socialism. Some scholars have recently argued that Khrushchev's genuine faith in the ability of socialism to overtake capitalism led him to believe in "all the Potyomkin villages of Socialist enthusiasm and transformation that Ulbricht staged for him during his official visits."[141] Yet others have pointed out that as early as August 1958 Soviet officials were alarmed by "the flight of the intelligentsia from the GDR," which inevitably took a serious toll on the East German economy. That very month, Khrushchev reportedly told Ulbricht, "we cannot compete with capitalism with open borders."[142] This statement, if Khrushchev truly made it, suggests that he too might have viewed the Main Economic Task as a temporary measure, a public relations palliative until the Berlin question was solved. But then one wonders if he approved of the timing of the collectivization campaign, particularly its increasing intensity after 1959, even as the GDR came closer to the edge of collapse. Or was he appalled by the mounting crisis, and did it cause him to consider a change of leadership within the SED in the hopes of getting Ulbricht off his back? These are questions only further research may answer.

In the end, Ulbricht got only part of what he wanted; the border was sealed, but West Berlin remained in the hands of Western authorities. This outcome, in the short run, meant an end to the refugee crisis, removing for a time much of the unbearable pressure on the SED to compete with West Germany on the battlefield of consumption. In the long run, of course, the West German challenge endured. Even if their citizens were now captive, SED leaders could never block out the images of abundance seeping through their "antifascist protection wall." As we now know, the relationship between dictatorship and demand was far from settled. And yet for our purposes the wall signifies an important break: never again would SED leaders adopt as official policy the goals they had proclaimed in the Main Economic Task; never again would they boast of East Germany's ability to surpass West Germany in individual consumption. In this sense, the building of the wall marks the end of a crucial chapter in the Cold War contest of prosperity.

Epilogue

I sit by the roadside.
The driver changes the wheel.
I do not like the place I have come from.
I do not like the place I am going to.
Why with impatience do I
Watch him changing the wheel?

Bertolt Brecht, "Changing the Wheel"[1]

It does no harm to have debts with West Germany.

Anastas Mikoyan, March 1961

In October 1960, in the atmosphere of heightened tension aroused by the Berlin crisis and in the wake of the great "socialist spring" in the countryside, which had done so much to undermine the food supply and with it the Main Economic Task, the East Berlin Magistrat held its annual festival *(Festtage)*. Over three thousand artists from all over the world came to participate and "fight," as *Neues Deutschland* explained, for the cause of peace and humanity. The newspaper cited the appearance of both the American singer Paul Robeson and the Soviet violinist David Oistrakh as "the most obvious symbol of the world-openness of our capital."[2] Another observer might have looked elsewhere for openness, perhaps to the as yet unsealed border over which more and more East Germans were crossing with no intention of returning, at least not any time soon.

As one would expect, the festival performances offered a combination of old and new, classic and contemporary. While the Staatsoper presented Verdi's *Don Carlos,* and the Komische Oper *La Traviata,* the Deutsches Theater staged Erwin Strittmatter's *Die Holländerbraut,* and the Maxim Gorky Theater mounted a production of Lion Feuchtwanger's adaptation of *Vasantasena.* Noteworthy as these productions were, perhaps the most popular event was the premier on the festival's final day of a new operetta-revue entitled *Messeschlager Gisela*, a tale of a young East German seamstress who aspires to become a fashion designer as she toils away at the fictional VEB Berliner Schick (People's-Owned Enterprise, Berliner Chic). In preparation for the Leipzig trade fair, the eponymous heroine designs a new dress, stylish yet practical, which, in the opinion of her co-workers, is sure to be the hit of the fair. But Gisela's boss, plant manager Kuckuck (his improbable name gives away the fact that he is the foil), disagrees, convinced that VEB Berliner Schick will attain world-class status *(Weltniveau)* only by outdoing the alleged excesses of western fashion designers. To that end, he designs his own absurd new dress, not only hideous but profligate in its waste of valuable material. Aptly, if unwittingly, he dubs it "Melone." Not surprisingly, as the plot unfolds in song and dance—featuring such titles as "Die Mode" (Fashion), "Selbstkritik ist mein Prinzip" (Self-Criticism is My Principle), and "Kleid für jede Frau" (Dress for Every Woman)—Kuckuck's Melone proves to be a flop, whereas Gisela's inspired creation is celebrated as a smashing success.

Messeschlager Gisela was a product of the moment. Only in the context of the Main Economic Task could one imagine a production so given over to the themes of fashion and consumption enjoying such a prominent occasion for its premier. The venue was perhaps no less important, for the production was staged at the Metropol Theater, located in the Friedrichstraße, just a few steps away from the train station where one crossed between East and West Berlin, a fact that might itself have been taken as a form of challenge to the West. The show was at least as successful as Gisela's fictional design, her "Kleid für jede Frau." Not only did the premiere sell out, but so did seventy-four subsequent performances over the course of the following ten months. As the Main Economic Task disintegrated at an ever-quickening pace, Gisela's triumph preserved a theatrical vision of its initial promise.

Signs of discomfort with the production, however, could be detected from the beginning, as it was greeted officially with a certain reserve. Although the review in *Neues Deutschland* offered some praise for the "successful attempt to mix operetta and revue in an amusing fashion," it criticized the show for concentrating too much on "the satirical depiction of negative types," on Kuckuck and his ilk, the obvious representatives of arrogant bureaucratism and slavish hankering after the products of western consumerism. The "positive figures," like Gisela, were consequently overshadowed, as was the larger "lesson on training for the collective, for socialist thought and action." This was no "irrelevant question," the reviewer emphasized, "but rather a central problem in the art of the socialist operetta."[3] An expectation of just this sort of reaction perhaps explains the all-too-familiar ambivalence about consumption permeating the subject matter itself. Clearly intended as a critique, however lighthearted, of prevailing conditions in the production and supply of clothing in East Germany, the piece was nevertheless careful not to go too far. Western fashion was characterized as distressingly decadent, those seeking to emulate it as morally deviant, if not politically suspect. Even Gisela's design embodied an idea ostensibly at odds with the tenets of western fashion; her "Kleid für jede Frau" would be just that, a dress for every woman and, as such, a clear rejection of western individualism, frivolity, and waste.

But by the time the Berlin Wall went up, even these ideological concessions could not save *Messeschlager Gisela*. The disjunction between the stupendous failure of the Main Economic Task and the musical reenactment of its professed goals had become too glaring for the authorities in East Berlin. At their "recommendation," the production came to an abrupt end, disappearing forever from the East German stage. It would not be performed again until after the wall came down, when in the late 1990s the increasingly widespread appetite for nostalgia *(Ostalgie)* gave rise to its revival in a reunited Berlin and several cities throughout the former GDR.[4] Gisela's return to the stage was ironic: what had once been enthusiastically embraced as a call for the greater satisfaction of legitimate material desires was now sought out in a spirit of nostalgia for the lost society in which those desires had so often been frustrated.

With the Berlin Wall in place and the flow of refugees to West Germany finally stanched, the problem of consumption did not go away. Most immediately, there remained the severe provisioning crisis that had helped to precipitate the sealing of the border; it could hardly be expected to disappear simply because the authorities rolled out their barbed wire on the night of August 12–13, 1961. In fact, the crisis persisted well into 1963, with drastic shortages in foodstuffs, manufactured goods, and semiluxuries. Meat and dairy products continued to be rationed by means of locally maintained customer lists—"steering measures," as functionaries euphemistically referred to them. Only by increasing the food supply with imports from capitalist countries and by raising the prices of certain goods to dampen demand was the regime able eventually to stabilize the situation.[5] Nevertheless, as Walter Ulbricht explained to his Soviet counterparts in May 1963, "even after the closing of the state borders, the high living standard [in West Germany] strongly affects the population of the GDR and its political attitudes."[6] Indeed, it would continue to do so until the collapse of the East German dictatorship. Although this is not the place to recount in detail the subsequent chapters in this ongoing story—there are already several works which do so[7]—our narrative would scarcely be complete without at least a glimpse ahead to later developments in their broader outlines as they stretched toward the fall of the wall in 1989.

In the mind of Walter Ulbricht, the wall was to be a temporary measure, one designed to provide greater breathing space. In closing off the option of flight, the regime would suspend the immediate pressures of unsatisfied consumer demand, giving itself time to increase productivity, pursue technological innovation, and, in turn, improve consumer supply. The economic history of East Germany in the 1960s is largely one of flirtation with reforms designed to achieve these aims. Ulbricht has long been viewed as a grim, prim, uncompromising Stalinist, stubbornly opposed to any deviation from Marxist-Leninist orthodoxy. (This image is essentially accurate for the years covered in this study.) However, since the opening of East Germany's state and party archives, our understanding of the East German leader during his last decade in power has been substantially revised.[8] It has now become clear that he was in fact the regime's leading proponent of the New Economic System (NES), as the reform package of the 1960s was initially called. NES was supposed to increase productivity by loosening up the rigid system of central planning and decision making; greater flexibility would be achieved through the introduction of "economic levers." Appealing to "material interest," the reform would make profit the primary measure for evaluating enterprise performance. The measure of profit, in turn, would be made possible by the introduction of more realistic—that is, market-oriented—prices. In fact, East German reformers, influenced by the work of the Soviet economist Evsei Liberman, were soon joined by reformers elsewhere in the Soviet bloc who pursued similar ideas.[9]

As recent findings have shown, however, the East German reform, such as it was, ended in total disappointment.[10] Prices were never really reformed; strict central control was only slightly and temporarily relinquished; and those most committed to the reform lacked support from Moscow, especially after Leonid Brezhnev replaced Khrushchev at the Soviet helm. To the modest extent that the reforms were introduced, however, they significantly complicated the process of planning and gave rise to anxiety among many party leaders and resentment among many economic planners. In 1967 Ulbricht acquiesced to his critics within the regime by introducing what was called the Economic System of Socialism, a much-diluted version of the original aims of NES. The cause of reform then suffered a crushing blow in 1968 with the invasion of Czechoslovakia, which triggered a reform backlash throughout the East bloc. By the end of the decade East Germany's leaders had quietly abandoned even the pretense of reform.

What did the abortive attempt at reform mean for consumers in East Germany? Essentially, more of what they had been experiencing since the mid-1950s. On the whole, the 1960s present a picture of continuity with the trends of the previous decade. As economic planners dithered over the nature of their proposed reforms, their long-term plans emphasized investment at the expense of consumption, pushing above all for accelerated growth in chemicals, metallurgy, and machine building.[11] However bold Ulbricht may have become as an economic reformer, he seems never to have lost his taste for the virtues of relative austerity. Consumption lost the high-profile status it had held during the brief but eventful years of the Main Economic Task, much as it had after the official demise of the New Course. Although one can certainly speak of progress in commodity supply (modern durables, for example, slowly entered more and more households), East German achievements seemed quite modest when compared with the ever-present and ever-advancing example of West Germany's material prosperity. Indeed, East German consumers continued to face chronic shortages, long lines, and poor-quality merchandise; and trade functionaries continued to struggle with the sadly familiar concatenation of excess purchasing power, an insufficient supply of desired commodities, and embarrassing *Überplanbestände.*

For its part, the regime contented itself with an equally familiar array of measures for addressing these difficulties. The HO, due to the end of rationing, had of course lost its special status as a site of higher-priced goods and thus as a crucial means of absorbing excess purchasing power. To make up for this loss, economic functionaries reinvented the HO anew—this time in the form of two new chains of luxury stores, *Exquisit* and *Delikat*. Where the first offered high-fashion clothing (much of it imported from the West) at artificially high prices based on heavy luxury taxes, the second sold luxury food items, also at inflated prices. As Philipp Heldmann has recently suggested, the regime thereby extended the tradition of the state-approved black market that had begun with the introduction of the HO in the late 1940s.[12]

One is struck by continuities in most other areas as well. The regime continued to make gestures, however halfhearted and underfunded, to providing more of the kinds of goods increasingly taken for granted in West Germany and western Europe. For example, in the 1960s the East German automobile industry introduced technological improvements in its two models, the Trabant and the Wartburg, and began increasing significantly the number of cars produced, albeit nowhere near sufficiently to meet demand.[13] In similar fashion, the East Germans followed developments in the West by establishing their own chain of fast-food restaurants specializing in grilled chicken. The Goldbroiler, as the restaurants were called, modeled themselves after the Wienerwald, a chain ubiquitous in Austria and West Germany.[14] Such efforts at modernizing the consumer landscape notwithstanding, the old problems bound up with consumer supply remained. Still burdened by their *Überplanbestände,* trade organs continued to carry out their end-of-season sales, offering their unwanted inventory at reduced prices. Similarly, demand researchers carried on with their thankless task, now working under the auspices of the new Institute for Demand Research in Leipzig (created in 1962 and renamed the Institute for Market Research in 1967). Although their efforts to ascertain consumer demand became more sophisticated as they incorporated consumer questionnaires, household budget studies, and other western techniques, the institute's researchers were in no position to remedy the unbalanced power relationship between trade and industry. Nor did their work have any influence on economic policy in general.

Real change came only with a change in leadership. By the beginning of the 1970s Ulbricht's position was much undermined by the failure of the economic reforms with which he had been so closely identified. In the last few years of his rule he had insisted on setting increasingly un-realistic economic targets. Obsessed with pushing forward the so-called scientific-technological revolution, he had pressured the Soviets for ad-ditional resources, arguing that the GDR would then be able to increase its productivity rate by 10 percent annually, a goal he was virtually alone in considering attainable. Such a policy, moreover, threatened to re-duce living standards in East Germany. At the Fourteenth Central Com-mittee Plenum in December 1970, Ulbricht again spoke out against consumerism and emphasized the need for renewed sacrifice. That very month increases in food prices and other austerity measures in Poland led to riots that drove the Polish leader, Władysław Gomułka, from power. The aging Ulbricht, now in ill health, seemed to be losing touch with reality. His illogical slogan to "overtake" West Germany "without catching up" (*Überholen ohne Einzuholen*) found no support in Moscow. His increasingly dictatorial manner, combined with his less-than-tactful assertions of the GDR's independence from the Soviet Union, also con-tributed to alienating the Soviet leadership. Once Erich Honecker and his supporters were ready to remove Ulbricht from power in 1971, they enjoyed Brezhnev's full support.[15]

Still, one might have been excused for expecting little to change when Ulbricht's successor presented his "Main Task" (*Hauptaufgabe*) at the SED's Eighth Party Congress in June 1971. Much of what Honecker had to say sounded entirely familiar: he promised a "new approach" to the provisioning of the population, offering immediate concessions to consumers; he announced a new round of wage increases; he called on trade representatives to "represent the needs of the population more vigorously against the forces of production"; he explained that in-creased productivity would make it possible to devote more resources to consumption needs.[16] Of course, all of this had been said before, nor was Honecker's *Hauptaufgabe* the first to be trumpeted at a party congress. And yet, as would become clear in the following years, his approach to the problems of consumption and material well-being dif-fered fundamentally from that of his predecessor in several key re-spects. Gone were the well-worn homilies on the virtues of sacrifice; gone was the vague vision of material plenty in some distant socialist utopia; gone also was the public boasting that the GDR would surpass West Germany in economic performance and per capita consumption. Instead, Honecker set out to offer the disaffected East German citizenry immediate improvements in the supply of consumer goods, combined with increased social spending and assurances of basic material security *(Geborgenheit)*. Under Honecker, the GDR entered the phase of "real existing socialism," in which, for reasons of political expediency and the legitimation of the new leadership, consumption would enjoy a new autonomy from the hitherto all-important demands of production. Living standards would improve, albeit modestly; the regime would thereby ensure that its citizens continued to acquiesce to its rule. In short, Honecker was imposing a trade-off: expanded consumption and material security in return for political quietude, if not loyalty. Walter Ulbricht had recognized that it was "politically dangerous" to demand unceasing sacrifice from the population. But he firmly believed that any potential unrest could always be countered with "the full authority of the party." Honecker, in contrast, took the view that one could "never govern against the workers."[17]

But how was the new leadership going to achieve the promised rise in living standards? How would it pay for what Ulbricht had always insisted could only be bought with increased productivity? Certainly not by pursuing market-oriented economic reforms such as those pondered in the 1960s. In fact, under Honecker the GDR experienced a consolidation of traditional, Soviet-type centralization in planning. The answer was actually rather simple, if ultimately disastrous: Honecker proceeded, with the indispensable help of his ingenious chief economic advisor, Günter Mittag, to import western consumer goods on a vastly expanded scale, to increase price subsidies and social expenditures to an unprecedented degree, and to pay for it all by borrowing from western creditors whatever the GDR could not itself afford with its own limited hard currency resources. Timothy Garton Ash has referred to this strategy as one of "reform substitution": "social benefits and consumer goods were offered to the people not as complements to a reform of the system but as substitutes for a reform of the system which the Party leadership considered would be too dangerous (for the Party leadership)."[18] It was hardly surprising then that Honecker's brand of socialism came to be referred to as "consumer socialism" or "jeans and Golf [Volkswagen] socialism." And in the short run, the strategy seemed to pay off. The first half of the 1970s was characterized by growing individual consumption and basic improvements in the overall quality of life for most East German citizens. Indeed, this may have been the best period of the GDR's history.[19] Nor was East Germany alone among Soviet bloc states in adopting this strategy, as Edward Gierek (Gomułka's successor) in Poland and Gustáv Husák in Czechoslovakia followed a similar path.[20]

In the long run, however, the Honecker-Mittag strategy was economically unsustainable. Within only a few years the GDR's trade deficit with the West soared. With imports far exceeding exports, East Germany was forced to take out loans, which only inflated its foreign debt further. Most of its imports, moreover, were devoted to immediate consumption, thus depriving the economy of badly needed resources for investment. As Jonathan Zatlin has neatly put it, "the GDR was not simply living beyond its means, but consuming its future—eating oranges instead of buying capital equipment to boost exports and pay for the oranges."[21] In 1970 the GDR's foreign debt had stood at a record one billion dollars, a source of considerable worry among party leaders, yet another serious item in the long list of grievances against Walter Ulbricht. But only ten years later that figure had risen twelve-fold. There were voices of warning within the regime, even from senior advisors. But Honecker, though a dilettante in economic matters, was able as party leader to block any serious challenge to his political-economic strategy.

As a consequence, however, he and Mittag were forced to redouble their efforts to increase East Germany's hard currency revenue. Only with western cash or credit would they be able to maintain their commitment to the Main Task (expanded and refurbished in 1976 within the parameters of the all too aptly named Unity of Economic and Social Policy)[22] and to service the GDR's dangerously expanding foreign debt. Much has been written since 1989 about East Germany's increasingly desperate scramble for hard currency during the Honecker years. The main features of this story are now well known: the widening of political and commercial contacts between the two German states, arising on the one hand from détente and West Germany's *Ostpolitik*, and on the other from the economic needs engendered by Honecker's policies; the easing of travel restrictions between the two Germanys, which greatly increased the number of West Germans (with their deutschmarks) visiting East Germany; the "buying free" *(Freikauf)* by West Germany of political prisoners in the GDR; the "transit fees" required for people traveling to and from West Berlin; the "twilight realms" of licit and illicit dealings presided over by the notorious Alexander Schalk-Golodkowski, who, among other things, headed East Germany's special agency of Commercial Coordination (*Bereich Kommerzielle Koordinierung* or *KoKo*);[23] Günter Mittag's program of export-led growth, which, in subordinating the import needs of East Germany's aging capital stock to the goal of debt reduction, "cannibaliz[ed] future production to satisfy immediate consumer demand";[24] the oil crises of the 1970s and the exploding inflation in prices for energy and raw materials on international markets, as a result of which the Soviets reduced their oil deliveries to East Germany *and* raised the price, thus intensifying the latter's need for hard currency; the Polish crisis of the early 1980s, which, triggered by an increase in meat prices, not only served as an all-too-effective cautionary example of the supreme risks inherent in reintroducing austerity measures but also revivified the specter of June 17, 1953, not that the memory of it had much faded from the minds of East Germany's still traumatized leaders; the crucial role played by East Germany's Intershops, those outposts of capitalist consumerism, where western goods were sold for western currency, the possession of which by East German citizens was legalized in 1974; and, of course, the so-called billion credits in West German loans negotiated between Franz Josef Strauß and Schalck-Golodkowski in 1983 and 1984, granted on highly favorable terms and guaranteed by the West German government, and without which the East Germans would have faced the immediate threat of insolvency and Erich Honecker would very likely have fallen from power, as had Edward Gierek in Poland in 1980.[25] Alas, for Gierek there was no rich, capitalist West Poland to turn to.

Such was the ironic and terribly awkward position in which the Honecker regime now found itself, that is, one of increasingly abject financial (and thus political) dependency on the capitalist enemy and his corrupting currency. To be sure, the survival of the East German state depended ultimately on the willingness of the Soviet Union to defend it, by force if necessary. Brezhnev had warned Honecker (and the other leaders of Eastern Europe) of the risks involved in becoming too indebted to the West. He pointed to the unrest in Poland as an example of what could happen if that debt reached "a dangerous level."[26] Within the GDR, meanwhile, the benefits for consumers of the Unity of Economic and Social Policy were much belied in the 1980s by the return of serious shortages in the provisioning of basic consumer supplies such as meat, dairy products, potatoes, toilet paper, and heating fuel.[27] What a striking contrast the Intershops presented, islands of plenty fully stocked with the haloed, come-hither products of capitalist abundance. Of course, in expanding the number of Intershops and in opening them to East German consumers, the regime fundamentally devalued its own currency and economic credibility. Unwittingly, it also invited its citizens to participate in the very "commodity fetishism" it officially denounced, as well as a corrosive new form of social stratification based on possession of that magic mode of exchange, the deutschmark.[28] Those with relatives or friends in the Federal Republic were perhaps most fortunate; those in the unlucky position of being without "West-contacts" offered a cynical play on Marx's once inspiring words of promise: "From each according to his ability, to each according to his needs!" These they rephrased: "To each according to his aunt's place of residence."

Over the course of the 1980s the regime slid ever closer to the point of financial and ideological bankruptcy. West German credits seemed to provide financial stabilization. Once it became clear, however, that Gorbachev's Soviet Union, unlike Brezhnev's, was not prepared to use force to prop up the satellite regimes of Eastern Europe, the fate not only of Honecker and his supporters but of the GDR itself was sealed. Honecker's "consumer socialism" had brought the East German economy to the brink of insolvency and ruin; in the process, it had opened the floodgates to the deutschmark, allowing the West German currency and all it promised to ingratiate itself into the everyday desires and frustrations of East German citizens. For those who in the fall and winter of 1989 welcomed the collapse of the SED dictatorship but who still hoped for the continued existence of an independent GDR, based perhaps on some more democratic form of socialism, the legacy of the Honecker regime was distinctly bitter: socialism thoroughly discredited, reunification all but inevitable.[29] The gravitational pull of West German prosperity was simply too strong to resist.

It is no exaggeration to say that the problem of consumption plagued the GDR for the entirety of its existence. Nor, it must be added, has the problem entirely disappeared in the new Germany, where in novel ways it continues to reflect divisions between East and West, perhaps most visibly in the form of a tenaciously guarded East German "identity" expressed through old, East German brand-name products (f6 cigarettes and Trabant automobiles), *Ostalgie* television programs, and *Ostrock* parties that recycle the still-much-loved East German hit parade. For many in the new *Bundesländer* reunification and its discontents have brought about an unexpected transformation: former emblems of frustrated desire have become cherished repositories for feelings of nostalgia.[30]

This book has tried to chart the emergence of the problem of consumption in East Germany during the years before the building of the Berlin Wall, focusing particular attention on its political significance in the context of the Cold War. While the other dictatorships of the Soviet bloc faced many of the same difficulties with regard to consumption as those confronting the SED regime, none did so under the same pressure to compete with a mirror image of itself increasingly enhanced in the ever-brightening neon glow of prosperity and freedom. To the leaders of the GDR it must have seemed as if the severed limbs (West Germany) were always mysteriously acquiring greater phantom power over the body itself (East Germany). Nowhere was the juxtaposition of opposing social systems more starkly posed than in divided Germany, and nowhere did the issue of material well-being play a more prominent role in the heated struggle for political legitimacy. As we have seen, between 1948 and 1961 the SED's consumption policies wavered back and forth, depending on the amount of pressure at any given moment to suspend the primary commitment to productivism by making concessions to consumerism. The SED took up the contest of prosperity slowly and grudgingly, profoundly reluctant to divert limited resources away from heavy industry, that sphere of the economy it consistently fetishized as the sole engine of real growth. Trade and consumption, in direct contrast, it dismissed as "unproductive." But as a result of the challenge posed by a new kind of prosperity in West Germany, combined with the open border that made it accessible to the millions of East Germans who chose to flee, SED leaders found themselves increasingly beholden to a standard of material well-being they could neither equal nor displace.

The SED's inability in the first fifteen years after the Second World War to develop a distinct, clearly articulated alternative idea for the organization of consumption in socialism was one of its great failures. Instead of elaborating such an idea, the party adhered to its productivist course, relegating consumption to the back burner and supplementing calls for sacrifice with feeble promises of abundance for all in some vague, distant future. But the provisioning hierarchies required by productivism—enshrined in Order no. 234—called into question the regime's commitment to eradicating social differences, while the chronic shortages and recurrent provisioning crises belied promises of long-term abundance. East German consumers complained incessantly: sacrifice for what? Nor did it help the SED that its sermons on the virtues of hard work and material austerity were underwritten by Soviet occupiers intent on extracting extensive reparations well into the 1950s, that is, at the very moment when West Germany was enjoying the benefits of Marshall Plan assistance. Identified by wide sections of the population as creatures of their Soviet sponsors, SED leaders were burdened from the outset by a considerable deficit in credibility and legitimacy.

The pressure on the regime to address consumer dissatisfaction became immense. Within the realm of officialdom itself there quickly emerged a consumer supply lobby pressing for greater attention to the material needs of East German consumers. If the officials in domestic trade who comprised that lobby were primarily motivated by the need to fulfill their sales plans, their efforts to advance their own interests simultaneously served to "represent" within the planning bureaucracy those of consumers as well. The cause of consumer supply drew much of its strength from the enticements of growing prosperity in West Germany and the mounting seriousness of the refugee crisis. When SED leaders found themselves forced to adopt more consumerist policies and poses, they did so in the terms and argumentation provided by the consumer supply lobby. And as we have seen, the SED's list of concessions to consumerism between 1948 and 1961 was a long one, including the introduction of the HO, the celebration of the Stalinallee as a glittering boulevard of socialist splendor, the array of measures bound up with the New Course, the widespread concern for a heightened level of *Verkaufskultur,* the statistical tracking of living standards, the system of demand research, the introduction of various retail innovations (the mail-order catalogue, the installment plan, the self-service store), and finally and most dramatically, the adoption of the Main Economic Task.

The consumption regime that emerged bit by bit in East Germany marked a distinct break with past German traditions characterized by cartels, suppressed wages, and artificially high prices for consumer goods. The main features of that regime, as we may now summarize them, were the following: subsidized low prices for goods that satisfied fundamental needs (basic foodstuffs, work clothing, children's clothing, rent, utilities); high taxes on and thus high prices for higher-end consumption goods (semiluxuries, fashionable clothing, furniture, and modern household durables); high wages relative to productivity; and a chronic disparity between purchasing power and commodity supply. The higher prices for "luxury" goods served two purposes: they helped to pay for the subsidized low prices for basic goods, and they drew a moral line between necessity and luxury. (Inadvertently, they also enhanced conditions for expressing social differences in the "workers' and peasants' state.") Meanwhile, fixed low prices for basic goods, intended to assure the satisfaction of basic needs, had the effect of inflating demand well beyond the extent to which it could be satisfied. As a consequence, East German economic planners were locked in an unending struggle with an intractable monetary overhang and an ever-present backlog of unsatisfied demand.

In certain respects, SED leaders shared the goals of the consumer supply lobby. They recognized the importance of appearances and *Verkaufskultur,* fully aware that the public face of socialism played a decisive role in the extent to which it appealed to fellow Germans in the West and to their own citizens. Similarly, consumerist endeavors sometimes helped to ease immediate economic problems: the HO helped to absorb excess purchasing power and to undermine the black market; the installment plan helped to move excess inventory. Other nods to consumerism neatly dovetailed with the SED's need to show that socialism was a vehicle of modernity. For example, the system of demand research, by communicating the particular needs and desires of consumers to producers, was supposed to bring the complex processes of production and consumption into a more rational, smoothly functioning alignment. Likewise, the self-service store would offer direct access to consumer goods and lend a distinctly modern profile to the East German retail landscape.

But concessions to consumerism had to be kept within strict limits. SED leaders were all too aware that resources were limited, that the shortage economy could provide only so much. The chronic weakness of domestic trade within the structure of East Germany's political economy marked the dividing line between the interests of SED leaders and those of the consumer supply lobby, a line that effectively limited the amount of internal pressure that could be brought to bear on the party to respond to consumer demand. Atomized consumers could go on voicing their individual complaints through letters of petition and grumbling at the sales counter, but their appeals had no claim on likely redress. Their demands remained subject to an unpredictable process of endless "adjustment," constantly requiring the indefinite suspension of initial desire—a kind of everyday, material frustration of what Václav Havel has called "the longing to live in truth."

Ultimately, SED leaders recognized consumerism as something alien to Marxism-Leninism, compatible with it, if at all, only in limited doses. Official dogma denounced consumerism as part and parcel of "the American way of life," of "monopoly capitalism," of "lying advertising," and of the generation of "false needs." Consumerism was inextricably bound up with individualism and the articulation of social distinctions, characteristics clearly at odds with the avowed ethos of collectivity in a "workers' and peasants' state." Economically, it held out the prospect of unbearable pressure on the planned economy to respond to the mercurial, unpredictable demands of individual consumers, demands increasingly driven by West Germany's more accelerated turnover of needs and desires. If given free reign, consumerism could effectively deprive the party of its control over the economy and thus over the development of society itself. The very idea of the Leninist vanguard party, with its privileged knowledge of history and its leading role in building Communism, would lose all relevance and justification. East Germany's leaders found themselves in an increasingly untenable situation: consumerism threatened their claims to power, yet the maintenance of power required periodic concessions to consumerism. These inherent tensions contained a tremendous potential for destabilization. In June 1953 the party could subdue them temporarily with the help of Soviet tanks; by August 1961 it could do so only by erecting the Berlin Wall. But in the long run, as we now know, even the wall fell short of rendering the dictatorship invulnerable to the pressures of demand.

Notes

Abbreviations

The following abbreviations for archives, government institutions, party organizations, and periodicals are used in the notes. See also the list of abbreviations for organizations on pages xi–xii.

BArch	Bundesarchiv, Berlin
DVHV	German Administration for Trade and Provisioning
DWK	German Economic Commission
Gbl der DDR	*Gesetzblatt der Deutschen Demokratischen Republik*
HVHV	Central Administration for Trade and Provisioning
KKB	Coordination and Control Agency for Domestic Trade
LAB	Landesarchiv, Berlin (Breite Strasse)
MdF	Ministry of Finances
MfHV	Ministry for Trade and Provisioning
MfL	Ministry for Light Industry
ND	*Neues Deutschland*
SAPMO-BArch	Stiftung Archiv der Parteien und Massenorganisation en der Deutschen Demokratischen Republik im Bundesarchiv
SKHV	State Commission for Trade and Provisioning
SPK	State Planning Commission
SZS	Staatliche Zentralverwaltung für Statistik
ZK	Central Committee of the SED
ZK Abt. HVA	Central Committee Department for Trade, Provisioning, and Foreign Trade

Zvbl   *Zentralverordnungsblatt: Amtliches Organ der Deutschen Wirtschaftskom-*
          mission und ihrer Hauptverwaltungen sowie der Deutschen Verwaltungen
          für Inneres, Justiz und Volksbildung

Introduction

1. Victor Homola, "Germany: A Chocolate Wall," *New York Times*, October 6, 1999, p. A12.

2. Jeffrey Kopstein, *The Politics of Economic Decline in East Germany, 1945–1989* (Chapel Hill: University of North Carolina Press, 1997); Charles Maier, *Dissolution: The Crisis of Communism and the End of East Germany* (Princeton, N.J.: Princeton University Press, 1997); Jonathan Zatlin, "The Currency of Socialism: Money in the GDR and German Unification, 1971–1989" (Ph.D. diss., University of California at Berkeley, 2000).

3. Scholars of consumption and consumer culture have only begun to turn their attention to the role of consumption in the early years of this struggle. See Katherine Pence, "From Rations to Fashions: The Gendered Politics of East and West German Consumption, 1945–1961" (Ph.D. diss., University of Michigan, 1999); Mark Landsman, "Dictatorship and Demand: East Germany between Productivism and Consumerism, 1948–1961" (Ph.D. diss., Columbia University, 2000); Judd Stitziel, "Fashioning Socialism: Clothing, Politics, and Consumer Culture in East Germany, 1948–1971" (Ph.D. diss., Johns Hopkins University, 2001); David Crew, ed., *Consuming Germany in the Cold War* (Oxford: Berg, 2003).

4. On the "proletarian mystique," see Adam B. Ulam, *The Bolsheviks: The Intellectual, Personal and Political History of the Triumph of Communism in Russia* (New York: Collier, 1968), p. 148. Ulam aptly describes Lenin as "the apostle of technology and efficiency, whose religion is production" (p. 146).

5. Quoted in Robert Skidelsky, *John Maynard Keynes: The Economist as Saviour, 1920–1937* (London: Macmillan, 1992), p. 519.

6. Karl Marx, "Critique of the Gotha Program," in Robert Tucker, ed., *The Marx-Engels Reader* (New York: Norton, 1978), p. 531.

7. Ibid., p. 530.

8. For a discussion of the history and usefulness of the terms "Sovietization" and "Americanization," see Konrad Jarausch and Hannes Siegrist, "Amerikanisierung und Sowjetisierung: Eine vergleichende Fragestellung zur deutsch-deutschen Nachkriegsgeschichte," in Konrad Jarausch and Hannes Siegrist, eds., *Amerikanisierung und Sowjetisierung in Deutschland 1945–1970* (Frankfurt: Campus, 1997).

9. See, for example, Michael Wildt, *Am Beginn der "Konsumgesellschaft"* (Hamburg: Ergebnisse Verlag, 1994); Arnold Sywottek, "The Americanization of Everyday Life? Early Trends in Consumer and Leisure-Time Behavior," in Michael Ermarth, ed., *America and the Shaping of German Society, 1945–1955* (Providence, R.I.: Berghahn Books, 1993); Axel Schildt, *Moderne Zeiten: Freizeit, Massenmedien und "Zeitgeist" in der Bundesrepublik der 50er Jahre* (Hamburg: Christians, 1995).

10. For differing views, see Volker R. Berghahn, "Ideas into Politics: The Case of Ludwig Erhard," in R. J. Bullen, H. Pogge von Strandmann, and A. B. Polonsky, eds., *Ideas into Politics: Aspects of European History 1880–1950* (London: Croom Helm, 1984); Ludolf Herbst, "Krisenüberwindung und Wirtschaftsneuordnung: Ludwig Erhards Beteiligung an den Nachkriegsplanungen am Ende des Zweiten Weltkrieges," *Vierteljahrshefte für Zeitgeschichte* 25, no. 3 (1977), pp. 305–340; Volker Hentschel, *Ludwig Erhard: Ein Politikerleben* (Munich: Olzog, 1996).

11. For a positive assessment of Erhard's postwar career and the social market economy in West Germany, see A. J. Nicholls, *Freedom with Responsibility: The Social Market Economy in Germany, 1918–1963* (Oxford: Oxford University Press, 1994).

12. Ludwig Erhard, *Wohlstand für alle* (Düsseldorf: Econ-Verlag, 1956), p. 168.

13. Ibid., p. 4.

14. On this theme, see Uta Poiger, *Jazz, Rock, and Rebels: Cold War Politics and American Culture in a Divided Germany* (Berkeley: University of California Press, 2000).

15. For an introduction to this subject, see Detlev Peukert, *The Weimar Republic: The Crisis of Classical Modernity* (New York: Hill and Wang, 1992), pp. 178–190.

16. See, for example, Jürgen Kuczynski and Bruno Schulz, "Der schwarze Markt," *Einheit* 3, no. 1 (1948), pp. 43–51; Otto Winzer, "Zur Lage in Berlin und den Aufgaben der Partei," *Einheit* 5, no. 9 (1950), pp. 830–841.

17. Mary Nolan, *Visions of Modernity: American Business and the Modernization of Germany* (New York: Oxford University Press, 1994), pp. 30–57.

18. Admittedly, there were exceptions among those Germans who visited the United States in these years. See, for example, Moritz Bonn, *Das Schicksal des deutschen Kapitalismus* (Berlin: S. Fischer, 1930).

19. The phrase is from Volker Berghahn, "Resisting the Pax Americana? West German Industry and the United States, 1945–55," in Ermarth, *America and the Shaping of German Society*, p. 97.

20. Victoria DeGrazia, "Changing Consumption Regimes in Europe, 1930–1970: Comparative Perspectives on the Distribution Problem," in Susan Strasser, Charles McGovern, and Matthias Judt, eds., *Getting and*

Spending: European and American Consumer Societies in the Twentieth Century (New York: Cambridge University Press, 1998).

21. See, for example, Vernon Aspaturian, "The Soviet Military-Industrial Complex— Does It Exist?" *Journal of International Affairs* 26, no. 1 (1972), pp. 1–28; Franklyn Griffiths and Gordon Skilling, eds., *Interest Groups in Soviet Politics* (Princeton, N.J.: Princeton University Press, 1971); János Kornai, *The Socialist System: The Political Economy of Communism* (Princeton, N.J.: Princeton University Press, 1992), pp. 418–420.

22. For discussions of the debate, see Ralph Jessen, "Die Gesellschaft im Staatssozializmus: Probleme einer Sozialgeschichte der DDR," *Geschichte und Gesellschaft* 21, no. 1 (1995), pp. 96–110; Thomas Lindenberger, "Die Diktatur der Grenzen: Zur Einleitung," in Thomas Lindenberger, ed., *Herrschaft und Eigen-Sinn in der Diktatur: Studien zur Gesellschaftsgeschichte der DDR* (Cologne: Böhlau, 1999); Konrad Jarausch, "Care and Coercion: The GDR as Welfare Dictatorship," in Konrad H. Jarausch, ed., *Dictatorship as Experience: Toward a Socio-Cultural History of the GDR* (New York: Berghahn Books, 1999).

23. This assumption becomes explicit in Lindenberger, "Die Diktatur der Grenzen," p. 20.

1. Production and Consumption

1. The literature on the occupation period is too extensive to list here. For a general account of the period, see Christoph Kleßmann, *Die doppelte Staatsgründung: Deutsche Geschichte 1945–1955* (Göttingen: Vandenhoeck & Ruprecht, 1991). On the Western zones, see Wolfgang Benz, *Von der Besatzungsherrschaft zur Bundesrepublik, Stationen einer Staatsgründung 1946–1949* (Frankfurt am Main: Fischer Taschenbuch, 1984). On the Soviet zone, see Norman M. Naimark, *The Russians in Germany: A History of the Soviet Zone of Occupation, 1945–1949* (Cambridge, Mass.: Harvard University Press, 1995).

2. See, respectively, Michael Wildt, *Der Traum vom Sattwerden: Hunger und Protest, Schwarzmarkt und Selbsthilfe in Hamburg 1945–1948* (Hamburg: USA-Verlag, 1986); Kleßmann, *Die doppelte Staatsgründung*; Rainer Gries, *Die Rationen-Gesellschaft: Versorgungskampf und Vergleichsmentalität: Leipzig, München und Köln* (Münster: Westfälisches Dampfboot, 1991); Paul Erker, *Ernährungskrise und Nachkriegsgesellschaft: Bauern und Arbeiterschaft in Bayern 1943–1953* (Stuttgart: Klett-Cotta, 1990).

3. Belinda Davis, *Home Fires Burning: Food, Politics, and Everyday Life in World War I Berlin* (Chapel Hill: University of North Carolina Press, 2000); Arnold Sywottek, "Konsumverhalten der Arbeiter und 'sozialistische'

Konsumgenossenschaften: Zur Geschichte der Arbeiterbewegung in der Weimarer Republik," in Albrecht Lehmann, ed., *Studien zur Arbeiterkultur* (Münster: F. Coppenrath, 1984); Karen Hagemann, "'Wir hatten mehr Notjahre als reichliche Jahre . . .': Lebenshaltung und Hausarbeit Hamburger Arbeiterfamilien in der Weimarer Republik," in Klaus Tenfelde, ed., *Arbeiter im 20: Jahrhundert* (Stuttgart: Klartext, 1991).

4. Ian Kershaw, *Hitler: 1889–1936 Hubris* (New York: Norton, 1998), pp. 306, 693.

5. Ibid., pp. 318, 404.

6. Timothy W. Mason, *Sozialpolitik im Dritten Reich: Arbeiterklasse und Volksgemeinschaft* (Opladen: Westdeutscher Verlag, 1978), chap. 3–6; Alf Lüdtke, "Hunger in der Grossen Depression: Hungererfahrungen und Hungerpolitik am Ende der Weimarer Republik," *Archiv für Sozialgeschichte* 27 (1987), pp. 174–175; Detlev Peukert, *Inside Nazi Germany: Conformity, Opposition, and Racism in Everyday Life* (New Haven, Conn.: Yale University Press, 1982), pp. 50–56; Michael Schneider, *Unterm Hakenkreuz: Arbeiter und Arbeiterbewegung 1933 bis 1939* (Bonn: J. H. W. Dietz, 1999), pp. 591–609.

7. Hartmut Berghoff, "Enticement and Deprivation: The Regulation of Consumption in Pre-War Nazi Germany," in Martin Daunton and Matthew Hilton, eds., *The Politics of Consumption: Material Culture and Citizenship in Europe and America* (Oxford: Berg, 2001).

8. Nancy Reagin, "Comparing Apples and Oranges: Housewives and the Politics of Consumption in Interwar Germany," in Susan Strasser, Charles McGovern, and Matthias Judt, eds., *Getting and Spending: European and American Consumer Societies in the Twentieth Century* (New York: Cambridge University Press, 1998).

9. Erker, *Ernährungskrise*, p. 24.

10. Michael Wildt, *Vom kleinen Wohlstand: Eine Konsumgeschichte der fünfziger Jahre* (Hamburg: Fischer Taschenbuch Verlag, 1994), p. 25.

11. On rationing and supply problems in the Western zones, see Erker, *Ernährungskrise;* Günter Trittel, *Hunger und Politik: Die Ernährungskrise in der Bizone 1945–1949* (Frankfurt am Main: Campus, 1990); John E. Farquharson, *The Western Allies and the Politics of Food: Agrarian Management in Postwar Germany* (Leamington: Berg, 1985).

12. Gries, *Die Rationen-Gesellschaft*, p. 94. Groups I and II included engineers, technicians, and workers in smelting furnaces, heavy industry, and mining; the presidents and vice presidents of the Länder and provincial governments; the mayors of Dresden, Leipzig, and Chemnitz; the leaders of the "antifascist" party organizations of the *Länder,* provinces, and large cities; the presidents of the transport and postal organizations; the

mayors of cities with more than thirty thousand inhabitants; leading doctors in large hospitals; professors; and especially well-known "antifascist" artists and intellectuals.

13. Ibid., pp. 198–201.
14. Alan Kramer, *The West German Economy 1945–1955* (New York: Berg, 1991), pp. 81–82.
15. Dr. Herta Ludwig, "Differenzierung in der Versorgung," *Die Versorgung* 2, no. 11 (1947), p. 54. On Soviet rationing practices, see Julie Hessler, "Culture of Shortages: A Social History of Soviet Trade" (Ph.D. diss., University of Chicago, 1996), chap. 3.
16. Wolfgang Zank, *Wirtschaft und Arbeit in Ostdeutschland 1945–1949: Probleme des Wiederaufbaus in der sowjetischen Besatzungszone Deutschlands* (Munich: Oldenbourg, 1987), p. 67. Place of residence also played a role in the provisioning of the Western zones. Gries, *Die Rationen-Gesellschaft*, pp. 278–280.
17. These representatives were recruited by local administrative offices. Rainer Gries has argued that in presiding over the allocation of ration cards, they acquired a political significance extending beyond questions of provisioning. Gries has compared them with the house and block wardens of the Nazi period. Gries, *Die Rationen-Gesellschaft*, pp. 77–78. Also see Thomas Scholze, "Zur Ernährungssituation der Berliner nach dem zweiten Weltkrieg: Ein Beitrag zur Erforschung des Großstadtalltags (1945–1952)," *Jahrbuch für Geschichte* 35 (1987), p. 544.
18. Only bread was allocated daily; salt, coffee, and tea were allocated monthly; potatoes and vegetables were allocated on an irregular basis. See Scholze, "Zur Ernährungssituation," p. 544.
19. Scholze, "Zur Ernährungssituation," pp. 547–549.
20. Ibid., p. 553. Also see Jörg Roesler, "The Black Market in Post-war Berlin and the Methods Used to Counteract it," *German History* 7, no. 1 (1989), pp. 92–107.
21. Scholze, "Zur Ernährungssituation," pp. 554–557. Charities also afforded some relief. For elderly and especially needy persons there were public soup kitchens *(Volksgaststätten)* offering warm meals, particularly in the winter. During the winter of 1948–49 there were still about nine hundred such soup kitchens in East Berlin.
22. The figure consistently demanded by the Soviet Union had been $10 billion. This is not, however, to suggest that the Soviet Union received nothing from the Western zones. Despite U.S. Military Governor Lucius Clay's reparation stop of May 1946, the United States and Britain continued to maintain deliveries of 25 percent of the dismantled plant from the Western zones to the Soviet Union. See Kramer, *The West German*

Economy, p. 119. On East German reparations to the Soviet Union, see Rainer Karlsch, *Allein bezahlt? Die Reparationsleistungen der SBZ-DDR, 1945–1953* (Berlin: C. Links Verlag, 1993); Naimark, *The Russians in Germany*, chap. 3.

23. Naimark, *The Russians in Germany*, p. 190.

24. Ibid., pp. 187, 193–195.

25. On planning in the Western zones, see Kramer, *The West German Economy*, pp. 121–123.

26. Bruno Leuschner, "Über die Richtlinien der KPD zur Wirtschaftspolitik," delivered at the Economics Conference of the KPD in Berlin on December 29, 1945, and collected in Bruno Leuschner, *Ökonomie und Klassenkampf: Ausgewählte Reden und Aufsätze 1945–1965* (East Berlin: Dietz, 1984), p. 19.

27. See Wolfgang Zank, "Wirtschaftliche Zentralverwaltungen und Deutsche Wirtschaftskommission," in Martin Broszat and Hermann Weber, eds., *SBZ-Handbuch: Staatliche Verwaltungen, Parteien, gesellschaftliche Organisationen und ihre Führungskräfte in der Sowjetischen Besatzungszone Deutschlands 1945–1949* (Munich: Oldenbourg, 1990), pp. 260–261.

28. Leo Skrzypczynski, president of the German Central Administration of Industry, was the exception. The German central administrations had been established in July 1945. Their relationships with their provincial *(Länder)* counterparts had been fraught with tension. Not satisfied with issuing general guidelines to the provincial governments, they pressed without much success for greater influence over implementation of policy. Naimark, *The Russians in Germany*, pp. 48–52.

29. This account of the sequence of events comes from Naimark, *The Russians in Germany*, pp. 52–55, and from Stefan Creuzberger, *Die sowjetische Besatzungsmacht und das politische System der SBZ* (Cologne: Böhlau, 1996), pp. 160–163.

30. For a fascinating collective biography of veteran German Communists, see Catherine Epstein, *The Last Revolutionaries: German Communists and Their Century* (Cambridge, Mass.: Harvard University Press, 2003).

31. For a first-hand account of this camp, see Arthur Koestler, *The Scum of the Earth* (London: Hutchinson, 1968).

32. Bernd-Rainer Barth, Christoph Links, and Helmut Müller-Enbergs, eds., *Wer war Wer in der DDR: Ein biographisches Handbuch* (Frankfurt am Main: Fischer Taschenbuch Verlag, 1995), p. 452.

33. Erich Gniffke, *Jahre mit Ulbricht* (Cologne: Verlag Wissenschaft und Politik, 1966), p. 124.

34. Naimark, *The Russians in Germany*, pp. 53–54; Zank, "Wirtschaftliche Zentralverwaltungen," pp. 265–266.

35. Protokoll Nr. 4 DWK Sitzung, July 28, 1947, BArch, DC-15/304, Bl. 30.

36. Ibid., Bl. 33.

37. The SMAD Administration for Foreign Trade closely controlled the zone's imports and exports. Imports consisted primarily of coal and other sources of fuel, while exports included significant amounts of textiles and clothing (RM 60 million in 1947 alone), which were in desperately short supply in the zone. Christoph Buchheim, "Wirtschaftliche Folgen der Integration in den RGW," in Christoph Buchheim, ed., *Wirtschaftliche Folgelasten des Krieges in der SBZ/DDR* (Baden-Baden: Nomos, 1995), pp. 341–347.

38. Ivan T. Berend, *Central and Eastern Europe, 1944–1993: Detour From the Periphery to the Periphery* (New York: Cambridge University Press, 1996), chap. 1–2; Alan H. Smith, *The Planned Economies of Eastern Europe* (New York: Holmes and Meier, 1983), chap. 2.

39. Zank, *Wirtschaft und Arbeit*, chap. 2.

40. Christoph Buchheim, "Kriegsfolgen und Wirtschaftswachstum in der SBZ/DDR," *Geschichte und Gesellschaft* 25, no. 4 (1999), pp. 515–517.

41. Farquharson, *The Western Allies and the Politics of Food*, pp. 120–122.

42. Ibid., p. 122. On tensions between the Western Allies with regard to control over the Ruhr and other German resources, see Alan S. Milward, *The Reconstruction of Western Europe, 1945–1951* (Berkeley: University of California Press, 1984), chap. 4.

43. Kramer, *The West German Economy*, p. 81.

44. Naimark, *The Russians in Germany*, p. 197.

45. Quoted in Trittel, *Hunger und Politik*, p. 8. Clay's quote comes from a memorandum dated April 11, 1946. George Kennan realized as early as the summer of 1945 that it was imperative "to lead our section of Germany—the section of which we and the British have accepted responsibility—to a form of independence so prosperous, so secure, so superior, that the East cannot threaten it." George Kennan, *Memoirs, 1925–1950* (New York: Pantheon, 1967), p. 258.

46. Quoted in Trittel, *Hunger und Politik*, p. 213.

47. Quoted in Peter Merseburger, *Der Schwierige Deutsche: Kurt Schumacher: Eine Biographie* (Stuttgart: Deutsche Verlags-Anstalt, 1995), p. 362.

48. Fred Oelßner, "Wirtschaftsplanung und Planwirtschaft: Einige kritische Bemerkungen zu dem Artikel von Rita Sprengel," *Einheit* 2, no. 8 (1947) pp. 761–762.

49. FDGB Groß-Berlin, "Denkschrift über die gesundheitlichen und wirtschaftlichen Folgen des Fehlens von Arbeitsschutzkleidung, Arbeitsschutzgeräten, Reinigungs- und Hautschutzmitteln sowie Berufskleidung und Schuhwerk," November 20, 1947, LAB, OB Rep. 101/121, Bl. 243–244, 255.

50. Naimark, *The Russians in Germany,* p. 196; Jeffrey Kopstein, *The Politics of Economic Decline in East Germany, 1945–1989* (Chapel Hill: University of North Carolina Press, 1997), p. 26.

51. Sheila Fitzpatrick, *Everyday Stalinism. Ordinary Life in Extraordinary Times: Soviet Russia in the 1930s* (New York: Oxford University Press, 1999), pp. 111–114; Hessler, "Culture of Shortages," pp. 111–114.

52. "Richtlinien zu Ziffer 9 des Befehles der SMAD Nr. 234 für die Durchführung der warmen Zusatzverpflegung in Werkküchen der Betriebe führender Industriezweige und des Transportwesens," BArch, DC-15/510, Bl. 123–126. Form A consisted of 100 grams bread, 50 grams processed foodstuffs, 200 grams potatoes, 150 grams vegetables, 5 grams ersatz coffee, as well as 50 grams meat and 10 grams fat twice per week. Form B consisted of 100 grams bread, 30 grams processed foodstuffs, 150 grams potatoes, 100 grams vegetables, 5 grams ersatz coffee.

53. The full text of the order was published in *Zvbl.,* January 15, 1948, pp. 1–10.

54. DVHV to Departments of Trade and Provisioning of all Länder governments, January 24, 1948, SAPMO-BArch, DY 30/ IV 2/602/85.

55. Ulbricht to all members of the Central Secretariat, "Maßnahmen zur Durchführung des Befehls Nr. 234 über Aufgaben und Arbeit der Volkskontrollorgane," November 21, 1947, SAPMO-BArch, NL 182/1198, Bl. 66; Ulbricht to Otto Meier, October 21, 1947, same file, Bl. 126.

56. DWK Abt. Wirtschaftsfragen, "Bericht über die erste Sitzung des Ausschußes zur Überwachung der Maßnahmen zum Befehl Nr. 234," SAPMO-BArch, NL 182/1198, Bl. 10–11.

57. DVHV, Schmincke to Ulbricht, December 8, 1947, SAPMO-BArch, NL 182/1198, Bl. 156–171.

58. DVHV, Handke to Verwaltung für Handel und Versorgung der SMAD, January 27, 1948, BArch, DC-15/510, Bl. 55.

59. "Bericht über die im Land Mecklenburg-Vorpommern festgestellten Maßnahmen zur Durchführung des Befehls Nr. 234," SAPMO-BArch, NL 182/1198, Bl. 369.

60. SED Abt. Wirtschaftspolitik, Kahn to Ulbricht, February 4, 1948, SAPMO-BArch, DY 30/ IV 2/602/85, p. 1.

61. Report from SED Landesvorstand Sachsen/Anhalt Abt. Frauen, March 16, 1948, BArch, DC-15/510, Bl. 76–80.

62. *Tribüne* to Ulbricht, November 12, 1947, SAPMO-BArch, NL 182/1198, Bl. 140.

63. The letters also allowed the regime to get some sense of popular opinion. On letters of petition generally, see Jonathan R. Zatlin, "Ausgaben und Eingaben: Das Petitionsrecht und der Untergang der DDR," *Zeitschrift für Geschichtswissenschaft* 45, no. 10 (1997), pp. 902–917.

64. Roughly translated, without the rhyme: "Give us something to eat. Then we can perform heavy labor and also endure." *Tribüne* to Ulbricht, November 12, 1947, SAPMO-BArch, NL 182/1198, Bl. 141–143.

65. Ibid., Bl. 146.

66. "Bericht über die Sitzung des Ausschußes zur Überwachung der Maßnahmen zum Befehl 234," February 23, 1948, BArch, DC-15/510, Bl. 71–72.

67. DWK Abt. Wirtschaftsfragen to Zentralsekretariat der SED, January 24, 1948, SAPMO-BArch, DY 30/ IV 2/602/85, p. 8.

68. Ibid., pp. 6–7.

69. Warnke to SED Abt. Wirtschaftspolitik, April 13, 1948, same file, p. 34.

2. The Contest Begins

1. Lutz Niethammer, ed., *"Hinterher merkt man, daß es richtig war, daß es schiefgegangen ist": Nachkriegserfahrungen im Ruhrgebiet: Lebensgeschichte und Sozialkultur im Ruhrgebiet 1930 bis 1960* (Bonn: J. H. W. Dietz, 1983), pp. 81–83.

2. On the currency reform, see Werner Abelshauser, *Wirtschaftsgeschichte der Bundesrepublik Deutschland 1945–1980* (Frankfurt am Main: Suhrkamp, 1983), pp. 46–53; Christoph Buchheim, "Die Währungsreform 1948 in Westdeutschland," *Vierteljahreshefte für Zeitgeschichte* 36, no. 2 (1988), pp. 189–231. On the initial hardships following the currency reform, see Michael Wildt, *Der Traum vom Sattwerden: Hunger und Protest, Schwarzmarkt und Selbsthilfe* (Hamburg: USA-Verlag, 1986), pp. 65–73.

3. Wildt, *Der Traum vom Sattwerden,* p. 67. According to Abelshauser, the cost of living index increased 14 percent in the second half of 1948. Abelshauser, *Wirtschaftsgeschichte,* p. 53.

4. Wildt, *Der Traum vom Sattwerden,* p. 68.

5. In the British zone the number of those unemployed increased from 216,647 in May to 308,644 in July 1948. Ibid., p. 69.

6. For recent examples, see Thomas Parrish, *Berlin in the Balance, 1945–1949* (Reading, Mass.: Perseus, 1998); Ann and John Tusa, *The Berlin Airlift* (New York: Atheneum, 1988).

7. William Stivers, "The Incomplete Blockade: Soviet Zone Supply of West Berlin, 1948–49," *Diplomatic History* 21, no. 4 (1997), pp. 569–602; Volker Koop, *Kein Kampf um Berlin? Deutsche Politik zur Zeit der Berlin-Blockade, 1948/1949* (Bonn: Bouvier, 1998).

8. Stivers, "The Incomplete Blockade," p. 579.

9. Eastmarks remained legal tender in the Western sectors of the city throughout the blockade. And with an exchange rate fluctuating be-

tween three and four eastmarks to one westmark, real costs were signifi-cantly diminished. As of March 20, 1949, however, all wages and salaries had to be paid entirely in westmarks, as a result of which business with the Soviet sector ceased to be very profitable.

10. Stivers, "The Incomplete Blockade," p. 595. Also see Koop, *Kein Kampf um Berlin?* pp. 211–223.

11. Stivers, "The Incomplete Blockade," pp. 570–571. Also see Koop, *Kein Kampf um Berlin?* pp. 229–230.

12. Stivers, "The Incomplete Blockade," p. 580. Koop, however, goes too far in his assertion that the HO was intended only, or even primarily, for West Berliners. After all, the stores were opened elsewhere in the Soviet zone as well. Koop, *Kein Kampf um Berlin?* pp. 186–190.

13. The exchange rate fluctuated between three and four to one, cutting the real cost of HO items to a fraction of their stated price. Stivers, "The Incomplete Blockade," p. 583.

14. Ibid., p. 584.

15. Ibid., pp. 574–575.

16. Ibid., p. 576.

17. "Organisationsplan der Unterabteilung lt. Befehl Nr. 80," LAB, Rep. 113/225. Letsch had been the mayor of the East Berlin district of Mitte.

18. In September the total number of West-sector residents registering for rations in East Berlin was 66,105; in October, the number had risen to 75,182. "Meldungen aus den Westsektoren," undated, LAB, Rep. 113/24.

19. Magistrat von Groß-Berlin, Abt. für Ernährung, Spangenberg to Büro des Oberbürgermeisters, December 13, 1948, LAB, OB-Rep. 101/659.

20. Abt. für Ernährung HV, Beschwerdestelle to Spangenberg, "Tätigkeits-bericht der Beschwerdestelle für die Zeit vom 24.1.–29.1.1949," LAB, Rep. 113/35.

21. Ebert, Aktennotiz, December 11, 1948, LAB, OB-Rep. 101/711, Bl. 29.

22. Abt. für Ernährung HV, Beschwerdestelle to Spangenberg, "Tätigkeits-bericht der Beschwerdestelle für die Zeit vom 24.1.–29.1.1949," LAB, Rep. 113/35.

23. Hauptprüfungsstelle, Dez. XI/I, Bezirk: Mitte, "Bericht betr.: Nachprü-fung der Beschwerde gegen den Berlin-Konsum, Krausenstr.," November 9, 1948, LAB, Rep. 113/107.

24. Letsch to Gubisch, August 20, 1948, LAB, Rep. 113/37.

25. Letsch to Gubisch, August 23, 1948, same file.

26. Abt. für Ernährung HB IV/I, Keyne to Letsch, September 14, 1948, LAB, Rep. 113/166; Keyne to Morawski, September 21, 1948, same file; Morawski to DWK, Stammler, September 22, 1948, same file.

27. Abt. für Ernährung HB IV/I, Keyne to Letsch, September 14, 1948, same file; Letsch and Morawski to Chef der Garnison und Militärkommandant der Stadt Berlin, Kotikow, September 16, 1948, same file; Ern. HB IV/I, "Vermerk Betr.: Unerledigte Anträge an die Zentralkommandatur," October 15, 1948, same file.

28. Abt. für Ernährung HV, Beschwerdestelle to Spangenberg, "Tätigkeitsbericht der Beschwerdestelle für die Zeit vom 27.12–31.12.1948," LAB, Rep. 113/35.

29. Abt. für Ernährung HV, Beschwerdestelle, "Tätigkeitsbericht der Beschwerdestelle für die Zeit vom 17.1–22.1.1949," "Tätigkeitsbericht der Beschwerdestelle für die Zeit vom 24.1.–29.1.1949," same file.

30. See Tusa and Tusa, *The Berlin Airlift,* pp. 239–242, 271–273.

31. The shortcomings of the supply scheme notwithstanding, Stivers perhaps goes too far when he describes the blockade in general as a "massive blunder." Although it was riddled with contradictions, and although when it ended, the West retained control over West Berlin and achieved a kind of symbolic "victory," the blockade did help Soviet and SED authorities consolidate their power over the economic and social life of the Soviet zone. Arguably, this was the main point of the blockade. Only more research in Soviet sources may tell. Stivers, "The Incomplete Blockade," pp. 594–596.

32. See, for example, "Westmächte vollenden Spaltung Deutschlands," *ND,* June 19, 1948, p. 1; Dr. Alfred Lemnitz, "Marshallplan und Währungsstrategie," *Einheit* 3, no. 8 (1948), pp. 693–695.

33. Dr. Alfred Lemnitz, "Die 'freie Marktwirtschaft,'" *Einheit* 3, no. 12 (1948), p. 1149.

34. Ibid., p. 1150. For similar arguments see H. K. J., "Schaufensterpolitik im Westen . . . und in der Ostzone?" *ND,* October 8, 1948, p. 3.; M. P., "Ein Bummel durch den 'Goldenen Westen'," *ND,* October 13, 1948, p. 4.

35. Hermann Zilles, "Von Kampf der Arbeiterklasse in Westdeutschland," *Einheit* 4, no. 1 (1949), p. 37

36. Willi Perk, "Das Preis- und Lohnproblem in Westdeutschland," *Einheit* 4, no. 1 (1949), pp. 47–48.

37. "Stenographische Niederschrift über die Sitzung des Wirtschaftspolitischen Ausschußes des Deutschen Volkskongreßes, May 5, 1948," SAPMO-BArch, NL 182/964. The German People's Congress Movement for Unity and a Just Peace, to give its full name, was initiated by the SED and the Soviets in 1947 as a means of hindering, or at least delaying, the formation of a West German state. Norman M. Naimark, *The Russians in Germany: A History of the Soviet Zone of Occupation, 1945–1949* (Cambridge, Mass.: Harvard University Press, 1995), pp. 56–58.

38. "Stenographische Niederschrift über die Sitzung des Wirtschaftspolitischen Ausschußes des Deutschen Volkskongreßes, May 5, 1948," SAPMO-BArch, NL 182/964, Bl. 46–47.

39. Ibid., Bl. 63.

40. Ibid., Bl. 64.

41. Bernd-Rainer Barth, Christoph Links, and Helmut Müller-Enbergs, eds., *Wer war Wer in der DDR: Ein biographisches Handbuch* (Frankfurt am Main: Fischer Taschenbuch Verlag, 1995), p. 421.

42. "Stenographische Niederschrift über die Sitzung des Wirtschaftspolitischen Ausschußes des Deutschen Volkskongreßes," May 5, 1948, SAPMO-BArch, NL 182/964, Bl. 65–67.

43. Ibid., Bl. 69. On Merker's later expulsion from the SED and subsequent arrest in connection with the Noel Field affair, see Peter Grieder, *The East German Leadership, 1946–1973: Conflict and Crisis* (Manchester: Manchester University Press, 1999), pp. 25–31. On Merker's role in postwar East German debates related to antifascism, the Holocaust, and the anticosmopolitan campaign of the early 1950s, see Jeffrey Herf, *Divided Memory: The Nazi Past in the Two Germanys* (Cambridge, Mass.: Harvard University Press, 1997), pp. 106–161.

44. Koval to Rau, June 21, 1948, BArch, DC-15/714, Bl. 10–11.

45. See "SMAD-Befehl Nr. 151/1948 über die Erhöhung der Lebensmittelnormen für die Bevölkerung der sowjetischen Besatzungszone Deutschlands" and "Deutsche Wirtschaftskommission Beschluß über die Erhöhung der Rationssätze in der sowjetischen Besatzungszone Deutschlands," both of which were published in *Zvbl,* October 2, 1948, pp. 427–429.

46. "Anordnung über die Verbesserung der Lebensmittelversorgung der Bevölkerung der sowjetischen Besatzungszone Deutschlands vom 4. Februar," *Zvbl,* February 19, 1949, p. 80.

47. Rau to Drofa, September 30, 1948, BArch, DC-15/714, Bl. 45.

48. Perelivchenko to Rau, October 20, 1948, same file, Bl. 52.

49. Rau to Drofa, November 12, 1948, same file, Bl. 61.

50. Kurmashev to Rau, December 14, 1948, same file, Bl. 183; "Anordnung über die Versorgung der Bevölkerung mit gewerblichen Gebrauchsgütern: Einführung der Punktkarten," *Zvbl,* December 27, 1948, pp. 584–585. A catalogue of point values for particular items was then published in *Zvbl,* February 4, 1949, pp. 38–42.

51. Rau to Koval, December 3, 1948, BArch, DC-15/714, Bl. 72.

52. Vermerk für Herrn Ganter-Gilmans, December 8, 1948, same file, Bl. 76

53. Sitnin to Rau, December 15, 1948, same file, Bl. 78.

54. SED Landesvorstand Saxon to SED Abt. Wirtschaftspolitik, Ulbricht, January 6, 1949, SAPMO-BArch, NL 182/1061, Bl. 240.

55. Konsum Hauptsekretariat to Zentralsekretariat der SED, January 6, 1949, SAPMO-BA, DY 30/IV 2/602/74, p. 13.

56. On national variations and similarities, see Joseph Rothschild, *Return to Diversity: A Political History of East Central Europe Since World War II* (New York: Oxford University Press, 1989), chap. 3; Ivan T. Berend, *Central and Eastern Europe, 1944–1993: Detour From the Periphery to the Periphery* (New York: Cambridge University Press, 1996), chap. 1–2.

57. On the development of the SED in these years, see Harold Hurwitz, *Die Stalinisierung der SED: Zum Verlust von Freiräumen und sozialdemokratischer Identität in den Vorständen, 1946–1949* (Opladen: Westdeutscher Verlag, 1997); Grieder, *The East German Leadership*, pp. 8–36.

58. See, for example, Walter Ulbricht, "Die Bedeutung des deutschen Planes," *Einheit* 3, no. 8 (1948), pp. 673–682; Herbert Warnke, "Die Gewerkschaften und der Wirtschaftsplan," *Einheit* 3, no. 8 (1948), pp. 682–689; Willi Stoph, "Bewußtsein und Produktion: Zur Frage der Erfüllung des Zweijahrplanes," *Einheit* 4, no. 2 (1949), pp. 97–105.

59. Herbert Warnke, "Die Hennecke Bewegung," *Einheit* 3, no. 12 (1948), p. 1127. On Stakhanovism in the Soviet Union, see Lewis H. Siegelbaum, *Stakhanovism and the Politics of Productivity in the USSR, 1935–1941* (Cambridge: Cambridge University Press, 1988).

60. "Thema des Tages: die Freien Läden," *ND*, November 13, 1948, p. 4.

61. Suppressed during the Nazi years, the consumer co-ops received official recognition with SMAD Order no. 176, issued on December 18, 1945. Already in May 1946, co-op membership exceeded 1 million. By 1948 there were a total of 290 co-ops in the Soviet zone. See Sabine Hödt, "Konsummarken kleben," in Neue Gesellschaft für Bildende Kunst, *Wunderwirtschaft: DDR-Konsumkultur in den 60er Jahren* (Cologne: Böhlau, 1996), pp. 122–123.

62. As a long-term goal, Soviet-zone authorities no doubt also viewed the new stores as yet another means of acquiring ever-greater control over the economy, hoping eventually to eliminate private retail. But this goal was not on the immediate agenda. Neither Soviet nor German officials mentioned it, either in public or private communications. In fact, state attempts to erode the share of private retail began to occur somewhat later and proceeded in staggered phases. See Andreas Pickel, *Radical Transitions: The Survival and Revival of Entrepreneurship in the GDR* (Boulder, Colo.: Westview, 1992).

63. Jörg Roesler, "The Black Market in Post-war Berlin and the Methods Used to Counteract it," *German History* 7, no. 1 (1989), pp. 92–107.

64. The Soviet-zone currency reform followed directly from the currency reform in the Western zones, where the old Reichsmarks were now worth-

less. To prevent them from flooding into the Soviet zone, Soviet officials ordered a currency reform for their own zone and the Soviet sector of Berlin on June 23, 1948. The new currency was distributed on the following day. On the effects of the currency reforms in West and East Berlin, see Michael Wolff, *Die Währungsreform in Berlin, 1948/49* (Berlin: Walter de Gruyter, 1991). On the connections between the Soviet-zone currency reform, the financial difficulties of the Soviet-zone economy, and the hoped-for role of the HOs in solving those difficulties, see Horst Barthel, "Die Einführung des doppelten Preissystems für Einzelhandelsverkaufspreise in der DDR durch die Schaffung der HO-Läden von 1948 bis 1950/51 als komplexe Maßnahme der Wirtschaftspolitik," *Jahrbuch für Geschichte* 31 (1984), pp. 273–297.

65. Katherine Pence, "Building Socialist Worker-Consumers: The Paradoxical Construction of the Handelsorganisation-HO, 1948," in Peter Hübner and Klaus Tenefelde, eds., *Arbeiter in der SBZ-DDR* (Essen: Klartext, 1999).

66. Ibid., p. 503.

67. Ibid., pp. 501, 517.

68. Ibid., pp. 505, 517–522.

69. "Besprechung bei der SMAD über die Errichtung von Staatlichen Läden," October 5, 1948, SAPMO-BArch, DY 30/ IV 2/602/76. Among those present at the meeting were Greta Kuckhoff, Dr. Karl Steiner (Deputy Leader of the Finance Administration), Heinz Schmincke (Central Administration of Trade and Provisioning), and Willi Stoph (SED Central Secretariat Department of Economic Policy).

70. On basic questions, see "Besprechung bei Herrn Maletin in Karlshorst," October 15, 1948, BArch, DC-15/731, Bl. 68–69. On quality standards, see Handelsorganisation HO, "Vermerk über eine Besprechung im Karlshorst," February 8, 1949, BArch, DL-1/739. For Soviet instruction in price policy, see Maletin to Rau, October 19, 1948, BArch, DC-15/714, Bl. 205–208; Maletin to Steiner, November 2, 1948, same file, Bl. 216–217; Sitnin to Rau, November 4, 1948, same file, Bl. 218–219.

71. On commercial stores and Soviet trade, see Sheila Fitzpatrick, *Everyday Stalinism: Ordinary Life in Extraordinary Times: Soviet Russia in the 1930s* (New York: Oxford University Press, 1999), pp. 54–58; Julie Hessler, "Culture of Shortages: A Social History of Soviet Trade" (Ph.D diss., University of Chicago, 1996), pp. 328–329.

72. HV der SMAD to Ganter-Gilmans, December 4, 1948, BArch, DL-1/429, Bl. 20; "Dienstanweisung der DWK über den Plan für den kommerziellen Handel im Jahr 1949," January 10, 1949, BArch, DL-1/732.

73. See, for example, Heinz Verleih, "Der Sowjethandel," *Die Versorgung* 5, no. 2 (1950), pp. 97–99.

74. Dr. Karl Steiner, "Freie Staatsläden zur Unterbietung des Schwarzmarkts," *Berliner Zeitung,* October 12, 1948, p. 5.

75. "Besprechung bei Herrn Maletin in Karlshorst," October 15, 1948, BArch, DC-15/731, Bl. 68–69.

76. See the correspondence in SAPMO-BArch, NL 182/951, Bl. 281–285.

77. "Kleiderkarte und freie Einkaufsläden," *ND,* October 16, 1948, p. 3.

78. "Freie Läden und Kleiderkarte," *ND,* October 27, 1948, p. 1. In fact, the foodstuffs sold in the HOs in 1949 included the following: bread and other baked goods; meat, sausage, and fish; butter, fat, oil and margarine; cheese, milk, and other dairy products; potatoes (excluding August to December); sugar and jam; fruit and vegetables; coffee and tea (excluding July to December); grain and processed foodstuffs. BArch, DE-2/895, Ministerium für Planung, Statistisches Zentralamt, Abt. IV, "Ergebnisse von Haushaltsrechnungen in der DDR für das Jahr 1949," August 1950.

79. Heinrich Rau, "Warum 'freie Einkaufsläden?'" *ND,* October 28, 1948, p. 5.

80. Erich Freund, "Grundsätzliches zu den freien Läden," *ND,* November 14, 1948, p. 4. For the screening of the article, see Freund to Wolf, November 6, 1948, SAPMO-BArch, DY 30/ IV 2/602/76.

81. Freund to Zentralsekretariat der SED, Abt. Wirtschaft, November 15, 1948, SAPMO-BArch, DY 30/IV 2/602/76.

82. "Besprechung bei Herrn Kurmashev," November 24, 1948, BArch, DC-15/717, Bl. 15–18.

83. "Denkschrift zur Frage der weiteren Entwicklung der HO 'Freie Läden,'" December 16, 1948, BArch, DL-1/739.

84. "Protokoll über die 1. Sitzung des Verwaltungsrates der Handelsorganisation-HO am 11.1.1949," BArch, DL-1/732. It was in this session that the "Freie Läden" formally adopted the official name, "Handelsorganisation HO."

85. Gabriele Baumgartner and Dieter Hebig, eds., *Biographisches Handbuch der SBZ/DDR, 1945–1990* (Munich: K. G. Sauer, 1997), 2: p. 909.

86. HO Zentrale Leitung, Streit to Kuckhoff, February 19, 1949, BArch, DL-1/739.

87. HO Zentrale Letiung, Streit to HVHV, Schmidt, March 29, 1949, same file. On increasing the principal capital of the HO, see "Beschluß über eine Änderung der Satzung der Handelsorganisation (HO) vom 16. März 1949," *Zvbl,* April 4, 1949, p. 167.

88. HVHV, Freund to Handelsorganisation HO, Abt. Organisation, February 25, 1949, BArch, DL-1/739.

89. Ganter-Gilmans to Handelsorganisation HO, January 31, 1949, same file.

90. For similar critiques, see "Protokoll über die 2. Sitzung des Verwaltungsrates der Handelsorganisation-HO am 22.4.49," BArch, DL-1/732;

Hauptverwaltung Wirtschaftsplanung, HA Warenverkehr & HVHV, HA Organisation/Kontrolle, "Bericht über die Informationsreise. Betr.: Warenumsatzplan vom 3.5.–4.5.1949," BArch, DC-15/79.

91. "'HO'! Das Tagegespräch von Berlin," *ND*, November 16, 1948, p. 4.
92. Barthel, "Die Einführung des doppelten Preissystems," p. 297; Wolfgang Zank, *Wirtschaft und Arbeit in Ostdeutschland 1945–1949: Probleme des Wiederaufbaus in der Sowjetischen Besatzungszone Deutschlands* (Munich: R. Oldenbourg, 1987), p. 69.
93. SED Abt. Werbung, Presse, Rundfunk to Ubricht, December 1, 1948, SAPMO-BArch, DY 30/ IV 2/602/76.
94. HVHV, Pressestelle to Ganter-Gilmans, Freund, Krüger, February 17, 1949, BArch, DL-1/739. Also see Pence, "Building Socialist-Worker Consumers," pp. 513–515.
95. SED Abt. Massenagitation to Pieck, Grotewohl, Ulbricht, Oelßner, February 15, 1949, SAPMO-BArch, NL 182/960, Bl. 535; Ulbricht to Rau, February 17, 1949, same file, Bl. 536.
96. "'Freie Läden'—populär geworden," *ND*, March 2, 1949, p. 2; Dr. Karl Steiner, "Preispolitik der freien Läden," *ND*, March 15, 1949, p. 3; H. W. Aust, "HO-Läden oder schwarzer Markt?" *Tägliche Rundschau*, May 4, 1949, p. 3.
97. "Protokoll über die 1. Sitzung des Verwaltungsrates der Handelsorganisation-HO am 11.1.1949," BArch, DL-1/732.
98. "Protokoll über die 2. Sitzung des Verwaltungsrates der Handelsorganisation-HO am 22.4.1949," same file.
99. SED Abt. Wirtschaftspolitik to Ulbricht, April 27, 1949, SAPMO-BArch, NL 182/960, Bl. 315.
100. Redaktion *Volksstimme* Magdeburg to ZK der SED, Presse Abt. Berlin, April 29, 1949, same file, Bl. 320. The Press Department then passed the information on to Ulbricht.
101. SED Abt. Wirtschaftspolitik, Stoph to Ulbricht, May 20, 1949, same file, Bl. 364–365.
102. HO Zentrale Leitung, Abt. Planung und Statistik to MfHV, Hauptabt. Handel und Versorgung, "Analyse über den Warenumsatz des IV. Quartals 1949 sowie des Jahres 1949," BArch, DL-1/2627, Bl. 1–7.
103. The shares of the other provinces were the following: Mecklenburg, 8.3 percent; Brandenburg, 10.8 percent; Saxony-Anhalt, 17.2 percent; Thuringia, 11.2 percent. Ibid., Bl. 3.
104. Hauptverwaltung Wirtschaftsplanung, "Erfüllungsbericht 1. Halbjahr 1949," undated (probably summer 1949), BArch, DC-15/590, Bl. 6.
105. The total planned retail sales for the zone was DM 10 billion, of which the HO was to contribute 2.2 billion and the consumer co-ops 2 billion.

The rest was to be provided by private retail. DWK, Hauptverwaltung Wirtschaftsplanung, "Volkswirtschaftsplan 1949, 1. Halbjahr des Zweijahrplanes—Plan des Warenumsatzes im Einzelhandel für die Zone und Länder," March 10, 1949, BArch, DE-1/28312, Bl. 1.

106. HO Zentrale Leitung, Abt. Organisation, "Übergabe Protokoll," April 30, 1949, BArch, DL-1/3185, Bl. 15. Figures for 1951 are from *Statistisches Jahrbuch der Deutschen Demokratischen Republik 1956* (East Berlin: VEB Deutscher Zentralverlag, 1957), pp. 492, 498.

107. "Stenographische Niederschrift der Rede des stellvertretenden Ministerpräsidenten Walter Ulbricht auf der Feierstunde anläßlich des einjährigen Bestehens der HO am 17. November 1949 in Berlin im Babylon," SAPMO-BArch, DY 30/IV 2/610/93, p. 1.

108. Ibid., p. 2.

109. Ibid., pp. 2–8.

110. Ibid., p. 9.

111. Barthels, "Die Einführung des doppelten Preissystems," p. 286.

112. Ibid., p. 296.

113. Roesler, "The Black Market in Post-war Berlin," pp. 106–107.

114. Zentrales Planungsamt, Hauptabteilung Kontrolle, "Kontrolle der Verwendung der Investitionsmittel bei der H. O.," March 21, 1950, BArch, DE-1/10078, Bl. 6. Also, excerpts from a December 1949 report on particular HO branches prepared by the Deutsche Investitionsbank, which was sent to the Investments Department of the Central Planning Office and then forwarded to Rau, same file, Bl. 3–4. With the official establishment of the German Democratic Republic as a state in October 1949, the DWK's Central Administration for Economic Planning (Hauptverwaltung für Wirtschaftsplanung) was succeeded by the Ministry for Planning.

115. "Gesetz über die Verbesserung der Versorgung der Bevölkerung und über die Pflichtablieferung landwirtschaftlicher Erzeugnisse im Jahre 1950. Vom 22. Februar 1950," *Gbl der DDR,* March 15, 1950, p. 165.

116. Handelsorganisation HO, Baender to Minister for Planning, Rau, April 18, 1950, BArch, DE-1/11317, Bl. 5–6.

117. Rau to Baender, same file, Bl. 7–8.

118. Baender to Rau, June 1, 1950, same file, Bl. 3; Baender to Ulbricht, May 31, 1950, same file, Bl. 10.

119. I have been unable to find precise figures on yearly investments in the HO either in archival materials or in statistical yearbooks. At the time of research, the files of the HO Zentrale Leitung were not yet accessible. When they are made accessible, it may be possible to obtain this information.

120. For example, see Leuschner's critique of Baender's investment proposals for 1951: Leuschner to Baender, October 30, 1950, BArch, DE-1/12113, Bl. 13.

3. The Planned and the Unplanned

1. See Jörg Roesler, *Die Herausbildung der sozialistischen Planwirtschaft in der DDR* (East Berlin: Akademie, 1978), chap. 1–3; Jeffrey Kopstein, *The Politics of Economic Decline in East Germany, 1945–1989* (Chapel Hill: University of North Carolina Press, 1997), chap. 1; Peter Hübner, *Konsens, Konflikt und Kompromiß: Soziale Arbeiterinteressen und Sozialpolitik in der SBZ/DDR, 1945–1970* (Berlin: Akademie, 1995), chap. 3.

2. HV Wirtschaftsplanung, "Kapitalinvestitionen für die Volkswirtschaft der SBZ 1949-Industrie (ohne SAG)," December 8, 1949, BArch, DC-15/586, Bl. 72; Statistisches Zentralamt to SPK, "Erfüllung des Volkswirtschaftsplanes 1950" ("Geheime Verschlußsache"), August 1, 1951, BArch, DE-1/28320, Bl. 20; "Investitionen," June 1952, BArch, DE-2/21568–0915396, Bl. A117–A120.

3. Jörg Roesler, "The Rise and Fall of the Planned Economy in the German Democratic Republic, 1945–89," *German History* 9, no. 1 (1991), pp. 49–50; Christoph Buchheim, "Wirtschaftliche Folgen der Integration der DDR in den RGW," in Christoph Buchheim, ed., *Wirtschaftliche Folgelasten des Krieges in der SBZ/DDR* (Baden-Baden: Nomos, 1995), pp. 348–351.

4. Klaus Zweiling, "Intelligenz und Arbeiterklasse," *Einheit* 4, no. 5 (1949), pp. 385–402; "Anordnung über die Verbesserung der Lebensmittelversorgung der Bevölkerung der sowjetischen Besatzungszone Deutschlands vom 4. Februar 1949," *Zvbl*, February 19, 1949, p. 80.

5. "Anordnung zur Aufhebung der bewirtschafteten Versorgung der Bevölkerung mit Gemüse," *Zvbl*, June 13, 1949, p. 406; "Anordnung zur Aufhebung der bewirtschafteten Versorgung der Bevölkerung mit Tabakwaren," *Zvbl*, June 17, 1949, p. 448; "Anordnung über die weitere Verbesserung der Lebensmittelversorgung der Bevölkerung der sowjetischen Besatzungszone," *Zvbl*, June 27, 1949, p. 475; "Verordnung über die Verbesserung der Versorgung der Bevölkerung mit Lebensmittel und Industriewaren," *Zvbl*, November 9, 1949, pp. 31–34.

6. See Jörg Roesler, "Privater Konsum in Ostdeutschland," in Axel Schildt and Arnold Sywottek, eds., *Modernisierung im Wiederaufbau. Die Westdeutsche Gesellschaft in der 50er Jahre* (Bonn: J. H. W. Dietz, 1993), p. 291. Rationing was finally lifted in the Soviet Union in December 1947, in France in 1949, in West Germany in January 1950, and in Great Britain in July 1954.

7. Ibid., p. 292.

8. SZS to MfHV, "Bericht über die Entwicklung der Einzelhandelspreise in der DDR in den Jahren 1950–1960, Vertrauliche Dienstsache," August 21, 1961, BArch DL-1/2700, Bl. 4–8.

9. In practice, prices were calculated on the basis of actual costs, due to the virtual absence of competition in the planned economy. Without competition to enforce efficiency there was no way to determine if socially unnecessary costs (for example, inefficient labor) emerged. János Kornai, *The Socialist System: The Political Economy of Communism* (Princeton, N.J.: Princeton University Press, 1992), pp. 149–150. For a more detailed discussion of price policy in the GDR in the 1950s, see Mark Landsman, "Preisgestaltung," in Dierk Hoffmann and Michael Schwartz, eds., *Geschichte der Sozialpolitik in Deutschland seit 1945. Bd. 8: Deutsche Demokratische Republik 1949–1961: Im Zeichen des Aufbaus des Sozialismus* (Baden-Baden: Nomos, 2004).

10. Bernd-Rainer Barth, Christoph Links, and Helmut Müller-Enbergs, eds., *Wer war Wer in der DDR: Ein biographisches Handbuch* (Frankfurt am Main: Fischer Taschenbuch, 1995), p. 210. It is not clear why Ganter-Gilmans, after being involved in Social Democratic politics in the 1920s and 1930s, was drawn to the CDU after the war.

11. Jochen Cerny, ed., *Wer war Wer–DDR: Ein biographisches Lexicon* (Berlin: C. Links Verlag, 1992), p. 165.

12. ZK Abt. Kaderfragen, SAPMO-BArch, DY 30/IV 2/11/172, Bl. 143–148; Andreas Herbst, Winfried Ranke, and Jürgen Winkler, eds., *So funktionierte die DDR: Lexicon der Funktionäre* (Reinbeck bei Hamburg: Rowohlt, 1994), 3: p. 90.

13. Krüger's Lebenslauf, SAPMO-BArch, DY 30/IV 2/11/174, Bl. 341–355.

14. In fact, high rates of turnover and attempts to advance people of working-class background resulted in a general lack of experience throughout the administration at all levels and not only in trade. See Roesler, *Die Herausbildung,* p. 4.

15. Initially, there was some variation in terminology. The plans produced by trade-and-provisioning planners sometimes went under the name of "*Versorgungsplan*" or "*Bedarfsplan.*" Eventually, by the early 1950s, the term settled upon was "*Warenbereitstellungsplan.*"

16. Koval to Rau, on "Versorgung mit Lebensmitteln und Gebrauchswaren," June 19, 1948, BArch, DC-15/42, Bl. 138; Leuschner to Ganter-Gilmans, May 10, 1949, BArch, DC-15/79.

17. HV Wirtschaftsplanung to Wittkowski, May 15, 1948, BArch, DC-15/584.

18. Leuschner to Ganter-Gilmans, October 1, 1948, BArch, DC-15/42; Ganter-Gilmans to HV Wirtschaftsplanung, May 10, 1949, BArch, DC-15/79.

19. Letter (origin unknown) to Ganter-Gilmans, dated November 1948,

BArch, DL-1/2504; Landesregierung Sachsen, Ministerium für Handel und Versorgung to HVHV, September 23, 1949, BArch, DL-1/620.

20. HV Wirtschaftsplanung, HA Warenverkehr, "Bericht über die Informationsreise. Betr.: Warenumsatzplan vom 3.5.–4.5.1949," BArch, DC-15/79.

21. "Wer schläft hier?" *ND,* September 15, 1949, p. 1.

22. Redaktion, *ND* to Ganter-Gilmans, September 20, 1949, BArch, DL-1/763/1.

23. For example, in November 1949, Ulbricht instructed Willi Stoph to plant a story in the press about problems in the production of work clothing. Ulbricht to Stoph, November 3, 1949, SAPMO-BArch, NL 182/960, Bl. 450.

24. Kopstein, *The Politics of Economic Decline,* pp. 29–32. On "soft budget constraint" generally, see Kornai, *The Socialist System,* pp. 140–145.

25. HV Wirtschaftsplanung to Wittkowski, September 21, 1949, BArch, DC-15/42, Bl. 124.

26. SED Zentralsekretariat, Frauensekretariat, Käthe Kern to SED Abt. Wirtschaft, Referat Handel und Versorgung, April 12, 1949, BArch, DL-1/765; "Bericht" from Erfurt, August 30, 1950, BArch, DE-1/10123, pp. 1–5.

27. HO Industriewaren, Zentrale Leitung to MfHV and Ministerium für Finanzen, September 17, 1951, BArch, DL-1/2747; HA Planung, HR Preispolitik to Frau Staatssekretär Krause, November 11, 1952, BArch, DL-1/2520, Bl. 7–10.

28. HVHV, "Versorgungsplan 2. Halbjahr. Prinzipien der Planerstellung und Durchführung der Verteilung," September 1, 1948, BArch, DL-1/620, pp. 1–2.

29. Ganter-Gilmans to HV Wirtschaftsplanung, May 10, 1949, BArch, DC-15/79; HVHV to HV Wirtschaftsplanung, July 7, 1949, BArch, DC-15/79, p. 2; MfHV, HA Planung, "Protokoll über die am 16.10.1952 durchgeführte Planabstimmung bei der Staatlichen Plankommission für den Planvorschlag 1953," October 17, 1952, BArch, DL-1/2520, Bl. 20–21.

30. The choice of the year 1936 may seem puzzling, given that it fell within the period of Nazi rule. Why would the GDR take as a benchmark a moment associated with National Socialist ascendancy and working-class prostration? On the other hand, 1936 was the last year before the full implementation of the Nazis' four-year economic plan, and, as such, it could be regarded as the last of the prewar years in which the German economy had not been primarily oriented toward war.

31. HV Wirtschaftsplanung, Wittkowski to Leuschner, June 3, 1948, BArch, DC-15/584, Bl. 34–35.

32. "Stenographische Niederschrift über die Beratung des Wirtschafts-

planes 1949/50 im Zentralsekretariat am 12.6.1948," BArch, DC-15/584, Bl. 50–51.

33. Christa Wolf, *The Quest for Christa T.* (New York: Farrar, Straus and Giroux, 1970), p. 51.

34. Catherine Epstein, *The Last Revolutionaries: German Communists and Their Century* (Cambridge, Mass.: Harvard University Press, 2003), p. 32.

35. For an introductory discussion of the position of women in the GDR during the Ulbricht years, see Donna Harsch, "Squaring the Circle: The Dilemmas and Evolution of Women's Policy," in Patrick Major and Jonathan Osmond, eds., *The Workers' and Peasants' State: Communism and Society in East Germany Under Ulbricht 1945–71"* (Manchester: Manchester University Press, 2002). On the related themes of gender, citizenship, and consumption in East and West Germany, see Katherine Pence, "From Rations to Fashions: The Gendered Politics of East and West German Consumption, 1945–1961" (Ph.D. diss., University of Michigan, 1999).

36. HA Versorgung to Rau, June 27, 1950, BArch, DE-1/11465.

37. Gesetz über den Fünfjahrplan, October 25, 1951, SAPMO-BArch, NL-182/965, Bl. 19.

38. HA Plankontrolle, "Kontrollbericht über die Versorgung der Bevölkerung Überprüfung vom 26.-30.8.50," September 1, 1950, BArch, DE-1/10123; plus a similar report from Erfurt, August 30, 1950, same file.

39. Hanna Wolf, "Wachsender Lebensstandard—ein Entwicklungsgesetz des Sozialismus," *Einheit* 5, no. 3 (1950), p. 247.

40. In West Berlin, where unemployment reached 14.5 percent in February 1950, officials resorted to advertising campaigns, appealing to West Berliners not to shop in East Berlin, where, with the favorable currrency exchange rate, they could buy consumer goods more cheaply. Pence, "From Rations to Fashions," chap. 5.

41. Alan Kramer, *The West German Economy, 1945–1955* (New York: Berg, 1991), pp. 145–146.

42. Quoted in Thomas Schwartz, "European Integration and the 'Special Relationship': Implementing the Marshall Plan in the Federal Republic," in Charles Maier and Günter Bischof, eds., *The Marshall Plan and Germany: West German Development Within the Framework of the European Recovery Program* (New York: Berg, 1991), p. 195.

43. According to Marshall Planners, "viablity" meant that the FRG would be able to achieve a balance of imports and exports without continued outside assistance by the end of 1952.

44. For the debate, see the essays collected in Hans-Jürgen Schröder, ed., *Marshall Plan und Westdeutscher Wiederaufstieg: Positionen-Kontroversen* (Stuttgart: Franz Steiner, 1990).

45. Kramer, *The West German Economy*, pp. 150–154; Michael J. Hogan, *The*

Marshall Plan: America, Britain, and the Reconstruction of Western Europe, 1947–1952 (New York: Cambridge University Press, 1987), pp. 431–432.

46. Charles Maier, "The Politics of Productivity: Foundations of American International Economic Policy after World War II," in Peter Katzenstein, ed., *Between Power and Plenty: Foreign Economic Policies of Advanced Industrial States* (Madison: University of Wisconsin Press, 1978), p. 23.

47. As Maier points out, "from an equal social product in 1938, [Europe's] societies had ploughed back only 12 percent." Ibid., p. 45.

48. Thomas Alan Schwartz, *America's Germany: John J. McCloy and the Federal Republic of Germany* (Cambridge, Mass.: Harvard University Press, 1991), pp. 99–100.

49. Hogan, *The Marshall Plan*, p. 415.

50. The phrase is Maier's in Maier and Bischof, eds., *The Marshall Plan and Germany*, p. 222.

51. Kramer, *The West German Economy*, pp. 200–203.

52. "Wage restraint" is Maier's phrase in "The Politics of Productivity," p. 44. Kramer goes further, speaking of "wage renunciation," in *The West German Economy*, p. 212. The position of organized labor was of course weakened by high unemployment rates; it is not surprising that wages grew more slowly than productivity.

53. Charles Maier, "The Two Postwar Eras and the Conditions for Stability in Twentieth-Century Western Europe," *The American Historical Review* 86, no. 2 (1981), p. 345.

54. Kramer, *The West German Economy*, p. 217.

55. Alan S. Milward, *The Reconstruction of Western Europe, 1945–1951* (Berkeley: University of California Press, 1984), p. 356; Schwartz, "European Integration and the 'Special Relationship,'" pp. 210–212.

56. Kramer, *The West German Economy*, pp. 214–219. Roesler, "Privater Konsum in Ostdeutschland," p. 294. According to official East German statistical yearbooks, up to (and including) 1953, well over half the expenditures of an "average four-person worker household" went to food. *Statistisches Jahrbuch der Deutschen Demokratischen Republik 1956* (East Berlin: VEB Deutscher Zentralverlag, 1957), p. 201. In West Germany, the percentage of disposable income spent on food by an average four-person worker household was already as low as 46.4 percent in 1950.

57. Pence, "From Rations to Fashions," pp. 454–456; Pence, "'You as a Woman Will Understand': Consumption, Gender and the Relationship Between State and Citizenry in the GDR's Crisis of 17 June 1953," *German History* 19, no. 2 (2001), pp. 218–252.

58. On the role played by trade officials in consumer advocacy in the 1960s, see Philipp Heldmann, "Konsumpolitik in der DDR: Jugendmode in den sechziger Jahren," in Hartmut Berghoff, ed., *Konsumpolitik: Die Re-*

gulierung des privaten Verbrauchs im 20. Jahrhundert (Göttingen: Vandenhoeck & Ruprecht, 1999).

59. Hans Paul Ganter-Gilmans, "Der Zweijahresplan und die Versorgungswirtschaft," *Die Versorgung* 3, no. 8 (1948), p. 1.

60. See, for example, Heinz Schmincke, "Der Handel mustert die Produktion," *Die Versorgung* 4, no. 9 (1949), pp. 17–18.

61. Dr. Carl Artur Werner, "Funktionen des Handels in der Versorgungswirtschaft," *Die Versorgung* 3, no. 12 (1948), pp. 67–69.

62. See, for example, Hans Striegan, "Bedarfsfeststellung und Produktionsplanung im Rahmen der Tätigkeit der Hauptverwaltung für Handel und Versorgung," *Die Versorgung* 4, no. 5 (1949), pp. 131–132. East German *Verkaufskultur* represented the adoption of a Soviet concept that scholars of Soviet trade have translated as "cultured trade." See Julie Hessler, "Culture of Shortages: A Social History of Soviet Trade" (Ph.D. diss., University of Chicago, 1996), chap. 6.

63. The consumer co-ops published their own periodicals with similar tips and advice. These included *Die Konsumverkaufsstelle*, which began appearing in 1949, as well as *Wir werben und Gestalten* and *Werben und Verkaufen*, both of which began appearing in the mid-1950s.

64. In the immediate postwar years denunciations of the black market were often tinged with overtones of anti-Semitism and racism, as those Jews and other foreigners remaining in Germany were associated in people's minds with the larger black market operations. Pence, "From Rations to Fashions," pp. 104–108.

65. Dorte Säckl, "Verkaufskultur—kein Schlagwort—sondern ein Begriff," *Der Handel* 1, no. 1 (1951), pp. 16–17.

66. The term *Reklame* had long carried negative connotations in German society. During the Nazi period advertisers felt the need to distinguish between *Reklame* and *Werbung*, at times insisting on a distinction between "Jewish" *Reklame* and "German" *Werbung*. Their hopes, however unrealized, were that under the auspices of Goebbels' Propaganda Ministry their industry would experience the modernization and professionalization its leading representatives so desired. See Hartmut Berghoff, "Von der 'Reklame' zur Verbrauchslenkung. Werbung im nationalsozialistischen Deutschland," in Berghoff, *Konsumpolitik*.

67. Säckl, "Verkaufskultur," p. 16.

68. Werner Kelch, "Neue Arbeitsmethoden in der Zusammenarbeit von Industrie und Handel," *Die Versorgung* 5, no. 10 (1950), pp. 230–232.

69. Prof. Horst Michel, "Guter Geschmack oder 'Geschmackssache': Ein Problem, das ernsthaft diskutiert werden sollte," *Der Handel* 1, no. 9 (1951), p. 280.

70. Anna Seghers, "Schönheit und Planung," written for the regular column

"Das Schaufenster unserer Zeit," *Die Waage* 1, no. 1 (1951), p. 13. *Die Waage* was an accompanying insert in all issues of *Der Handel,* starting in October 1951.

71. Sigrid Meuschel, *Legitimation und Parteiherrschaft in der DDR* (Frankfurt am Main, 1992), p. 39.

72. Berghoff, "Von der 'Reklame' zur Verbrauchslenkung," pp. 98–109.

73. Sheila Fitzpatrick, *Everyday Stalinism: Ordinary Life in Extraordinary Times: Soviet Russia in the 1930s* (New York: Oxford University Press, 1999), pp. 90–95.

74. Ibid., pp. 104–105. Also see Sheila Fitzpatrick, "Becoming Cultured: Socialist Realism and the Representation of Privilege and Taste" in Sheila Fitzpatrick, *The Cultural Front: Power and Culture in Revolutionary Russia* (Ithaca, N.Y.: Cornell University Press, 1992). Of course, many remained unconvinced by such arguments. For the classic critiques of privileged ruling groups in socialist societies, see Leon Trotsky, *The Revolution Betrayed* (New York: Merit, 1965); Milovan Djilas, *The New Class: An Analysis of the Communist System* (San Diego: Harcourt Brace Jovanovich, 1983).

75. Nadezhda Mandelstam, *Hope Abandoned* (New York: Atheneum, 1989), p. 193.

76. Heinz Verleih, "Der Sowjethandel," *Die Versorgung* 5, no. 2 (1950), p. 1. Sometimes Soviet articles were translated and published in East German trade journals. See, for example, S. V. Serebryakov, "Warenverkauf und Betreuung der Käufer," *Die Waage* 2, no. 21 (1952), pp. 289–290. Also, translated versions of Soviet literature on trade were published in East Germany; between 1949 and 1952 over seventy such works were published in the GDR by the Staatlicher Handelsverlag. MfHV, "Literaturverzeichnis," BArch, DL-1/1002, Bl. 102–107.

77. Greta Kuckhoff, "Der Handel muss wissenschaftlich arbeiten," *Die Versorgung* 5, no. 11 (1950), p. 243. The East Germans, meanwhile, were hardly alone among East-bloc countries in adopting the Soviet understanding of the relationship between consumption and culture. On similar discussions in postwar Poland, see David Crowley, "Warsaw's Shops, Stalinism and the Thaw," in Susan E. Reid and David Crowley, eds., *Style and Socialism: Modernity and Material Culture in Post-War Eastern Europe* (Oxford: Berg, 2000).

78. On the practice, methods, and results of industrial labor competitions, see Kopstein, *The Politics of Economic Decline,* chap. 1; Jörg Roesler, "Die Produktionsbrigaden in der Industrie der DDR: Zentrum der Arbeitswelt?" in Hartmut Kaelble, Jürgen Kocka, and Hartmut Zwahr, eds., *Sozialgeschichte der DDR* (Stuttgart: Klett-Cotta, 1994); and Alf Lüdtke, "'Helden der Arbeit'—Mühen beim Arbeiten: Zur mismutigen Loyalität von Industriearbeitern in der DDR," in Kaelble, *Sozialgeschichte der DDR.*

79. "Verkaufskultur-Wettbewerb," *Der Handel* 1, no. 1 (1951), p. 23.

80. Dörte Säckl, "Einen Tag lang unterwegs mit dem Verkaufsinstrukteur," *Der Handel* 1, no. 2 (1951), pp. 49–50.

81. Dr. Karl Hamann, "Handel und Versorgung im Fünfjahrplan," *Der Handel* 1, no. 9 (1951), p. 266.

82. T., "Verkaufskultur-Wettbewerb mit Hindernissen," *Der Handel* 1, no. 6 (1951), pp. 192–193.

83. According to Rolf Steininger, Stalin's note of March 10 constituted a serious offer, and, therefore, there was a chance for German reunification in 1952. Rolf Steininger, *The German Question: The Stalin Note of 1952 and the Problem of Reunification* (New York: Columbia University Press, 1990). Recent research in the Russian archives, however, has yielded information supporting those who would argue that Stalin never expected a positive response from the West and that the note was essentially propaganda intended for the German public. See Gerhard Wettig, "Stalin and German Reunification: Archival Evidence on Soviet Foreign Policy in Spring 1950," *The Historical Journal* 37, no. 2 (1994), pp. 411–419.

84. For the classic account of June 17 as a worker's uprising, see Arnulf Baring, *Uprising in East Germany: June 17, 1953* (London, NLB, 1972). For recent works that support and add to Baring's analysis, see Torsten Diedrich, *Der 17. Juni 1953 in der DDR: Bewaffnete Gewalt gegen das Volk* (Berlin: Dietz, 1991); Ilse Spittmann and Karl Wilhelm Fricke, eds., *17. Juni 1953: Arbeiteraufstand in der DDR* (Cologne: Verlag Wissenschaft und Politik, 1982); Nadia Stulz-Herrnstadt, ed., *Das Herrnstadt Dokument: Das Politbüro der SED und die Geschichte des 17. Juni 1953* (Hamburg: Rowohlt, 1990). For recent attempts to question Baring's focus on workers and to portray the event more broadly as a "people's uprising," see Manfred Hagen, *DDR—Juni '53: Die erste Volkserhebung im Stalinismus* (Stuttgart: Franz Steiner, 1992); Ilko-Sascha Kowalczuk, Armin Mitter, and Stefan Wolle, eds., *Der Tag X–17. Juni 1953: Die "innere Staatsgründung" der DDR als Ergebnis der Krise 1952/54* (Berlin: C. Links Verlag, 1995). For a brief but insightful summary of all of these aspects of the June uprising, see Mary Fulbrook, *Anatomy of a Dictatorship: Inside the GDR, 1949–1989* (Oxford: Oxford University Press, 1995), pp. 177–187.

85. Diedrich, *Der 17. Juni 1953*, p. 25.

86. Christoph Buchheim, "Wirtschaftliche Hintergründe des Arbeiteraufstandes vom 17. Juni in der DDR," *Vierteljahrshefte für Zeitgeschichte* 38, no. 3 (1990), pp. 427–428.

87. Diedrich, *Der 17. Juni 1953*, pp. 30–40.

88. Ibid., p. 418. Several further factors accelerated flight from the GDR. The regime intensified its ideological campaign against the churches and tightened its controls over intellectuals and artists. There were also attempts to impose physical barriers to contact with West Germany, such as the creation of a five-kilometer-wide border strip and the stopping of streetcar traffic between East and West Berlin in January 1953. Hermann Weber, *Geschichte der DDR*, original ed. (Deutscher Taschenbuch Verlag, 1999), pp. 227–231; Diedrich, *Der 17. Juni 1953*, p. 43. On the transformation of East German agrarian society, see Jonathan Osmond, "From *Junker* Estate to Co-operative Farm: East German Agrarian Society, 1945–61," in Major and Osmond, *The Workers' and Peasants' State*.

89. Kopstein, *The Politics of Economic Decline*, p. 35. According to Kopstein, by April 1953 nearly 40 percent of the wealthier farmers in East Germany had fled.

90. Jan Foitzik, "Die stalinistischen 'Säuberungen' in den ostmitteleuropäischen kommunistischen Parteien," in Hermann Weber and Dietrich Staritz, eds., *Kommunisten verfolgen Kommunisten: stalinistischer Terror und "Saüberungen in den kommunistischen Parteien Europas seit den dreißiger Jahren* (Berlin: Akademie, 1993). Foitzik estimates that by 1951, nearly 350,000 former SPD members were either purged from or left the SED. Among those leading East German officials caught up in the hysteria were Franz Dahlem, a member of the SED Politburo, and Karl Hamann, the LDP leader and minister for trade and provisioning. On the purges, also see Peter Grieder, *The East German Leadership, 1946–1973: Conflict and Crisis* (Manchester: Manchester University Press, 1999), pp. 17–36; Epstein, *The Last Revolutionaries*, pp. 130–157.

91. In fact, the old Frankfurter Allee had been renamed Stalinallee in December 1949, on the occasion of Stalin's seventieth birthday. Plans for the National Construction Program, meanwhile, were first proposed in November 1951. See Herbert Nicolaus and Alexander Obeth, *Die Stalinallee: Geschichte einer deutschen Straße* (Berlin: Verlag für Bauwesen, 1997), pp. 55, 127–128.

92. Beschluß des Politbüros vom 20. Januar 1953, "Die Aufgaben des Handels unter den Bedingungen der Schaffung der Grundlagen des Sozialismus in der DDR," SAPMO-BArch, DY 30 J IV 2/2–258, Bl. 36; MfHV, "Direktive zur Verbesserung der Arbeit im Ministerium und im Apparat des Minsteriums für Handel und Versorgung," July 24, 1952, BArch, DL-1/1009, Bl. 9–11.

93. Protokoll der Sitzung des Kollegiums des Ministeriums für Handel und Versorgung vom 8. November 1952, BArch, DL-1/1007, Bl. 4–11, 13–17.

The Kollegium was created in August 1952. See MfHV, Schaumberg to Abt. Wirtschaftsfragen der SKK, September 24, 1952, BArch, DL-1/1001, Bl. 390.

94. MfHV, HA I Planung, HR Koordinierung, "Begründung zum Planvorschlag 'Entwicklung des Handelnetzes für HO und Konsum 1953,'" November 6, 1952, BArch, DL-1/2520, Bl. 12.

95. MfHV, HA Planung, "Protokoll über die am 16.10.1952 durchgeführte Planabstimmung bei der Staatlichen Plankommission für den Planvorschlag 1953," BArch, DL-1/2520, Bl. 20–21.

96. MfHV, "Protokoll über die am 10. März 1953 stattgefundene Arbeitstagung mit den Abteilungsleitern für Handel und Versorgung der Räte der Bezirke, den Leitern der Zentral- und Bezirksverwaltungen der HO sowie den Leitern der Großhandelskontore," BArch, DL-1/1211, Bl. 2.

97. "Entwicklung des privaten Einzelhandels 1952/1953," October 29, 1952, SAPMO-BArch, J IV 2/202/45, pp. 2–3.

98. GB Handel, Abt. 3, "Protokoll von der Besprechung am 12.9.1952 in Leipzig, DHZ Niederlassung Textil," BArch, DC-5/1, pp. 1–3.

99. Senf to Strampfer, "Aktennotiz Betr.: Fettversorgung der Bevölkerung Erfurt in der HO," October 13, 1952, same file.

100. Vehma to Staatssekretär Strampfer, "Aktennotiz Betr.: Saisonbedingte Versorgung der Bevölkerung mit Baumwoll-Untertrikotagen," October 20, 1952, same file.

101. Vehma, "Bericht über die Reise am 4. und 5.12.1952 nach Chemnitz," December 6, 1952, BArch, DC-6/20, Bl. 11–12.

102. HO Industriewaren, Rostock-Stadt to Operativen Bezirksstab der HO, Rostock, November 13, 1952, BArch, DC-5/4, pp. 1–6; HA Planung, HR Preispolitik to Frau Staatssekretär Krause, November 11, 1952, BArch, DL-1/2520, Bl. 7–10.

103. "Millionenbeträge liegen in der HO fest," *Berliner Zeitung*, November 6, 1952. Planners in the SPK, meanwhile, were complaining about their lack of control over price policy. Through the press and through rumor they learned of several price reductions carried out without their approval. SPK, Planung der Preise to Leitung der Betriebs-Parteiorganisation zu Händen des Gen. Apel, December 15, 1952, BArch, DE-1/12114, Bl. 1–4.

104. Ulbricht to Grotewohl, October 31, 1952, SAPMO-BArch, NL 182/991, Bl. 82.

105. SED, Bezirksleitung Chemnitz, Sekretär Buchheim to Ulbricht, December 6, 1952, same file, Bl. 88–89.

106. Leuschner to Herrn Minister Ziller, Dr. Feldmann, Dr. Hamann,

Handke, July 1, 1952, BArch, DE-1/12103. Leuschner also forwarded the above letter to the KKB. Leuschner to KKB, Strampfer, July 2, 1952, BArch, DC-6/39.

107. For copies of the lists, see BArch, DC-6/39. On subsequent planning, see Zentralverwaltung der HO, HO-Industriewaren to MfHV, Herrn Staatsekretär Baender, September 18, 1952, BArch, DL-1/3054, Bl. 298; MfHV, "Protokoll der Hauptabteilungsleiter-Dienstbesprechung am 5.10.1952," BArch, DL-1/1496, Bl. 4.

108. HO Industriewaren, Landesleitung Thüringen, "Begründung zum Planvorschlag Entwicklungsplan der Handelsorgane HO-J Volks-wirtschaftsplan 1953" ("vertrauliche Dienstsache"), August 27, 1952, BArch, DL-1/2519, Bl. 1.

109. Nicolaus and Obeth, *Die Stalinallee,* p. 243.

110. MfHV, draft "Nationales Aufbauprogram Stalinallee," July 4, 1952, BArch, DL-1/3054, Bl. 438–440.

111. Nicolaus and Obeth, *Die Stalinallee,* p. 242.

112. Ibid., pp. 243–244.

113. SPK, Warenumsatz und Lebensmittelbilanzen, Abt. Lebensmittelbi-lanzen, "Berichterstattung über die Versorgungssituation im I. Quartal und die sich daraus ergebenden Maßnahmen," February 5, 1953, BArch, DE-1/7186, Bl. 31–36.

114. SKHV, Strampfer to ZK, Baeger, "Bericht über die Versorgungslage," February 10, 1953, BArch, DC-6/81, pp. 4–5; MfHV, "Protokoll über die am 10. März 1953 stattgefundene Arbeitstagung mit den Abtei-lungsleitern für Handel und Versorgung der Räte der Bezirke, den Leitern der Zentral- und Bezirksverwaltungen der HO sowie den Lei-tern der Großhandelskontore," BArch, DL-1/1211, Bl. 1–4.

115. "Statut der 'Staatlichen Kommission für Handel und Versorgung' vom 30. April 1953," *Gbl der DDR,* May 22, 1953, pp. 734–735. Its members included the minister for trade and provisioning, the state secretary for the food and semiluxuries industries, the minister of agriculture, the minister for light industry, and the deputy chairman of the SPK. "An-lage Nr. 11 zum Protokoll Nr. 4/53 vom 20. Januar 1953," SAPMO-BArch, DY 30 J IV 2/2–258, Bl. 62.

116. Herbst, *So funktionierte die DDR,* p. 299. On Schmidt's role as head of the SKHV, see Pence, "'You as a Woman Will Understand.'"

117. MfHV, "Protokoll über die Kollegiumssitzung am Freitag, den 17.4.1953," BArch, DL-1/1012, Bl. 2–3.

118. "Protokoll Nr. 17/53 der Siztung des Politbüros am 24. März 1953," SAPMO-BArch, DY 30 J IV 2/2A-255, Bl. 91; "Anlage Nr. 1 zum Pro-tokoll Nr. 18/53 vom 26. März 1953, Maßnahmen zur Sicherung der

Versorgung der Bevölkerung mit den wichtigsten Nahrungsmitteln," SAPMO-BArch, DY 30 J IV 2/2–272, Bl. 1–6.

119. SPK, "Beschlußentwurf Massenbedarfsartikeln," BArch, DE-1/7190, Bl. 24–29; SPK, "Beschluß zur Verbesserung der Versorgung der Bevölkerung mit Massenbedarfsgütern," BArch, DE-1/1828, Bl. 1–10; "Analge Nr. 1 zum Protokoll Nr. 26/53 vom 12. Mai. Beschluß zur Verbesserung der Versorgung der Bevölkerung mit Massenbedarfsgütern," SAPMO-BArch, DY 30 J IV 2/2–280, Bl. 11–20.

120. *Wörterbuch der Ökonomie Sozialismus* (East Berlin: Dietz, 1969), p. 521.

121. "Analge Nr. 1 zum Protokoll Nr. 26/53 vom 12. Mai. Beschluß zur Verbesserung der Versorgung der Bevölkerung mit Massenbedarfsgütern," SAPMO-BArch, DY 30 J IV 2/2–280, Bl. 11.

122. Grieder, *The East German Leadership*, pp. 53–66.

123. "Stenographische Niederschrift der 13. Tagung des Zentralkomitees am Mittwoch, dem 13., und Donnerstag, dem 14. Mai 1953 im Zentralhaus der Einheit," SAPMO-BArch, DY 30 J IV 2/1/115, Bl. 155.

124. Ibid., Bl. 156.

125. Ibid., Bl. 157. In the Soviet Union, she claimed, light and chemical industries were fully capable of producing fabrics in the colors and quality desired by consumers. She demanded to know why this was not possible in the GDR. Similarly, it was the Czech shoe industry that produced "affordable, fashionable and seasonally appropriate shoes that are happily bought by our population." Why were so few East German firms able to produce equally desired shoes?

126. Baring, *Uprising in East Germany*, pp. 26–27.

127. "Kommuniqué des Politbüros vom 9. Juni 1953," in *Dokumente der Sozialistischen Einheitspartei Deutschlands* (East Berlin: Dietz, 1954), 4: pp. 428–431.

128. "Es wird Zeit, den Holzhammer beiseite zu legen," *ND*, June 14, 1953; Otto Lehmann "Zu einigen schädlichen Erscheinungen bei der Erhöhung der Arbeitsnormen," *Die Tribüne*, June 16, 1953.

4. The Rise, Decline, and Afterlife of the New Course

1. For recent accounts of this struggle, see Peter Grieder, *The East German Leadership, 1946–1973: Conflict and Crisis* (Manchester: Manchester University Press, 1999) pp. 53–85; Catherine Epstein, *The Last Revolutionaries: German Communists and Their Century* (Cambridge, Mass.: Harvard University Press, 2003), pp. 158–163.

2. See, for example, Hermann Weber, *Geschichte der DDR*, original ed. (Munich: Deutscher Taschenbuch Verlag, 1999), p. 173; Sigrid Meuschel,

Legitimation und Parteiherrschaft in der DDR (Frankfurt am Main: Suhrkamp, 1992), p. 145.

3. "Kommuniqué des Politbüros vom 9. Juni 1953," in *Dokumente der Sozialistischen Einheitspartei Deutschlands* (East Berlin: Dietz, 1954), 4: p. 428.

4. The ordinances were published in *Gbl der DDR,* June 19, 1953, pp. 805–808.

5. Torsten Diedrich, *Der 17. Juni 1953 in der DDR: Bewaffnete Gewalt gegen das Volk* (Berlin: Dietz, 1991), p. 64.

6. Grieder, *The East German Leadership,* p. 71.

7. Diedrich, *Der 17. Juni 1953,* pp. 66–67.

8. Mary Fulbrook, *Anatomy of a Dictatorship: Inside the GDR, 1949–1989* (Oxford: Oxford University Press, 1995), p. 183.

9. MfHV, Wach to Abt. Handel, Nahrungs und Genußmittelindustrie der SKK, June 18, 1953, BArch, DL-1/1002, Bl. 72–73.

10. "Über die Lage und die unmittelbaren Aufgaben der Partei," in *Dokumente der Sozialistischen Einheitspartei Deutschlands,* pp. 437–439.

11. Ibid., p. 443.

12. Ibid., p. 445.

13. "Protokoll Nr. 40/53 der Sitzung des Politbüros des Zentralkomitees am 21. Juni 1953," SAPMO-BArch, DY 30 J IV 2/2–294, Bl. 2.

14. Dietrich Staritz, *Geschichte der DDR,* expanded ed. (Frankfurt am Main: Suhrkamp, 1996), p. 127.

15. "Protokoll Nr. 46/53 der Sitzung des Politbüros des Zentralkomitees am 4. Juli 1953," SAPMO-BArch, DY 30 J IV 2/2–300, Bl. 1–3. The commission included Heinrich Rau, Bruno Leuschner, Elli Schmidt, Gerhard Ziller, Kurt Gregor, and Willy Rumpf.

16. Andreas Herbst, Winfried Ranke, and Jürgen Winkler, eds., *So funktionierte die DDR,* vol. 3 (Reinbek bei Hamburg: Rowohlt, 1994), p. 356.

17. SPK, Opitz to Wach, July 4, 1953, BArch, DL-1/2750, Bl. 135–136. In fact, Wach was not alone. The minister of light industry was also calling for price reductions for goods sitting in inventory because shoppers refused to pay what they considered to be exceedingly high prices. MfL, Feldmann to Wach, August 31, 1953, same file, Bl. 142–144.

18. SPK, untitled report on price reductions after June 17, 1953, dated October 16, 1953, BArch, DE-1/6068, Bl. 21.

19. "Zur weiteren Verbesserung der Lebenshaltung der Arbeiter," in *Dokumente der Sozialistischen Einheitspartei Deutschlands,* p. 448.

20. "Neue Preissenkung vom Ministerrat beschlossen," *ND,* July 25, 1953, p. 1. The ordinances were published in *Gbl der DDR,* July 27, 1953, pp. 885–888.

21. "Stenographische Niederschrift der 15. Tagung des Zentralkomitees

vom 24.-26. Juli 1953 in Berlin, Haus der Einheit, 12. Uhr—Unkorrigiert!" SAPMO-BArch, DY 30/ IV 2/1/119, Bl. 25–26, 66.

22. Ibid., Bl. 66.

23. "Der neue Kurs und die Aufgaben der Partei," in *Dokumente der Sozialistische Einheitspartei Deutschlands,* p. 459.

24. Ibid., p. 467.

25. Ernst Lange, "Die politische Bedeutung und die Aufgaben des Handels," *Einheit* 8, no. 9 (1953), pp. 1085–1092; Leitartikel, "Wichtige wirtschaftliche Aufgaben des neuen Kurses," *Einheit* 8, no. 11 (1953), pp. 1239–1247; Leitartikel, "1954–das Jahr der großen Initiative," *Einheit* 9, no. 1 (1954), pp. 20–25; Ernst Lange, "Die Aufgaben der Lebensmittelindustrie bei der Durchführung des neuen Kurses," *Einheit* 9, no. 4 (1954), pp. 365–371.

26. Lange, "Die politische Bedeutung und die Aufgaben des Handels," p. 1085.

27. A. I. Mikojan, "Die Verbindung mit dem Volke enger gestalten," *Der Handel* 3, no. 24 (1953), pp. 665–666; A. I. Mikojan, "Die Verkaufskultur heben! Aus der Rede A. I. Mikojans über die neuen Aufgaben des Handels in der UdSSR," *ND,* November 12, 1953, p. 5.

28. ZK Abt. HVA to Ulbricht, April 8, 1954, SAPMO-BArch, NL 182/991, Bl. 106–109. Mikoyan's visits were reported in the press: "A. I. Mikojan besuchte die Stalinallee," *ND,* April 8, 1954, p. 8; "Genosse Mikojan be suchte das HO-Warenhaus am Alexanderplatz," *ND,* April 9, 1954, p. 2.

29. "Beschluß des Ministerrats zur Durchführung der Verordnung über die weitere Senkung von Preisen bei Lebensmitteln und Industriewaren," October 24, 1953, BArch, DE-1/6068, Bl. 59–60; "Verordnung über die weitere Senkung von Preisen bei Lebensmitteln, Genußmitteln und Verbrauchsgütern," *Gbl der DDR,* October 26, 1953, pp. 1059–1060.

30. "Kommuniqué über die außerordentliche Sitzung des Ministerrats der Deutschen Demokratischen Republik am Sonnabend, dem 24. Oktober 1953," *Tägliche Rundschau,* October 25, 1953, p. 1. Leuschner did not say how the deliveries were to be paid for.

31. For a broad sampling of before-and-after prices, see *Tägliche Rundschau,* October 25, 1953, pp. 1–2.

32. SZS to MfHV, "Bericht über die Entwicklung der Einzelhandelspreise in der DDR in den Jahren 1950–1960, Vertrauliche Dienstsache," August 21, 1961, BArch, DL-1/2700, Bl. 4–5.

33. I. Zblowski, "Größerer Reichtum für alle—das ist die neue Preissenkung!" *Tägliche Rundschau,* October 28, 1953, p. 3; "Westdeutsche Teuerung in Mark und Pfennigen," *Tägliche Rundschau,* October 29,

1953, p. 3. In fact, as discussed, even East German statisticians came to the conclusion, in internal reports, that the cost of living was considerably higher in East Germany than in West Germany.

34. "Preisherabsetzung weckt neue Initiative," *Tägliche Rundschau*, October 27, 1953, p. 1.

35. Zblowski, "Größerer Reichtum für alle," p. 3.

36. Volker R. Berghahn, *The Americanisation of West German Industry, 1945–1973* (Cambridge: Cambridge University Press, 1986), pp. 13–26.

37. Jeffrey Kopstein, *The Politics of Economic Decline in East Germany, 1945–1989* (Chapel Hill: University of North Carolina Press, 1997), p. 38.

38. Sekretariat des Hohen Kommissars der UdSSR in Deutschland to MfHV, Wach, October 30, 1953, BArch, DL-1/1002, Bl. 35. For the article in question, see B. Kern, "Mehr Bedarfsgüter für die Bevölkerung!" *Tägliche Rundschau*, October 31, 1953, pp. 1–2. Two days earlier, the *Tägliche Rundschau* had published an article on mass-demand-goods production in the Soviet Union: "Produktion von Massenbedarfsgütern bedeutend vergrößert. Beschluß des Ministerrats der UdSSR und des ZK der KPdSU," *Tägliche Rundschau*, October 29, 1953, p. 1.

39. MfHV, "Bericht über die Sitzung der Kommission der Versorgung der Bevölkerung," November 4, 1953, BArch, DE-1/18599, pp. 1–4; SPK, "Volkswirtschaftsplan 1954, Warenumsatz im Einzelhandel" ("vertrauliche Dienstsache"), May 28, 1954, BArch, DL-1/2546, Bl. 9.

40. MfHV, "Bericht über die Sitzung der Kommission der Versorgung der Bevölkerung," November 4, 1953, BArch, DE-1/18599, pp. 5–7.

41. "Verordnung über die Erhöhung und Verbesserung der Produktion von Verbrauchsgütern für die Bevölkerung vom 17. Dezember 1953," *Gbl der DDR*, December 31, 1953, pp. 1315–1329. On Soviet involvement, see "Bemerkungen zum Entwurf einer Verordnung des Ministerrats der DDR 'über die Steigerung und Verbesserung der Produktion von Massenbedarfsgütern,'" December 11, 1953, SAPMO-BArch, J IV 2/202/46, pp. 1–3.

42. MfL, ZA Planung, Oemisch (Planungsleiter) to SPK, Arbeitsgruppe Massenbedarfsgüter, January 7, 1954, BArch, DE-1/29148, pp. 1–2.

43. SPK, Stellvtr. des Vorsitzenden, Binz to SPK, Leiter der Abt. Massenbedarfsgüter, Wange, February 20, 1954, BArch, DE-1/29147.

44. Leuschner to Ulbricht, January 18, 1954, SAPMO-BArch, J IV 2/202/39, pp. 1–7.

45. "Die Lage in der Versorgung der Bevölkerung bei Nichterfüllung der Aufgaben im Außenhandel," March 13, 1954, SAPMO-BArch, J IV 2/202/46, pp. 1–5.

46. Ibid., p. 4.

47. Walter Ulbricht, "Die gegenwärtige Lage und der Kampf um das neue Deutschland," *ND*, April 1, 1954, p. 3.

48. "Anlage Nr. 2 zum Protokoll Nr. 7/54 von 25. Mai 1954–Beschluß über die neuen Aufgaben zur Durchführung des Volkswirtschaftsplanes 1954," SAPMO-BArch, DY 30 J IV 2/2–363, Bl. 13.

49. ZK Abt. HVA, Sektor Handel to Ulbricht and Ziller (über Gen. Lange), April 9, 1954, SAPMO-BArch, NL 182/991, Bl. 110.

50. MfHV, Abt. Bedarfsforschung und Umsatzplanung, "Entwurf: Vorschlag zur Kontrollziffer 1955 für den Warenumsatz," March 15, 1954 ("vertrauliche Dienstsache"), BArch, DL-1/2558, Bl. 147–150; SPK, "Volkswirtschaftsplan 1954, Warenumsatz im Einzelhandel," May 28, 1954 ("vertrauliche Dienstsache"), BArch, MfHV, DL-1/2546, Bl. 1–2.

51. *Statistisches Jahrbuch der Deutschen Demokratischen Republik 1956* (East Berlin: VEB Deutscher Zentralverlag, 1957), p. 488.

52. See, for example, SPK, Warenumsatz und Warenbereitstellung to Arbeitsgruppe Massenbedarfsgüter, August 6, 1954, BArch, DE-1/29159, pp. 1–2.

53. MfHV, Abt. Fahrzeuge, EBM und sonst-Holzbearbeitung to MfHV, HA Sonst. Industriewaren, November 30, 1954, BArch, DC-20/1853, Bl. 18. The report was also critical of wholesalers and retailers. Low fulfillment of the commodity supply plans had made many willing to accept poor-quality products from manufacturers, products which simply expanded their inventory, since consumers refused to buy them.

54. "Anlage 1 zum Protokoll der 172. Sitzung d. Reg. v. 14.10.54–Beschluß über die Sicherung der Produktion von Massenbedarfsgütern im Jahre 1954/55 vom 14. Oktober 1954," BArch, DC-20 I/3–239, Bl. 15–20. The new ordinance aimed its criticism primarily at the Ministries of Machine Building and Light Industry for respective shortfalls of DM 50 million and DM 30 million in the first half of 1954.

55. SPK, Gruppe Massenbedarfsgüter, Wange to Stellvtr. des Vorsitzendes, Gen. Opitz, February 2, 1955, BArch, DE-1/29159; HA Kontrolle, Gruppe III, "Stellungnahme zur Durchführung des Massenbedarfsgüterprogramms im Jahre 1955," April 5, 1955, BArch, DC-20/1861, Bl. 4–5.

56. Ulbricht and Grotewohl to Central Committee of the Communist Party of the Soviet Union, Khrushchev, February 17, 1955, SAPMO-BArch, J IV 2/202/39, pp. 1–13. The total volume of foreign trade was expected to decline from 10.4 billion rubles in 1954 to 9.1 billion in 1955, with imports falling from 4.8 billion to 4.0 billion rubles.

57. Unfortunately, there is no comprehensive study of East Germany's hard currency problems, particularly for the 1950s and 1960s. On the GDR's hard currency debt in the 1970s and 1980s and on attempts to augment

its hard currency intake, see Kopstein, *The Politics of Economic Decline,* chap. 3; Charles Maier, *Dissolution: The Crisis of Communism and the End of East Germany* (Princeton, N.J.: Princeton University Press, 1997), chap. 2; Jonathan Zatlin, "Consuming Ideology: Socialist Consumerism and the Intershops, 1970–1989," in Peter Hübner and Klaus Tenefelde, eds., *Arbeiter in der SBZ-DDR* (Essen: Klartext, 1999); Timothy Garton Ash, *In Europe's Name: Germany and the Divided Continent* (New York: Vintage, 1993), pp. 141–162.

58. Khrushchev to SED Central Committee, March 30, 1955, SAPMO-BArch, J IV 2/202/39, p. 1.

59. Khrushchev to Ulbricht and Grotewohl, May 3, 1955, SAPMO-BArch, J IV 2/202/39, pp. 1–3.

60. SPK, Wittkowski to Ulbricht, May 7, 1955, same file; Ulbricht and Grotewohl to Khrushchev, May 9, 1955, same file.

61. SPK, Leuschner to Ulbricht, June 20, 1955, SAPMO-BArch, J IV 2/202/47, pp. 1–2; adjoining report, "Grundlage für die Ausarbeitung der Direktive zur Aufstellung des zweiten Fünfjahrplanes 1956 bis 1960," same file, pp. 1–3.

62. SPK, Leuschner to Ulbricht, June 20, 1955, "Grundlage für die Ausarbeitung der Direktive zur Aufstellung des zweiten Fünfjahrplanes 1956 bis 1960," SAPMO-BArch, J IV 2/202/47, p. 3.

63. Arnold Sywottek, "The Americanization of Everyday Life? Early Trends in Consumer and Leisure-Time Behavior," in Michael Ermarth, ed., *America and the Shaping of German Society, 1945–1955* (Providence, R.I.: Berghahn Books, 1993), p. 150. Also see Michael Wildt, *Vom kleinen Wohlstand: Eine Konsumgeschichte der fünfziger Jahre* (Frankfurt am Main: Fischer Taschenbuch, 1996); Axel Schildt, *Moderne Zeiten: Freizeit, Massenmedien und 'Zeitgeist' in der Bundesrepublik der 50er Jahre* (Hamburg: Christians, 1995).

64. See, for example, Alessandro Pizzorno, "The Individualistic Mobilization of Europe," *Daedalus* 93, no. 1 (1964), pp. 217–221.

65. As of 1953, East Germans wishing to visit the Federal Republic required official permission. Still, in 1956 2.5 million East Germans visited the Federal Republic (West Berlin and West Germany). And although in 1957 East German officials made it more difficult to travel to West Germany, approximately seven hundred thousand were still able to visit in 1958. In addition, 25 percent of West Berlin's university students lived in East Berlin. Wolfgang Ribbe, *Geschichte Berlins,* Bd. 2 (Munich: C. H. Beck, 1987), pp. 1086–1088.

66. Conversely, a little over twelve thousand West Berliners worked in East Berlin. Ibid., p. 1086.

67. Ibid., p. 1088. For their part, West Berliners regularly took advantage of cultural offerings in East Berlin, visiting the Berliner Ensemble and the Komische Oper, among other cultural institutions.

68. Sywottek, "The Americanization of Everyday Life?" p. 149; Wildt, *Vom kleinen Wohlstand,* pp. 172–176.

69. Wildt, *Vom kleinen Wohlstand,* pp. 167–170.

70. Ibid., pp. 156–161.

71. Sywottek, "The Americanization of Everyday Life?" pp. 148–149.

72. Wildt, *Vom kleinen Wohlstand,* p. 53.

73. Georg Bergler, "Das Verhalten des Verbrauchers im modernen Markte," in Georg Bergler, *Verbrauchsforschung zwischen Mensch und Wirtschaft* (Munich: Moderne Industrie, 1961), p. 92.

74. Ibid., pp. 90–91. Of course, Bergler had an interest in emphasizing the changing behavior of consumers and the competitiveness of the market, both of which implied a heightened need for market research. But he hardly needed to exaggerate; by 1956 market research had already become a well-established element in West German distribution and marketing practices. As Volker Berghahn has suggested, "the Fordist recipe" of linking mass production and mass consumption "found wide acceptance in the 1950s" among industrial elites. It was generally recognized that rationalized, streamlined production now required rationalized forms of distribution. Volker Berghahn, "Resisting the Pax Americana? West German Industry and the United States, 1945–55," in Ermarth, *America and the Shaping of German Society,* p. 97.

75. "Bericht über die Erfahrungen des Versandhandels," July 26, 1956, BArch, DL-1/3133, MfHV, Bl. 11. In this report, for example, mention is made of a delegation sent to the well-known West German mail-order firm, Neckermann.

76. Annette Kaminsky, "'Keine Zeit verlaufen—beim Versandhaus kaufen,'" in Neue Gesellschaft für Bildende Kunst, *Wunderwirtschaft: DDR-Konsumkultur in den 60er Jahren* (Cologne: Böhlau, 1996), pp. 124–126.

77. MfHV, Abt. Warenhäuser und Versandhandel, "Bericht über die Tätigkeit des Versandhauses Leipzig," January 19, 1957, BArch, DL-1/3040, Bl. 37, 42–43.

78. Annette Kaminsky, *Kaufrausch: Die Geschichte der ostdeutschen Versandhäuser* (Berlin: C. Links Verlag, 1998), pp. 22–24.

79. MfHV, "Bericht über die Erfahrungen des Versandhandels," July 27, 1956, BArch, DL-1/3040, Bl. 54–63.

80. MfHV, Stellvertreter des Ministers, Einzelhandel (Bormann), "Aktenvermerk über die Beratung betr. Versandhandel," September 9, 1957, same file, Bl. 1–2.

81. MfHV, report on turnover, October 2, 1958, BArch, DL-1/2670, Bl. 1–8.

82. For contemporary descriptions of the installment plan in capitalist economies, see Erich Krauss, *Der Teilzahlungskauf* (East Berlin: VEB Deutscher Zentralverlag, 1956), pp. 10–70; Hermann Fürst, "Teilzahlung mit Überlegung," *Der Handel* 3, no. 2 (1954), p. 9.

83. There were already existing credit options, but they entailed prohibitively restrictive conditions. It was necessary to save at least 50 percent of the total price in a special bank account, and then, after receiving credit for the rest, one had to pay back the loan within one year. In practice, only those with high incomes were able to meet these requirements. Fürst, "Teilzahlung," p. 9; ZK Abt. Planung und Finanzen to Ulbricht, August 5, 1953, SAPMO-BArch, NL 182/991, Bl. 95.

84. Deutsche Investitionsbank, Franz Ulbrieg to Ulbricht, July 20, 1953, SAPMO-BArch, NL 182/991, Bl. 97–99. Ulbricht had received a similar, if somewhat less adamant, letter from East Germany's Central Bank on July 13, 1953. Same file, Bl. 100.

85. In fact, East Germany was only a few years ahead of the Soviet Union, which introduced the installment plan in late 1959. Roger Skurski, *Soviet Marketing and Economic Development* (London: Macmillan, 1983), p. 143.

86. "Anordnung über die Finanzierung des Kaufs von Möbeln und anderen langlebigen Gebrauchsgütern vom 26. October," reprinted in Krauss, *Der Teilzahlungskauf,* pp. 96–98.

87. The intital list of goods one could buy on credit, assuming they were available, consisted of the following: furniture, ovens and stoves, sewing machines, radios, TVs, rugs, vacuum cleaners, bicycles, motorcycles, automobiles, typewriters, outboard motorboats, accordions, and cameras.

88. Krauss, *Der Teilzahlungskauf,* pp. 74–76.

89. Quoted in Peter Horvath, "Die Teilzahlungskredite als Begleiterscheinung des westdeutschen 'Wirtschaftswunders,'" in *Zeitschrift für Unternehmensgeschichte* 37, no. 1 (1992), pp. 25, 34, 47.

90. "Die Entwicklung des Einzelhandels in Westberlin," March 16, 1956, LAB, Rep. 113/480, pp. 11–12.

91. SPK (Meiser) to MfHV, Stellvertreter des Ministers, Schneiderheinze, July 31, 1956, BArch, DE-1/25182.

92. MdF, HA Geldumlauf und Kredite, Becker to MdF, Stellvertreter des Ministers, Rothe, July 26, 1956, BArch, DN-1/900; MdF, Rothe to ZK Abt. Planung und Finanzen, June 9, 1956, same file; MdF, Rothe to VdK, der Vorstand, May 15, 1956, same file; MdF, Rumpf to Stellvertreter des Ministerrates, Oelßner, August 1956, same file.

93. The banks continued to supply the credit, but retailers now controlled its dispensation. Consumers no longer had to worry about where the

credit came from. The types of goods included remained unchanged. Krauss, *Der Teilzahlungskauf,* pp. 88–90, 103–106.

94. MdF, HA Geldumlauf und Kreidte, Becker, "Leitungsmaterial für Stellvertreter des Ministers Rothe," January 24, 1957, BArch, DN-1/900, pp. 1–4. The HO accounted for 55 percent of the purchases, the co-ops for 45 percent.

95. SPK, HA Planung und Finanzen, "Protokoll über die am 1.2.1957 stattgefundene Besprechung über das Teilzahlungsgeschäft," February 1, 1957, BArch, DN-1/900; SPK, HA Materialbilanzierung der Leichtindustrie, "Analyse der Erfüllung der Bereitstellungspläne für die Bevölkerung der wichtigsten Waren der Leichtindustrie im 1. Halbjahr 1957," August 12, 1957, BArch, DE-1/3731, Bl. 16; Deutsche Notenbank to MdF, Gremler, March 26, 1958, BArch, DN-1/901, p. 2.

96. Deutsche Notenbank to MdF, Gremler, March 26, 1958, BArch, DN-1/901, pp. 1–6. In total, 1.2 million installment plan contracts were processed in 1957.

97. "Protokoll über die konstituierende Sitzung der Regierungskommission für Konsumgüterproduktion und Versorgung der Bevölkerung am 12.12.1955," BArch, DE-1/24201.

98. Oelßner Sekretariat to Sekretariat der Volkskammer der DDR, January 2, 1957, Kurzbiographie, SAPMO-BArch, NY 4215/1, Bl. 11; Oelßner to Verlag Die Wirtschaft Berlin, August 13, 1945, Kurzbiographie, same file, Bl. 29. Also see Epstein, *The Last Revolutionaries,* pp. 34–37; Gabriele Baumgartner and Dieter Hebig, eds., *Biographisches Handbuch der SBZ/DDR, 1945–1990* (Munich: K. G. Sauer, 1997), p. 613. For memories of Oelßner in Moscow, see Wolfgang Leonhard, *Die Revolution entlässt ihre Kinder* (Munich: Wilhelm Heyne Verlag, 1981), p. 369.

99. Karl Schirdewan was a member of the Politburo and Central Committee Secretary for Cadre Questions *(Kaderfragen)*; Ernst Wollweber was a member of the Central Committee and minister for state security. Both men, along with Oelßner and others, lost their leading state and party positions. On the power struggles within the SED in the mid-to-late 1950s, see Grieder, *The East German Leadership,* pp. 114–132; Epstein, *The Last Revolutionaries,* pp. 159–162, 169–177.

100. MfL, ZA Technologie, "Protokoll über die Besprechung am 5.7.1956 beim Stellv. d. Vors. des Ministerrats Professor Fred Oelßner," July 11, 1956, SAPMO-BArch, DY 30/ IV 2/609/94, p. 1.

101. Sektor Leichtindustrie, Textil, "Berichterstattung über die Probleme der Textilindustrie und ihre angestrebte Lösung," May 14, 1956, SAPMO-BArch, DY 30/ IV 2/609/8, p. 7. The author of another report from the same SED department complained bitterly that GDR invest-

ment in the textile industry in 1955 and 1956 amounted to about DM 70 million annually, while in West Germany the comparable figure came to more than DM 400 million. ZK Abt. Leicht- und Lebensmittelindustrie, "Zu einigen Fragen der Textilindustrie im 2. Fünfjahrplan," March 7, 1956 ("streng vertraulich!"), SAPMO-BArch, DY 30/ IV 2/609/94, p. 8.

102. Magistrat von Groß-Berlin, Abt. Handel und Versorgung, "Die Entwicklung des Einzelhandels in Westberlin," March 16, 1956, LAB, Rep. 113/480, pp. 7–10.

103. SZS to SPK, December 9, 1954, draft of "Verordnung über die Durchführung der Statistik des Lebensstandards der Bevölkerung," BArch, DE-1/12766, p. 1.

104. Quoted in Michael Lemke, *Die Berlinkrise 1958 bis 1963: Interessen und Handlungsspielräume der SED im Ost-West-Konflikt* (Berlin: Akademie, 1995), pp. 46–47.

105. Quoted in William J. Tompson, *Khrushchev: A Political Life* (New York: St. Martin's Press, 1995), p. 160.

106. See Lemke, *Die Berlinkrise,* pp. 46–47.

107. Vladislav Zubok, "Khrushchev and the Berlin Crisis (1958–1962)," Working Paper no. 6, May 1993, *Cold War International History Project* (CWIHP), p. 3.

108. As a 1957 report from the SPK explained, "until now there has been no methodology or any kind of index system in this area." SPK, Perspektivplanung-Lebensstandard, "Thesen über ein Kennziffersystem für die Planung des Lebensstandards," January 22, 1957, BArch, DE-1/3493, Bl. 1.

109. In 1958, for the first time, the official Travel Office *(Reisebüro)* organized trips to socialist countries for five thousand GDR citizens. Jörg Roelser, "Wandlungen in Arbeit und Freizeit der DDR-Bevölkerung Mitte der sechziger Jahre," *Zeitschrift für Geschichtswissenschaft* 37, no. 12 (1989), p. 1067. Indicative of how limited the phenomenon was, official statistical yearbooks on the 1950s provide no information on travel abroad, either to socialist or capitalist countries; the category does not exist. By 1960, however, they show that 107,742 East Germans traveled in the East bloc. By 1963 that number grew to 239,700. *Statistisches Jahrbuch der Deutschen Demokratichen Republik 1964* (East Berlin: VEB Deutscher Zentralverlag, 1965), p. 469.

110. Grieder, *The East German Leadership,* pp. 108, 119–120.

111. SZS, HA VI-Volkswirtschaftliche Gesamtübersichten, "Die Entwicklung des Lebensstandards der Werktätigen in der Periode des 1. Fünfjahrplanes," May 1956, BArch, DE-2/31413–0921988, p. 4.

112. According to the report, real wages in 1955 were 24.2 percent higher than in 1936; and where the first Five-Year Plan had foreseen a 28 percent fall in the prices for most consumer goods, they had, in fact, fallen 32 percent. As a result, taking 1936 prices as a basis, the cost of living index for middle-income groups had fallen from 327 to 203 percent. Ibid., pp. 27–28.

113. *Statistisches Jahrbuch der Deutschen Demokratischen Republik 1956* (East Berlin: VEB Deutscher Zentralverlag), p. 203.

114. Jörg Roesler, "Privater Konsum in Ostdeutschland 1950–1960," in Arnold Sywottek and Axel Schildt, eds., Modernisierung im Wiederaufbau: Die Westdeutsche Gesallschaft der 50er Jahre (Bonn: J. H. W. Dietz, 1993), pp. 295–297.

115. SZS, HA VI-Volkswirtschaftliche Gesamtübersichten, "Die Entwicklung des Lebensstandards der Werktätigen in der Periode des 1. Fünfjahrplanes," May 1956, BArch, DE-2/31413–0921988, p. 29.

116. Ibid., p. 69. Also see SZS, "Statistischer Bericht über die Entwicklung des Lebensstandards in der Deutschen Demokratischen Republik und in der Bundesrepublik Deutschlands," probably 1956, BArch, DE-1/11791.

117. Between 1950 and 1952, the annual number of refugees fleeing to West Germany hovered between 165,000 and 198,000. In 1953, due to the provisioning crisis, that figure exploded to over 330,000. In 1954 the number declined to 184,000, most likely as a result of the New Course. But in 1955 the number of refugees again rose sharply to nearly 253,000, a level at which it more or less remained until 1958, when the SED proclaimed its Main Economic Task of surpassing West Germany in per capita consumption. For figures on flight to West Germany, see Weber, *Geschichte der DDR*, p. 220.

118. ZK der SED to Khrushchev and Bulganin, May 19, 1956, SAPMO-BArch, J IV 2/202/39, p. 1.

5. Demand Research

1. There is a growing literature (too extensive to list here) that addresses the history of marketing generally. For works on Germany, see Dirk Reinhardt, *Von der Reklame zum Marketing: Geschichte der Wirtschaftswerbung in Deutschland* (Berlin: Akademie, 1993); Rainer Gries, Volker Ilgen, and Dirk Schindelbeck, eds., *"Ins Gehirn der Masse kriechen"! Werbung und Mentalitätsgeschichte* (Darmstadt: Wissenschaftliche Buchgesellschaft, 1995); Dirk Schindelbeck, "'Asbach Uralt' und 'soziale Marktwirtschaft': Zur Kulturgeschichte der Werbeagentur in Deutschland

am Beispiel von Hanns W. Brose (1899–1971)," *Zeitschrift für Unternehmensgeschichte* 40, no. 4 (1995) pp. 235–252; Michael Wildt, *Vom kleinen Wohlstand: Eine Konsumgeschichte der fünfziger Jahre* (Frankfurt am Main: Fischer Taschenbuch, 1996). These works, however, have little, if anything, to say about market research.

2. On advertising in Soviet-type systems, see Philip Hanson, *Advertising and Socialism: The Nature and Extent of Consumer Advertising in the Soviet Union, Poland, Hungary, and Yugoslavia* (London: Macmillan, 1974). But as with the literature on market economies, this work has little to say about market research.

3. For a brief summary on the period between the late nineteenth century and the Nazi years, see Reinhardt, *Von der Reklame zum Marketing,* pp. 44–48.

4. Georg Bergler, *Die Entwicklung der Verbrauchsforschung in Deutschland und die Gesellschaft für Konsumforschung bis zum Jahre 1945* (Kallmünz: Lassleben, 1959–1960).

5. Ibid., pp. 6–21.

6. Ibid., p. 48; Georg Bergler, "Wilhelm Vershofen, Meister und Begründer der europäischen Marktforschung," *Werberundschau* 35, no. 40 (1960) pp. 17–20.

7. A. J. Nicholls, *Freedom with Responsibility: The Social Market Economy in Germany, 1918–1963* (Oxford: Oxford University Press, 1994), pp. 76, 116.

8. Volker Hentschel, *Ludwig Erhard: Ein Politikerleben* (Munich: Olzog, 1996), pp. 17–18. Unfortunately, there is no biography of Vershofen; in the secondary literature he is discussed primarily in terms of his connection with Erhard.

9. Georg Bergler, "Der Beitrag Wilhelm Vershofens zur Marktforschung," in Georg Bergler, *Verbrauchsforschung zwischen Mensch und Wirtschaft* (Munich: Moderne Industrie, 1961), p. 23.

10. Simmel's thoughts on the subject are well represented in his essays on fashion and adornment. "Fashion" was first published in English in *International Quarterly* 10 (1904), pp. 130–155; "Adornment" is reprinted in Kurt Wolff, ed. and trans., *The Sociology of Georg Simmel* (Glencoe, Ill.: Free Press, 1950).

11. Wilhelm Vershofen, *Wirtschaft als Schicksal und Aufgabe* (Darmstadt: O. Reichl, 1930), p. 237.

12. Bergler, *Die Entwicklung,* pp. 64–65.

13. Ibid., pp. 144–153.

14. Ibid., pp. 87–88, 120–144, 182–184.

15. The nature of the relationship between the society and the Nazi regime, hardly clear, requires further research. Bergler certainly had an interest in minimizing any possible shared agenda. Dirk Reinhardt, however,

suggests that the regime tried to enlist the institute in its attempts to achieve economic autarchy, hoping in particular that the institute would help to realize the goal of "consumption guidance." He also points out that the Advertising Council of the German Economy, created by the Nazis and placed under the Ministry of Propaganda, was represented on the board of the society. Reinhardt, *Von der Reklame zum Marketing*, p. 140. Also see Hartmut Berghoff, "Von der Reklame zur 'Verbrauchslenkung': Werbung im nationalsozialistischen Deutschland," in Hartmut Berghoff, ed., *Konsumpolitik: Die Regulierung des privaten Verbrauchs im 20. Jahrhundert* (Göttingen: Vandenhoek & Ruprecht, 1999), pp. 98–99.

16. Grete Wittkowski, "Die Entfaltung der Masseninitiative im volkseigenen und genossenschaftlichen Handel," *Einheit* 6, no. 12 (1951), p. 1592.

17. Wittkowski's Lebenslauf and Kurzbiographie, SAPMO-BArch, DY 30/ IV 2/11/v.1820, Bl. 1–12. Wittkowski's setback was temporary. In 1954 she not only resumed her position as Leuschner's deputy in the SPK, but was also elected to the SED Central Committee.

18. Wittkowski, "Die Entfaltung," p. 1589.

19. Ibid., p. 1592.

20. "Die Ergebnisse der ersten Monate des Fünfjahrplans: Entschließung des Zentralkomitees der sozialistischen Einheitspartei Deutschlands auf der 6. Tagung am 13., 14. und 15. Juni 1951," *ND*, June 23, 1951, p. 4.

21. See, for example, Dr. Gerhard Last, "Marktbeobachtung und Bedarfsanalyse," *Die Versorgung* 4, no. 8 (1949), pp. 1–2.

22. On planning meetings, see HO Hausmitteilung, Landesleitung Thüringen to HO Lebensmittel, Zentrale Leitung, Abt. Marktbeobachtung, June 20, 1952, BArch, DL-1/3297, Bl. 26; HO Lebensmittel, Landesleitung Thüringen, Abt. Marktbeobachtung, "Protokoll über die Arbeitsbesprechung der Abt. Marktforschung am 26.6.1952," same file, Bl. 18–24; MfHV, HA I Planung, Protokoll über die Tagung der Planer am 27.7.1952 im Haus der Ministerien, July 22, 1952, BArch, DL-1/2520, Bl.36–52.

23. Werner Kelch, "Zur Marktbeobachtung im Einzelhandel," *Der Handel* 2, no. 1 (1952), p. 19. Unfortunately, very little is known about Kelch himself.

24. Wolfgang Heinrichs, "Zu einigen Problemen der marxistisch-leninistischen Theorie der Bedarfsforschung," *Der Handel* 2, no. 9 (1952), p. 220.

25. Werner Kelch, "Die Organisation der Bedarfsermittlung im gesellschaftlichen Einzelhandel," *Der Handel* 2, no. 2 (1952), p. 289.

26. The Soviet source invoked for demand research was a work by the economist S. V. Serebryakov, translated into German and published under the title *Organisation und Technik des Sowjethandels*. On this work, see Hans Bloch, "Einiges zu den Richtlinien für eine systematische Bedarfsermittlung," *Der Handel* 2, no. 18 (1952), p. 434.

27. See Kelch, "Die Organisation," parts 1 and 2 in *Der Handel* 2, nos. 12 and 13 (1952), pp. 289–292, 310–313. On guidelines passed down to the local levels, see HO-Industriewaren, Landesleitung Sachsen, Betr.: Arbeitsrichtlinien für GB 1–Bedarfsermittlung, "Aufgaben der Abt. Bedarfsermittlung," June 13, 1952, BArch, DC-5/9; MfHV, Baender, "Richtlinien für den organisatorischen Aufbau einer systematischen Bedarfsermittlung im gesellschaftlichen Handel," July 15, 1952, BArch, DL-1/3297.

28. It is a sad loss for historians and other scholars of East Germany that these books no longer exist. Stored temporarily in local archives, they were periodically disposed of. One can assume, however, that the information they contained about the complaints and opinions of consumers is more or less reproduced in many of the countless letters of complaint (*Beschwerdebriefe*) still sitting in German archives, federal and regional. Other sources suggest that the books were alternately ignored, used for communicating complaints, and used for making "provocative observations." Wilhelm Hilger, "Der HO in das Stammbuch geschrieben," *Der Handel* 1, no. 12 (1951), p. 278; Staatliche Handelsinspektion, "Die Einwirkung des Handels auf die Produktion," December 16, 1954, BArch, DC-20/1640, p. 1.

29. As they did with so many aspects of the administrative functioning of the economy, East German economic planners began tinkering almost immediately with the system just described. But their modifications were never so drastic as to alter its basic character. See, for example, MfHV, "Richtlinien für den organisatorischen Aufbau einer systematischen Bedarfsermittlung im gesellschaftlichen Einzelhandel," November 6, 1952, BArch, DL-1/2600; MfHV, Abt. Bedarfsforschung und Umsatzplanung, "Anleitung für die monatliche Berichterstattung ausgewählter Verkaufsstellen über die Bedarfsermittlung," February 25, 1953, BArch, DL-1/2603, Bl. 8–9.

30. MfHV, Kelch, "Bedarfsermittlung Februar 1953," BArch, DE-1/27359, pp. 1–12.

31. MfHV, Kelch, "Bedarfsermittlung Februar 1953," BArch, DE-1/27358, pp. 1–26. Though in a different file, this is the second half of the report cited in note 30.

32. My italics. Neither the precise style nor the provenance of the "California" shoes is clear. The appellation is, nevertheless, worth noting.

33. "Bedarfsforschung für Monat Juli 1953," September 3, 1953, BArch, DL-1/2602, Bl. 1–2; MfHV, Abt. Bedarfsforschung und Umsatzplanung, "Bericht über die Bedarfsermittlung im September 1953," October 19, 1953, BArch, DL-1/2604, Bl. 159–171, 186–193.

34. Describing the woeful state of affairs in a particular furniture fabric store, one report concluded, "One can hopefully imagine the kinds of scenes that occur in the store; the customers become very nasty *[gemein]*." MfHV, Abt. Umsatzplanung, Bedarfsforschung und Handelsstatistik, "Ergebnisse der Bedarfsforschung im III/54," undated, BArch, DE-1/27357, p. 21.

35. Were market researchers in West Germany concerned with these questions? The paucity of literature on the subject makes direct comparisons difficult. One may, however, assume that these questions were asked, since market researchers in prewar Germany had posed them in their questionnaires and interviews with consumers. See Georg Bergler, *Die Entwicklung*, pp. 87–88, 120–144. For an interesting, though tendentious, attempt to cast West German market research in the Foucauldian language of discipline and surveillance, see Erica Carter, *How German Is She? Postwar West German Reconstruction and the Consuming Woman* (Ann Arbor: University of Michigan Press, 1997), chap. 3. For their part, East German demand researchers began to utilize questionnaires and interviews in later years. Ina Merkel, *Utopie und Bedürfnis: Die Geschichte der Konsumkultur in der DDR* (Cologne: Böhlau, 1999), pp. 144–147. Unfortunately, Merkel provides little detail on the types of questions asked and, thus, the kinds of information sought. Nor does she discuss the fate of their findings within the planning bureaucracy.

36. VdK eGmbH, Berlin, "Bedarfsermittlung für den Monat November 1953," December 18, 1953, BArch, DE-1/28639, Bl. 11.

37. See, for example, the editors' introduction, "In den zweiten Jahrgang," *Die Versorgung* 2, no. 8 (1947), pp. 1–2; Paul Friedländer, "Zwei Jahre Konsumgenossenschaften in der Ostzone," *Die Versorgung* 3, no. 1 (1948), pp. 88–89; Heinz Schmincke, "Der Handel mustert die Produktion," *Die Versorgung* 4, no. 9 (1949), pp. 17–18; Werner Kelch, "Neue Arbeitsmethode in der Zusammenarbeit von Industrie und Handel," *Die Versorgung* 5, no. 10 (1950), pp. 230–232.

38. SPK, Planung der Warenzirkulation, Pehlemann to Leuschner, July 17, 1951, BArch, DE-1/25158, pp. 1–2.

39. The laws were published in *Gbl der DDR*, December 17, 1951, pp. 1141–1145.

40. In addition to the Central State Contract Court in Berlin, there were originally five regional courts, one for each *Land:* But with the dissolution of the *Länder* as administrative units in July 1952 and their replacement with fifteen districts *(Bezirke)*, including Berlin, the *Länder* courts were replaced with fifteen district courts.

41. Daniel John Meador, *Impressions of Law in East Germany: Legal Education*

and Legal Systems in the German Democratic Republic (Charlottesville: University Press of Virginia, 1986), pp. 159–168.

42. Siegrfried Baumgartl, "Kontrolle des Abschlußes und der Erfüllung der Verträge," *Der Handel* 2, no. 2 (1952), p. 43; Helmut Lepke, "Die Einkaufsabteilungen der HO im Vertragssystem," *Der Handel* 2, no. 2 (1952), pp. 44–45.

43. Genossenschaftsverband, HA IB-Industriewaren, Abt. Textilien to Zentrale Kommission für Staatliche Kontrolle, Betr.: mangelhafte Warenbereitstellung, May 3, 1952, BArch, DE-1/25158, pp. 1–2.

44. "Der volkseigene Großhandel muß seine Arbeit verbessern," *Der Handel* 2, no. 11 (1952), pp. 265–266.

45. K. Hänel, "Die Anwendung des allgemeinen Vertragssystems muß verändert werden," *Der Handel* 3, no. 20 (1953), pp. 528–529.

46. Protokoll der 19. Sitzung des Kollegiums, Sept. 2, 1955, BArch, DL-1/1089, Bl. 4–7; MfHV, draft of "Analyse über die Durchführung des Volkswirtschaftsplanes 1954, Planteil Warenumsatz," January 11, 1955, BArch, DL-1/2552/1, Bl. 1–2.

47. "Der Analyse auf dem Gebiete des Handels," September 16, 1955, SAPMO-BArch, DY 30 IV/ 2/610/108; HA Warenumsatz- und Warenbereitstellung, Vermerk! Betr.: Globalverträge, February 1, 1956, BArch, DE-1/25185; "Ergebnisse der Beratung der Kommission für Handel und Versorgung über das Entstehen und die Verhinderung von Überplanbeständen in Konsumgütern," probably late 1955, BArch, DE-1/24104, pp. 1–2.

48. On these phenomena, see Janos Kornai, *The Socialist System: The Political Economy of Communism* (Princeton, N.J.: Princeton University Press, 1992), pp. 140–148.

49. Ibid., pp. 118–124.

50. "Funktionen des Handels mit gewerblichen Gebrauchsgütern," *Die Versorgung* 2, no. 9 (1947), pp. 24–25; Anton Kemmer, "Versorgung der Bevölkerung mit Textil- und Schuhwaren," *Die Versorgung* 2, no. 11 (1947), pp. 50–52; Heinz Schmincke, "Versorgung der Werktätigen mit Textilien und Schuhwaren," *Die Versorgung* 3, no. 5 (1948), pp. 145–146.

51. The official figure is 27.9 percent. In addition to private retailers, private craftsmen, who sold their wares directly to consumers, accounted for 9 percent of total retail sales in 1952. In 1959 private retailers and craftsmen still accounted for 24.7 percent of total retail sales. *Statistisches Jahrbuch der Deutschen Demokratischen Republik 1959* (Berlin: VEB Deutscher Zentralverlag, 1960), p. 539.

52. On the development of wholesale trade, see "Großhandel. Strukturelle Entwicklung seit 1945," ("Vertrauliche Dienstsache"), BArch, DE-1/3534, Bl. 42–43.

53. Ibid., Bl. 42–43; SPK, Abt. Handel und Versorgung, Hieke, Stellvtr. des Vorsitzenden & Leiter der Abt. Versorgung, "Vorlage über Maßnahmen zur weiteren Entwicklung des sozialistischen Großhandels mit Konsumgütern in der DDR," June 10, 1958, BArch, DE-1/7329, Bl. 201.

54. On the DHZs, see "Verordnung über die Verbesserung der Arbeit der Deutschen Handelszentralen vom 6. Dezember 1951," *Gbl der DDR,* December 17, 1951, pp. 1145–1147; Günter Manz, "Zur Entwicklung des Staatlichen Großhandels," *Der Handel* 1, no. 12 (1951), pp. 271–273.

55. MfHV, HA Staatlicher Einzelhandel, Abt. HO-Industriewaren, Hauptabteilungsleiter Iwanik to Staatssekretariat für Koordinierung des Binnenhandels, Staatssekretär Strampfer, June 23, 1952, BArch, DC-5/8, pp. 2–3. In addition, the report pointed out, the DHZ very often sold goods cheaper to private retailers, waiving the sales tax it normally passed on to the HO.

56. SKHV, "Bericht über die Kontrollfahrt nach Berlin, Chemnitz und umliegende Orte mit Textilindustrie vom 30. August bis 6. September 1952," September 8, 1952, BArch, DC-6/20, Bl. 29. In response to trade rejecting its deliveries, industry also turned to foreign trade organs, channeling goods originally intended for domestic consumption into exports. "Protokoll der Beratung zwischen den leitenden Funktionären des Ministeriums für Handel und Versorgung und des Ministeriums für Leichtindustrie beim Stellvertreter des Vorsitzenden des Ministerrates Prof. Fred Oelßner," June 24, 1957, BArch, DC-20/1278, pp. 1–6.

57. *Der Handel,* Ehrenpfordt to MfHV, Koll. Schacher, February 9, 1954, BArch, DL-1/2903, Bl. 37.

58. "Stenographische Niederschrift der 15. Tagung des Zentralkomitees der SED vom 24.-26. Juli 1953, 3. Verhandlungtag, Sonntag," July 26, 1953, SAPMO-BArch, DY 30/ IV 2/1/120, Bl. 157.

59. Präsidium des Ministerrats, "Beschluß Betr.: Überleitung des Großhandels mit Waren der individuellen Konsumtion in die Verantwortlichkeit des Ministeriums für Handel und Versorgung," October 1953, BArch, DL-1/2905, Bl. 227.

60. "Großhandel: Strukturelle Entwicklung seit 1945," ("Vertrauliche Dienstsache"), BArch, DE-1/3534, Bl. 42–43.

61. SPK, Abt. Handel und Versorgung, Hieke, Stellv. des Vorsitzenden & Leiter der Abt. Versorgung, "Vorlage über Maßnahmen zur Weiteren Entwicklung des sozialistischen Großhandels mit Konsumgütern in der DDR," June 10, 1958, BArch, DE-1/7329, Bl. 202. The Ministry for Trade and Provisioning had been seeking for some time to draw private retail into its control, thereby removing the competition. See MfHV, Office of the Minister to Sekretariat Prof. Fred Oelßner, July 10, 1957, "Vorlage

für einen Beschluß des Politbüros des Zentralkomitees der SED," July 8, 1957, BArch, DC-20/1285, pp. 1–2.

62. MfHV, Paul Baender to Otto Stauch, September 28, 1951, BArch, DL-1/3054, Bl. 287; Baender to ZK der SED, Abt. Wirtschaftspolitik, Kurt Wolf, September 28, 1951, same file, Bl. 286; subsequent correspondence in this file between the MfHV, the SPK, and the SED, Bl. 260–276.

63. "Richtlinien für die Schaffung von den Industrie-Ministerien unterstellten Verkaufsläden," September 5, 1951, BArch, DL-1/3054, Bl. 288.

64. See *Statistisches Jahrbuch der Deutschen Demokratischen Republik 1959* (East Berlin: VEB Deutscher Zentralverlag, 1960), pp. 538–539.

65. List of stores already existing and those to be set up in 1954, September 22, 1953, LAB, Rep. 113/637.

66. "Handel: Warenumsatz des Einzelhandels. Strukturelle Entwicklung seit 1945" ("Vertrauliche Dienstsache"), BArch, DE-1/3534, Bl. 8.

67. Even the industry stores lacked the desired "influence on production," as a result of which their offerings were not always as impressive as they were supposed to be. MfL to MfHV, "Richtlinien zur Verbesserung der Tätigkeit der Industrieläden im Bereich des Ministeriums für Leichtindustrie," July 12, 1956, BArch, DL-1/3060, Bl. 122–123.

68. See the extensive correspondence in LAB, Rep. 113/634.

69. "Reorganisation der Industrieläden—Eingliederung in das Netz des volkseigenen Einzelhandels," not dated (probably late 1956 or early 1957), BArch, DL-1/3060, Bl. 67–71.

70. Ministerium für Allgemeinen Maschinenbau, Wunderlich to MfHV, Wach, December 19, 1956, BArch, DL-1/3060, Bl. 23; Ministerium für Chemische Industrie, Winkler to Wach, January 7, 1957, same file, Bl. 21; Ministerium für Lebensmittelindustrie, Westphal to Wach, January 16, 1957, same file, Bl. 19–20; MfL, Feldmann to Wach, January 7, 1957, same file, Bl. 15–18.

71. For the entire exchange, see Wittkowski to Lange, January 28, 1959, SAPMO-BArch, DY 30/ IV 2/610/79; Krüger to Wach, December 17, 1958, same file; Wach to Krüger, January 14, 1959, same file.

72. SPK, HA Maschinenbau, "Analyse über den Stand der Konsumgüterproduktion," January 13, 1955, BArch, DE-1/29159, pp. 1–5. Meanwhile, the Minister for General Machine Building, Helmut Wunderlich, tried to deflect criticism by reporting to the SPK the failures of the Ministry for Transport to fulfill its obligations in the area of mass-demand goods. Wunderlich to SPK, Opitz, "Analyse über die Produktion von Massenbedarfsgütern im Jahre 1954," January 11, 1955, same file, pp. 1–4.

73. MfHV, Staatssekretär Dressel, "Bericht über die Erfüllung des Volkswirtschaftsplanes 1. Halbjahr 1956," BArch, DE-1/24201, pp. 1–11.

74. Ibid., pp. 3–4.

75. "Abschrift der Rede des Stellv. des Vorsitzenden des Ministerrates, Gen. Fred Oelßner, in der Ministerratstagung vom 16.8.56," BArch, DE-1/12769, pp. 2–3.

76. My italics. These lines were underlined by the official reading this copy of Oelßner's speech. Ibid., p. 2.

77. Unique among SED leaders, Oelßner was sympathetic during these years to the ideas of reformist economists such as Fritz Behrens and Günther Kohlmey, particularly on the question of price policy. Peter C. Caldwell, *Dictatorship, State Planning, and Social Theory in the German Democratic Republic* (New York: Cambridge University Press, 2003), pp. 42–44.

78. Autorenkollektiv, *Preispolitik und Preisbildung in der Deutschen Demokratischen Republik* (East Berlin: Verlag Die Wirtschaft, 1961), pp. 215–221.

79. HO Industriewaren, Zentrale Leitung to MfHV and MdF, September 17, 1951, BArch, DL-1/2747; HA Planung, HR Preispolitik to Frau Staatssekretär Krause, November 11, 1952, BArch, DL-1/2520, Bl. 7–10; HO Industriewaren, Rostock-Stadt an Operativen Bezirksstab der HO, Rostock, "Betr.: Abbau von Überplanbeständen, Umsatzerfüllung und Preisangleichung," November 13, 1952, BArch, DC-5/4; "Ergebnisse der Beratungen der Kommission für Handel und Versorgung über das Entstehen und die Verhinderung von Überplanbeständen in Konsumgütern," probably late 1955, BArch, DE-1/24104; HO Warenhaus Dessau to ZK der SED, Büro des 1. Sekretärs Walter Ulbricht, Götsche, May 11, 1957, BArch, DC-20/1264.

80. *"Biwa-Läden"* was short for *Läden für billige Waren* (stores for cheap goods). On the sales and the stores, see Judd Stitziel, "Fashioning Socialism: Clothing, Politics, and Consumer Culture in East Germany, 1948–1971" (Ph.D. diss., Johns Hopkins University, 2001), pp. 307–318, 321–332.

81. On East Germany's private sector, see Andreas Pickel, *Radical Transitions: The Survival and Revival of Entrepreneurship in the GDR* (Boulder, Colo.: Westview, 1992); Anders Aslund, *Private Enterprise in Eastern Europe: The Non-Agricultural Private Sector in Poland and the GDR, 1945–1983* (New York: St. Martin's Press, 1985).

82. There were attempts to establish uniform fixed prices in the 1950s, but they were largely unsuccessful. On the difficulties involved, see Büro der Regierungskommission für Preise (Dr. Baum) to ZK Abt. Planung und Finanzen (Pfütze), October 28, 1959, SAPMO-BArch, DY 30/ IV 2/6.08/70, Bl. 255–256. Also see Stitziel, "Fashioning Socialism," pp. 277–285; André Steiner, *Die DDR Wirtschaftsreform der sechziger Jahre: Kon-*

flikt zwischen Effizienz- und Machtkalkül (Berlin: Akademie, 1999), pp. 187–190.

83. ZK Abt. Planung und Finanzen (Müller) to Apel, June 25, 1958, SAPMO-BArch, DY 30/ IV 2/2.029/65, Bl. 18–19. I am indebted to Philipp Heldmann for generously sharing with me his research and insights on price policy. On the role of subsidies and taxes in consumer prices, see his essay, "Negotiating Consumption in a Dictatorship: Consumption Politics in the GDR in the 1950s and 1960s," in Martin Daunton and Matthew Hilton, eds., *The Politics of Consumption: Material Culture and Citizenship in Europe and America* (Oxford: Berg, 2001), pp. 197–199.

84. SZS, HA Volkswirtschaftliche Übersichten, "Analyse der Berichtsbilanz der Geldeinnahmen und -ausgaben der Bevölkerung für das Jahr 1955" ("Vertrauliche Verschlußsache") April 1956, BArch, DE-2/22415 (0036984), p. 37.

85. Redaktion *Die Wirtschaft,* Abt. Leichtindustrie, Dr. Hanke to Oelßner, May 23, 1956, BArch, DC-20/478. Dr. Hartwig's article was entitled, "Vermeidung von Überplanbeständen und Qualitätsverbesserung bei Konsumgütern," pp. 1, 5.

86. Ibid., p. 4. Hartwig cited Fred Oelßner, "Die Werttheorie und unsere Preispolitik," *Einheit* 10, no. 12 (1955), p. 1172. In this article, Oelßner argued for a more flexible price policy allowing for more easily instituted price reductions for those consumption goods that failed to sell and contributed to excess inventory.

87. Hartwig, "Vermeidung von Überplanbeständen," pp. 6–8. In addition, Hartwig was skeptical of trade's ability to ascertain demand with any real precision due to the need to conclude contracts months in advance of deliveries. What was required, he believed, was a far more flexible system, allowing for swifter communication and reaction time between trade and industry. Ibid., pp. 4–6.

88. "Protokoll der Beratung zwischen den leitenden Funktionären des Ministeriums für Handel und Versorgung und des Ministeriums für Leichtindustrie beim Stellvertreter des Vorsitzenden des Ministerrates Prof. Fred Oelßner," June 24, 1957, BArch, DC-20/1278, pp. 1–6.

89. "Diskussionsbeitrag: Beseitigung der sprunghaften Annahme der Waren durch den Handel," typewritten note following a handwritten note signed by Hoepner, June 28, 1956, BArch, DE-1/25185.

90. As Jeffrey Kopstein has argued, after the June 1953 uprising, attempts to impose discipline on the shop floor were abandoned, and labor unrest remained limited and sporadic. Although Kopstein discusses primarily heavy industry enterprises, it is reasonable to assume a similar, if not exaggerated, pattern for enterprises producing consumer goods, which,

after all, occupied a much lower place on the list of SED priorities. See Jeffrey Kopstein, *The Politics of Economic Decline in East Germany, 1945–1989* (Chapel Hill: University of North Carolina Press, 1997), p. 38.

91. On "demand adjustment," see Kornai, *The Socialist System*, pp. 234–240.

92. Hermann Weber, *Geschichte der DDR*, original ed. (Munich: Deutscher Taschenbuch Verlag, 1999), p. 220. For a thoughtful discussion of this phenomenon, see Corey Ross, "Before the Wall: East Germans, Communist Authority and the Mass Exodus to the West," *Historical Journal* 45, no. 4 (2002), pp. 459–480.

93. Albert O. Hirschman, *Exit, Voice, and Loyalty: Responses to Decline in Firms, Organizations, and States* (Cambridge, Mass.: Harvard University Press, 1970). For Hirschman's application of the concepts of "exit" and "voice" to the events of 1989, see Albert O. Hirschman, "Exit, Voice, and the Fate of the German Democratic Republic: An Essay in Conceptual History," *World Politics* 45, no. 2 (1993), pp. 173–202.

94. The total cost of this bloodletting would be impossible to quantify in all its aspects. According to one estimate, the loss merely in terms of educational investments, up to 1957, came to DM 22.5 billion. Volker R. Berghahn, *Modern Germany: Society, Economy and Politics in the Twentieth Century* (Cambridge: Cambridge University Press, 1987), p. 227.

6. Crisis Revisited

1. *Protokoll der Verhandlungen des V. Parteitages der Sozialistischen Einheitspartei Deutschlands. 10. bis 16. Juli 1958* (East Berlin: Dietz, 1959), 1: p. 71.

2. Ina Merkel, *Utopie und Bedürfnis: Die Geschichte der Konsumkultur in der DDR* (Cologne: Böhlau, 1999); Katherine Pence, "From Rations to Fashions: The Gendered Politics of East and West German Consumption" (Ph.D. diss., University of Michigan, 1999), chap. 8. Merkel addresses individual aspects of the Main Economic Task but does so in an atomized fashion, leaving them detached from one another and unconnected to the broader political context. Pence offers a brief discussion of the Main Economic Task, equally unconnected to the wider context.

3. Hope M. Harrison, "Ulbricht and the Concrete 'Rose': New Archival Evidence on the Dynamics of Soviet–East German Relations and the Berlin Crisis, 1958–1961" (Cold War International History Project Working Paper No. 5, Washington, D.C.: International Center for Scholars, May 1993); James G. Richter, *Khrushchev's Double Bind: International Pressures and Domestic Coalition Politics* (Baltimore, Md.: Johns Hopkins University Press, 1994), chap. 5; Michael Lemke, *Die Berlinkrise 1958 bis 1963: Interessen und Handlungsspielräume der SED im Ost-West-Konflikt* (Berlin: Aka-

demie, 1995); Vladislov Zubok and Constantine Pleshakov, *Inside the Kremlin's Cold War: From Stalin To Khrushchev* (Cambridge, Mass.: Harvard University Press, 1996), chap. 6, 8; Marc Trachtenberg, *A Constructed Peace: The Making of the European Settlement, 1945–1963* (Princeton, N.J.: Princeton University Press, 1999), chap. 7–8.

4. "Gesetz über die Abschaffung der Lebensmittelkarten vom 28. Mai 1958," *Gbl der DDR*, May 29, 1958, pp. 413–415.

5. Hermann Weber, *Geschichte der DDR*, original ed. (Munich: Deutscher Taschenbuch Verlag, 1999), p. 201.

6. MfHV, Wach to 1. Stellvertreter des Vorstizenden des Ministerrates, Sekretariat Ulbricht, z.Hd. des Gen. Gotsche, July 12, 1957, BArch, DL-1/3771.

7. Büro des Präsidiums des Ministerrates, Grotewohl to MfHV, Dressel, October 17, 1957, BArch, DL-1/3774, Bl. 2. The commission included Gerhart Ziller, Otto Lehmann, Hermann Streit, Willy Rumpf, Gerhard Lucht, and Ernst Lange.

8. "Analyse der Haushaltsrechnungen von August 1957" ("Vertrauliche Verschlußsache"), BArch, DL-1/3772, Bl. 84–92.

9. Wolfgang Ribbe, ed., *Geschichte Berlins* (Munich: C. H. Beck, 1987), 2: p. 1086.

10. MfHV, Säverin, "Untersuchungskomplex: Auswirkung der Aufhebung der Rationierung auf Einkäufe durch Westberliner," September 14, 1957, BArch, DL-1/3771, Bl. 74–80.

11. "Die Hauptprobleme aus der bisherigen Arbeit der zentralen Kommission zur Vorbereitung der Aufhebung der Rationierung," SAPMO-BArch, DY 30/ IV 2/2A-607, pp. 1–2; "Zwischenbericht an das Politbüro über die Arbeit der zentralen Kommission der Aufhebung der Rationierung," December 28, 1957, same file, p. 9.

12. Lemke, *Die Berlinkrise*, pp. 53–54.

13. Ulbricht to Khrushchev, May 12, 1958, SAPMO-BArch, J IV 2/202/39, p. 4.

14. Patrice Poutrus, "Lebensmittelkonsum, Versorgungskrisen und die Entscheidung für den 'Goldbroiler,'" *Archiv für Sozialgeschichte* 39 (1999), p. 397.

15. Ministry summaries of reports from Bezirke, all dated May 29, 1958, BArch, DL-1/3774, Bl. 92, 98, 118; "Vermerk über Unzulänglichkeiten bei der Bereitstellung der notwendigen Unterlagen bei der Abschaffung der Lebensmittelkarten," same file, Bl. 116; similar summaries of reports from Bezirke, BArch, DL-1/3776, Bl. 1, 2, 6, 11.

16. ZK Abt. Planung und Finanzen (Müller) to Apel, April 28, 1958, SAPMO-BArch, DY 30/ IV 2/2.029/65, Bl. 5. Also see Poutrus, "Lebensmittelkonsum," p. 397.

17. Protokoll Nr. 34/58 der Sitzung des Politbüros des Zentralkomitees am

Dienstag, dem 19.8.58, Anlage Nr. 1 Neue Fragen der Versorgung der Bevölkerung mit Konsumgütern, insbesondere mit Nahrungsmitteln nach der Abschaffung der Lebensmittelkarten, SAPMO-BArch, DY 30/ J IV 2/2/606, Bl. 8–13, 20–22.

18. *Protokoll der Verhandlungen,* p. 68. Christoph Kleßmann is quite right to point out that the Main Economic Task loses a little of its drama when one realizes that the proposed comparison was between East Germany's working population and West Germany's entire population. See Christoph Kleßmann, *Zwei Staaten, Eine Nation: Deutsche Geschichte, 1955–1970* (Göttingen: Vandenhoeck & Ruprecht, 1988), p. 310. As shown below, however, he is wrong to assume that in specifying "important" consumption goods the SED was confining the Main Economic Task only to basic consumption goods. In fact, the Main Economic Task embraced modern consumer durables as well and in so doing constituted a bold and unprecedented promise.

19. Lemke, *Die Berlinkrise,* p. 56.

20. André Steiner, "Vom Überholen eingeholt: Zur Wirtschaftskrise 1960/ 61 in der DDR," in Burghard Ciesla, Michael Lemke, and Thomas Lindenberger, eds., *Sterben für Berlin? Die Berliner Krisen 1948 : 1958* (Berlin: Metropol, 2000), pp. 247–248. In his discussion, Steiner focuses mostly on the production side of the Main Economic Task, largely omitting the Berlin Crisis and the collectivization of agriculture.

21. Quoted in Zubok and Pleshakov, *Inside The Kremlin's Cold War,* p. 192.

22. Quoted in William Taubman, *Khrushchev: The Man and His Era* (New York: Norton, 2003), p. 379.

23. Steiner's speculations about the state of mind of the SED leadership are not backed up by sufficient evidence. Moreover, his discussion touches only intermittently on the development of consumption policy during the years of the Main Economic Task. In his recent biography of Khrushchev, William Taubman emphasizes the "fragility" of the Soviet leader's "euphoria" over Sputnik. Taubman, *Khrushchev,* p. 378.

24. The regime's reports on the mood of the population indicated considerable skepticism regarding the Main Economic Task. Patrick Major, "Vor und nach dem 13. August 1961: Reaktionen der DDR-Bevölkerung auf den Bau der Berliner Mauer," *Archiv für Sozialgeschichte* 39 (1999), pp. 331–332.

25. In 1957, 261,622 people fled; in 1958, 204,092; in 1959, 143,917. Weber, *Geschichte der DDR,* p. 220. Admittedly, the decline began before the announcement of the Main Economic Task, in part due to a tightening of visa controls imposed at the end of 1957. Corey Ross, "Before the Wall: East Germans, Communist Authority, and the Mass Exodus to the West," *Historical Journal* 45, no. 2 (2002), p. 462.

26. MfHV, Forschungsinstitut, Forschungsgruppe Warenbewegung, "Teil-ergebnis zum Forschungsauftrag: Rationelle Formen der Warenbe-wegung von Konsumgütern von der Produktion zum volkseigenen Einzelhandel: Ergebnisse der Untersuchungen des Teilabschnittes Waren-bewegung Haushaltskühlschränke," March 31, 1958, BArch, DL-1/2666, Bl. 1–20; SPK, HA Perspektivplanung, draft "Konzeption über die Ent-wicklung des Lebensstandards der Bevölkerung 1965, 1970, 1975," Feb-ruary 14, 1958, BArch, DE-1/3492, Bl. 3–5.

27. Michael Wildt, *Vom kleinen Wohlstand: Eine Konsumgeschichte der fünfziger Jahre* (Frankfurt am Main: Fischer Taschenbuch, 1996), pp. 124–125; Arnold Sywottek, "The Americanization of Everyday Life? Early Trends in Consumer and Leisure-Time Behavior" in Michael Ermarth, ed., *America and the Shaping of German Society, 1945–1955* (Providence, R.I.: Berg, 1993), p. 147. On East Germany, see SPK, HA Perspektivplanung, Fachgebiet Lebensstandard, report on the standard of living, the title page of which is missing, November 1960, BArch, DE-1/3487, Bl. 11.

28. My italics. These lines were underlined by the official reading the letter. Frau B. to *Berliner Zeitung*, "Bärchen," March 9, 1957, LAB, Rep. 113/ 362. Presumably the newspaper forwarded the letter to the Magistrat's Department for Trade and Provisioning.

29. Frau B. to Leiter der Abt. Handel und Versorgung, Herrn Karsten, April 10, 1958, same file.

30. In 1958, 6.2 percent of East German households had television sets. In West Germany, the figure was 13 percent. SPK, HA Perspektivplanung, Fachgebiet Lebensstandard, report on the standard of living, the title page of which is missing, November 1960, BArch, DE-1/3487, Bl. 11. It is worth noting that despite Frau B.'s difficulties, East German perfor-mance in supplying TVs was considerably better than it was in supplying refrigerators and washing machines. The discrepancy suggests a clear dif-ference in priorities; television, after all, provided a new, exceptionally powerful medium for pedagogy, more often than not a higher-ranking imperative than material well-being in the SED hierarchy of concerns.

31. Leiter der Abt. Handel und Versorgung, Karsten to Frau B., April 17, 1958, LAB, Rep. 113/362.

32. Frau B. to Stadtrat Schneider, June 6, 1958, same file.

33. Stadtrat Schneider to Frau B., June 9, 1958, same file.

34. See Janos Kornai, *The Socialist System: The Political Economy of Socialism* (Princeton, N.J.: Princeton University Press, 1992), pp. 140–148.

35. Protokoll der Sitzung der Wirtschaftskommission des Politbüros, un-dated (probably fall 1958), SAPMO-BArch, DY 30/ IV 2/2.101/1, Bl. 77.

36. For biographical information on Apel, see Peter Grieder, *The East German*

Leadership, 1946–1973: Conflict and Crisis (Manchester: Manchester University Press, 1999), p. 162; Andreas Herbst, Gerd-Rüdiger Stephan, and Jürgen Winkler, eds., *Die SED: Geschichte, Organisation, Politik: Ein Handbuch* (Berlin: Dietz, 1997), p. 898.

37. The SPK carried out before-and-after studies comparing the consumption of recently unrationed commodities. Studying different-sized households with varying incomes, it noted significant increases in the monthly consumption of meat, butter, margarine, and milk. SPK, HA Perspektivplanung, "Zur Entwicklung des Pro-Kopf-Verbrauches an wichtigen Nahrungsmitteln in Haushalten von Arbeitern und Angestellten im Vergleich der Monate April und November 1958," BArch, DE-1/ 3492, Bl. 17–19.

38. Poutrus, "Lebensmittelkonsum," pp. 398–411.

39. Leuschner to Grotewohl, November 11, 1958, BArch, DC-20/1861, Bl. 195–200; ZK Abt. HVA, Ernst Lange, "Information an die Mitglieder und Kandidaten des Politbüros," November 12, 1958, SAPMO-BArch, DY 30/ IV 2/2.029/86, Bl. 142.

40. Ulbricht and Grotewohl to Khrushchev, January 31, 1959, SAPMO-BArch, J IV 2/202/29.

41. SPK, Leuschner to Ulbricht, March 3, 1959, SAPMO-BArch, J IV 2/ 202/29.

42. Lange to Apel, March 13, 1959, SAPMO-BArch, DY 30/ IV 2/2.029/85, Bl. 64–67.

43. Wittkowski to Apel, "Information über die Versorgung mit Textilien und Schuhwaren des 1. Halbjahres 1959 und die Sicherung einer bedarfsgerechten Versorgung im 2. Halbjahr 1959," July 1959, SAPMO-BArch, DY 30/ IV 2/2.029/86, Bl. 238–244.

44. SZS, "Über den Lebensstandard und seine statistische Quantifizierbarkeit," undated (probably spring 1959), BArch, DE-1/3563, Bl. 13.

45. SZS, "Protokoll über die Tagung des Arbeitskreises "Statistik des Lebensstandards" am 10.6.1959, June 11, 1959," same file, Bl. 19–22.

46. SZS, Sektor Lebensstandard und Wirtschaftsrechnungen, Protokoll der Tagung des Arbeitskreises Lebensstandard am 16.9.1959, September 29, 1959, same file, Bl. 30. As their own internal studies show, GDR statisticians were well aware that the cost of living in East Germany continued to exceed that of West Germany. SZS, Sektor Lebensstandard und Wirtschaftsrechnungen, "Die Entwicklung und das Niveau der Lebenshaltungskosten in 4-Personen Arbeiter und Angestelltenhaushaltungen der DDR und der Westzone" ("Nur für den Dienstgebrauch Nicht zur Veröffentlichung"), July 29, 1959, BArch, DE-1/3564, Bl. 17–41.

47. (Draft) "Beschluß des Präsidiums des Ministerrates zu Fragen des Handels und der Versorgung," November 1958, BArch, DL-1/1373, Bl. 19.

48. Among those firms studied were Quelle and Neckermann. "Bericht über die durchgeführte Informationsreise nach Westdeutschland: Studium Versandhandel" ("Vertraulich! Empfänger haftet für sichere Aufbewährung!"), May 10, 1960, SAPMO-BArch, DY 30/ IV 2/610/134, pp. 1–8. Leading SED officials also studied closely West German mail-order catalogues. ZK Abt. Planung und Finanzen, Schürer to Apel, May 25, 1961, SAPMO-BArch, DY 30/ IV 2/2.029/65, Bl. 292–294. The new house opened in Karl-Marx-Stadt on January 1, 1961. Its original name, "Konsum-Versandhandel Karl-Marx-Stadt," was later changed to "*konsument*-Versandhaus." Annette Kaminsky, *Kaufrausch: Die Geschichte der ostdeutschen Versandhäuser* (Berlin: C. Links Verlag, 1998), p. 39.

49. See Wildt, *Vom kleinen Wohlstand,* chap. 8.

50. Ibid., pp. 151–155.

51. "Die Entwicklung des Einzelhandels in Westberlin," March 16, 1956, LAB, Rep. 113/480, pp. 10–11.

52. MfHV, "Protokoll der Dienstbesprechung," November 28, 1955, BArch, DL-1/1593, Bl. 2.

53. Magistrat, Abt. Handel und Versorgung, "Analyse der ersten Selbstbedienungsverkaufsstellen in Berlin für die Zeit vom Dezember 1956 bis Februar 1957," April 2, 1957, LAB, Rep. 113/386, pp. 1–9.

54. Magistrat, Abt. Handel und Versorgung, Abteilungsleiter, Karsten, "Aktenvermerk Betr.: Bildung einer Arbeitsgruppe zur Untersuchung der bisherigen Entwicklung des Selbstbedienungssystems in der Deutschen Demokratischen Republik, Ermittlung des geeigneten Selbstbedienungssystems für den Berliner Handel und Ausarbeitung eines Planes zur Umgestaltung von Verkaufsstellen im demokratischen Sektor von Groß-Berlin auf Selbstbedienung," May 22, 1957, same file, pp. 1–3. Study trips to Czechoslovakia and Austria were also proposed.

55. Anlage zur Magistratsvorlage, "Programm zur Einrichtung von Selbst- und Teilselbstbedienungsverkaufsstellen in der Zeit von 1958 bis 1960 im staatlichen Einzelhandel," Magistratsvorlage dated January 29, 1958, LAB, Rep. 113/641.

56. For official East German treatments of this theme, see Werner Prendel and Bruno Wilms, *Selbstbedienungsläden: Lebensmittel. Arbeitsmaterial und Grundsätze für Verkaufsorganisation, Arbeitsorganisation, Einrichtung, Anlage und Aufrüstung* (East Berlin: Verlag Die Wirtschaft, 1958); Julius Mader, *Die Selbstbedienung im Lebensmittel-Einzelhandel* (East Berlin: Volk und Wissen Volkseigener Verlag, 1960).

57. Magistrat, Abt. Handel und Versorgung, Abteilungsleiter, Karsten to MfHV, May 16, 1959, LAB, Rep. 113/641.

58. ZK Abt. HVA to MfHV, Merkel, April 17, 1959, SAPMO-BArch, DY 30/ IV 2/610/91.

59. SZS, "Handelsberichterstattung 1959: Anzahl, Umsatz, Verkaufsraum-fläche und Verkaufskräfte der Verkaufsstellen (ohne Gaststätten) nach Branchen—Stichtag Sept. 30, 1959" ("vertrauliche Dienstsache"), December 11, 1959, BArch, DE-2/22471 (0050421). The figure of 399 did, however, include 80 "partial" self-service stores *(Teilselbstbedienung)*.

60. SZS, Abt. Handel, Transport-Nachrichtenwesen, "Bericht über die Struktur der Kauf- und Warenhäuser der volkseigenen (HO) und des konsumgenossenschaftlichen Einzelhandels nach Verkaufsabteilungen, deren Verkaufsraumfläche und der derzeitigen Bedienungsform" ("vertrauliche Dienstsache"), undated, BArch, DE-2/21434 (0040266), p. 6; "Tabelle 3–Gegenüberstellung der Anzahl der Verkaufsstellen u. der Anzahl der Verkaufsabteilungen der Kauf- und Warenhäuser des sozial Einzelhandels (HO und Konsum) nach Branchengruppen und Bedienungsform," same file, p. 10. The exact number of self-service stores was 12,912, of which the largest number sold foodstuffs and semiluxuries (10,482). The concentration of these items in self-service stores was also characteristic of West Germany. Wildt, *Vom kleinen Wohlstand,* p. 154.

61. MfHV, Forschungsinstitut für den Binnenhandel der DDR, Anneliee Albrecht and Hans Dietrich, "Aktuelle Probleme der Bedarfsforschung im sozialistischen Handel und im Staatsapparat," undated (probably late 1958 or early 1959), BArch, DL-1/3779, Bl. 48–49.

62. Nor did these reports come only from trade officials. See, for example, Zentrale Kommission für Staatliche Kontrolle, "Informationsbericht über Kontrollergebnisse hinsichtlich der vom Staats- und Wirtschaftsapparat eingeleiteten Maßnahmen zur Erfüllung des Planes und der Verpflichtungen zur Produktion von zusätzlichen industriellen Konsumgütern," October 13, 1958, BArch, DE-1/12357, pp. 1–8, 15–18; Sektor Maschinenbau to Abt. Leichtindustrie, Sonnenburg, February 14, 1958, SAPMO-BArch, DY 30/ IV 2/609/13, pp. 1–2; ZK Abt. Leicht- und Lebensmittelindustrie, "Informationsbericht über die Lage in der Textilindustrie der Deutschen Demokratischen Republik," December 17, 1959, SAPMO-BArch, DY 30/ IV 2/609/8, pp. 2–6, 9–13.

63. Apel to Leuschner, August 22, 1959, BArch, DE-1/12113, Bl.10.

64. For a recent discussion of the American National Exhibition and the "kitchen debate," see Walter Hixson, *Parting the Curtain: Propaganda, Culture, and the Cold War, 1945–1961* (New York: St. Martin's Press, 1997), chap. 6.

65. Politbüro, "Anlage Nr. 7 zum Protokoll Nr. 26 vom 26. Mai 1959, Betr.: Durchführung einer Handelskonferenz—einzuberufen durch das Zentralkomitees der SED und dem Ministerium für Handel und Versorgung," SAPMO-BArch, DY 30/ J IV 2/2/650, Bl. 29. Originally

intended for July 9–10, the conference was actually held on July 30–31, 1959.

66. On the drafting of programmatic theses, see the correspondence in SAPMO-BArch, DY 30/ IV 2/610/88. On the planning of press coverage, see the correspondence in SAPMO-BArch, DY 30/ IV 2/610/91.

67. On the statistical makeup and breakdown of the participants, see "Analge 1" to the protocol of the Politburo meeting of August 11, 1959, SAPMO-BArch, DY 30/ J IV 2/2A/713.

68. "Kultur Program anläßlich der Handelskonferenz des Zentralkomitees der Sozialistischen Einheitspartei Deutschlands und des Ministeriums für Handel und Versorgung," SAPMO-BArch, DY 30/ IV 2/610/92.

69. Merkel's speech set this conciliatory tone from the outset. "Protokoll nach dem Redestenogram, Handelskonferenz am 30. und 31. Juli in Leipzig in der Messehalle II der Technischen Messe," same file, pp. 3–8. Only at one point did Merkel refer to "several responsible functionaries in production, who neglect in the rudest manner the needs of the population." Ibid., p. 12. For formulaic and innocuous comments by Wittkowski and Feldmann, see same file, pp. 57–60, 137–139.

70. Ibid., p. 19.

71. Ibid., p. 202.

72. Ibid., p. 203.

73. MfHV, Bereich Lebensmittel, "Kurzanalyse über die Gründe der im III./ 1959 aufgetretenen Schwierigkeiten in der Versorgung mit einigen wichtigen Warenarten," October 1, 1959, SAPMO-BArch, DY 30/ IV 2/ 2.029/149, Bl. 40–43.

74. Wittkowski to Leuschner, November 17, 1959, SAPMO-BArch, DY 30/ IV 2/610/79.

75. The figures on the collectivization of agriculture are readily available in Weber, *Geschichte der DDR*, p. 215. On the collectivization campaign of 1958–1960, see Arnd Bauerkämper, *Ländliche Gesellschaft in der kommunistischen Diktatur: Zwangsmodernisierung und Tradition in Brandenburg, 1945–1963* (Cologne: Böhlau, 2002), pp. 181–194; Corey Ross, *Constructing Socialism at the Grass Roots: The Transformation of East Germany, 1945–1965* (Basingstoke: Macmillan, 2000), pp. 110–124.

76. See, for example, Wittkowski, "Information für die Mitglieder und Kandidaten des Politbüros (Auswirkungen auf die Versorgung der Bevölkerung aufgrund der Information der Landwirtschaft vom 11.7.1959)," SAPMO-BArch, DY 30/ IV 2/2.029/86, Bl. 234–235. The report attributed shortfalls in milk, butter, and cheese to drought. Shortfalls of over 30 percent in the production of fruit and vegetables received no explanation.

77. Protokoll der Sitzung der Wirtschaftskommission des Politbüros am 7. Juli 1960, SAPMO-BArch, DY 30/ IV 2/2.101/17, Bl. 33.

78. Weber, *Geschichte der DDR*, p. 215.

79. Protokoll der Sitzung der Wirtschaftskommission des Politbüros am 7. Juli 1960, SAPMO-BArch, DY 30/ IV 2/2.101/17, Bl. 42.

80. Poutrus, "Lebensmittelkonsum," pp. 400–401; Lemke, *Die Berliner Krise*, p. 57.

81. "Information über die gegenwärtige Versorgungslage," June 1960, SAPMO-BArch, DY 30/ J IV 2/2A/758, pp. 1–3.

82. Politbüro, draft of "Beschluß vom . . . über Maßnahmen auf dem Gebiet der Versorgung der Bevölkerung" ("Persönliche Verschlußsache"), June 21, 1960, SAPMO-BArch, DY 30/ J IV 2/2A/759.

83. Zentrale Kommission für Staatliche Kontrolle, Eberling to Ernst Lange, July 26, 1960, SAPMO-BArch, DY 30/ IV 2/610/83, pp. 1–5.

84. "Analyse über die eingegangenen Bevölkerungsbeschwerden im 2. Halbjahr 1959," February 13, 1960, SAPMO-BArch, DY 30/ IV 2/610/10, pp. 1–3; "Analyse über die eingegangene Bevölkerungspost im II. und III. Quartal 1960," December 13, 1960, BArch, DC-20 I/3/318, pp. 1–2.

85. VdK, Gerhard Lucht to Ernst Lange, February 26, 1960, SAPMO-BArch, DY 30/ IV 2/610/134; MfHV, Merkel to Magistrat von Groß Berlin, Stadtrat Mallickh, July 22, 1960, LAB, OB-Rep. 101/1859, Bl. 11; Stadtrat Mallickh to Rat des Bezirkes Rostock, July 21, 1960, LAB, OB-Rep. 101/ 1859, Bl. 12.

86. Leuschner, "Ergebnis der Beratungen über die ökonomischen Fragen," June 17, 1959, SAPMO-BArch, J IV/ 2/202/29, p. 2. In order to reach the plan's output goals, Leuschner pointed out that production in certain branches of textiles, leather goods and semiluxuries would have to be lowered due to dependency on imports of raw materials.

87. Ibid., pp. 1–4.

88. "Stenographische Niederschrift der 6. Tagung des Zentralkomitees der SED im Amtsitz des Präsidenten der DDR, Berlin-Niederschönhausen am 18. und 19. September, 1959," SAPMO-BArch, DY 30/ IV 2/1/222, Bl. 70.

89. For the most part, the craft trades had hitherto escaped the processes of expropriation and socialization that had long since taken over the larger industries of East Germany. But between 1958 and 1961, that portion of the craft trades still in private hands declined from 93 percent to 65 percent. Weber, *Geschichte der DDR*, p. 215.

90. Wirtschaftskommission des Politbüros, stenographic protocol, undated (probably fall 1958), SAPMO-BArch, DY 30/ IV 2/2.101/1, Bl. 162–163.

91. ZK Abt. Planung und Finanzen, Fritz Müller, "Probleme, die sich aus

dem 6. Plenum des Zentralkomitees für die Arbeit der Abteilung Planung und Finanzen ergeben und die Methoden der Lösung," October 17, 1959, SAPMO-BArch, DY 30/ IV 2/2.029/65, Bl. 143.

92. SPK, "Programm zur Verbesserung der Versorgung der Bevölkerung mit den tausend kleinen Dingen des täglichen Bedarfs, mit Reparaturen und Dienstleistungen," December 12, 1959, SAPMO-BArch, DY 30/ IV 2/2.029/95, Bl. 23.

93. SED Bezirksleitung Groß-Berlin, Willi Schmidt to Apel, November 19, 1959, SAPMO-BArch, DY 30/ IV 2/2.029/112, Bl. 71–80; "Bericht über die Reise einer Studiengruppe nach Schweden in der Zeit vom 28.10–7.11.1959," November 12, 1959, SAPMO-BArch, DY 30/ IV 2/610/110, Bl. 3–12.

94. "Beschluß über das Programm zur Verbesserung der Versorgung der Bevölkerung mit den tausend kleinen Dingen des täglichen Bedarfs, mit Reparaturen und Dienstleistungen vom 11. Februar 1960," BArch, DC-20 I/3/318.

95. MfHV, Protokoll der Dienstbesprechung unter Leitung des Gen. Schneiderheinze, October 29, 1959, BArch, DL-1/1425, Bl. 4–10; SPK, Wittkowski, "Vorlage für die Staatliche Plankommission," stamped November 25, 1959, SAPMO-BArch, DY 30/ IV 2/610/110.

96. SPK, Wittkowski to Leuschner, "Kurze Übersicht über den Stand bei der Durchführung des Programms der 1000 kleinen Dingen des täglichen Bedarfs nach einigen Schwerpunkten," March 24, 1960, BArch, DE-1/12110, Bl. 6–8; SPK to ZK Abt. HVA "Bericht über die Erfüllung des Ministerratsbeschlußes 1000 kleine Dinge, Reparaturen und Dienstleistungen," September 21, 1960, SAPMO-BArch, DY 30/ IV 2/610/110, pp. 1–2.

97. Protokoll der Sitzung der Wirtschaftskommission des Politbüros am 7. Juli 1960, SAPMO-BArch, DY 30/ IV 2/2.101/17, Bl. 14.

98. Ibid., Bl. 41.

99. "Untersuchungen über die Planung und Bilanzierung industrieller Konsumgüter (einschließlich tausend kleine Dinge)," December 12, 1960, SAPMO-BArch, DY 30/ IV 2/609/7, pp. 1–9; Protokoll der Sitzung der Wirtschaftskommission des Politbüros am 4. November 1960, SAPMO-BArch, DY 30/ IV 2/2.101/20, Bl. 160–161; "Zur Qualitätsentwicklung der Massenbedarfsgüter (1000 kleine Dinge)," December 12, 1960, SAPMO-BArch, DY 30/ IV 2/610/110, pp. 1–3.

100. SZS, "Zusammenstellung von statistischem Material zu den Fragen der Versorgung der Bevölkerung mit den 'Tausend kleinen Dingen des täglichen Bedarfs' für das Jahr 1960" ("Vertrauliche Dienstsache"), March 30, 1961, BArch, DE-2/21450 (0040749), Bl. VII.

101. Ibid., Bl. I, IV-V, 1–3.

102. Fillinger to Lange, March 2, 1960, sending draft of "Vorläufige Arbeits-ordnung über die Versorgung in wichtigen Industriezentren und Großbetrieben," SAPMO-BArch, DY 30/ IV 2/610/125, p. 1.

103. MfHV, Bereich Organisation und Technik, Stellvertreter des Ministers, "Vermerk Betr.: Aussprache beim Gen. Ernst Lange, ZK der SED, am 8.8.59," August 10, 1959, SAPMO-BArch, DY 30/ IV 2/610/125, pp. 1–3.

104. Apel to Merkel, October 17, 1959, BArch, DL-1/3872, Bl. 61.

105. That list consisted primarily of enterprises in heavy industry, raw mate-rials, energy, and chemicals. MfHV, Bereich Lebensmittel, Wunder, "Vermerk für Genossin Müller," August 29, 1960, SAPMO-BArch, DY 30/ IV 2/610/125, pp. 1–3.

106. Priority provisioning was implemented, for example, at the VEB Leuna-Werke Walter Ulbricht. MfHV, Bereich Lebensmittel, Stellvertreter des Ministers, "Bericht über die Durchführung der Anordnung über die Ver-sorgung in wichtigen Großbetrieben und Industriezentren," May 2, 1960, SAPMO-BArch, DY 30/ IV 2/610/125, pp. 1–8.

107. Quoted in Taubman, *Khrushchev*, p. 397.

108. This finding has been most forcefully presented in Harrison, "Ulbricht and the Concrete 'Rose.'" Similar conclusions are reached in A. James McAdams, *Germany Divided: From the Wall to Reunification* (Princeton, N.J.: Princeton University Press, 1993), pp. 29–30, 48–49.

109. On Khrushchev's desire for a German peace settlement as part of a broader peace offensive intended to make possible cuts in Soviet de-fense spending, which in turn would allow for greater expenditures on Soviet domestic needs, see Richter, *Khrushchev's Double Bind*, chap. 5. For an account emphasizing Soviet fears of West Germany acquiring nuclear arms, see Trachtenberg, *A Constructed Peace*, chap. 7.

110. Each of these factors is discussed at length in Hope M. Harrison, *Driv-ing the Soviets up the Wall: Soviet-East German Relations, 1953–1961* (Princeton, N.J.: Princeton University Press, 2003).

111. For example, in January 1961, an East German delegation landed un-expectedly in Moscow while on its way to China for a visit about which the Soviets had not been informed. Ibid., pp. 164–165.

112. Steiner, "Vom Überholen eingeholt," pp. 254–256. As Steiner also points out, labor shortages forced the regime into allowing wages to rise more quickly than planned to keep workers from leaving their jobs. Higher wages, however, could not be balanced with an increase in the supply of consumer goods. As a result, the gap between purchasing power and commodity supply only widened further.

113. Patrick Major, "Torschlußpanik und Mauerbau: 'Republikflucht' als Symptom der zweiten Berlinkrise," in Ciesla, *Sterben für Berlin?*, pp. 226–227.

114. ZK Abt. HVA to Ulbricht, September 23, 1960, SAPMO-BArch, NL 182/1061, Bl. 279–281. Ulbricht was simultaneously receiving similar information from Leuschner. Leuschner to Ulbricht, September 21, 1960, same file, Bl. 275.

115. MfHV, Merkel to Lange, July 30, 1960, SAPMO-BArch, DY 30/ IV 2/ 610/77. On East German disappointments with COMECON in these years, see Lemke, *Die Berlinkrise*, pp. 83–92. On the advantages and disadvantages of COMECON for the GDR generally, see Christoph Buchheim, "Wirtschaftliche Folgen der Integration der DDR in den RGW," in Christoph Buchheim, ed., *Wirtschaftliche Folgelasten des Krieges in der SBZ/DDR* (Baden-Baden: Nomos, 1995).

116. Lemke, *Die Berlinkrise*, pp. 58–59. In the late 1950s the GDR's economy had become dependent on West Germany for imports of modern components for machines, chemicals and electronics. West German industry, meanwhile, was divided on the trade stop. Jörg Roesler, "Handelsgeschäfte im Kalten Krieg: Die wirtschaftliche Motivationen für den deutsch-deutschen Handel zwischen 1949 und 1961," in Buchheim, *Wirtschaftliche Folgelasten*, pp. 204–210.

117. ZK Abt. Agitation und Propaganda, "Information (50) über die Lage in der Versorgung der Bevölkerung und über Diskussionen in der Bevölkerung zu Versorgungsschwierigkeiten" ("Nur für den Dienstgebrauch im Parteiapparat"), November 3, 1960, SAPMO-BArch, DY 30/ IV 2/2.029/93, Bl. 1–7.

118. Protokoll der Sitzung der Wirtschaftskommission des Politbüros am 4. November 1960, SAPMO-BArch, DY 30/ IV 2/2.101/20, Bl. 140–141, 150.

119. Ibid., Bl. 150–161.

120. Ibid., Bl. 158.

121. Protokoll der Sitzung der Wirtschaftskommission des Politbüros am 16. Juni 1961, SAPMO-BArch, DY 30/IV 2/2.101/24, Bl. 141.

122. The number of East Germans fleeing to the West increased from 143,917 in 1959 to 199,188 in 1960. Weber, *Geschichte der DDR*, p. 220.

123. In some areas, rationing of certain goods had already been reintroduced. For instance, in Dresden sugar cubes had been rationed since the second quarter of the year. Protokoll der Sitzung der Wirtschaftskommission des Politbüros am 4. November 1960, SAPMO-BArch, DY 30/ IV 2/2.101/20, Bl. 137. Also see Poutrus, "Lebensmittelkonsum," p. 402.

124. "Record of Meeting of Comrade N. S. Khrushchev with Comrade W. Ulbricht, 30 November 1960," published in Harrison, "Ulbricht and the Concrete 'Rose,'" Appendix A, pp. 4, 6.

125. Grieder, *The East German Leadership*, p. 129.

126. Ulbricht to Khrushchev, January 18, 1961, published in Harrison, "Ulbricht and the Concrete 'Rose,'" Appendix B, pp. 7–8.

127. For a description of this process, see Lemke, *Die Berlinkrise*, pp. 64–69.

128. "Aktenvermerk: über eine Unterredung zwischen den Genossen Mikojan und Rau anläßlich der Unterzeichnung des Abkommens am 23.2.1961 in Moskau," March 3, 1961, SAPMO-BArch, J IV 2/202/30. Mikoyan had also suggested as much to Leuschner in January 1961. See Lemke, *Die Berlinkrise*, p. 65.

129. "Niederschrift über die Wirtschaftsverhandlungen der Regierungsdelegationen der UdSSR unter Leitung des Stellvertreters des Vorsitzenden des Ministerrates Gen. Sassjadko, und der DDR unter Leitung des Stellvertreters des Vorsitzenden des Ministerrates, Gen. Leuschner, am 22.4.1961," April 23, 1961, SAPMO-BArch, J IV 2/202/30, p. 11.

130. "Anlage 1a zum Protokoll Nr. 11 vom 9./10. März 1961–Aussprache im Politbüro über den Volkswirtschaftsplan," SAPMO-BArch, DY 30/ J IV 2/2/753 (Bd. 1), Bl. 48–53, 88–90; ZK Abt. HVA to Apel, May 20, 1961, SAPMO-BArch, DY 30/ IV 2/2.029/87, Bl. 22–27.

131. Merkel to Wittkowski, May 29, 1961, SAPMO-BArch, DY 30/ IV 2/ 2.029/93, Bl. 133.

132. ZK Abt. Parteiorgane, "Information über die Stimmung der Bevölkerung zur Versorgungslage in Berlin und im Bezirk Potsdam," May 19, 1961, SAPMO-BArch, DY 30/ IV 2/610/29, p. 3.

133. Ernst Lange to Willi Stoph, May 16, 1961, SAPMO-BArch, DY 30/ IV 2/ 610/79. In fact, Merkel had already issued instructions to introduce one meatless day per week in restaurants and hotels, and two per week in work kitchens, schools, and canteens; these measures resulted in protests. Merkel, *Utopie und Bedürfnis*, p. 78.

134. In these months 67 store managers and 697 sales-people quit their jobs in Berlin. Lange to Apel, June 23, 1961, SAPMO-BArch, DY 30/ IV 2/ 610/87, Bl. 35.

135. Harrison, "Ulbricht and the Concrete 'Rose,'" p. 31.

136. Harrison, *Driving the Soviets up the Wall*, pp. 186–187.

137. Major, "Vor und nach dem 13. August," pp. 331–338.

138. Harrison, "Ulbricht, Khrushchev, and the Berlin Wall," pp. 339–341.

139. Some western observers suspected that the SED was encouraging people to flee as a pretext for tightening the screws. Zubok and Pleshakov, *Inside the Kremlin's Cold War*, p. 196.

140. Soviet observers in East Germany regularly conveyed their concerns about Ulbricht's recklessness. Richter, *Khrushchev's Double Bind*, p. 142.

141. Zubok and Pleshakov, *Inside the Kremlin's Cold War*, p. 197.

142. Quoted in Richter, *Khrushchev's Double Bind*, p. 116.

Epilogue

1. Bertolt Brecht, "Der Radwechsel," translated by Michael Hamburger, collected in *Bertolt Brecht Poems*, edited by John Willett and Ralph Mannheim with the cooperation of Erich Fried (London: Eyre Methuen Ltd., 1976), p. 439.

2. Karl-Heinz Hagen, "Weltoffene Hauptstadt: Berliner Festtage 1960 mit internationalem Glanz," *ND*, October 28, 1960, p. 4.

3. Hansjürgen Schaefer, "Messeschlager Gisela: Uraufführung im Berliner Metropol-Theater," *ND*, October 26, 1960, p. 4.

4. I had the good fortune to see the revival staged at Berlin's Neuköllner Oper in 1998.

5. Patrice Poutrus, "Lebensmittelkonsum, Versorgungskrisen und die Entscheidung für den 'Goldbroiler,'" *Archiv für Sozialgeschichte* 39 (1999), pp. 406–415.

6. Quoted in Jeffrey Kopstein, *The Politics of Economic Decline in East Germany, 1945–1989* (Chapel Hill: University of North Carolina Press, 1997), p. 48.

7. On the 1960s, see Philipp Heldmann, *Herrschaft, Wirtschaft, Anoraks: Konsumpolitik in der DDR der Sechzigerjahre Göttingen:* Vandenhoeck & Ruprecht, 2004); Patrice Poutrus, *Die Erfindung des Goldbroilers: Über den Zusammenhang zwischen Herrschaftssicherung und Konsumentwicklung in der DDR* (Cologne: Böhlau, 2002); Ina Merkel, *Utopie und Bedürfnis: Die Konsumkultur in der DDR* (Cologne: Böhlau, 1999). On the Honecker years, see Kopstein, *The Politics of Economic Decline;* Charles Maier, *Dissolution: The Crisis of Communism and the End of East Germany* (Princeton, N.J.: Princeton University Press, 1997); Jonathan Zatlin, "The Currency of Socialism: Money in the GDR and German Unification, 1971–1989" (Ph.D. diss., University of California at Berkeley, 2000).

8. Kopstein, *The Politics of Economic Decline,* chap. 2; Peter Grieder, *The East German Leadership 1946–1973: Conflict and Crisis* (Manchester: Manchester University Press, 1999), chap. 4; Monika Kaiser, *Machtwechsel von Ulbricht zu Honecker: Funktionsmechanismen der SED-Diktatur in Konfliktsituationen, 1962 bis 1972* (Berlin: Akademie, 1997), pp. 57–64; Mario Frank, *Walter Ulbricht: Eine deutsche Biographie* (Berlin: Siedler, 2001), pp. 351–357.

9. On reforms elsewhere in Eastern Europe in the 1960s, see Alan H.

Smith, *The Planned Economies of Eastern Europe* (New York: Holmes and Meier, 1983), pp. 54–80; Ivan T. Berend, *Central and Eastern Europe, 1944–1993: Detour from the Periphery to the Periphery* (New York: Cambridge University Press, 1996), pp. 136–152.

10. Much has been written in recent years about the fate and significance of the reforms of the 1960s. For differing interpretations, all of which nevertheless emphasize its limited implementation and ultimate demise, see André Steiner, *Die DDR-Wirtschaftsreform der sechziger Jahre: Konflikt zwischen Effizienz- und Machtkalkül* (Berlin: Akademie, 1999); Heldmann, *Herrschaft, Wirtschaft, Anoraks;* Kopstein, *The Politics of Economic Decline,* chap. 2; Grieder, *The East German Leadership,* pp. 160–170; Maier, *Dissolution,* pp. 87–92.

11. Heldmann, *Herrschaft, Wirtschaft, Anoraks,* pp. 62–69.

12. Ibid., pp. 285–295. On the failure of the 1960s reforms to affect consumer price policy in general, see pp. 268–270.

13. Both cars were originally introduced in the latter half of the 1950s, but production did not exceed one hundred thousand until 1966. Jonathan Zatlin, "The Vehicle of Desire: The Trabant, the Wartburg, and the End of the GDR," *German History* 15, no. 3 (1997), pp. 364–367.

14. On the Goldbroiler, see Poutrus, *Die Erfindung des Goldbroilers.*

15. For recent works on the change in leadership, see Grieder, *The East German Leadership,* chap. 4; Kaiser, *Machtwechsel von Ulbricht zu Honecker;* Jochen Staadt, "Walter Ulbrichts letzter Machtkampf," *Deutschland Archiv* 29 (1996), pp. 686–700; Jochen Stelkens, "Machtwechsel in Ost-Berlin: Der Sturz Walter Ulbrichts 1971," *Vierteljahrshefte für Zeitgeschichte* 45, no. 4 (1997), pp. 503–533; Frank, *Walter Ulbricht,* pp. 385–427.

16. Erich Honecker, "Bericht des Zentralkomitees der Sozialistischen Einheitspartei Deutschlands an den VIII. Parteitag der SED," in *Protokoll der Verhandlungen des VIII. Parteitages der Sozialistischen Einheitspartei Deutschlands* (East Berlin: Dietz, 1971), pp. 62–66.

17. Quoted in Christoph Boyer and Peter Skyba, "Sozial- und Konsumpolitik als Stabilisierungsstrategie: Zur Genese der 'Einheit von Wirtschafts- und Sozialpolitik' in der DDR," *Deutschland Archiv* 32, no. 4 (1999), pp. 583–584.

18. Timothy Garten Ash, *In Europe's Name: Germany and the Divided Continent* (New York: Vintage), pp. 187–188.

19. So Kopstein suggests in *The Politics of Economic Decline,* pp. 83–84.

20. Ash, *In Europe's Name,* pp. 187–188.

21. Jonathan Zatlin, "Consuming Ideology: Socialist Consumerism and the Intershops, 1970–1989," in Peter Hübner and Klaus Tenfelde, eds., *Arbeiter in der SBZ-DDR* (Essen: Klartext, 1999), p. 560.

22. Presented at the SED's Ninth Party Congress in May 1976, the Unity of

Economic and Social Policy called for increased social expenditures, including an ambitious new housing program that seriously attempted to address the long-neglected problem of insufficient housing in East Germany. On the significance of these policies for the legitimacy of the regime, see Sigrid Meuschel, *Legitimation und Parteiherrschaft: Zum Paradox von Stabilität und Revolution in der DDR 1945–1989* (Frankfurt am Main: Suhrkamp, 1992), pp. 221–241; Hans Günter Hockerts, "Soziale Errungenschaften? Zum sozialpolitischen Legitimitätsanspruch der zweiten deutschen Diktatur," in Jürgen Kocka, Hans-Jürgen Puhle, and Klaus Tenfelde, eds., *Von der Arbeiterbewegung zum modernen Sozialstaat* (Munich: Sauer, 1994); Boyer and Skyba, "Sozial- und Konsumpolitik als Stabilisierungsstrategie."

23. On these developments, see Ash, *In Europe's Name*, chap. 2–4; "twilight realms" is his phrase, p. 158.

24. Zatlin, "The Currency of Socialism," p. 168.

25. In addition to the accounts in Ash and Zatlin, also see Kopstein, *The Politics of Economic Decline*, chap. 2–3, and Maier, *Dissolution*, chap. 2.

26. Quoted in Ash, *In Europe's Name*, p. 157.

27. Zatlin, "The Currency of Socialism," chap. 3–4.

28. On the "corrosive social effects of the Intershops," see Zatlin, "Consuming Ideology," pp. 566–572.

29. On hopes to "renew" the GDR or to find a "Third Way" between socialism and capitalism, see Konrad H. Jarausch, *The Rush to German Unity* (New York: Oxford University Press, 1994), pp. 77–94.

30. Outside Germany, the phenomenon of *Ostalgie* has become most widely known through the success of the recent film, *Good Bye Lenin!*. In Germany, however, the phenomenon has been a matter of widespread public discussion almost since the wall fell. On the many disappointments bound up with reunification, see Jarausch, *The Rush to German Unity*, pp. 137–156; Fritz Stern, "Freedom and its Discontents: The Travails of the New Germany," in Fritz Stern, *Einstein's German World* (Princeton, N.J.: Princeton University Press, 1999). On *Ostalgie* television programs, see Christoph Dieckmann, "Honis heitere Welt," *Die Zeit*, August 28, 2003.

Index

Adenauer, Konrad, 89, 201, 204

Advertising, 9–10; American influence on, 150, 222; improving on, 93–97; lack of, 53; methods of, 123, 134, 136, 186; the need for, 64

Agriculture: forced collectivization of, 101, 191–192

Allocations, special, 21

American National Exhibition (Kitchen debate), 189

"Americanism": German prejudices about, 8

American-style mass culture, 7

"Antifascist bloc of democratic parties," 14

Apel, Erich, 173, 183–185, 189, 192, 196–198, 200–201

Appeal (petition), letters of, 35

Association for Consumer Cooperatives (VdK), 159

Austerity and sacrifice: role of in communism, 5

Baender, Paul, 71

Bergler, Georg, 150

Beria, Lavrenti, 109–110

Berlin Blockade, 39–41

Berlin Crisis, The, 198–204

Berlin Wall, 1–2, 204, 210; symbolic meaning of, 1

Bizone (US and British zones), 24

Black market: HO shops as solution for, 56, 71; prices of basic foodstuffs, 22

Border (between East and West), 204

Border Crossers (*Grenzgänger*), 134

Buchwitz, Otto, 54

Byrnes, James F., 28–29

Capital goods: Soviet emphasis on, 17

CARE (Cooperative for American Remittances to Europe), 28

CDU (Christian Democratic Party), 14

Centralized economic planning: first Five-Year Plan, 32, 76, 88, 97, 146; Main Economic Task, 178; provisioning failures of, 82–88; Second Five-Year Plan, 132–133; SED need for, 23–24; Seven-Year Plan, 194, 205; Two-Year Plan, 85–86

Christian Democratic Party (CDU), 14

Class (social) stratification: in traditional views of consumption, 9

Clay, Lucius (US Military Governor), 28–29

Clothing: allocation under Order no. 234, 33–34

Clothing, protective: denial of, 30

Coal exports: Western zones' ceiling for, 27